D1561043

FRACTAL CITIES

ἀγεῶμέτρητος μηδεὶζ εχσίτω
Let no one enter who does not know geometry

Anon, Inscription on the door of Plato's Academy
at Athens, although often accredited to Plato himself

Elias Philosophus, *In Aristotelis Categoria Commentaria, 118.18*
(A. Busse Ed. *Comm. in Arist. Greaca*, Berlin, 1900, XVIII, i.)
From *The Oxford Dictionary of Quotations*, 1979, 3rd Edition.

FRACTAL CITIES

A Geometry of Form and Function

MICHAEL BATTY
National Center for Geographic Information and Analysis,
State University of New York, Buffalo, New York, USA

and

PAUL LONGLEY
Department of Geography, University of Bristol, Bristol, UK

ACADEMIC PRESS
Harcourt Brace & Company, Publishers
London   San Diego   New York
Boston   Sydney   Tokyo   Toronto

ACADEMIC PRESS LIMITED
24–28 Oval Road
LONDON NW1 7DX

U.S. Edition Published by
ACADEMIC PRESS INC.
San Diego, CA 92101

This book is printed on acid free paper

A catalogue record for this book is available from the British Library

ISBN 0-12-455570-5

Typeset by Photo·graphics, Honiton, Devon
Printed in Great Britain by the Bath Press, Bath, Avon

Preface

Fractal geometry was invented almost single handedly by Benoit Mandelbrot over a thirty year period from 1950. It burst onto the academic stage 10 or so years ago through its ability to generate highly realistic computer graphic scenes of the natural world, which were popularized in Mandelbrot's (1983) remarkable book. At the same time, it was becoming central to the reawakening of interest in the science of form in the fields of physics and biology. In mathematics too, the new geometry was instrumental in visualizing solution spaces of dynamic systems whose behavior could no longer be regarded as smooth, but discontinuous and chaotic. The key insight emanating from these diverse origins revolves around the idea that the world is chaotic, discontinuous, irregular in its superficial physical form but that beneath this first impression lies an order which is regular, unyielding and of infinite complexity. But this is an order that has been simplified away in terms of the continuous and the smooth in all previous attempts at scientific understanding. In this sense, the world must now be seen as largely fractal. Non-fractal or smooth renditions of it and the science that accompanies this is thus the science of the special case.

It is hard to impress the importance of this insight but in the last decade, fractal geometry has found its way into many sciences and arts. Everything from Stephen Hawking's theories of the universe to George Lucas's *Star Wars* movies and popular novels such as Michael Crichton's *Jurassic Park* seem to be touched by fractals, while statements of its importance to science and modern society abound. John A. Wheeler says that:

"No one is considered scientifically literate today who does not know what a Gaussian distribution is, or the meaning and scope of the concept of entropy. It is possible to believe that no one will be considered scientifically literate tomorrow who is not equally familiar with fractals"

while Hugh Kenner describes the field as being

". . .as big a picture as this century has seen".

James Gleick in his book *Chaos* says that: ". . .twentieth-century science will be remembered for just three things: relativity, quantum mechanics and chaos", and this includes the geometry of chaos – fractals. The superlatives continue and readers could be forgiven for throwing up their hands in horror at yet more hype about fractals.

The time has come however for these ideas to be absorbed into the mainstream of science. Recently, with the dust settling, many applications of fractal geometry are being developed in diverse fields and researchers are finding that fractal ideas have been part of our consciousness, certainly from the time of the Italian Renaissance, but probably as far back as the Greeks, and maybe before. What fractal geometry does is to provide a framework for tying together previously unconnected and diverse concepts, thus enabling the assembly of a 'bigger' picture. Cities yield some of the best examples of fractals. For generations, architects and planners have attempted to impose a simple, smooth, visual order on cities in the belief that such order counters the disorder and dysfunction which cities reveal when they develop 'naturally'. All the great Utopias from Plato onwards have sought to impose the geometry of Euclid on the city as an example of man's triumph over nature. In this way, art has been separated from science. But this viewpoint has always been opposed in some measure. In the last 50 years, with the realization that social and economic order belies the physical form of cities, the idea that the naturally or organically growing city is optimal in countless ways which we have hitherto ignored, has grown in strength. In short, our view now about the shape and form of cities is that their irregularity and messiness is simply a superficial manifestation of a deeper order. And as we will argue here, fractal geometry has much to say about this.

This book presents an initial attempt to apply fractal geometry to cities. In fact, we go beyond this and argue that cities are fractal in form, and that much of our pre-existing urban theory is a theory of the fractal city. As befits a beginning, this book is very much an introductory statement and, as we argue throughout, these ideas are simply crude snapshots of a much bigger picture which we hope others will steer their research towards. In terms of theory, we show here that the architect's physical determinism concerning the city can be captured and elaborated in terms of fractals while the geographer's concern for the economic theory of location is entirely consistent with the use of fractal ideas. We live in an era when physical determinism is still disreputable as architects and city planners seek to minimize the impact of designs which manifestly interfere with the social and economic fabric of cities in countless unanticipated and undesirable ways. But physical form does determine the quality of life in cities. We see fractal geometry as providing a new hope for understanding the power of determinism, as well as new methods for enabling the synthesis of urban density with central place theory, new ways of visualizing the impact of human decision-making on cities, and perhaps most of all, new goals for achieving the good society through manipulating and planning city form.

One of the central themes of this book is based on the need to 'visualize' complex spatial phenomena, in our case cities. Visualization has come hard on the heels of developments in computer graphics during the 1980s and now forms a major force in advancing science whose systems are spatial in some sense, and whose form reveals infinite complexity. Urban theory has not advanced to the extent it might because the intrinsic complexity and extensiveness of data has been difficult to grasp just as the results of modeling such complexity have been difficult to absorb and evaluate. Computer graphics as scientific visualization thus blazes a path within science from which we can learn how to make progress through studying examples and applications from many diverse fields. Although our focus is on cities, we see the examples in this book as being as relevant to biology and astronomy, say, as to our own more limited domain just as we see the entire field of visualization as helping us to fashion computer graphics to our own problems. We thus consider that creative advances in visualization are unlikely to be restricted to any particular field, metaphors and analogies between one field and another being the way forward. In this sense, our text is part picture book from which those interested in graphics and visualization might draw some inspiration. It is through pictures that our ideas can be most readily and clearly articulated, and there is perhaps something about the icons we employ that might encourage the sort of interdisciplinary research which is central to our own field.

Our book also provides a gentle introduction to fractal geometry and it is our hope that through this medium, the more general scientific reader will find much of interest here. Cities, as we said earlier, are fine example of fractals and we believe that this book could be used in courses which teach their rudiments, especially to those whose mathematics is at the 'beginning calculus' level. Moreover, it is our view that fractals are as much a part of the artificial as the natural world, that they are writ large in social and well as physical systems. Thus we hope that our treatment might be of use to social scientists whose concern in some way is with space, and, of course, to geographers, urban economists, planners, engineers, designers, mathematicians, and computer scientists.

Let us say a few words about the origins of the book. For one of us (Batty), fractals go back a long way to the 1960s through ideas in location theory involving power laws in rank-size and central place theory. In fact, the first edition of Peter Haggett's *Locational Analysis in Human Geography* published in 1965 was full of references to the effect of form on location and cities. Mandelbrot's work in this area was known to us at that time, and again in 1974, Michael Dacey pointed out its relevance to us. Mandelbrot's first edition of his book *Fractals: Form, Chance, and Dimension* published in 1977 escaped us but in 1981, Lionel March mentioned it and from then on, fractals seemed to be always with us. Of course, it was clearly the emergence of computer graphics which fueled the fire and by the time Mandelbrot published his second English edition *The Fractal Geometry of Nature* in 1982, the movement was in full swing.

It is unlikely that we would have begun work in this area unless one us (Batty again) had not attempted to train himself in computer graphics in the early 1980s. Almost accidentally, an attempt at generating Mandelbrot's fractal planet on a very small (32K RAM) microcomputer yielded a remarkable and startling realism (as shown in Plate 3.5). From then on we were hooked. Paul Longley began his university career in Bristol in 1977 in the same year Peter Haggett produced the much enlarged second edition of his book which captured much of the synthesis forged within locational analysis during the 1960s and 1970s. After lecturing in the Universities of Karlsruhe and Reading, he joined Michael Batty in Cardiff in 1984 and as part of a project to develop computers in city planning and building on our past work in urban models, we cultivated these interests from 1986 on.

Many people have helped us with this book. Its production would not have been possible without the skills and efforts of our technical staff. Tracey Dinnock drew some of the figures, Martin Morris and Nathan Webster took many of the photographs, and Andrew Edwards assembled hardware and software when we were both associated with the Department of City and Regional Planning at the University of Wales in Cardiff. Tony Philpott and Simon Godden have helped us more recently with the final production of the book in the Department of Geography at the University of Bristol. Kate Brewin, our editor at Academic Press, has been most supportive.

This work has been partly financed by two major research grants; that awarded to Cardiff for the Wales and South West Regional Research Laboratory by the Economic and Social Research Council (WA504–28–5006: 1986–1991) and that to State University of New York at Buffalo for the National Center for Geographic Information and Analysis by the National Science Foundation (SES-88–10917: 1988–1993). The National Center for Supercomputing Applications at the University of Illinois in Urbana-Champaign financed one of us to begin work on the fractal simulations reported in Chapter 4 in the summer of 1986 and we thank Larry Smarr, David Boyce and Lew Hopkins for making this visit possible. We also thank Kwang Sik Kim of Sung Kyun Kwam University in Seoul, Korea, for help on Chapter 9, and John Shepherd of Birkbeck College in the University of London for his cooperation on the research that led to use of the East Anglia and South East England data sets in Chapter 10.

We have benefited immeasurably from discussions and comments with our academic colleagues. In Cardiff, Ian Bracken kept us sane and his help is directly reflected in the two color plates (7.1 and 7.2) which he produced for this book. Huw Williams has been a source of great inspiration and we thank him for discussion on many topics in physics and transport such as 'spin glasses' and much else besides. David Martin provided sobering comments by reading the book in its entirety. Both in Cardiff and in Buffalo, Stewart Fotheringham worked with us on diffusion-limited aggregation, besides tempting one of us, in part, to leave those hallowed shores for the New World.

In Buffalo itself, Mike Woldenberg, the source of all historical wisdom on fractals and allometry, continues to engage us in vibrant discussion while David Mark injected us with an equally influential skepticism. Yichun Xie helped with C and UNIX and was responsible for the computer analysis of the North East US cities examples in Chapter 7. Pierre Frankhauser of the Universite de Franche-Comte, Besancon, read the complete manuscript and gave us comments at a late stage when we met him in Buffalo and Budapest. We thank all these colleagues and friends, and many who go unremarked, for their help. In as controversial a set of applications as these, they bear no responsibility other than sharpening us to the criticism.

This book has been a long time in the making. It was begun in earnest when Paul Longley spent a semester of study leave at Buffalo in late 1991. A lot of the earlier work was done when we in the University of Wales at Cardiff in one of the most dynamic and turbulent environments we are ever likely to encounter. It was in that place that this started and at times, we wondered whether we and the research would survive it. But it is a testament to the power of ideas, especially good ones such as fractals, that they (and we) did do so, and nothing would be more satisfying to us than if just a few of these were to be picked up by others in our field and made still more applicable.

Finally, we thank our respective families, Sue and Daniel, and Mandy, who cheerfully tolerated the writing of this book, amidst important domestic events such as countless houses and house moves, GCSEs, and marriage. We dedicate it to them.

Michael Batty   **Paul Longley**

Acknowledgements

We thank the authors and publishers for permission to reprint the following figures: figures X and XX from Abercrombie, P. (1945) *Greater London Plan 1944*, HMSO, London; figures 2 and 3 from Arlinghaus, S. L., and Nysteun, J. D. (1990) Geometry of Boundary Exchanges, *The Geographical Review*, **80**, 21–31; figures 1436 and 1437 from Benevolo, L. (1980) *The History of the City*, The MIT Press, Cambridge, MA; figure 2 from Benguigui, L., and Daoud, M. (1991) Is the Suburban Railway System a Fractal? *Geographical Analysis*, **23**, 362–368; the figure on page 54 of Berthon, S., and Robinson, A. (1991) *The Shape of the World: The Mapping and Discovery of the Earth*, Rand McNally, Chicago, IL; the figure on page ii of Chapin, F. S., and Weiss, S. F. (Editors)(1962) *Urban Growth Dynamics: In a Regional Cluster of Cities*, John Wiley and Sons, New York; figure 3.1 from Dantzig, G. B., and Saaty, T. L. (1973) *Compact City: A Plan for a Livable Urban Environment*, W. H. Freeman and Company, San Francisco, CA; figures 236 and 237 Doxiadis, C. A. (1968) *Ekistics: An Introduction to the Science of Human Settlements*, Hutchinson, London; figures 3.61 and 4.1 from Frankhauser, P. (1994) *La Fractalite Des Structures Urbaines*, Villes Collection, Anthropos, Paris, France; the figures on pages 262, 263, and 426 of Gallion, A. B., and Eisner, S. (1950, 1975) *The Urban Pattern: City Planning and Design*, Van Nostrand Reinhold Company, New York; figure 1 from Goodchild, M. F. and Mark, D. M. (1987) The Fractal Nature of Geographic Phenomena, *Annals of the Association of American Geographers*, **77**, 265–278;

Figures 24 and 25 from Keeble, L. (1959) *Principles and Practice of Town and Country Planning*, The Estates Gazette, London; figures 153, 163, and 193 from Kostof, S. (1991) *The City Shaped: Urban Patterns and Meanings Throughout History*, Little, Brown and Company, Boston, MA; the figures on pages 21 and 22 from McGuire, M. (1991) *An Eye For Fractals: A Graphic and Photographic Essay*, Addison-Wesley Publishing Company, New York; figures 4.11, 4.77, 5.11, 5.12, 5.13, 5.14, 5.15, 5.17, 5.32 and 7.15 from Morris, A. E. J. (1979) *History of Urban Form: Before the Industrial Revolutions*, Longmans Scientific and Technical, London; New York; figures 84, 119, 289, and 291 from Reps, J. W. (1965) *The Making of Urban America: A History of City Planning in the United States*, Princeton University Press, Princeton, NJ; the figure on page 259 of Vance, J. E. (1990) *The Continuing City: Urban Morphology in Western Civilization*, The Johns Hopkins University Press, Baltimore, MD.

We thank The Glamorgan Archive Service for permission to reprint the following maps of Cardiff: by John Speed 1610, Cardiff in the late 1830s by John Wood, Cardiff in 1851, and District Plan of Cardiff and Penarth 1869.

We thank Ian Braecken for plates 7.1 and 7.2, and Keith Horsfield for the plaster cast of the lung reproduced in Fig. 2.15(a). These plates and figures were made available especially for this book.

Some of this material has been published by ourselves before as journal articles and we thank the editors and publishers for permission to reprint and revise selected parts of the following: *Area*, **19**, 215–221, 1987; *Computers and GeoSciences*, **15**, 167–183, 1989; *Environment and Planning A*, **18**, 1143–1179, 1986; **21**, 1447–1472, 1989; **23**, 511–544, 1991; *Environment and Planning B*, **14**, 123–134, 1987; *15*, 461–488, 1988; *Regional Studies*, **26**, 437–452, 1992; *Transactions of the Institute of British Geographers*, **16**, 75–94, 1991; *Urban Studies*, **29**, 1043–1070, 1992.

Contents

List of Figures

List of Tables

List of Color Plates

Introduction

Fractal geometry will make you see everything differently. (Barnsley, 1988a, p. 1.)

Our view of cities is changing. One hundred years ago, cities were understood and planned as physical artifacts with predominant concern for their architecture and their aesthetics. It was widely agreed that their physical form was the ultimate determinant of their social and economic functioning, and the quality of life therein. As the 20th century wore on, this view weakened as attention turned to their economic structure and the efficiency of their organization, but until the 1960s, the physical viewpoint remained central, notwithstanding a gradual shift from aesthetic concerns to locational efficiency.

Prevailing views and approaches then changed dramatically. During the last 25 years, attention has been focussed upon the institutional structure of cities, on social processes and class conflict, on urban poverty and deprivation, on their diverse roles in the local and global economy. After a century of sustained effort at their understanding, our knowledge is still partial and fragmentary, based on a kaleidoscope of viewpoints and ideologies. What, however, is widely accepted, perhaps a little reluctantly by some, is that cities are mirrors and microcosms of society and culture at large, with every viewpoint contributing something to their understanding. Yet in this quest, there have been few successes in evolving our understanding from one approach to another. Consequently, the physicalism based on the idea of cities as being 'architecture-writ-large' cannot be easily related to the theory of cities as social or economic or institutional systems – social processes are not easy to relate to spatial form – and thus our current understanding is overwhelmed by their complexity and diversity.

Yet there is a curious paradox in all of this. We know instinctively that the physical form of cities is the ultimate result of a multitude of social and economic processes, constrained and shaped by the geometry of the natural and man-made world. We know that urban problems are manifest in the first instance in physical and spatial terms. We also know that many, if not most, of the instruments we have at our disposal for designing better cities are physical in form and intent. But there is still no widespread consensus as to the importance of form, geometry, layout, and configuration which characterize the physical city. Physicalism has fallen out of fashion in many fields in the last 50 years. This now appears to be changing too, and there is new hope that a more profound understanding of physical form in science generally is about to emerge. In this, there are important implications for how we might develop a new understanding of the form of cities. The challenge we set ourselves in this book is to address these possibilities.

These movements are clearly a part of more fundamental secular trends in the way we fashion knowledge and science and apply it in society. One hundred years ago, there was great optimism, great certainty that science and technology would lead us to the good society. Today we know different. That certainty and optimism has dissolved and has been replaced by a degree of uncertainty and a skepticism as to whether our science can ever yield the answers. This change is not only a social effect of the difficulties realized in the application of technology, but has also emerged from science itself. The quest for comprehensiveness through systems thinking which came to dominate science by the mid-20th century led to the profound discovery that even the simplest physical systems can admit uncertainty in their predictions. The emergence of catastrophe theory, and now chaos, first in mathematics and then in countless applied areas, is testament to this change. The current concern for complexity and diversity, for micro–macro and local–global properties of systems, for treating the world simultaneously on many levels, is reinforcing these trends, while the gradual realization that there is order in chaos, is taking science and mathematics to new levels of abstraction, far away from the most elemental of human intuitions from whence springs the original thirst for knowledge.

Fractal geometry is part of this change. For the first time, a formal framework for the geometry of the real world rather than for its abstraction into pure mathematics has been established which enables us to understand order and regularity in what, at first sight, appears irregular and disordered. Rather than starting with function and progressing to form, fractal geometry enables us to search out functions and processes which give rise to the man-made and natural patterns we observe in the real world, thus helping us not only to describe and understand reality a little better but to progress our forecasts and predictions of how the real world might evolve. Geometry is no longer conceived in terms of straight lines – the geometry of Euclid – but can now admit irregularity without abandoning continuity, thus relaxing the severity of mathematics to encompass what is natural and essential. The application of this geometry to cities is immediate. Planned cities are cast in the geometry of Euclid but by far the majority, those which are unplanned or planned less, show no such simplicity of form. Moreover, all cities contain some organic growth, even planned cities are adapted to their context in more natural ways once the plan comes to be implemented, and in any case, the extent to which human decision-making is ordered or planned is always a matter of degree. In this sense then, all cities show some irregularity in most of their parts and are thus ideal candidates for the application of fractal geometry.

This book is but a beginning in the quest to develop a robust and relevant geometry for the spatial organization of cities. Much of the material we introduce here is speculative and informal, in that it is part of an ongoing research program which we hope will develop and grow as the logic of these arguments is appreciated. We will sketch out how fractal geometry might be applied to cities in many ways; first in terms of visualizing urban form through computer models and computer graphics, and then through the measurement of patterns in real cities and their dynamic simulation. We will illustrate these ideas with hypothetical and real cities and with simulations or models. We will focus on physical forms such as city boundaries, networks, hierarchies, urban texture, and the density of population amongst many structural concepts. We will deal with real, ideal and hypothetical concepts, showing how these might be best applied to yield general insights into urban form and functioning. It is not our intention to provide a blueprint for a new theory of cities. This may come eventually from fractal geometry, but as we continually emphasize, this is merely a beginning.

At the very outset, we must give the reader a brief but cogent idea of fractal geometry and its relevance to cities. Fractals, a term coined by their originator Benoit Mandelbrot (1983), are objects of any kind whose spatial form is nowhere smooth, hence termed 'irregular', and whose irregularity repeats itself geometrically across many scales. In short, the irregularity of form is similar from scale to scale, and the object is said to possess the property of self-similarity or scale-invariance. It is the geometry of such objects which is fractal, and any system which can be visualized or analyzed geometrically, whether it be real or a product of our mathematical imagination, can be fractal if it has these characteristics. We do not wish to preempt our discussion in Chapters 2 and 3 but when we refer to an object as being irregular, we do not mean that it is disordered or chaotic, but that it is not smooth in the sense in which Euclidean geometry articulates the world.

Because fractal objects are not smooth, their geometry poses certain basic conundrums. The classic example is the coastline. Coastlines are never straight, nor do they twist and turn in such a way that they enclose space completely. But on an intuitive level, they are something more than the straight line which has a Euclidean dimension of 1 and something less than the plane in which they exist which has a dimension of 2. We could guess, and in fact we would be correct, that their dimension was between 1 and 2, fractional rather than integral, thus opening up the possibility that the Euclidean dimensions of 1 and 2 are simply extremes or special cases which bound a continuum of fractional or fractal dimensions. In Chapter 2, we will imply that this argument can be generalized to any dimension, and that although coastlines and terrain are fractal in the familiar realm of space–time, fractals exist in higher dimensions, in mathematical space, where their visualization only makes sense to abstract analysis. The conundrums emerge for all fractals whose measurement which is usually based upon the integral part of their fractal dimension, no longer accords to this Euclidean logic. For coastlines, for example, this means that their length in the linear dimension is infinite although the area that they enclose is bounded. More, much more of this, in Chapter 2.

In this book, we will restrict our discussion to fractals which exist in the continuum from points to lines to planes to volumes which are all geometric notions useful in describing the city. Thus our geometry is a literal one and not one abstracted from these real properties of the city. In fact, most of our analysis of the geometry of cities, of urban form, will deal with boundaries and areas. We will not consider the city in its third dimension which might also be regarded as fractal – the skyline of Manhattan for example – although in a sense, the third dimension will enter implicitly when we deal with population densities in later chapters. Our applications to cities also reveal the essential logic of fractal geometry. If fractals are self-similar in that their geometry repeats itself on many levels or scales, it is clear that a stable process or set of processes is operating to form the geometry. For example, coastlines and terrain are determined by geomorphic processes of weathering and erosion. Cities of different sizes are associated with specialization due to economies of scale, and so on. Of course, if we can demonstrate that an object is fractal, this gives us some hope that we can narrow our search for those functions and processes which give rise to different forms.

Cities have quite distinct fractal structure in that their functions are self-similar across many orders or scales. The idea of neighborhoods, districts and sectors inside cities, the concept of different orders of transport net, and the ordering of cities in the central place hierarchy which mirrors the economic dependence of the local on the global and vice versa, all provide examples of fractal structure which form the cornerstones of urban geography and spatial economics. Hierarchical distributions of city size in the form of Pareto or rank-size rules have long been considered the iron laws of spatial systems, while distributions and density profiles inside the city are fractal in nature. We will not attempt to rewrite the entire edifice of urban theory in fractal geometry within this book although we will touch upon such theory at many points. This may disappoint some who feel that these ideas are suggestive enough to demand such a reworking. But ours is a different quest, once again a beginning, a demonstration of what is possible. We hope to lay out some promising trails, but doubtless, we will trace some false ones. And we are not too arrogant to confess that there are many aspects and implications of fractal geometry which lie beyond our expertise and must be taken up by others, with different interests and objectives in mind. Finally there are many aspects of cities which can be interpreted as fractal in the geometric sense, and as yet there is no coherent theory to pull all this diversity together. Nor need there be, for if fractal geometry is to be truly general like any geometry, its applicability to even similar systems of interest will be likewise diverse. In so far as integrated theory exists to which fractal geometry can be applied, this integration will be in terms of the system itself and not its geometry.

The cities, and systems of cities, which we will consider range from the hypothetical to the real. Those which are hypothetical exist as idealized abstractions and are mainly introduced in the earlier chapters where we are concerned with laying the foundations of fractal geometry. These enable us to explore how we might develop appropriate techniques for measuring and modeling fractal distributions. However, most examples in this book are concerned with real cities. From Chapter 5 on, we will develop methods for describing and measuring fractal properties of cities which exist at cross-sections in time, in terms of boundaries to entire cities, and to the land uses which they comprise, as well as the urban textures which reflect their spatial juxtapositioning. We then launch into a study of the fractal city proper, measuring its growth over time, its processes of growth, and ways in which we might model this growth, connecting all these ideas up with urban economic theory in the form of population densities on the one hand, and systems of cities which compose central place theory on the other. Our exposition will begin with the superficial geometry of the city but will then expand to examine its internal functions and its positioning within the wider hierarchy of city sizes.

We will begin in Chapter 1 by reviewing what we know about the shape of cities, about urban form, particularly emphasizing the distinctions between 'planned' or 'regular' cities, and 'organic' or 'irregular' cities. This is a matter of degree, of course, but our argument will establish the case for a fractal geometry of cities, and we will show how the concepts of hierarchy and self-similarity particularly, comprise the structure of knowledge in this domain. Our next three chapters lay the foundations for a fractal theory of cities largely, but not exclusively, based on hypothetical or at least highly abstracted city shapes. In Chapter 2, we outline the rudiments of fractal geometry, presenting classic well-defined 'deterministic' fractals such as space-filling curves, trees and hierarchies of various kinds, emphasizing the appropriate mathematics of shape, scale and dimension, and methods for constructing fractals through recursion and iteration. In Chapter 3, we generalize these ideas to fractals whose properties must be measured statistically, concentrating largely on methods for estimating the fractal dimension of coastlines and terrain, as well as on appropriate techniques for their generation. We then use these techniques to simulate the patterning and texture of land use in a large city with an emphasis on visualization using computer graphics. We take these ideas much further in Chapter 4 where we set up a laboratory for visualizing different urban forms which are possible using these types of model, and finally we apply these ideas to a real example – residential housing location in London.

Chapters 2–4 explain the use of fractals in visualization and in simulation rather than in measurement, but in the next two chapters we change tack to consider much more specific methods of measurement and estimation. In Chapter 5, we rework the classic fractal as the boundary of an urban area – the edge of the city, while in Chapter 6, we extend these ideas to sets of many fractal objects, in this case, those land uses which comprise the elements of the city which exist within its urban boundary. This introduces a key theme into this discussion, namely the distinction between methods for estimating the fractal dimension of a single object, and methods for estimating the dimension of a set of many objects, and the ways these are related. By this point, we have introduced enough theory and method to begin the construction of fully-fledged dynamic models of the city and systems of cities using fractal geometry, and this we accomplish in the rest of this book.

Chapter 7 is one of the most important for there we lay the groundwork for a theory of the fractal city in contrast to the discussion hitherto which has been pitched around the idea of fractal theory applied to cities. We begin by examining the form of several cities around the world, focussing upon their fractal properties in terms of the way their development fills available space. The model we propose builds on the ideas already introduced but is set within the context of the growing city and the way development generates regular gradations of density associated with its space-filling. We then propose a more general model based on the idea of limited diffusion of growth – the so-called diffusion-limited aggregation (DLA) model which is widely used in non-equilibrium physics – and we spend the rest of this chapter fitting it to real examples. We then extend and generalize the model in Chapter 8 to provide a new laboratory for generating a range of different urban forms and we select one which best fits the form of the city of Cardiff, thus providing simple, but nevertheless suggestive, simulations of urban growth and form. In Chapters 9 and 10, we embed these ideas first into the theory of urban population densities and then into central place theory. In Chapter 9, we show how fractals provide a new and enriched view of density theory, implying functional forms different from those used traditionally, but also providing more informed methods for measuring and estimating density functions than those used hitherto. In Chapter 10, we generalize these density and scaling relations to a system of cities, to the central place hierarchy, and show how constraints on their form influence the pattern of settlement at the regional level. In both these chapters, we complete our theory of the fractal city by extending its scaling relations to embrace both density theory and urban allometry.

Our conclusions are brief but directed, mainly pulling together the many threads we have sought to weave but also charting plans for the future. We reflect there upon the purpose of this work. Clearly fractal geometry enables us to link form to function which is our initial motivation, and at least, it shows us how we might approach this quest. What we do not intend here is to suggest models which are immediately applicable in a policy context, for our concern is much more with demonstrating an approach. At one level, this might be adapted to specific contexts, at another, it might simply suggest how we think about cities. Furthermore, we can even argue that fractal methods are more applicable to the generic city than to actual or particular cities, and in this sense, are mainly expository rather than applicable. But we will not take this discussion any further here for these are issues that the reader must decide.

Before we begin, we must say something briefly about the mathematical notation we will use. Throughout the book, we will use a standard set of definitions to refer to geometrical entities: distances, numbers of objects or populations, lines, areas, and densities. The overall linear size of an object will be defined by the variable R and its reference at any explicit point by r; these are typically distances in cities whose size is measured thus. The numbers of objects, usually associated with a system of size R is given by N, in turn referenced in terms of its parts by n. Length of lines and areas are denoted by L and A respectively, while density, defined as N/A, is given as ρ. Each of these variables might be indexed by size or distance r or R to which they refer, or discretely by integers in the range i, j, k, l, m and n depending upon context. With respect to dimension, the fractal dimension is defined as D while the Euclidean or integer dimension is E. Note that we will use d as a measure of discrete distance, not as part of the continuum $r \subset R$, and that the statistical measure of fit or coefficient of determination r^2 should not be confused with size or distance r. In Chapter 10, E_k is also used to define the length of the envelope of an urban area specific to settlement k. All other variables and parameters will not be completely standardized but defined chapter by chapter, although some attempt will be made to make their usage unique. Equations which are numbered are always referred to explicitly in the text by their number; those which are not do not have any lesser significance but are simply not referred to in the text.

1

The Shape of Cities: Geometry, Morphology, Complexity and Form

Why have cities not, long since, been identified, understood and treated as problems of organized complexity? If the people concerned with the life sciences were able to identify their difficult problems as problems of organized complexity, why have people professionally concerned with cities not identified the *kind* of problems they had? (Jacobs, 1961, p. 434.)

1.1 Understanding Cities

When Jane Jacobs posed her prescient question over 30 years ago, our understanding of cities was still dominated by the search for a visual order. As our immediate knowledge of the city is visual, it is perhaps explicable that urban problems which manifest themselves in cities are first associated with the destruction of visual order and harmony. The clear consequence of this has been the quest to solve, or at least alleviate, these problems by reimposing this order or developing it anew through city planning and design. Indeed, modern city planning still takes its inspiration from works such as Camillo Sitte's (1889, 1965) *City Planning, According to Artistic Principles*, which was published a little over 100 years ago. As long as man has sought to interpret the city, this has been mainly though the visual arts and architecture, culminating in the present century in the ideologies of the Garden City, the City Beautiful, and the Modern Movement. This deeply ingrained view of the city has had a profound influence on less artistic, more humanistic and somewhat more explicitly scientific approaches which in turn have sought to see the city through the need to assert statistical order in terms of homogeneity of its structure and the suppression of 'undesirable' diversity. Indeed, since Jane Jacobs elaborated her thesis, our understanding now augmented by the realization that the city presents a kaleidoscope of complexity, has hardly changed; planning and design still seek to impose a simplistic order on situations which defy our proper understanding and which we can only perceive as disordered.

Yet throughout history, there has always been an alternative view. From ancient times, towns and cities have been classified into those which grow 'naturally' or 'organically' and those which are 'artificial' or 'planned'. The distinction between these types is manyfold and often blurred, and of course there exists a continuum from organic to planned growth, many if not most towns being formed from elements of both. One of the key distinctions involves the speed at which cities change, while another relates to the scale of their development. Organically growing cities develop much more slowly than those which are planned. Cities which grow naturally are formed from a myriad of individual decisions at a much smaller scale than those which lead to planned growth which invariably embody the actions of somewhat larger agencies. Planned cities or their parts are usually more monumental, more focussed and more regular, reflecting the will of one upon the many or, at best, reflecting the will of the majority through their elected representatives. Finally, organic change involves both growth and decline, while planned change is more asymmetric, frequently embodying growth but rarely dealing with decline. Thus in this sense, a more complete picture of urban development is based on a backcloth of natural or organic growth interwoven both in space and time by planned development.

These distinctions articulate themselves in clear visual ways. Organically growing towns seem to fit their natural landscape more comfortably in that if decisions are smaller in scale, they reflect the properties of nature more closely as well as reflecting more intense concerns at the local level. The degree of overall control and coordination between such individual decisions is usually less explicit while the overall resources which govern such development are mobilized separately in their parts without regard to any economies of scale which might be generated centrally. The development which occurs is much less systematic and often irregular in form, and such irregularity of form conflicts with our intuition and predisposition to thinking in terms of the simplistic geometrical order based on the geometry of Euclid and the Greeks. Moreover, it is naturally growing cities which have led to the various biological analogies so popular in describing city growth since the work of Geddes (1915, 1949). Planned growth appears more man-made in that the patterns produced are more regular, reflecting more control over the natural landscape, and the mobilization and coordination of much larger quantities of resources devoted to the development in question. In history, such planned developments are invariably centered upon the areas of towns associated with political or religious power – palace and temple complexes, or with rapidly developing colonial towns, while in the modern age, retail and industrial developments in contrast to residential display some of the same regularity. However, it is impossible to identify solely organic or planned towns, for these two classes of development merge into one another in many different parts of the city and at many different scales.

In terms of the doctrine of visual and statistical order, organic towns when viewed in plan form resemble cell growth, weaving in and out of the landscape, closely following the terrain and other natural features, embodying the technology of movement through main transport routes, like spider webs or tree-like forms focussed on centers which usually contain the origin of growth. Their geometry seems irregular, although as we will be at pains to emphasize throughout this book, this should not imply 'disorder'. In contrast, planned towns display a geometry of straight lines and smooth curves, built on a directness of movement which can only be imposed from above, embodying some sense of man's direct control over nature through technology. Until this century, such planned developments were either parts of larger towns or very small complete towns, more at the scale of the village; although with the institutionalization of large scale urban planning in the last 80 years, much more grandiose plans for entire cities such as the British New Towns or capital cities such as Chandigargh and Brasilia have been attempted which embody a more perfect geometry. Nevertheless, most towns and cities provide a blend of both, usually containing elements of the planned within a backcloth of organic growth. One of the clearest and perhaps surprising examples is the Athens of the fifth century BC where the acropolis, the agora and straight streets such as the Panathenaic way were but isolated elements in a city whose ". . . corresponding architectural growth was . . . slow and unsystematic and irregular" (Wycherley, 1962).

These differences between organic and planned growth strike at the very core of the way cities are developed and manifest themselves in every way we might conceive their study. In this context, we will concentrate on the geometry of cities, on their spatial properties as displayed mainly in two dimensions through their plans, and in this sense, we will emphasize their shape. Nevertheless, we are confident that our approach does not stand aside from the mainstream, but maps closely onto other ways of understanding cities through diverse disciplines within the arts, humanities, the social and the engineering sciences. Our starting point in this chapter will be the ways in which traditional and popular geometry has been fashioned to extend our understanding of cities. Wherever planned development has taken place, man has invoked the doctrine of visual order and imposed simple, regular geometrical forms or shapes on cities using the geometry of Euclid and drawing inspiration from such city building as far back as the Greeks. Yet during this century, and particularly since scholars, such as Jane Jacobs amongst others, have drawn our attention to the poverty of city planning in this ancient tradition, the paradigm of the visual order has come under intense scrutiny.

In parallel, the idea that naturally growing cities are in fact more workable, more efficient and more equitable, indeed more democratic, has gained credence as we have begun to probe the complexity which composes the way cities evolve and function. In the last 30 years, the gradual relaxation of the theoretical structures imposed on us through classical physics, mathematics and art which assume that whatever theory we develop must be simple, clear, workable and mechanistic, is leading to very new approaches to knowledge which appear more promising in the study of complex systems such as cities than anything hitherto. New approaches to time which embody discontinuity and to space which embody irregularity are becoming established and changing the philosophies to which we have traditionally ascribed. In this book, we will wholeheartedly embrace these new paradigms and demonstrate how we can begin to think of cities as systems of organized complexity whose geometry betrays a complexity of scale and form of which we have hitherto been largely unaware. To this end, we will suggest how urban theorists and city planners alike might move their world view a little closer to what we see as the 'true reality' of the ways cities develop and should be developed.

We will begin by tracing the various changing conceptions of how space and time have been abstracted across the broad sweep of human history. Our tendency to continually abstract through simplification manifests itself in the way we use mathematics to portray order and regularity, the way we conceive time as a continuous flow, and the way we perceive space as composed of simple geometries. But this is rapidly changing and we are entering a time when many of these traditional notions are being intensely scrutinized. In our quest to refocus the study of cities using these new ideas, we will first trace the juxtaposition of planned and organic urban forms and the ways these conceptions have dominated the study of urban form throughout history. From this review will emerge a deeper sense of how the morphology of cities should be understood in terms of their form and process, scale and shape, their statics and dynamics; and this will enable us to map out our approach which builds our understanding of urban form about the new geometry of the irregular – fractal geometry.

In essence the shift engendered by this approach is fundamental in that a theory of the fractal city breaks directly with the tradition that sees cities as simple, ordered structures, expressible by smooth lines and shapes which describe their overall morphology and the disposition of their elements. The change we seek to impress moves us closer to the view that cities are complex organisms, evolving and changing according to local rules and conditions which manifest more global order across many scales and times. In this, our view of cities is closer to modern biology than it is to either the visual arts or classical economics which have both influenced the study of cities and their planning so profoundly over the last century (Steadman, 1979). Nevertheless, our emphasis will still, in the first instance, be upon approaching the study of cities through their geometry and form, but always with this broader and deeper context in mind.

1.2 Ancient and Traditional Conceptions of Space

From the earliest examples of the written record, there is evidence that man has always made sense of the world through powerful simplifying abstractions which seek out the underlying principles and order in our experiences and perceptions. The power to abstract is one which probably sets man aside from the rest of the animal kingdom and it is clear that the ability to impress order and structure on diverse phenomena though casting aside detail irrelevant to the quest in hand, is strongly correlated with our conventional view of human progress. In short, abstraction leads to theory and theory enables the kernel of any phenomena to be isolated, defined and thence explained. From prehistory, such abstraction has been associated with the power to simplify the world visually and from the earliest cave paintings, man has sought to impose smooth geometry on art so that its meaning can be communicated in the simplest and most effective way.

Ten thousand years ago, the first towns developed when man moved from a nomadic existence to a society and economy based on more settled agriculture. This was what Toffler (1981) has called 'the first wave', beginning in the 'fertile crescent' centered upon the Rivers Euphrates and Tigris, in ancient Babylon. The evidence of man's attempts at visual abstraction and geometrical simplification of both natural and artificial phenomena come fast and furious from these times. Although this revolution was marked more by the natural or 'organic' growth of towns, there are many examples of 'planned' developments where man imposed his simple geometry on the land and upon the processes through which cities were sustained. The first cities show evidence of straight streets, of ordered land uses separated from one another, of vistas and monuments associated with the visual display of political and economic power in temple and palace complexes, of routes radiating from central places and of well-developed hierarchies of city systems consistent with elaborate agricultural and market economies. The earliest excavations have revealed urban agglomerations existing around 2500 BC; the Babylonian city of Ur, Harrapan cities along the Indus such as Mohenjo-daro and ancient Egyptian palaces as at Tel-el-Amarna all attest to the imposition of geometrically ordered streets and buildings following gridiron plans and focussed upon central points such as markets and temples (Morris, 1979).

In fact, there is no sense in the written record of any time when man's spatial sense of order was any less developed than in modern times, although the association of geometrical order with science and with the means to impose that order through technology has changed substantially since the first urban civilizations emerged. The Egyptians considered the world to be a flat plane yet the notion that the world might be round in some sense has been imbedded deep in our psyche since prehistory. The first known map of the world inscribed on a Sumerian clay tablet around 1500 BC, shows the familiar concentric and perhaps egocentric view of society, in that case centered in a circle about Babylon. This convention of centering or focussing social and economic activity in space around some powerful focus such as a city repeats itself throughout history when maps are made and plans proposed, and it has only been in the present century that there has been any sustained effort at thinking ourselves out of this traditional perspective.

It was the Greeks who first developed our visual senses to the point where art and science came to be treated as one, and where the imposition of geometry upon nature was first interpreted though the medium of science. It was the Greeks who first conceived of the earth as a sphere, and who first developed the requisite geometrical science to both demonstrate and use this understanding for the process of building cities. A long line of Greek scientists and geometers assembled a science and geometry which ultimately provided the foundation for the modern age and which essentially still dominates architecture and city planning to this day. The spherical model of the cosmos developed by Thales, Pythagoras, Herodotus amongst others and demonstrated using devastating measurement techniques by Eratosthenes, changed man's conception of space but more in matter of degree than kind. In fact, the notion that the earth might be a perfect sphere further impressed the idea that the 'true' geometry, the 'perfect' geometry, which was that which represented the highest form of art was that based upon the point, the line, the circle, the sphere and diverse combinations of the regular, in contrast to the irregular which remained beyond understanding (Berthon and Robinson, 1991).

During Greek and Roman times, the distinction between 'regular planned' and 'irregular organic' forms of urban settlement first appeared. In fact as we noted earlier, most towns grew organically as the product of many individual decisions made according to local rules and circumstances. But the Greeks and Romans left a legacy of planned towns, largely through their efforts at colonizing the known world, and it is there that the first examples of regular town plans based on the gridiron form make their appearance as at Miletus and Priene in present-day Asia Minor. The Roman military camp which could be assembled in a matter of hours also imposed geometrical order on places where none had been hitherto, and as technology developed to a larger scale, this geometry became imposed upon the wider landscape though long straight roads, walls and other man-made barriers as well as through large-scale agricultural cultivation. When the Roman world collapsed and Europe descended into her dark ages, what was left in terms of our knowledge and understanding of space was extensive and widely recorded in many treatises: Ptolemy's *Geography*, Vitruvius's *De Architectura*, and of course Euclid's magnificent exposition in his *Elements of Geometry* written some 300 BC, all of which rang down the ages to be rediscovered during Europe's Renaissance, precursor to the modern age.

For almost a thousand years from the division of the Roman Empire until the Crusades, the formal knowledge of geometry and science bequeathed upon us by the Greeks lay dormant in the monasteries or in the east in Constantinople where the crossroads with Islam gave it another twist through the development of algebra. In fact, the geometry was so deep-seated that it remained central to mainstream religious thought. There is a beautiful example of man's sense of the world and its geometry in the map produced by Isidore, the seventh century archbishop of Seville, which shows the world as round but formed as three continents, Asia, Europe and Africa, divided by the Mediterranean Sea, and the Rivers Nile and Don which we show in Figure 1.1. Isidore's map is more abstract than many before such as Ptolemy's, but it does reveal the extreme abstraction which has persisted until this present century in much map making, especially at the local scale. In the 13th and 14th centuries, Europe began to wake from its long sleep, trade revived, and the world view of society dominated for so long by religion came under increasing scrutiny. With this, the geometry and the science of the Greeks was rediscovered, literally reborn and almost immediately new advances were made in the development of geometry though the discovery of perspective. But it was in science that the real revolution in our perceptions of space came from, this time around.

Although the idea that the earth was a sphere had been known to the Greeks, the notion that the earth was center of the universe was central to religious belief, particularly to Christianity. However, the model of the universe based on interlocking spheres did not accord to observations of the motions of the planets and modern science from the 15th century generated increasingly precise observations of these motions. The great intuition, however, as to how these orbits fit together was made by Newton in the late 17th century and published in his *Principia* which established not only

Figure 1.1. A seventh century world geometry (from Berthon and Robinson, 1991).

the laws of gravitation which held for the observable solar system, but also the physical principles for diverse physical phenomena at many scales. Much of Newton's science and that of his contemporaries was deeply rooted in the notion of a perfect geometry. However, it was not the mechanics established by his insights, but the mathematics which he fashioned to present his science, which reinforced Euclid's view, still our conventional world view of geometry. In essence, Newton's mechanics depended upon the principle of continuity. Both space and time had to be continuous in the simplest possible sense for his theories to triumph. In short, the scale of physical systems and the forces which might change their scale could not admit any discontinuity which might change their form. Mass, for example, should be capable of being accelerated continuously, and if the force responsible were to cease, so would the acceleration and movement, but at a continually decreasing rate. This was the kind of science that embodied the principle of continuity, enshrined in the mathematics of the calculus which Newton and his contemporary Leibnitz invented to make all this possible. Such systems were said to change in a linear, continuous fashion both in terms of the space and scale they occupied and by which they were defined, and within the time frame of their existence.

During the 19th century, this type of physics based on the mechanics of Newton and the geometry of Euclid became the cornerstone of modern science. In other areas such as in biology, Darwin's theories of continuous evolution through survival of the fittest were also fashioned into the Newtonian mould, while the emergent social sciences began their quest to develop a science akin to physics based on reducing every phenomenon to continuously varying structures based on simple causal relations, embodying ideas of strong equilibrium and convergence. In short, by the end of the 19th century, the broad structure of science and associated knowledge was underpinned by concepts of pure geometry, the theory of continuous variation, the notion that all systems had some underlying simple set of forces, and the idea that their understanding could be pursued through successive reductionism. This was the 'majestic clockwork' as

Bronowski (1973) amongst others has referred to it. The world, however, was about to change, casting a doubt upon our age-old and perhaps superficial abilities to simplify through immediate and intuitive abstraction.

1.3 The New Science of Space and Time

At this point, it is worth posing a series of dichotomies which are not only useful in summarizing the changes to various world views which are relevant to our quest for a better understanding of space and time but are central to the changes in viewpoint which we will imply in the theory of fractal cities to be developed in this book. First we must contrast the notions of *simplicity* and *complexity*. Science stands at an edge between reality and mind, in perpetual tension between the need to simplify in order to understand and the need to provide a requisite variety in our theory to meet the perceived complexity. In one sense, however, the emphasis is more on simplicity, for great science, it is argued, seeks to provide the most parsimonious, hence the simplest and most elegant explanation, and success is thus judged through Occam's razor. In fact, we will argue that the science which is emerging everywhere in the late 20th century has found that previous standards of parsimony no longer admit the requisite explanation and thus we are now being forced to move to a higher threshold. In this sense then, our theories are becoming more complicated as well as dealing with new orders of complexity.

A second distinction is between *reductionism* and *holism*. Reductionist thinking has dominated physics and economics until quite recently, as indeed it has done biology, but there is a general and growing consensus that more holistic theory is needed which seeks to synthesize, not simply by aggregating the fine detail but by enabling the emergence of higher level form and function associated with new causes and forces. That 'the whole is more than the sum of the parts' may be a long-worn cliche of general systems theory, but ultimate explanations are no longer likely to be found in the quest for knowing more and more about less and less. To some extent, these issues smack of vitalism, and one small corner of our quest to counter this depends upon the logic of the ideas developed here. We have already mentioned our third distinction – the emphasis in Newtonian science upon the idea of continuity and the polarization of the *continuous* with the *discontinuous*. In essence, classical science has been entirely ineffective in coping with systems which display some abrupt change in behavior and in recent times, it would appear that more and more systems in very different domains manifest behavior patterns which cannot be treated using any kind of continuous formalism. In one sense, the idea that space is not continuous applies directly to cities, in that smooth change in physical form is clearly an abstraction when it comes to measuring and observing how the urban form evolves and shapes spatial organization. For a long time, science has been content to derive theory for idealized situations within the laboratory or within highly controlled situations, but increasingly, such science has been shown to be inapplicable to the real world, and continuity is one of the central problems inhibiting its applicability.

A fourth distinction involves the degree of homogeneity or heterogeneity which systems display, in essence the degree to which systems manifest *uniformity* or *diversity*. Systems which are intrinsically diverse and heterogeneous have for long been treated as being beyond science in some sense, while those systems for which the most pleasing explanations have been found are those which are well-behaved, controllable, homogeneous and ordered – that is, uniform in some sense. However, increasingly even the simplest systems betray a degree of complexity which departs from our traditional perceptions of uniformity and new theories are beginning to directly address the issue of explaining rather than suppressing diversity. A fifth dichotomy relates *certainty* to *uncertainty*. As we have begun to explain more and more, it seems that we are certain about less and less, that is, that our knowledge seems increasingly contingent upon time and space, upon the unique and the ephemeral. How is it, we ask, that the bounds of what we know seem to retreat a little faster than the rate at which we generate new ideas and insights? Is this progress? As we will argue throughout this book, this insight in itself is probably progress of a kind in a world of infinite variety and complexity, one whose nature we have only just begun to recognize.

Lastly, let us dwell briefly on the contrast between the *regular* and the *irregular*. In this book, we will be using this distinction in a very specific sense to draw out the differences between urban form conceived and perceived using the geometry of Euclid with that using the geometry of Mandelbrot (1983), the founder of fractal geometry, the geometry of the irregular. But the distinction is deeper and more far-reaching than this in that our penchant to abstract is strongly rooted in searching out the regular and dismissing the irregular. In short, we are predisposed to filter out that which we cannot cast into the geometry and the science of the regular although in doing so, we are in danger of casting out the very essence of what we need to explain. Science is only just beginning to grasp the notion that it is the irregular, the complex, the diverse, the uncertain, the whole system which is the proper domain of inquiry and to which we must reorient our quest.

In fact, at the end of the 19th century, classical physics was challenged, not by any of these opposites that are implied in the distinctions we have just sketched, but by the need to address basic forces in *relative* rather than *absolute* terms. Two different sources of anomaly emerged. First physical observations of phenomena involving the speed of light such as planetary orbits no longer seemed to fit Newtonian theory, while the conceptual problem of reconciling the space–time frameworks of observers light years apart loomed large. It was Einstein's intuition to visualize such problems and reconcile them by showing that the space–time continuum could no longer be treated as the absolute mould within which the universe existed if observers were to see the same thing at different positions in time and space. This represented the first loosening of a framework which had dominated scientific assumption since prehistory and as such represented the biggest challenge to man's intuitive grasp of the universe so far.

The second came close on its heels and involved not the very large but the very small. The continuing reductionism of physics took a major step forward in the late 19th century when the idea of the atom and its constituent parts became an intense focus of concern. As more and more particles came to be discovered – first the electron, then the proton, neutron and so on, a new framework for explaining the position of each was required, and with this came the startling conclusion that the actual position of such subatomic particles was uncertain. Because physical observations of position in time and space could only be made with physical forces, their actual position was fundamentally influenced by the parameters of the measuring device, and so was born the principle of uncertainty attributed to Heisenberg, a central postulate of the quantum theory. In fact, this notion of uncertainty was probably easier to accept in the social world where experience suggested that direct observation of phenomena often had an influence on the nature of that phenomena, and thus physicists were simply learning that the more remote the phenomena from direct observation, the more uncertain the outcome of that observation, a simple enough concept but one that again rocked long-held assumptions of the scientific world.

Reaction against reductionism too has been forced onto the agenda in many fields during the present century. In physics, there has been little success to date with the development of unified theory linking the very small to the very large, although there are intense efforts at the present time and there are signs of breakthrough. However, in less dramatic domains, particularly in the social and biological sciences, the idea that the whole system need be understood has become paramount. Aggregating micro to macro theory has proved to be virtually impossible in economics for example. Systems which contain many elements have required frameworks for their reconciliation which construct the whole from the parts and from the mid-century, the development of general systems theory has become significant. At first such theory was static in focus, intent upon explaining the form and function of systems at an instant of time, although in the last two decades such systems theory has been deeply enriched with new ideas concerning system dynamics and behavior. Moreover, the notion that systems might operate almost entirely using local forces which ultimately add up or aggregate to global order has also gained ground as it has become clearer that the very small and the very large can be different aspects of the same underlying system phenomena.

These changes in world view have had quite profound effects on our scientific approach to space. Throughout the 20th century, the idea of visualizing phenomena beyond the first three physical, and fourth, temporal, dimensions has become important. In many disciplines, the focus has been upon dimensions other than the four basic ones where space and time have been seen as simply the matrix within which more interesting and significant actions and forces exist, and this has been particularly the case in the social sciences. In economics for example, the predominant concern has been with the way various actors and agencies establish a competitive equilibrium through networks of markets and monetary allocation, such theories being largely independent of the space in which such systems exist and largely suppressing the temporal dynamics of such behavior in rigid assumptions concerning convergence and equilibrium. Anything which threatens to destroy the elegance of the equilibrium such as the imperfections posed by space and time have been ruled out of court. It is thus no surprise that economics has little or nothing to say about most current economic events which thrive upon such imperfections and although such theory is under intense scrutiny at present, it will take at least a generation for economics to reestablish its theoretical sights.

The same has been true for other social sciences, sociology and psychology for example where the space–time matrix has been simply assumed to be a given, neutral with respect to its effects upon the phenomena under study. This lack of a geometrical perspective in the social domain has been both liberating and constraining. It has meant in fact that social science has long avoided the trap of physical determinism but at the same time it has meant that the physical constraints of space and time have had little influence in social explanation where often such influence is important. In the study of cities for example, it has kept the social and artistic approaches separate except through the pragmatism of geography, and it has inhibited the development of a theory of city systems which is a relevant synthesis of social process and spatial form. In practice, this dichotomy can be seen at its most extreme when commentators and researchers dealing with the same subject using the same jargon present their ideas in diametric opposition through entirely visual or entirely verbal media. Urban theorists from the social domain have found the visual paradigm to be empty for their study of social process while those from the visual arts have found social processes to be impossible to relate to the manipulation of physical space which represents the long-standing medium for city planning and design.

Yet changes in our conceptions of space and time which see irregularity and discontinuity as reflecting a new underlying order and system do perhaps provide a fresh perspective as to the impact of physical determinants on social and economic processes. The emergence during the last 20 years of a mathematics and a geometry in which discontinuous change can be ordered in terms of catastrophes and bifurcations and where sudden change can be easily accounted for, has helped show the importance of formal dynamics to many fields. More recently, the development of theories of chaos in which deterministic systems generate behavior paths which are unique and never repeat themselves are finding enormous applicability in qualitative studies of system behavior and structure in the social and biological sciences. In fact, there are many physical systems such as the weather which are subject to the same underlying complexity and the notion of an intrinsic order based on strange attractors which can only be envisaged in the higher geometry of their mathematical space has become central to the study of many real systems. In biology too, the notion of smooth change or evolution has also been informed by these theories which explain the importance of punctuated equilibrium, sudden species development and ecological catastrophe. And in all of this, the smooth geometry associated with Euclid which has dominated our thinking for so long is giving way to a geometry of the irregular which is still ordered but where the order repeats itself across many scales and through many times and where such irregularity is clearly consistent with observations and measurements of our most interesting systems.

All of these changes in world view are tied up with the emerging science of complexity (Lewin, 1992), in turn being different facets of the kaleidoscope of complexity which science seeks to understand. When Jane Jacobs (1961) wrote about the need to understand cities as problems of organized complexity, she was invoking ideas from general systems theory, of a more speculative kind and associated with the writings of Warren Weaver (1967). Weaver argued, as we have done here, that science developed from the 17th to the 19th centuries dealing with problems of simplicity, two-body problems amenable to linear mathematics and strict determinism. The emergence of quantum theory shifted this balance to problems of disorganized complexity where the predominant characteristic method of explanation was statistical. But between, there lay many problems amenable to neither approach, ". . . problems which involve dealing simultaneously with a sizable number of factors which are interrelated into an organic whole" (Weaver, 1967). In short, such systems are those in which the emergence of organization is reflected in their form or morphology. We are now in a position to begin to develop some of these ideas in our study of cities, but before we do so, it is worth reviewing examples and principles of the geometry describing a range of city shapes beginning with the planned city, the city of the ideal, the city of pure geometry.

1.4 The City of Pure Geometry

If there has been any significant change in our visual sense of the city through history, this has been in the nature of the way it has been abstracted and represented. From a contemporary perspective, there appears to have been increasingly abstract representation of urban phenomena in visual terms as we delve further into the past which manifests itself in less realism and greater simplicity than is now acceptable. Currently, with more media to record than at any time in history through photographs, digital imagery and the like, city plans and maps from the past seem to abstract away too much while portraying some detail in almost surrealistic ways. Mapping, now perhaps, is also considerably more single-minded in purpose, and the sort of detail contained in historical maps relating to people and events as well as places suggest that the visual records of the past were for somewhat different and more comprehensive purposes than those we employ today.

An excellent example of this visual simplicity is contained in one of the earliest town plans known which represents the shape of an Assyrian military encampment and the segregation of its land uses some 2000 BC (Kostof, 1991). In Figure 1.2, we show this plan which depicts a circular and fortified town, divided by two axes into four quarters where the pictures in each symbolize the usage of these areas. The plan was embodied as a relief on the wall of a temple in Nimrud (in present-day Iraq) and as such is one in a long line of gridiron plans used for rapid development most obviously associated with military camps, but also widely used for colonization. This Assyrian example, in fact, shows all the elements which repeat themselves throughout history in terms of imposing and developing cities based on pure geometry: the circle which invariably encloses and bounds development as well as focussing upon the core, the straight streets and routes which form the structure of the grid, the blocks which represent the

Figure 1.2.   The earliest depiction of the city of pure geometry (from Kostof, 1991).

interstices within the grid, the clear segregation of uses which is often imposed within such planned forms, and the fortified outer wall which was a feature of many cities until the present century when the technology of war went beyond this need.

The first evidence we have of highly ordered geometric forms is associated with either very rapid physical development, such as in military camps, or with more monumental, larger scale building related to the demonstration of political–religious–economic power within the city, such as in palace and temple complexes. For example, the camps used by workers to construct the pyramids and other monuments in ancient Egypt were laid out according to the strict principles of the grid, while colonial cities from the earliest Greek civilizations represented a more permanent but nevertheless rapid application of the same principles. Miletus and Priene are the archetypes, but there are many other examples which have been documented (Morris, 1979; Wycherley, 1962). The grid is also repeated in the development of larger complexes associated with the display of wealth and power throughout the ancient civilizations. All the important cities of the ancient world, Babylon, Knossos, Mycenae, Athens and of course, Rome, provide much evidence of a well-ordered geometry largely built around the gridiron as a basis for the construction of temples, market places, civic buildings and organized leisure in terms of sport and drama.

It is of interest that circular geometries are much less obvious and by association, much less used in city building up to the middle ages. Circular forms in a sense represent a natural bound for any city which is based on some central focus around which the major economic and political activity takes place. In this sense, most cities when examined in terms of their boundaries and edges, unless heavily constrained by physical features, are organized in some circular form, perhaps distorted along transport routes into a star shape, about some central point, usually the origin of growth. In fact, it is hard to find many examples where such circularity has been invoked as the basis of a geometrical order in towns before the medieval era. The Greeks did introduce radiality into their grids occasionally and there was some preoccupation with the use of the circle in theater complexes and stadia. The Romans did the same with their circuses and also in more detailed building through their invention and widespread use of the semi-circular arch. But it was not until the late middle ages and the Renaissance that cities really began to exploit the geometry of the pure circle. This perhaps was due to the lesser control over the geometry through the then available building technology although it is more likely that this may have been a purely aesthetic difference between ancient and modern, a difference in taste.

The best examples, of course, of the use of the grid come from the Roman military camp or *castra*, which is still the basis of many towns plans in contemporary Europe as evidenced best in England in towns ending with the word – *chester*. The main axes – the decumanus and the cardo – of such grids marked out the center of the camp where dwelt the legate, the legionary commander, and as the Assyrian map suggests arrayed around this were more specialized uses serving the legion, with the barracks banished to the edge of the camp often with recreation (the circus, amphitheater, etc.) beyond the wall. The Roman camp also marks the typical scale at which town plans were visualized and depicted up to these times. Although towns could be depicted in terms of their growth at a scale which abstracted away from the actual building and streets, this was very rare. The norm was to represent the town in terms of buildings and streets, and often to impose the geometry of the straight line on forms that clearly did not meet such geometrical purity in reality. However, the size of typical towns up until the modern age was so small and their form so compact that the sort of exploding metropolis reminiscent of the growth of London or the eastern seaboard of the United States which will be examples of our concern here, simply did not exist. This too goes some way in explaining their typical depiction.

The descent of Europe into its dark and middle ages led to the disappearance of the city of pure geometry. Towns looked inward; their form was compact although irregular and idiosyncratic, buildings huddled around the center which by now was church and market square. In fact, the notion of the circular city was much in evidence during these times to be fashioned a little later during Europe's Renaissance in more geometric form. In some instances, in the case of planned towns, for military purposes of control at borders, for example, the grid was still being used as it was wherever speed of development dictated its use, a fine example being the crusader port of Aigues-Mortes in the Rhone delta (Kostof, 1991). But what did develop quite distinctly during this period was a concern and fascination for elaborate fortifications based on regular but discontinuous geometries which maximized the amount of space available for the defense of a town.

A clear example of the succession of styles from Roman to medieval and beyond can be seen in the growth of the town of Regensburg on the southern bank of the River Danube which we illustrate in Figure 1.3 (Morris, 1979). In the year 350, the Roman settlement displays the clear grid of the

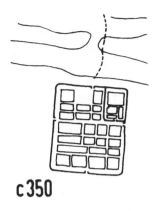

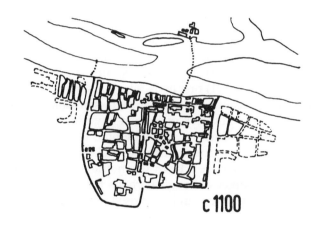

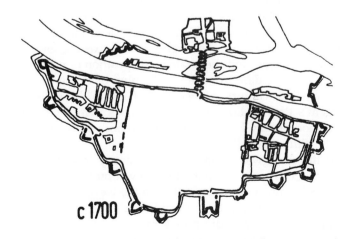

Figure 1.3.   A succession of geometries: Regensberg from Roman times (from Morris, 1979).

original castra while by 1100, although this has collapsed into the huddle of medieval buildings, the effect of the original grid is still apparent. The fortifications which encircled the town by 1700 represented a tight bound on growth, although the focus of the town is clearer in its approximately circular expansion from the original center of settlement. The fortifications based on regularly spaced triangular displacements from the straight wall represent the classic style of fortifying towns to increase the wall space available for their defense and as such represent a kind of space-filling phenomenon which as we shall see in the next chapter, is reminiscent of the regular fractal called the Koch or snowflake curve.

The Renaissance, however, was the time of high theory for the city of pure geometry. The rediscovery of the architecture of Greece and Rome through the written works of scholars such as Vitruvius (Bacon, 1967) led to massive experimentation and speculation on ideal town forms. Combined with developments in the architecture of fortification, the discovery of perspective which generated the need for a radial focus in the plan as well as within the three-dimensional massing of the city, and the need for regularly laid out city blocks, ideal town plans were much more ambitious than anything previously and such was the strength of commitment and belief in the new order, that the ideal became real in many instances. Figure 1.4 shows two such ideals; the first in 1.4(a) is based on Vitruvius's (republished 1521) first book which is somewhat perplexing in that it established an ideal in the circular plan, something as we have remarked, that did not exist in Greek or Roman city building. The second plan in Figure 1.4(b) is that which was actually built for the city of Palma Nuova outside Venice usually accredited to the Italian architect Scamozzi (Morris, 1979).

Many similar ideal town geometries were suggested as we will note in the next chapter although perhaps the finest which was built is Naarden in Holland whose plan is as close to the original as any. In fact, many such ideas were incorporated into existing cities such as we see at Regensburg in Figure 1.3 as well as in much larger cities such as Paris, Rome and Vienna where idealized fortifications were continually under construction. Examples of more regular circular geometries also date from this time, one of the best examples being Karlsruhe which we picture in Figure 1.5 (Morris, 1979; Kostof, 1991). Nevertheless the circular town form was embodied much more thoroughly within existing towns in the form of foci for radial streets and the strategic disposition of circles and squares. Excellent examples date from the replanning of Rome under Pope Sixtus V in the late 16th century, Hausmann's Paris in the mid-19th century, Nash's Regent's Park in London, and l'Enfant's plan for Washington DC which was modified by Ellicott, the last two both being implemented during the early 19th century.

If the circle was to gain the ascendancy in Baroque Europe, it was the grid that complete dominated the development of American cities from the late 18th century onwards. Cities in the New World resembled those in the old until the early 19th century when rapid expansion led to widespread application of the gridiron as a matter largely of speed and convenience, and perhaps through a sense of modernity – a break with the past. New York or rather Manhattan island is the example *par excellence*. Town after town which was laid out in the western expansion of settlement in North

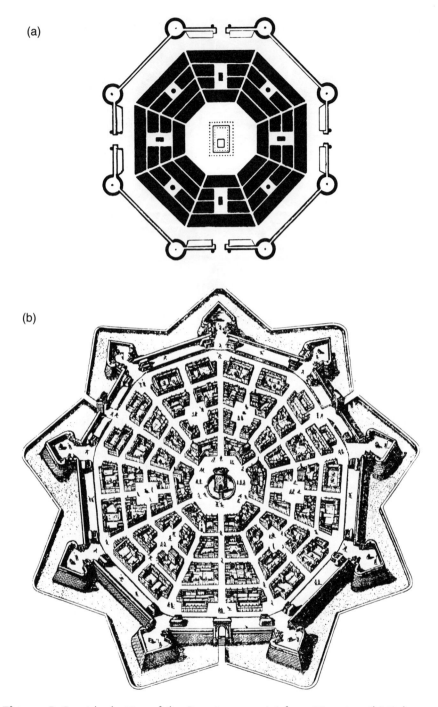

Figure 1.4.   Ideal cities of the Renaissance: (a) from Vitruvius; (b) Palma Nuova after Scamozzi (from Morris, 1979).

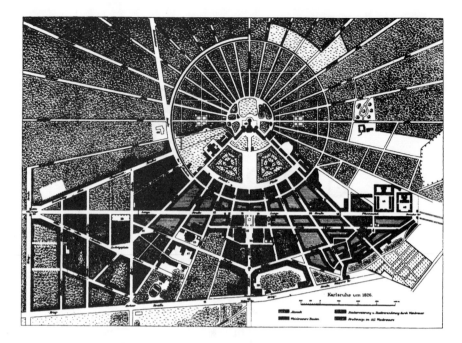

Figure 1.5. Circular towns: Karlsruhe (from Morris, 1979).

America conformed to the grid as Reps' (1965) *The Making of Urban America* so clearly demonstrates. Yet during these years too, there are few documented examples of how geometrically ordered plan forms actually developed; that is, concerning the extent to which such plans were modified. As we have reiterated throughout this chapter, such plans usually only exist for a snapshot in time and as such, once implemented do in fact begin to adapt to the physical and other constraints of settlement as well as to the actions of individuals working with a different purpose to that of larger agencies. Two examples of the extent to which pure geometry guided development, however, are worth illustrating. First, the town of Savannah, Georgia, was laid out in gridiron fashion in the 1730s by colonists from England and with surprising commitment given the rapid development during these years, the residents of Savannah grew their town according to the grid for the next 100 years. The evolution of the town is shown in Figure 1.6 and is one of the very few examples of urban growth clearly built on purely geometric principles.

The second example is more prosaic and it concerns the development of a circular town in southern Ohio named Circleville. Circular town forms as we have indicated are almost entirely absent from the New World although in the 1820s, such a form was adopted for this land on which had stood circular Indian mounds which may have influenced the shape of the plan and the naming of the town. However for diverse reasons, some clearly related to the use of space, the plan was 'redeveloped' some 20 years after it had first been laid out so that it might conform to the more standard grid. Remarkably, the agency responsible for carrying out this change was called the 'Circleville Squaring Company' and its actions are clearly recorded in the systematic transformation of the circular town plan into a

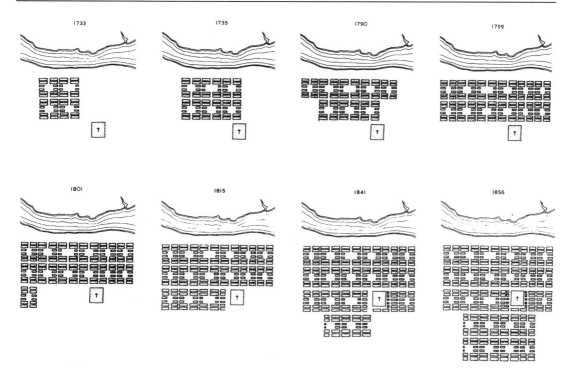

Figure 1.6.   Regular cellular growth: Savannah 1733–1856 (from Reps, 1965).

grid as illustrated in Figure 1.7. Aside from the somewhat idiosyncratic example this poses, it does show the power of pure geometry in city building as well as reinforcing our popular and deeply-ingrained perception of what constitutes 'good design'.

During the present century, there has been a distinct shift to geometries which combine perfect circles and squares and the like with more sinuous although still smooth curves. There has also, in the last 50 years, been a major shift towards conceiving cities in terms of ideal network geometries based on communications routes, largely road systems. Architects and urban designers have exuded more confidence too in their quest to build the city of pure geometry, suggesting larger and larger idealizations of the old ideas. In the late 19th century, more abstract conceptions of the ideal city system based on social and economic ideas of utopia became important in movements such as the Garden Cities (Howard, 1898). These are so significant that we will deal with them in a later section for what they imply concerning urban form is pitched at a different spatial scale from the ideas of this and the next section. But we must point to the most significant of the 20th century physical utopias and we will begin with Le Corbusier.

The *Ville Radieuse* is perhaps the most important of Corbusier's statements about the future city and in essence, it is based not on any specific notion of grid or circle, but upon the idea that the city should exploit its third dimension much more effectively through tall blocks, thus releasing the ground space for recreation and leisure. In fact, Corbusier's ideas are best seen in his plan for the Indian capital of Chandigargh which is illustrated in Figure 1.8(a). The form in fact is one based on a grid, the scale of

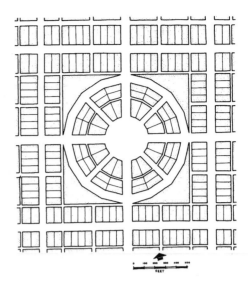

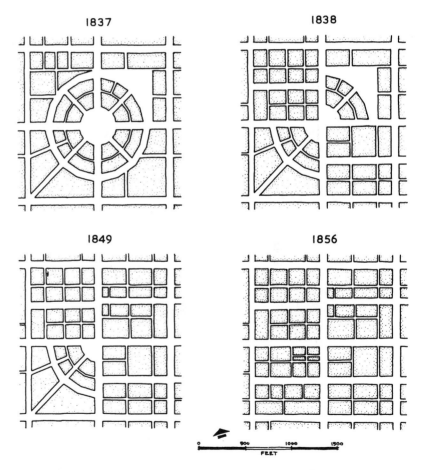

Figure 1.7. The squaring of Circleville 1810–1856 (from Reps, 1965).

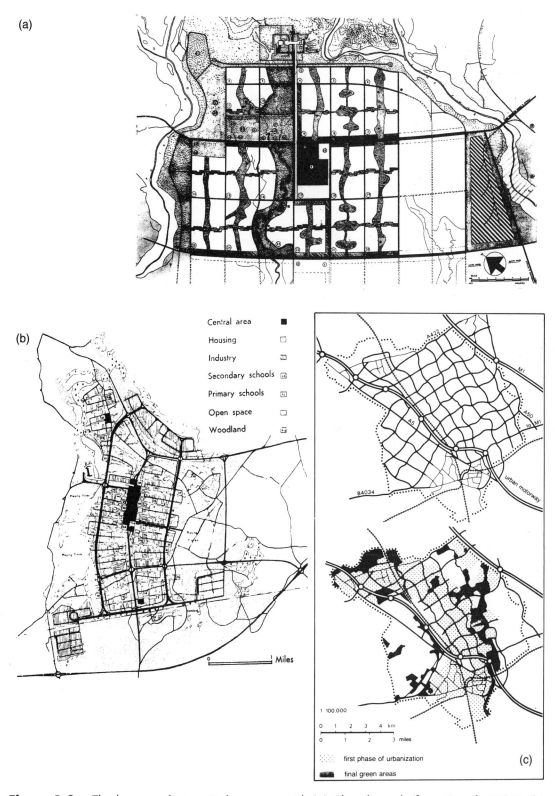

Figure 1.8. The large scale twentieth century grid: (a) Chandigargh (from Kostof, 1991); (b) Hook New Town (from Keeble, 1959); (c) Milton Keynes (from Benevolo, 1980).

its conception is much greater than anything we have illustrated so far in this chapter but its form is still rooted very firmly within conventional Euclidean geometry. However, the plan like so many in the 20th century is more comprehensive, emphasizing strict segregation of uses, as well as a separate landscape – a green grid – which is the complement of the urban transportation and neighborhood grid. Similar types of grid can be seen in some of the British New Towns which we also illustrate in Figures 1.8(b) and (c).

In contrast, Frank Lloyd Wright's *Broadacre City* is a city of low density which sacrifices the rigor of communal tower block living to a more individualist, American style, although he too casts his ideas into a rigid grid. Many other geometric schemes have been suggested since the beginning of the industrial era based on exploiting single principles of urban development: transport around which the linear city such as Sonia y Mata's *Cuidad Lineal* was fashioned in a proposal in 1882 and its application to existing city forms as in the MARS plan for London in the early 1940s, integrated service provision as in Frank Lloyd Wright's later and somewhat extreme reaction to his own *Broadacre City* through the idea of mile high residential superblocks, and in Dantzig and Saaty's (1973) *Compact City* in which all services are concentrated in a city of five or so levels, but built entirely in purely geometric and organized fashion as a machine for living. We illustrate these conceptions in Figure 1.9 where it is now clear that the emphasis has changed a little. The geometry of the ideal town has been relaxed slightly during the 20th century; it is more curvilinear, but still linear nonetheless. It is more organized around new transportation technologies and it is more concerned with land uses and activities than with specific building shapes. However, these ideals are still largely visual in organization and intent, and rarely portray any sense of urban evolution which is so important to the development of cities. We will, however, shift our focus, still concentrating on the visual form of cities in two not three dimensions, but now examining cities which are not dominated by pure geometry, those for which their development is often assumed to be more 'natural'.

1.5 The Organic City

Organic cities do not display obvious signs that their geometry has been planned in the large, although they may well be a product of many detailed and individual decisions which have been coordinated in the small. Therefore it is probably more a hindrance than a help to think of organic cities as being 'unplanned' in contrast to those that have been 'planned', as this represents only the most superficial of reactions to urban form. Thus we will avoid any association between 'organic' cities and the notions of uncoordinated or uncontrolled growth, although we will follow at least the spirit if not the word of Kostof (1991) who characterizes the organic city as:

... 'chance-grown', 'generated' (as against 'imposed'), or, to underline one of the evident determinants of its pattern, 'geomorphic'. It is presumed to develop without the benefit of designers, subject to no master plan but the passage of time, the lay

(a)

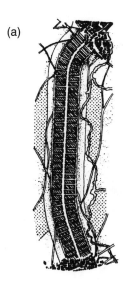

(b)

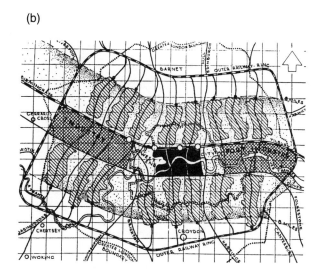

Figure 1.9. Experimental urban geometries: (a) Cuidad Lineal (from Keeble, 1959); (b) The MARS Plan for London (from Keeble, 1959);

A	County Seat Administration	H	Small Industry	R Orchards
B	Airport	J	Small Farms	S Homes and Apartments
C	Sports	K	Park	
D	Professional Offices	L	Motor Inn	T Temple and Cemetery
E	Stadium	M	Industry	U Research
F	Hotel	N	Merchandising	V Zoo
G	Sanitarium	P	Railroad	W Schools

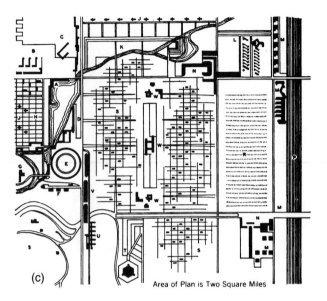

(c)

Area of Plan is Two Square Miles

(d)

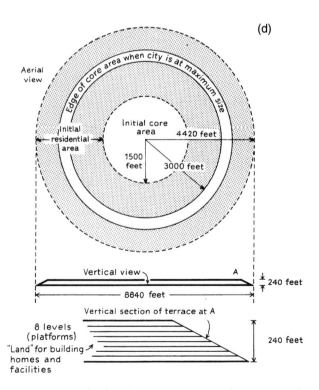

Figure 1.9. Experimental urban geometries (contd.): (c) Broadacre City (from Gallion and Eisner, 1950, 1975); (d) Compact City (from Dantzig and Saaty, 1973).

of the land, and the daily life of the citizens. The resultant form is irregular, non-geometric, 'organic', with an incidence of crooked and curved streets and randomly defined open spaces. To stress process over time in the making of such city-forms, one speaks of 'unplanned evolution' or 'instinctive growth'. (Kostof, 1991.)

The biological metaphor in city planning has been used since the 16th century, from a time when man first began to move beyond myth to a scientific study of the body and when analogy became one of the dominant ways of making progress in the sciences (Steadman, 1979). In one sense, the idea of the organic city follows this metaphor, especially reinforced in the notion that the organic cities adapt to individual social and economic preferences, to the constraints of the natural landscape, and to the dominant technology of the city. The metaphor has been exploited as cities have grown exponentially in population especially over the last 300 years, and as activities have begun to restructure themselves more quickly through decentralization of functions and increasing locational specialization. The idea of the city as being composed of a 'heart' – the central business district (CBD), of 'arteries' and 'veins' in terms of the hierarchy of transport and communications routes, of 'lungs' in terms of green space and so on, has been writ large across the face of urban analysis and city planning over the last 100 years.

Yet there has been a subtle and growing contradiction between this metaphor and the dominant practice of city planning: although the metaphor has been widely embraced, it has been used both to argue that cities are sometimes poorly-adapted, sometimes well-adapted – that cities should be planned according to the metaphor or against it – that the evolution of cities shows good fit with their requirements or not, and that cities show stability or are pathological in their evolution, exhibiting more cancerous than balanced growth. There is little consistency between these points of view and the preoccupation with the design of cities in visual terms. In fact, in this book, although we will not exploit the terminology of the biological metaphor, much of what we will argue is entirely consistent with it in seeking an understanding of the city which is deeper and less superficially visual than that associated with the traditional geometric model. It is in this sense too, that our interpretation of the city is tilted more towards the organic than the city of pure geometry.

Clearly, cities display a mixture of these two styles, although for over 95% of those which exist and have existed, their form would be seen as being more organic than purely geometric. This is in stark contrast to those cities which are illustrated as examples in the education of city planners where the dominant model is the geometric, cities planned in the large. In fact, examples of cities which developed organically up until the middle ages are conspicuously absent from the historical, certainly the visual record. This may be due to the small size of towns in ancient times, but it is also due to the way towns were represented visually and perhaps of the particular biases which the ancients had toward urban form. However, in modern times, the bias has changed in that towns are now subject to very different levels of organizational control, and building and transport technology than before. Thus there are elements of 'conscious' planning on at least one level in every town, although little or no evidence of planning at higher scales where the focus is upon the growth of entire towns and cities in their urban region.

As we have implied, there is a major problem of representation when we come to examine the visual history of town form. Not only has the type of artistic representation changed as we can clearly see when we examine the forms shown in the figures in this chapter, but the scale at which towns are depicted has altered as they have grown through time, with many more scales of possible representation now than at earlier periods of history. Moreover, the focus of representation has changed. Town plans and maps now are clearly geared to more functional purposes than they were centuries ago and there are a greater variety of possible types of urban map. There are also differences between plans which are designed to show geometric form which often embody yet-to-be-realized ideas in contrast to existing plans which are part of the historical record and rarely designed to show such ideal conceptions.

The biggest differences, however, between urban forms through history are due to size and scale. Before the modern age, most cities were small and compact, with higher densities, much smaller space standards than now, often by orders of magnitude (witness the barracks space in a typical Roman fort), and transport technologies which were much more limited in terms of their ability to move people and goods as well as in their access by ordinary citizens. By far the biggest city before the 17th century was the Rome of the later Empire which at its peak had over one million inhabitants. But Rome was an anachronism. The size of the city was a symptom of the malaise of the Empire for the technology of the civilization was simply unable to sustain such a system. By contrast, the Greek city states rarely grew to larger than 20,000 with only Athens and Syracuse growing to 50,000. Thus before the modern age, urban form was dramatically constrained in contrast to the physical urbanization of the last 200 years. In this view then, the conception of what we might call organic is not independent of either history or culture.

In terms of our present-day notion of organic growth, we only begin to see such forms in the city during the middle ages, and even then the kinds of explosive growth which characterize present-day cities only began in the early 19th century. It has almost been as though there is now 'too much' to plan in contrast to the past, that economic growth and scientific change have reached a threshold in terms of urban growth, beyond which the organic analogy only applies. However, it is more likely that our conception of growth has changed. In history, organic form is associated with slow growth, akin to the gradual accretion of cells, their gradual replacement and renewal which are much closer packed than the way similar units of development are added to and deleted from cities today. Cities now are clearly more dispersed, the use of land is across a much wider range of functions and our concept of irregularity which is embodied in the differences between slow and faster cell growth, is also different. These distinctions are also reflected in the range of urban forms present today in that some cultures where social and economic norms are closer to those of the past than in the west still generate cities which are organic in the older, slower growing sense. For example, the cities of Islam still contain elements of town form which are unaffected by modern technologies and social organization, although such elements rarely exist now in isolation from more modern forms of town. In short, what this implies is that the theories and models which we advocate here are restricted very much to western cultures whose cities are still largely industrial in structure, although rapidly changing to the post-industrial. We do, however, consider that the principles of fractal geometry which we will be developing here are relevant to cities of any time and any culture, but the examples which we have chosen and the scales at which these are depicted are very much rooted in contemporary patterns of urban growth in the west at the city and regional level.

Another important issue relates to the way the organic and geometric principles of urban form vary with respect to scale. At one scale, the city might appear to be ordered in terms of pure geometry while at another it may appear to have no such planned order and be the product of a multitude of local decisions. The example *par excellence* once again is New York. Manhattan developed organically until the early 19th century when the commissioners of the city laid out the island on a regular grid about which all development then took place. But in the wider urban region, development east through Long Island, on the Jersey shore, into Westchester and Connecticut to the north east was not planned on any form of grid, and at this scale of the city region, the growth looks 'unplanned' and explosive. Zooming out even further to megalopolis – the eastern seaboard (Gottman, 1961) – the organic analogy holds although the region contains much pure geometric planning at the local scale in cities such as Washington, Philadelphia and Baltimore. At this wider scale, there has been less contention about the merits of geometric planning although the 20th century has witnessed many attempts at such large scale urban planning as we demonstrated in the last section and illustrated in Figures 1.8 and 1.9. However, notwithstanding our focus on irregularity and organic growth at the urban scale and above in this book, fractal geometry is still applicable at lower scales, and in Chapters 2, 7 and 10 we will indicate how such geometry might be used at these finer scales.

The basic organic model involves the growth of a town from some center of initial growth or seed, the growth proceeding in compact form around the center in waves of development like the rings of a tree. This growth, however, is likely to be distorted by radial lines of transportation along which growth often proceeds faster due to increased access to the center, the ultimate form of town thus resembling some star-like shape. In fact, this model presumes that growth is not constrained by the need for some defensive wall, and until the middle ages and even beyond, such walls tended to minimize distortions forced by the radial and nodal structure of the town in its region. Although there may not have been any overall geometric plan to such early towns, their small size and the intensity of use and density of development must have led to considerable coordination and control of development in social and economic terms which would have had an impact physically. This model represents an abstraction from real growth, but it has become the basis of the organic metaphor: a clear example of the growth and form produced are illustrated in Figure 1.10, taken from Doxiadis's (1968) *Ekistics* which still represents one of the most complete statements of the organic approach to city planning.

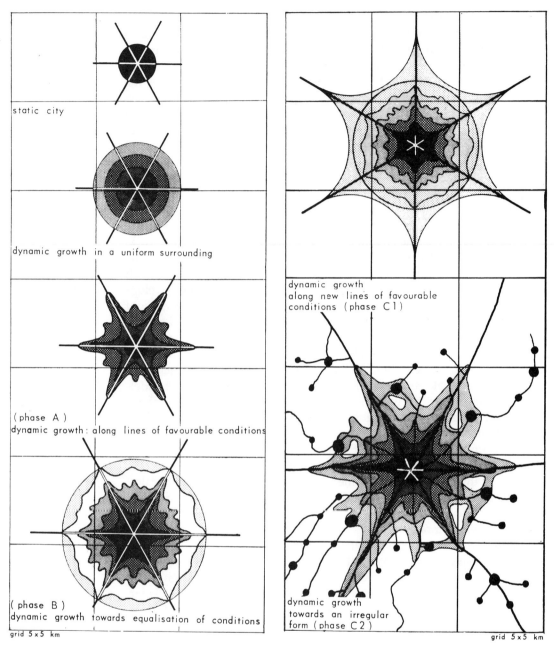

Figure 1.10. The shape of the organically growing city (from Doxiadis, 1968).

The earliest examples of towns in Sumeria demonstrated such slow organic growth in that cells of development composing the town were added incrementally but were highly clustered and continually adapted to the dictates of the physical site. For example, the town of Catal Huyuk (Benevolo, 1980) dating from 6500 BC was built as an accumulation of residential houses all attached to one another but successively adapted in both two- and three-dimensional space across different levels. Such towns are still characteristic of those today in the Middle East and parts of Africa; they were inward looking, based almost entirely on pedestrian traffic, with some sense of regularity in terms of the use of straight lines to demarcate property, but closely hugging the landscape and with no sense of overall visual unity in plan form. In so far as the visual quality of such organic development can be applauded, it is in terms of its informality, its idiosyncracies and its picturesque properties and occasionally in its exploitation of dramatic natural features, but never in terms of the power of its geometry. As we have implied, from these times there are hardly any examples of organic growth which are faster than the century by century adaptation characteristic of these types of town. Where organic growth was faster and larger in scale as in the Athens of Pericles or in second century Rome, the emphasis was not upon transport and decentralization and dispersion of functions, but on adapting the site to the most cultured art and architecture in an effort to mesh the pure geometry of building with the natural geometry of the landscape.

By the middle ages, the slow accretion and adaptation of development to its site so characteristic of the medieval town was well established and there are several illustrative examples. We have already seen the evolution of Regensburg in Figure 1.3 from its Roman grid in the fourth century to its replacement by a huddled mass of different sized and shaped buildings by the year 1100. The development is characteristic of the high feudalism which made its mark on the medieval market town too. A more picturesque example taken from southern Bohemia around 1300 is the town of Cesky Krumlov (Morris, 1979) which shows how the meander of the river, the topography of the river valley in which it sits and the circuitous nature of the transport routes have molded its urban form. There is no sense of the grid or the circle in this type of town, although had this been the New World of the 19th century, a grid would certainly have been imposed with interesting consequences. The town and its medieval development are shown in Figure 1.11. Finally, the medieval town also represents the last example of very slow organic growth where towns were compact and constrained behind their walls in a period of comparative stability when population and economic growth was modest but slow.

By the 17th century, Europe and the Americas were on their way to the industrial era where better transport systems and building technologies were to ultimately lead to much bigger and much lower density cities. The city wall went first, thus enabling the town to begin to conform to its classic star-like shape. In Figure 1.12(a), we show the form of Boston in 1640 (from Reps, 1965), which is reminiscent of the medieval English village, although showing clear evidence of the extent to which the cluster of buildings and space is no longer necessary. This is as good an example of the embryonic radially- concentric modern city as any we can portray. Its form is reinforced by another 80 years of growth in John Bonner's 1722 map (Vance, 1990) shown in Figure 1.12(b), but this illustrates the way in which the 'pictorial' map provides a somewhat less clear way of presenting the salient characteristics of form – the radially concentric nature of the transport pattern and the disposition of development. Nevertheless, like Cesky Krumlov, Boston shows no sense of pure geometry in its plan, but it does show form closely adapted to its physical site.

Figure 1.11. Medieval organic growth in Cesky Krumlov (from Morris, 1979).

Although we are unable to present a clear map of the development of Rome in the late Empire, an excellent illustration of urban development in the early 19th century is Clarke's 1832 map which is given in Figure 1.13. Many of the features of organic and geometric form which we have noted in these last two sections are illustrated here; amongst these, are the clear radial structure of the city in its straight roads focussing upon the Palatine Hill, the slow cell-like growth of Rome itself and its medieval development, the distinct Roman monumental architecture of the Coliseum, forum, stadium and so on, and the geometric planning of Pope Sixtus V in the late Renaissance. The wall is still intact to a degree, but the city is spreading across the Tiber and outside its wall, much more characteristic of the present century than earlier ones. There is substantial evidence of the dual mix of traditions of city building in this map, but with an emphasis already on

(a)

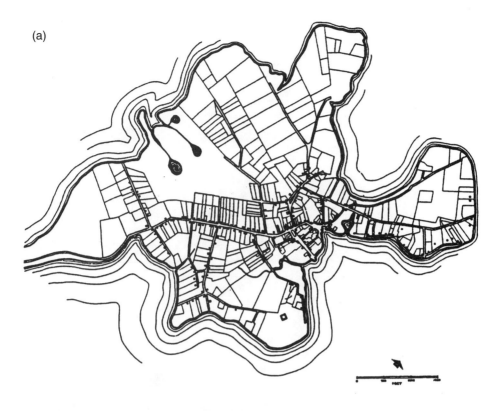

(b)

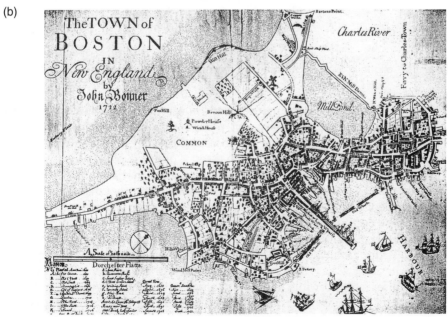

Figure 1.12.   Seventeenth century Boston: (a) in 1640 (from Reps, 1965); (b) John Bonner's 1722 map (from Vance, 1990).

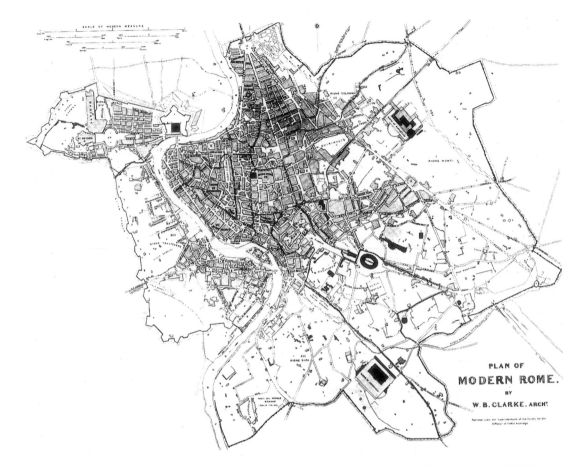

Figure 1.13.   The organic growth of Rome by the early19th century (from Morris, 1979).

the power of individual decisions concerning development in contrast to earlier and grander geometric plans for coordination.

Only at this point are we in a position to examine the kinds of urban form which will determine the essence of our explanations in this book. As we have indicated, we do not have a clear and unambiguous time series of urban development in terms of visual (or for that matter any other) form except from old maps, and these are never consistent from time period to time period. However, to give some sense of evolution of urban form over the last 200 years, we show in Figure 1.14 a series of maps for the town of Cardiff from the mid-18th century to the modern day, all reproduced at different scales, showing the way urban development has been depicted differently over this period and also the type of irregularity of form which is the norm rather than the exception in terms of the modern city. We have not abstracted from these maps because we do so in later chapters where we use Cardiff extensively as one of our examples. In fact, in Plate 5.1 (see color section), we show the growth of the city from the late 1880s to 1949 in four stages taken from the relevant maps within the series given in Figure 1.14.

By the mid-20th century, the notion of examining urban form at a larger

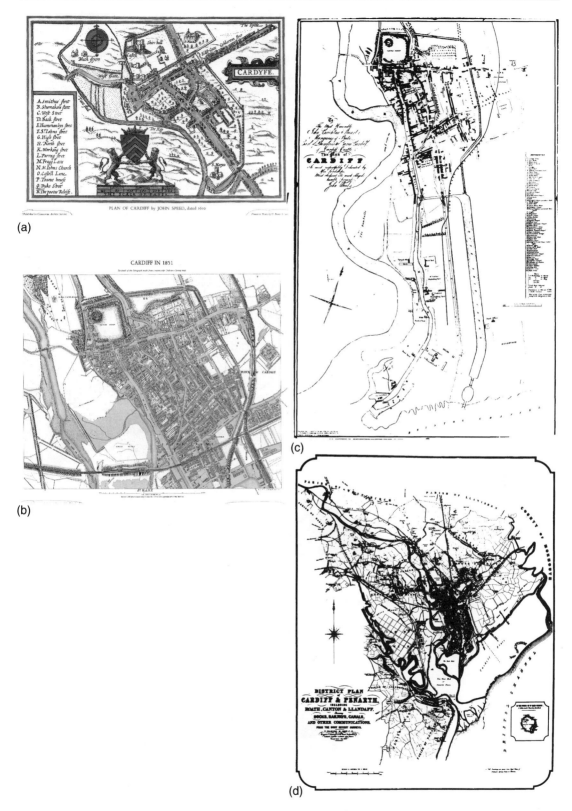

Figure 1.14. The growth of Cardiff, Wales, from the mid-18th century (from the National Museum of Wales).

scale, that of the city and its region, had been well established. In Figure 1.15, we show a diagram from the first edition (1950) of Gallion and Eisner's (1975) book *The Urban Pattern* which is entitled 'The Exploding Metropolis', where the caption implying that such growth is disordered, hence undesirable, both illustrates the predominant concerns of the urban analyst and the ideologies of the city planner. These are the kinds of patterns which we will begin to measure and explain from the next chapter on in our quest to convince that this type of form reveals a degree of order which is considerably deeper than the superficial order associated with the city of pure geometry. Moreover, although we will not dwell very much in this book upon the way in which cities grow and merge forming larger metropolitan areas and urban regions, conurbations in Geddes' (1915, 1949) terms, our analysis and ideas will be entirely consistent with these examples.

The reader is encouraged to skim the figures in later chapters to get some idea of the kinds of forms we will be investigating here, although we will conclude this section with what we consider to be an example of the archetypical urban form for which a theory of the fractal city is most appropriate. Figure 1.16 shows five urban clusters without any scale. There are several points to make here. This pattern of urban development shows no evidence of planned growth, it is radially concentric in structure, it shows

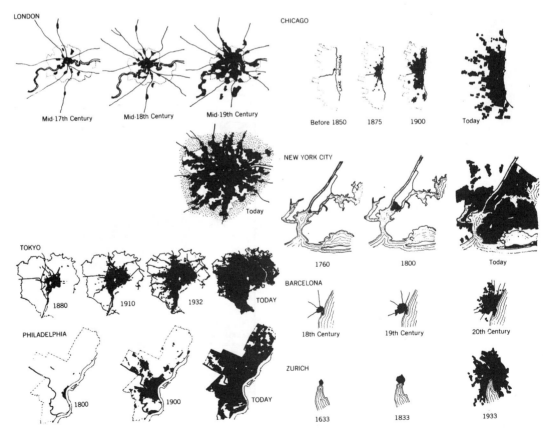

Figure 1.15. The exploding metropolis (from Gallion and Eisner, 1950, 1975).

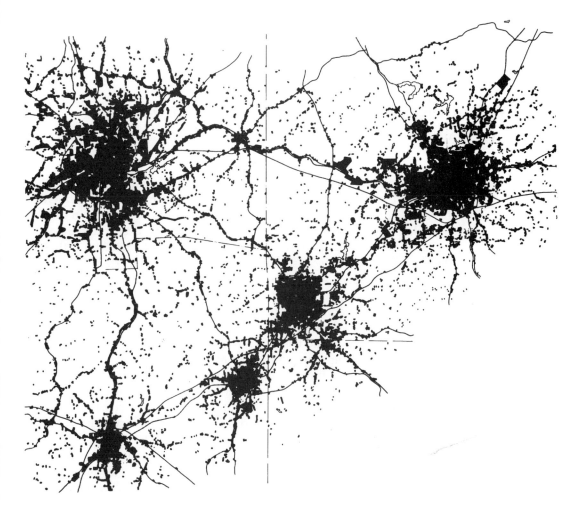

Figure 1.16. Contemporary urban growth patterns (from Chapin and Weiss, 1962).

clusters growing together and it could be at any scale from that of an urban region the size of Tokyo to a cluster of villages and market towns in rural England such as those, for example, we illustrate in Chapter 10. In fact, it is the pattern of urban development in 1958 for five towns in North Carolina – Winston-Salem, Greensboro, High Point, Thomasville and Lexington – taken from Chapin and Weiss (1962). The scale is in fact about 50 miles in the horizontal direction but it could be much larger. This clearly indicates that although our focus is, to an extent, scale dependent, that is, emphasizing urban growth at the city scale up, the patterns we are concerned with do have a degree of scale independence, and our analysis is not restricted to a narrow range which limits the use of our theories and techniques. This whole question of scale will be exceedingly important to our subsequent analysis, and in the next chapter we explore its implications in considerable detail. But it is important to accept that in the application of geometry to human artifacts such as cities, definitions and approaches are always contingent upon the mode of inquiry, the culture to which the analysis applies, and the time at which the application is made. In this sense then, our ideas about the fractal city are appropriate now, and although the principles are likely to be enduring, the examples will change as the approach develops.

1.6 Morphology: Growth and Form, Form and Function

We have made use of the word 'form' extensively already without attempting any definition, for in one sense, the term is self-evident: as D'Arcy Thompson (1917, 1961) implies, form means shape, and in this context, shape pertains to the way cities can be observed and understood in terms of their spatial pattern. In fact, we will need to reflect a little more deeply on the word because our usage here implies a certain approach to geometry and space as well as process and function. Whyte (1968) sums this up when he says: "The word 'form' has many meanings, such as shape, configuration, structure, pattern, organization, and system of relations. We are here interested in these properties only in so far as they are clearly set in space", and this is the usage we will follow here. Form is broader than shape *per se*, although our immediate and first attack on its measurement and understanding is through the notion of shape, in "the outward appearance of things" (Arnheim, 1968). In terms of the study of cities, form will represent the spatial pattern of elements composing the city in terms of its networks, buildings, spaces, defined through its geometry mainly, but not exclusively, in two rather than three dimensions. Yet form can never merely be conceived in terms of these local properties but has a wider significance or gestalt, a more global significance in the way cities grow and change.

The analytic study of form of which this book is a part is always more than it seems at first sight. Form is the resultant of many forces or determinants interacting in a diverse manner through space and time, thus causing the system to evolve in novel and often surprising ways. D'Arcy Thompson (1917, 1961) best sums it up when he says: "In short, the form of an object is a 'diagram of forces'", and in this sense, the study of form without the processes which give rise to it is meaningless. The association of process with form has two clear dimensions. The first is 'growth' which is loosely used in biology and even in city planning to embrace all types of change, and involves the notion that forms evolve through growth, that objects are transformed through the diverse interaction of their forces. This has led to the term 'organic form'. The second dimension relates to function. The various processes which contain the forces which determine form have specific functions and a study of form from the static viewpoint, form at one snapshot in time for example, is often rooted in the quest to understand function. This approach has been widely exploited throughout the arts and sciences, especially in the first half of the 20th century. 'Form Follows Function' has been the battle cry of the Modern Movement in Architecture, although it is somewhat ironic that in its application to city planning by designers such as Corbusier and Wright, the plans produced have rarely followed the motto faithfully, forms being developed which embody the most minimalist, hence the most restrictive of functions. Indeed, it is the task of this chapter and of this book to demonstrate the poverty of urban analysis and city planning which seeks such a rigid interpretation of form.

The term morphology was first coined by Goethe in 1827 as 'the study of unity of type of organic form' (noted in March and Steadman, 1971). Morphology is thus the study of form and process, growth and form, form and function and as Goethe stated: "The formative process is the supreme process, indeed the only one, alike in nature and art" (quoted in Whyte, 1968). Form too is always more than shape, and we will follow Whyte (1968) who speaks of *spatial form* which he defines as comprising external form or visible shape, and internal form which is structure. This brings us back full circle to the idea of form being some manifestation of system with structure being the underlying or invisible form which explains the external urban form, the form which is the subject of our immediate and casual observation. Systems are often studied in terms of their statics or their dynamics, the first implying structure, the second behavior usually in the context of changing structures. Our first grasp of systems, at least those that in some sense are external to us, is in terms of their structure from which we proceed to infer their behavior in the quest to understand their dynamics. In fact, it is system structure of which form is the most superficial characteristic which often provides the basis for classification, the beginnings of scientific study through appropriate description and measurement.

System structures are defined as being composed of elements and relations, the elements being the basic components of the system, the relations defining the way the elements interact and function. Various decompositions of the system into sets of elements define subsystems which it may be possible to associate with, and arrange into, a distinct hierarchy. The various elements, and aggregations thereof into subsystems, may reflect the same form but at different system levels of the hierarchy, and if this conception of organizing the system this way is spatial in any sense, these subassemblies may be *replications of the same form at different scales*. This is an important point for it reflects one of the principles which we will use in the sequel to develop our idea that cities are fractal in form.

There are, however, many ways to describe the elements of the city which usually depend upon the disciplinary perspective of the theory being invoked. Many of these are spatial, although what constitute the key elements will determine whether or not the city system can be subdivided into a strictly spatial hierarchy. For example, the city might be conceived in terms of activity systems of land uses which do not group easily into spatially distinct parts, or in terms of social-organizational groupings which are not obviously spatial in their most significant variations. In fact, many of these systemic descriptions may map only partially onto the strict spatial organization of the city, and thus we consider the approach to be developed here consistent with a variety of related urban theory which is not explicitly spatial. However, the most obvious way to describe cities is in terms of the way they develop. Hamlets become villages, villages towns, towns cities and cities urban regions, all involving a growth and compounding of spatial forces which leave their mark on the evolution of form. The reverse processes of decline are also evident, while in terms of such change, discontinuities and strange cycles can occur, for the evolution is far from remorseless. The basic component or building block of cities is a unit of development, often housing, sometimes called a 'block', smaller than the neighborhood, and these can be usually assembled into a hierarchy of both distinct and overlapping spatial areas. Together with the various communications networks which link these components and all the related functions such as employment, commerce, education, recreation which have their own hierarchies and networks, these compose a complex but rich spatial ordering which manifests itself in a geometry which cannot be captured in the traditions of Euclid. However, from this brief description, it is important to draw out the idea that system structure can be described by relations organized as networks and/or hierarchies, and this will be the path we follow in the rest of this book.

There are many more problems in finding as convenient a representation for the dynamic processes which evolve the city through its functions. Processes are never immediately obvious, or directly observable, and our measurement of them is subject to an uncertainty principle. We do not have time here to speculate on the wide array of theories and methods used to study urban processes which are the subject of inquiry throughout the social sciences. All we can say is that many of the current approaches which at some point enable an understanding and prediction of urban spatial form can be seen as consistent with the ideas we pursue here. For example, the idea of a hierarchy of urban space which results from growth of cities and the development of systems of cities is a basic ordering principle of general systems enabling stable growth and change. Systems, when changed, are changed at the level of their cells rather than more globally, and in this sense, contain a degree of spatial resilience which is manifested in the persistence of their form (Simon, 1969). Moreover, such cellular or local growth by the successive addition or deletion of basic elements also leads to a fitness of the resultant form to its context or environment which can be destroyed through too rapid growth or intervention at an inappropriate level. This is Alexander's (1964) thesis in which he argues that good design or good decision-making in a broader sense must be based on an understanding of the ways the system evolves through the elements within its hierarchy.

Therefore our approach to urban form will be through tracing the 'invisible structure' of relations which underlie the external form or outward appearance of cities, using ideas involving hierarchies and networks and searching for functions which are consistent with the shape of cities and their evolution. We can sketch out such a structure from the top down, illustrating how urban space can be seen as both a hierarchy and a network which in fact represent different sides of the same coin. In Figure 1.17, we show how this is done, beginning with an idealized square geometry, successively subdividing the space in binary terms (1.17(a)), tracing out a perfect and symmetric hierarchy (1.17(b)). The subdivision can also be traced out as a network on the square space as in Figure 1.17(c), and a comparison of (b) and (c) shows that the hierarchy is the network and vice versa. In a simple way the hierarchy might be considered an inverted tree, and the network the same tree in plan form. As we shall see in Chapter 2, such hierarchies provide models of trees and vice versa. We should also note that the system of relations we show in Figure 1.17 is independent of

a)   b)   c)

Disaggregation   **Hierarchy**   **Network**

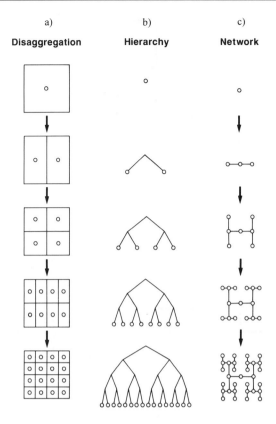

Figure 1.17. Spatial disaggregation: strict subdivision, hierarchy and network structure.

the actual shape of the space to which we apply it: that is, it serves to define either the organic city or the city of pure geometry although as we shall see, it does cast a different light upon the idea of organic form.

If we take a bottom-up approach to the same set of relations, the idea of a distinct hierarchy immediately collapses. As a generating device the hierarchy is efficient, but if we pose the question as to how the elemental units – the most basic grid squares in Figure 1.17 – might aggregate, it is likely that the hierarchy would not capture the degree of diversity within such a structure. If the rule be assumed that each unit aggregates with its nearest neighbor, with the new units overlapping one another in that each element can now belong to one or more aggregate, then what emerges is the semi-lattice structure which we show in Figure 1.18. This is an order of magnitude more complex than the hierarchy; it demonstrates a richness of structure which is in fact still very restrictive in terms of what types of aggregate space might be present in a town, and it is but one of a multitude of possible lattice-like structures. In fact, this is what Alexander (1965) in his famous article 'A City is Not a Tree' suggests is the difference between artificial cities and naturally evolving ones. He says: "What is the inner nature, the ordering principle, which distinguishes the artificial city from the natural city? You will have guessed from my title what I believe this ordering principle to be. I believe that a natural city has the organization

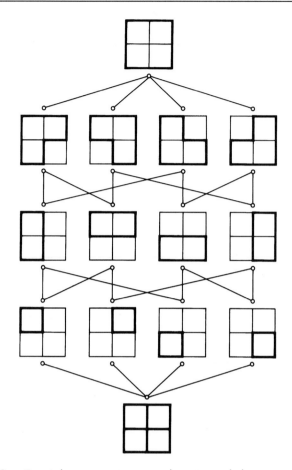

Figure 1.18. Spatial aggregation: overlapping subdivision and lattice structure.

of a semi-lattice; but that when we organize a city artificially, we organize it as a tree".

It is but a short step from Alexander's ideas to the notion that organic cities are not only cities which display an 'irregular' geometry but also cities where that underlying structure of the geometry of its relationships is also 'irregular', or at least asymmetric in the sense of the difference between a lattice and tree. In fact, Alexander (1965) goes on to say that: ". . . whenever a city is 'thought out' instead of 'grown', it is bound to get a tree-like structure". Thus in terms of Jane Jacobs' (1961) arguments, the doctrine of visual order is doubly at fault for not only imposing a rigid geometry which goes against the natural grain, but also for imposing rigidity of social and functional structure, both of which are highly unrealistic and thus increase rather than diminish the problems they seek to solve. We have raised a theme and an expectation concerning an appropriate geometry of cities which it may appear in subsequent chapters we cannot address or meet. Our succeeding ideas will be dominated by hierarchies and networks, some of which will overlap but most of which will not. However, the complexity we seek to address will take much more than the ideas of this book to report, for this is but a beginning, and the approach we seek to establish is in fact entirely consistent with lattice structures as overlapping hierarchies. The functions we will fit and the patterns we will generate may at first seem strictly hierarchical, but as we will show, this is only the most superficial reaction to the ideas we will introduce. Hierarchies are useful generating principles as we will see in the next section, but the phenomena we seek to explain are always richer, and the models we use always capable of dealing with deeper complexity.

1.7 Urban Hierarchies

Hierarchies, we have argued, are basic organizing devices for describing and measuring the importance of urban functions across many spatial scales. As they are a property of general systems, their import extends beyond individual cities to systems of cities, and thus they present us with the framework for linking local to global and vice versa. In fact, it is the lattice which provides a more appropriate descriptor for this captures the richness of overlap between scales and the somewhat blurred nature of any definition of a distinct and unambiguous scaling. Yet the strict non-overlapping hierarchy which Alexander (1965) rightly ascribes as having been used extensively to purge the natural complexity and variety of cities, is still useful as an initial foray into the way we might organize the relation of scales, one to another, and the fact that we can simplify scales according to a strict hierarchical order does not exclude a richer order from existing within the hierarchy.

Spatial hierarchies relate elements of city systems and systems of cities at successive scales where elements of urban structure are repeated in diverse ways across the range (Berry, 1964). The key idea in this book and the basis of fractal geometry involves identifying systems in which elements are repeated in a *similar* fashion from scale to scale. If this similarity is strong in a geometric sense, then it is referred to as *self-similarity* or in its weaker form as *self-affinity*. We will define these characteristics of the new geometry in Chapter 2 but the idea is all pervasive in the context of cities. In terms of their description, then we will follow a top-down approach in contrast to their generation which always occurs from the ground up. The classic example in the city relates to those routine functions such as retail and commercial services whose frequency and scale of provision is closely tied to the same characteristics of the places where they locate. The largest focus is the CBD, while a loose hierarchy of centers exists throughout the city with lesser numbers of district centers, larger numbers of neighborhood centers, even more local centers and so on, with a size and spacing commensurate with their position in the hierarchy. The same structure exists for the educational and leisure system which is differentiated according to the finer grained differences between functions.

On this basis, cities are usually organized into neighborhoods, typically from 5000 to 10,000 in population, enough to support basic educational and retail functions. Indeed the theory of the ideal city from Plato on has focussed around town sizes which are rarely more than 50,000, often less, implying that a balanced urban structure would be one which contains no more than about 10 neighborhoods (Keeble, 1959). Districts usually comprise two or three neighborhoods, but the differentiation does not end there. Larger towns might comprise smaller, and so on up the hierarchy, while the various transport systems used to enable communication consist of a hierarchy of distributors from primary or trunk down to local, often involving overlapping networks which are further differentiated according to mode (Buchanan *et al.*, 1963).

The smallest examples of urban hierarchies are contained in residential housing layouts where the clearest are those in which vehicle and pedestrian transport is segregated. The layout at Radburn, New Jersey, designed in the late 1920s by Clarence Stein and Henry Wright in the Garden Cities tradition is the prototype (Kostof, 1991). In such layouts where pedestrian routes rarely intersect with vehicular, the networks follow a strict hierarchy and although, in practice, these layouts are generated this way, they are obviously used in a somewhat more flexible fashion. It is in the British New Towns and 1950s housing development that the most archetypical examples can be found. Figure 1.19 provides an example from the town of Coventry where we show the layout simplified as a plan of the road system (1.19(a)), the actual layout of housing (1.19(b)), and the road system as a hierarchy (1.19(c)). Note that Figure 1.19(a) contains an implicit hierarchy of roads where pedestrians can move within the major housing blocks without crossing them, and that these types of layout are reminiscent of many towns in Africa and the Middle East where cul-de-sacs are used extensively to constrain movement.

These layouts are clearly generated artificially, notwithstanding the existence of similar plans which have evolved more naturally. However, various descriptions of cities in terms of the clustering of their neighborhoods and districts also follow strict hierarchies. Abercrombie (1945) in his *Greater London Plan* organized the metropolis into several distinct districts as we show in Figure 1.20, while this idea is also the basis of the development of a hierarchy of small towns, arranged as satellites around an existing central city which is the essence of Howard's (1898, 1965) Garden Cities idea. The kind of geometry which this settlement structure implies is shown in Figure 1.21, and from this there is a clear link to theories of systems of cities which rely upon the notion of a hierarchy of city sizes and hinterlands. Howard's conception of the dependence of small 'new' towns on the central city, at least in the way such settlements were sized and spaced, is clearly consistent with the theory of central places due to Christaller (1933, 1966). By way of conclusion to this section and to systems of relations which we will use in the sequel, we will now show how such theories are consistent with these ideas of hierarchy and city structure at the more local level.

The simplest geometric form of a system of cities is based on an entirely regular grid of basic settlement types – neighborhoods or villages say – which are systematically aggregated into all encompassing regions at successive levels up the hierarchy. We will proceed using this bottom-up approach which is consistent with the way small settlements grow into larger ones, although such systems are often described in the reverse direction. Let us assume a regular landscape of basic urban units which are arranged on a square lattice or grid as in Figure 1.22. In fact, if we assume

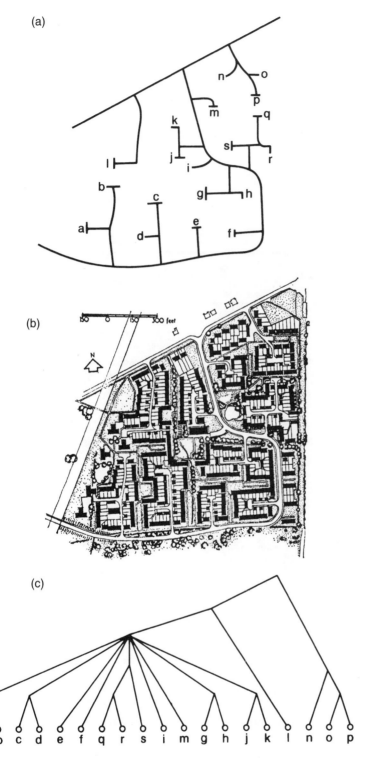

Figure 1.19. Residential layout as hierarchy (after Keeble, 1959).

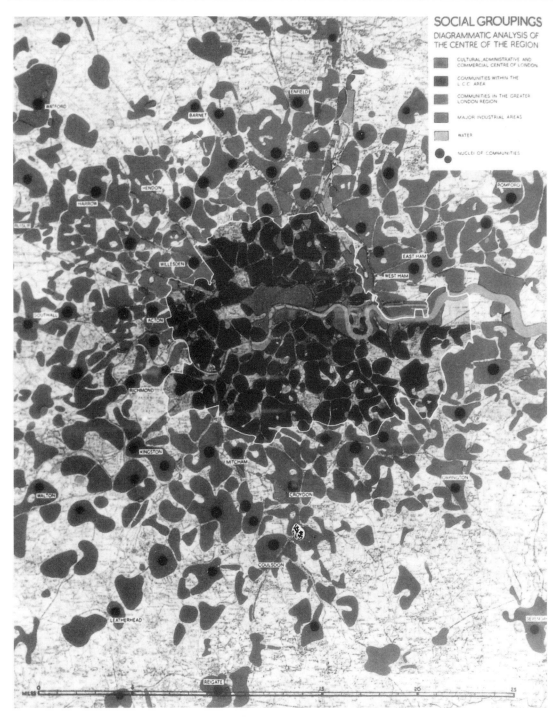

Figure 1.20. The hierarchy of social districts in London (from Abercrombie, 1945).

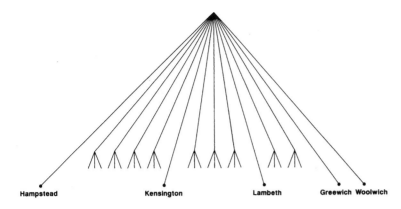

Hampstead   Kensington   Lambeth   Greewich Woolwich

Figure 1.20. Continued.

that these units grow from the smallest seeds, then their areas of influence overlap and the most efficient demarcation between them is clearly the grid; that is, the packing of such hinterlands is most likely to be a grid in this case as shown in Figure 1.22(a). A central place system emerges by defining regularly spaced central places at successive levels of hierarchy, the places in question at each level existing as similar centrally placed locations at all lower levels. The process of aggregating about one major central place in the square grid is shown in Figure 1.22(b).

The number of basic units generated as the aggregation proceeds through levels $i = 0, 1, 2, 3, \ldots$ is given by n^i where n is the number of units in the first aggregate $i = 1$. In the case of the grid in Figure 1.22(b), $n = 9$ (which is formed from an inner grid of 3^2) and thus the sequence of 1, 9, 81, 729, 6561, $\ldots$ units in typical regions $i = 0, 1, 2, 3, 4, \ldots$ can be formed. The number of units in these regions is given by the recursive relation

$$n^i = n^{i-1}n, \quad i = 0, 1, 2, \ldots, n^0 = 1, \tag{1.1}$$

from which a total population N_i can be calculated in proportion to n^i, where we assume a constant population density ρ. This can be written as

$$N_i = \rho n^i = N_{i-1}n, \quad N_0 = 1. \tag{1.2}$$

From equation (1.2), it is easy to derive another recursive relation relating any earlier aggregation of basic units to a later one, that is smaller aggregates to larger ones. Then noting that $N_{i-1} = N_i/n$

$$N_{i-(j-1)} = \frac{N_i}{n^{(j-1)}}, \quad j = 1, 2, 3, \ldots \tag{1.3}$$

where j is now the 'rank' in the hierarchy with i, the largest index region or the base being associated with the first rank $j = 1$ and so on down the cascade. In essence, equation (1.3) is a rank-size rule of the kind associated with hierarchies based on the Pareto frequency distribution of city sizes (Zipf, 1949). In short, equations (1.1) to (1.3) are power or scaling laws, but with their powers being the ranks or scales themselves. The more usual and simpler rank-size rule is of the form

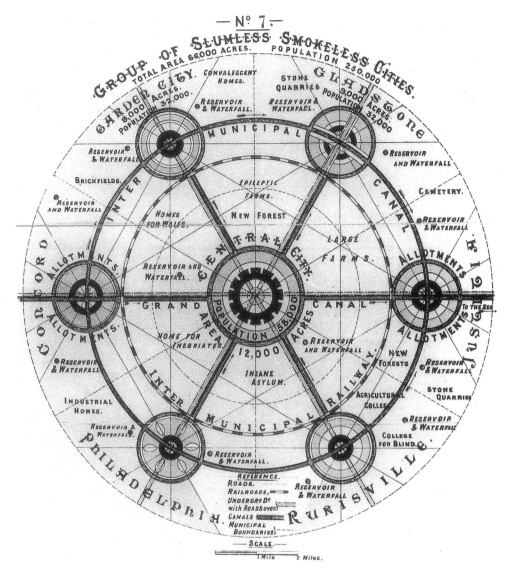

Figure 1.21. Ebenezer Howard's ideal system of social cities (after Howard, 1898, 1965, from Kostof, 1991).

$$N_{i-(j-1)} = \frac{N_i}{j^\tau}, \quad j = 1, 2, 3, \dots \tag{1.4}$$

where τ is some power usually greater than unity. From equations (1.3) and (1.4), for any level j, $\tau = \{[(j-1)\log(n)]/\log(j)\}$. There are various ways in which equation (1.3) might conform to the simple rank-size rule implied by equation (1.4), most obviously by setting the density of population ρ as some function of the scale or rank. This we will indicate in Chapter 10 where we show how τ might be a function of the fractal dimension D. But for the moment, it is sufficient to note that hierarchies generate power laws and that power laws are one of the bases of fractal geometry.

The hierarchy which is generated in this way is shown in Figure 1.22(c),

(a)

(b)

(c)

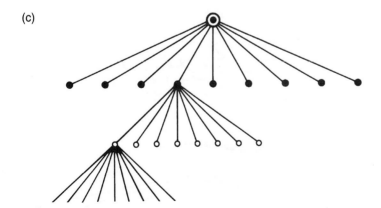

Figure 1.22. Grid geometry and the hierarchy of central places.

and we are immediately drawn to suggesting how this might be made more realistic. If we transform the underlying grid of points to a triangular rather than square net, we generate a packing of basic units which is hexagonal, not square, this now being the geometrical basis of central place theory (Christaller, 1933, 1966). In the square grid system in Figure 1.22, n was the basic number of settlement units which was dependent upon a central place at the next order of hierarchy, in that case n being equal to 9. The usual approach is to assume that hinterlands defining the dependence of places on a center, share basic settlement units, and in Figure 1.23 we show how

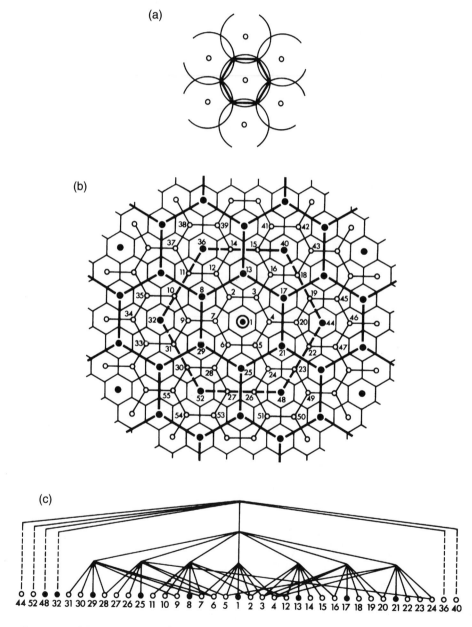

Figure 1.23.   Hexagonal geometry and the lattice of central places.

this might be so. Figure 1.23(a) shows the basic hexagonal packing while 1.23(b) shows the way successive hinterlands are constructed with each of six places defining the hexagonal trade area around each center at a given level in the hierarchy, being shared with two other adjacent hinterlands. In this case, the number of dependent settlements within each aggregate at a given level of hierarchy is $n = [1 + (1/3)6] = 3$. Different aggregations which still employ a hexagonal geometry are possible with $n = 4, 7, 9, 12$ and so on, these being called central place systems with given k values, the k defined here as n, the number of dependent settlements between each level (Haggett, Cliff, and Frey, 1977).

In the case of the system shown in Figure 1.23(b), this is based on the most minimal of hexagonal tessellations which, using equation (1.2), generates a sequence of 3, 9, 27, 81, 243, . . . basic settlement units at successive levels of hierarchy. Moreover, because of the split dependence of centers on adjacent hinterlands, the hierarchy is, in fact, a lattice of overlapping regions, and this is shown in Figure 1.23(c). It is possible to further increase the realism of these types of systems. By letting the integer n vary at different levels i, and over space, considerable distortions in the central place landscape can be produced (Isard, 1956). The theory is one of the cornerstones of human geography, and although we will show at various points in this book how this structure is consistent with fractal geometry, we have introduced enough to give the reader a flavor of how it might connect to the theories we will espouse here. In fact, the development of central place theory and fractal geometry constitutes a study in its own right, and already a beginning has been made by Arlinghaus (1985). To complete this rapid but long survey of the geometry of cities, we will now focus the conclusions to this chapter on the need for introducing a geometry of the irregular into city systems, noting briefly how these might be linked to other formal approaches to urban design which have emerged over the last 20 years.

1.8 A New Geometry

In this chapter, we have reviewed the study of shape in two ways: first, in terms of the simplest geometry used by those intent on developing the doctrine of visual order, and second, in terms of more abstract geometrical relations, hierarchies and networks, used by those seeking a deeper meaning to spatial order in the city. Whilst Euclidean geometries are largely descriptive and difficult to link to the underlying processes of growth explicitly, the geometry of relations used to show how space and shape within the city is ordered, does begin to suggest ways of unravelling the complexity of urban form. But there have been a succession of approaches to urban form developed over the last 20 years which build on more systematic, mathematical ideas, linking surface to underlying structure and process. We have already noted the coincidence of hierarchical ideas in design pioneered by Alexander (1964), for example, with those in human geography based on central place theory, and it is worth noting that the formality of these ideas has been even further relaxed by Alexander *et al.*

(1977) amongst others in the search for appropriate frameworks for explaining the diversity and richness of urban form. This stream of work will continue to inform the ideas presented in later chapters.

Several formal approaches to shape and layout from the architectural to the city level are built around the ideas of relations or connectivity, a natural starting point being the theory of networks or graphs (March and Steadman, 1971). The idea of a graph as the dual of continuous spatial subdivision has become the basis of architectural morphology in terms of building plans (Steadman, 1983), while more recent work has sought to develop the theory of spatial order using shape grammars built on the basic ideas of mathematical linguistics originally inspired by Chomsky (March and Stiny, 1985). These approaches do not, however, directly broach the notion that form is complex and irregular but ordered, and hence explicable. Perhaps the emphasis within architecture on the ultimate order imposed by Euclidean geometry in building structures has inhibited discussion of irregularity in form which exists at every scale, but only becomes strongly apparent at the larger scales of the city and the metropolis. In this sense, architecture is rooted in the idea of the planned form in contrast to more naturally evolving 'organic' structure, and as Steadman (1979) implies, the biological analogy, although exploited in a casual way, has had less impact on the way designers design. In fact, the development of shape grammars and their linking to cellular automata implies that at the level of buildings, such approaches could well begin to address concepts of irregularity and growth if developments in complexity theory from this perspective gain influence as appears likely at present.

Two other approaches are worth noting. Hillier and Hanson's (1984) approach to spatial form is at a slightly higher scale than the architectural, and they base their ideas on measuring the actual network qualities of neighborhoods and districts up to entire cities. Their approach turns space inside out with a strong emphasis on the way buildings are connected through their external spaces, employing many statistics associated with the patterns of connectivity described using graph theory. Ideas of growth and change are more central to their approach which is clearly based on a concern for the organic in contrast to planned evolution of city systems. Finally, we should note the emerging body of work on treating building and urban systems and their design using cognitive theory, particularly knowledge-based systems which in turn link these ideas back to shape grammars and the morphology of graphs (Coyne *et al.*, 1990).

Yet there is a need for a geometry that grapples directly with the notion that most cities display organic or natural growth, that form cannot be properly described, let alone explained, using Euclidean geometry, that urban form must be related to the underlying theories of the city which form the conventional wisdom of urban economics and human geography. We have implied that such an approach would grapple with the geometry of the irregular but at this point we must also recognize that there are many types of regularity, which do not fit within the traditional Euclidean paradigm, often incorrectly attributed to geometries of the 'irregular'. Such a geometry must deal directly with the notion that our assumptions of continuity when it comes to urban form must be more sophisticated, that shape is not continuous and manifests many discontinuities at the levels of lines and surfaces, but that the way we articulate its dimensions as discrete or discontinuous is too strict an order and must be relaxed to embrace the notion of continuous variation.

This would be a geometry that went beyond the superficial description of form, that built on the essential idea of linking form to function, of form to process, of statics to dynamics, a geometry commensurate with D'Arcy Thompson's (1917, 1961) original quest for a geometry of growth and form. That geometry has emerged during the last 20 years in the geometry of fractions, of shapes that do not display the clean lines and continuity of Euclidean geometry. As Porter and Gleick (1990) in their book *Nature's Chaos* so vividly portray, the geometry which has emerged, fractal geometry, is as much about the artificial world as the natural. They say:

A painter hoping to represent the choppy ocean surface can hardly settle for a regular array of scalloped brush strokes, but somehow must suggest waves on a multiplicity of scales. A scientist puts aside an unconscious bias toward smooth Euclidean shapes and linear calculations. An urban planner learns that the best cities grow dynamically, not neatly, into complex, jagged, interwoven networks, with different kinds of housing and different kinds of economic uses all jumbled together.

This is a geometry of order on many scales, a geometry of organized complexity which we will begin to develop and apply in the next chapter.

2

Size and Shape, Scale and Dimension

We are here face to face with the crucial paradox of knowledge. Year by year we devise more precise instruments with which to observe nature with more fineness. And when we look at the observations, we are discomforted to see that they are all still fuzzy and we feel that they are as uncertain as ever. We seem to be running after a goal which lurches away from us to infinity every time we come within sight of it. (Bronowski, 1973, p. 256.)

2.1 Scale, Hierarchy and Self-Similarity

We have already seen in Chapter 1 that cities are organized hierarchically into distinct neighborhoods, their spatial extent depending upon the economic functions which they offer to their surrounding population. This hierarchy of functions exists throughout the city, with the more specialized serving larger areas of the city than those which meet more immediate and local needs. The centers and their hinterlands which form this hierarchy have many elements in common in functional terms which are repeated across several spatial scales, and in this sense, districts of different sizes at different levels in the hierarchy have a similar structure. Moreover, the hierarchy of functions exists for economic necessity, and the growth of cities not only occurs through the addition of units of development at the most basic scale, but through increasing specialization of key centers, thus raising their importance in the hierarchy. These mechanisms of urban growth also ensure that the city is stable, in the sense portrayed in the previous chapter where hierarchical differentiation was associated with the process of building resilient systems (Simon, 1969).

Cities are primarily vehicles for bringing people together to engage in the exchange of ideas and material goods, and city size depends upon the level at which the city exists in the entire hierarchy of size from the smallest hamlet to the most global city. But large cities grow from the tiniest seeds, and the nature of economic production and consumption which are related to each other in the market is directly based on the level of population the market can support and vice versa. Perhaps incredibly, the way spatial markets are organized across the range of spatial scales is virtually identical. When consumers purchase goods in retail outlets, the same structures and mechanisms are used at whatever level of the hierarchy such transactions take place. Such structures which repeat themselves at different levels of the hierarchy and which in turn are associated with different scales and sizes are said to be *self-similar*. Moreover, it is this property of self-similarity that is writ large in the shape and form of cities, and provides the rationale for a new geometry of cities which is to be elaborated in this book.

To make progress in tracing the link between urban form and function, we must now embark upon a more structured analysis of city systems. In this chapter, we will outline the rudiments of this new geometry of form and function which has been developed over the last two decades, and which we anticipated in our introduction and in the previous chapter. This geometry has been christened by its greatest advocate, Benoit Mandelbrot (1983), as a 'geometry of nature', and although its most graphic examples exist in nature, it is increasingly being used to explore the ways in which artificial or man-made systems develop and are organized. In this book, we will speculate on how this geometry can be applied to cities, and in this chapter we will present its rudiments, concentrating on natural forms, but gradually introducing and demonstrating man-made forms which have similar properties.

When we talk of geometry, we usually talk of a geometry based on the straight line, the geometry of Euclid upon which our concept of dimension is based. Although most natural shapes that we can imagine are clearly not composed of straight lines, we are able to approximate any object to the desired degree by representing it as straight line segments. However, we can only make formal sense of such objects if we can represent the entire form of the object in ways in which we might apply the calculus of Newton and Leibnitz, and invariably with real objects this is not possible. It is sometimes possible to make progress by studying gross simplifications of natural objects in which form is continuous and differentiable, but we are so accustomed to assuming that our understanding of natural objects must be based on atomistic principles that we often assume away any pattern and order which does not fit our Euclidean–Newtonian methods of analysis. In short, our understanding of natural form and how it relates to function has been woefully limited, usually lying beyond analysis.

During the last 20 years, there has emerged a geometry of nature based on the very assumption that objects whose structure is irregular in Euclidean terms, often display patterns within this irregularity which are as ordered as those in simpler objects composed of straight lines. Objects composed of a multitude of lines which are nowhere smooth may well manifest order in more aggregative terms than the sorts of simple objects which are dealt with in mathematics. Such objects which show the same kind of irregularity at many scales have been called *fractals* (from the Latin adjective *fractus* meaning 'broken') by their inventor and popularizer Mandelbrot (1983, 1990) and the geometry which has emerged in their study is called 'fractal geometry'. In essence, a fractal is an object whose irregularity as a non-smooth form, is repeated across many scales, and in this sense, systems such as cities which manifest discrete self-similarity are ideal candidates for such study. A somewhat looser definition is given by Lauwerier (1991) who says that "A *fractal* is a geometrical figure that consists of an identical motif repeating itself on an ever-reduced scale". Cities with their manifest self-similarity of market area and repeating orders of centers and neighborhoods meet these criteria and form the set of fractal objects which we will explore in this book.

The best way to begin describing fractals is by example. A coastline and a mountain are examples of natural fractals, a crumpled piece of paper an example of an artificial one. However, such irregularity which characterizes these objects is not entirely without order and this order is to be found in fractals in terms of the following three principles. First, fractals are always *self-similar*, at least in some general sense. On whatever scale, and within a given range you examine a fractal, it will always appear to have the same shape or same degree of irregularity. The 'whole' will always be manifest in the 'parts'; look at a piece of rock broken off a mountain and you can see the mountain in the part. Look at the twigs on the branches of a tree and you can see the whole tree in these, albeit at a much reduced scale.

Second, fractals can always be described in terms of a *hierarchy* of self-similar components. Fractals are ordered hierarchically across many scales and the tree is the classic example. In fact, the tree is a literal interpretation of the term hierarchy and as such, it represents the most fundamental of fractals. There are many other examples of hierarchy: as we indicated in the last chapter, the organization and spacing of cities as central places is such an order while the configuration of districts and neighborhoods, and spatial distribution of roads and other communications are hierarchically structured. The third principle relates to the *irregularity* of form. Here by irregularity we mean forms which are continuous but nowhere smooth, hence non-differentiable in terms of the calculus. This point is so important that we must elaborate upon it further.

If you try to describe a coastline, you will encounter the following problem. If you measure its length from a map, the map will have been constructed at a scale which omits lower level detail. If you actually measure the length by walking along the beach, you will face a problem of knowing what scale or yardstick to use and deciding whether to measure around every rock and pebble. In essence, what you will get will be a length which is dependent on the scale you use, and as you use finer and finer scales down to microscopic levels even, the length of the coastline will continue to increase. We are forced to conclude that the coastline's length is 'infinitely' long or rather, that its absolute length has no meaning and the length given is always relative to the scale of measurement.

This conundrum has been known for a very long time. Richardson (1961) wrote about it for coastlines and national boundaries, while the geographer Andreas Penck (1894) alluded to it (Nysteun, 1966; Perkal, 1958a). There is some evidence that Leonardo da Vinci knew about it (Stevens, 1974) and if Leonardo knew about it, so probably did the Greeks. But it was not until the mid-1960s that the problem was raised formally and explicitly by Mandelbrot (1967). Building on Richardson's (1961) paper, Mandelbrot in an article entitled "How Long is the Coast of Britain?" argued that if the length of a straight line is absolute with Euclidean dimension 1, and the area of a plane is absolute with dimension 2, then something like a coastline which twists about in the plane must intuitively have a dimension between 1 and 2; in short a fractional or fractal dimension. Thus Mandelbrot was arguing that fractals were not only irregular lines like coastlines with self-similarity across a range of scales or orders in a hierarchy, but were also characterized by fractional dimension. Mountains would thus have fractal dimensions between 2 and 3, as if they were sculpted out of a solid block, more than the plane but less than the volume (cube). Fractals, however, would not be restricted to simply the dimensions we can visualize between the point and the volume but could exist between any adjacent pairs of higher dimensions. Indeed, as Mandelbrot (1967) argued, such objects are more likely to be the rule than the exception with Euclidean being a special case of fractal geometry. Most objects would thus have fractional, not integral dimension.

In this chapter, we will illustrate this geometry using idealized forms. In other words, we will present fractal geometry in terms of objects which are well-specified and manifest similarity across scales which we can model exactly. This is in contrast to most of the fractals illustrated in the rest of this book which will not be exact in terms of their self-similarity, but manifest similarities across scales which are ordered only in terms of their statistical distribution. In the sequel, we will begin by exploring the simplest of deterministic fractals – the Koch curve – and then we will use this to derive the basic mathematics used to describe fractal forms, in particular, emphasizing the meaning of fractal dimension. We will explore one-dimensional curves which fill two-dimensional space, hierarchies and tree structures, and we will then outline a rather different approach to fractals based upon repeated transformations used to generate their form at every scale. This approach which is largely due to Barnsley (1988a) is called *Iterated Function Systems* (IFS) and it provides a powerful way of illustrating the critical properties of fractals.

In this book, we will be speculating on the measurement of urban form in two ways: first in terms of boundaries around and within cities, and second, in terms of the way cities grow and fill the space available to them. Our ideas will be largely restricted to those fractals which exist between the one dimension of the line and the two dimensions of the plane. Our mathematics will be elementary, requiring no more than high school algebra and calculus, and when we introduce some trickier development we will explicitly present our algebra through all the needed steps. Another feature of our approach and indeed of the development of fractals generally is that it is easiest to work with them using computer graphics. Indeed some say that without computer graphics, fractals would certainly not have come alive in the last 20 years. We will thus present many computer graphics to illustrate these ideas, some of which will be in gray tones or black and white, and others in color (see color plate section).

2.2 The Geometry of the Koch Curve

To construct the simplest fractals we follow Mandelbrot (1983) in starting with a geometric object which we call an *initiator*. To this we apply a motif which repeats itself at every scale calling this the *generator*. We construct the fractal by applying the generator to the initiator, deriving a geometric object which can be considered to be composed of several initiators at the next level of hierarchy or scale down. Applying the generator once again at this new scale results in a further elaboration of the object's geometry at yet a finer scale, and the process is thus continued indefinitely towards the limit. In practice, the iteration or recursion is stopped at a level below which further scaled copies of the original object are no longer visible in terms of the scale at which the fractal is being viewed. In essence, however, the true fractal only exists in the limit, and thus what we see is simply an approximation to it.

We illustrate this process in Figure 2.1 for the non-rectifiable curve introduced by Helge von Koch in 1904, where we show the initiator – a straight line, and the generator which replaces the line by four copies of itself arranged as a continuous line but scaled so that each copy is one third the length of the initiator. The recursion which defines the process is shown as a hierarchy, or cascade as we will term it, in Figure 2.1. The tree which defines this cascade is indicative of the generative process which at each level replaces each part of the object by four smaller parts. As we have already implied, the tree which defines the cascade is itself a fractal, and in the rest of this chapter we will define all our fractals in terms of initiators, generators and the cascade which forms the process of application. In some fractals, we will see their geometry in terms of the cascading tree much more clearly than in others.

The Koch curve is an excellent example of a line which is scaled up in length at each iteration through replacing each straight line acting as its initiator by a line four thirds the length of the initiator, ordered in four continuous straight line segments. An even better illustration of this process for our purposes is given by the Koch island whose construction and the first three levels of its cascade is illustrated in Figure 2.2. In this case, the initiator is an equilateral triangle – the island, and the generator consists of scaling the triangle to one which is one third the length of each of the initiator's sides, and then 'gluing' each smaller copy of the triangle to each of the initiator's sides. Each side of the Koch island is thus a Koch curve which in the limit defines a fractal. It is easy to see that the Koch island is composed of smaller and smaller Koch islands which are identical motifs scaled successively by the same ratios. It is in this sense then that we speak

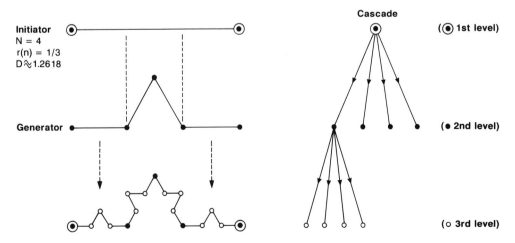

Figure 2.1. The construction of the Koch curve.

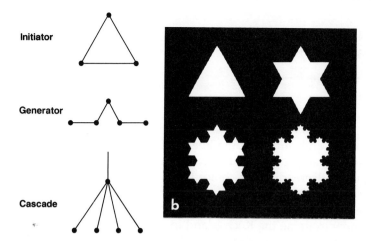

Figure 2.2. The Koch island.

of 'self-similarity'. We also illustrate the island after four cascades in Plate 2.1. In the Koch curve, the endlessly repeating motifs are strictly self-similar in that the scaling imposed by the generator does not stretch the object in one direction over another. In fact, objects which are stretched or distorted and scaled in the manner of fractals at successive scales are still fractals in our use of the term, although their scaling is said to embrace the property of self-affinity rather than self-similarity. We will encounter examples of these later in this chapter; in practice, most real fractals in nature and in the man-made world display self-affinity rather than strict self-similarity.

The Koch island represents one of the best fractals with which to illustrate the various conundrums which throw into doubt our Euclidean conceptions of space and dimension. Figure 2.1 suggests that the length of the Koch curve like the coastline of Britain is infinitely long, whereas Figure 2.2 and Plate 2.1 suggest that the area of the Koch island composed of three Koch curves is in fact bounded. We can illustrate these intuitions formally as follows. Let the length of the initial Koch curve which is each side of the original Koch island be defined as r. As Figure 2.1 implies, each side of the generator has length $r/3$ and consists of four copies of the initiator. Then we can define the increasing length of the Koch curve as follows. The length of the original line is

$$L_0 = r.$$ (2.1)

Applying the generator to the initiator results in a line L_1 which is 4/3 the length of L_0:

$$L_1 = \frac{4}{3} L_0 = \frac{4}{3} r,$$ (2.2)

and subsequent recursion gives

$$L_2 = \frac{4}{3} L_1 = \left(\frac{4}{3}\right)^2 r,$$ (2.3)

$\vdots$ $\vdots$

$$L_k = \frac{4}{3} L_{k-1} = \left(\frac{4}{3}\right)^k r.$$

(2.4)

It is clear that as $k \to \infty$, then

$$\lim_{k \to \infty} L_k = \left(\frac{4}{3}\right)^k r \to \infty.$$

(2.5)

To all intents and purposes, the line is of infinite length like the coastline of Britain in Mandelbrot's early writing on fractals. In fact, the Koch curve is a somewhat serendipitous choice for as Mandelbrot (1967) shows, it has a fractal dimension close to the coastline of Britain, thus providing a graphic example of this conundrum concerning length.

If we now examine the Koch island in Figure 2.2, then it is clear that the perimeter of the island is three times the length of a single Koch curve and thus we must replace the length r with $3r$ in equations (2.1) to (2.5) above. We will now examine the area of this island and show that despite its perimeter being of infinite length, its area converges to a finite value. To show this, first let us define the area of the initiating equilateral triangle as A_0 and with each side given as r, the area is

$$A_0 = \frac{\sqrt{3}}{4} r^2.$$

(2.6)

On the first iteration, three equilateral triangles are added to each of the three sides of the initiator and the area of each defined as $\tilde{A}_1$ is

$$\tilde{A}_1 = \frac{\sqrt{3}}{4} \left(\frac{1}{3}r\right)^2$$

(2.7)

and the area of the three triangles A_1 is given as

$$A_1 = \frac{1}{3} \frac{\sqrt{3}}{4} r^2.$$

(2.8)

Clearly $A_1 < A_0$ and thus the sum of areas so far given as $\bar{A}_1$

$$\bar{A}_1 = A_0 + A_1 = \frac{\sqrt{3}}{4} r^2 \left(1 + \frac{1}{3}\right).$$

(2.9)

At each stage of the recursion $3 \times 4^{k-1}$ triangles are added and the cumulative total area to k is thus

$$\bar{A}_k = A_0 + A_1 + 4A_2 + \dots + 4^{k-1} A_k.$$

(2.10)

A_k is defined as

$$A_k = \frac{1}{3^{2k}} \frac{\sqrt{3}}{4} r^2 = \frac{1}{3^{2k}} A_0,$$

(2.11)

and this simplifies to

$$A_k = \frac{\sqrt{3}}{12} r^2 \left(\frac{4}{9}\right)^{k-1}.$$

(2.12)

The cumulative total area on iteration k can now be written as

$$\bar{A}_k = \frac{\sqrt{3}}{4} r^2 + \frac{\sqrt{3}}{12} r^2 \left\{ 1 + \frac{4}{9} + \left(\frac{4}{9}\right)^2 + \dots + \left(\frac{4}{9}\right)^{k-1} \right\}. \tag{2.13}$$

Equation (2.13) can be written more compactly as

$$\bar{A}_k = \frac{\sqrt{3}}{4} r^2 + \frac{\sqrt{3}}{12} r^2 \sum_{j=0}^{k-1} \left(\frac{4}{9}\right)^j. \tag{2.14}$$

The summation term in equation (2.14) is a converging geometric series which can easily be shown to sum to 9/5 as $k \to \infty$, and thus the limit of equation (2.10) is given as

$$A = \lim_{k \to \infty} \bar{A}_k = \frac{\sqrt{3}}{4} r^2 + \frac{\sqrt{3}}{12} r^2 \frac{9}{5}$$

$$= \frac{2\sqrt{3}}{5} r^2 = \frac{8}{5} A_0. \tag{2.15}$$

Equivalent summations are given in Woronow (1981) and by Peitgen, Jurgens and Saupe (1992).

2.3 Length, Area and Fractal Dimension

The mathematical argument presented above in equations (2.1) to (2.15) is a formal statement of the coastline conundrum. Although the length of the curve which bounds the Koch island increases without bound as the scale is reduced – becomes finer, the area of the island converges to a finite value which is $0.693r^2$. If the length of the curve converged, then its dimension would clearly be 1 and the area it enclosed 2 but in the case of the Koch curve, it is apparent that length measured in the conventional Euclidean sense is unbounded. In an attempt to unravel the paradox of infinite length and finite area, let us restate the generation of the Koch curve in the following way. We will first repeat equation (2.4) as

$$L_k = \left(\frac{4}{3}\right)^k r. \tag{2.4}$$

Now this length in (2.4) is made up of the number of copies of the initiator used in generating the curve which we call N_k and the scaling ratio r_k applied to the original line length r which gives the length of each line in the N_k copies. Therefore length L_k is defined as

$$L_k = N_k r_k, \tag{2.16}$$

from which it is clear that $N_k = 4^k$ and $r_k = r/3^k$.

In Table 2.1, we show the increase in N_k in comparison to r_k as well as the length L_k for both the Koch curve in equation (2.16) and the straight line, where N_k is divided into the same number of parts as the inverse of

Table 2.1. Scaling properties of the Koch curve

Iteration k	Koch curve				Straight line			
	N_k	r_k	r_k^{-1}	$N_k r_k$	N_k	r_k	r_k^{-1}	$N_k r_k$
0	1	1	1	1	1	1	1	1
1	4	1/3	3	1.333	4	1/4	4	1
2	16	1/9	9	1.777	16	1/16	16	1
3	64	1/27	27	2.370	64	1/64	64	1
⋮	⋮	⋮						⋮

the individual length of each part r_k^{-1}. It is clear that for the Koch curve, the number of copies N_k increases at a much faster rate than the inverse r_k^{-1}. This can be seen by examining $N_k r_k$ which for the straight line is a constant, whereas for the Koch curve is increasing. If we were to predict the number of copies N_k generated from the number of parts r_k^{-1} the initiator is divided into, then it is clear that r_k^{-1} would need to be raised to a power D greater than unity. That is

$$N_k = (r_k^{-1})^D = r_k^{-D}. \tag{2.17}$$

For a straight line, $D = 1$ while for the Koch curve the similarity factor r_k must scale as a power $D > 1$. Now if we substitute N_k in equation (2.17) into equation (2.16), the equation for the length of the line becomes

$$L_k = N_k r_k = r_k^{(1-D)}. \tag{2.18}$$

If the parameter D is equal to 1 then equation (2.18) gives a constant (unit) length, while if $D > 1$, L_k is unbounded. Moreover, it is intuitively obvious that D plays the role of dimension in these equations and as such, we have now demonstrated that the Koch curve has a dimension which is greater than 1, hence must be fractional, not integral in value.

In strictly self-similar curves, the dimension D can be calculated exactly, for the recursion which generates the curve is itself identical at each level or scale. Then taking the log of equation (2.17), the dimension D at any level k called D_k is given as

$$D_k = -\frac{\log N_k}{\log r_k} = \frac{\log N_k}{\log (1/r_k)}. \tag{2.19}$$

In the case of the Koch curve where we assume without loss of generality that $r = 1$, then $N_k = 4^k$ and $(1/r_k) = 3^k$, and equation (2.19) reduces to

$$D = D_k = \frac{\log 4}{\log 3} \cong 1.262,$$

which is the value of the fractal dimension. This bears out our intuition that the Koch curve has a dimension nearer 1 than 2 in that the curve departs from the straight line significantly but does not fill very much of the two-dimensional space.

There are many different types of fractal dimension (Falconer, 1990; Takayasu, 1990). The one we have derived is often called the 'similarity dimension' which is only defined for strictly self-similar objects. In this context, we will use the notion of the fractal dimension in its generic sense for we will define such dimensions in a variety of contexts, and as our purpose is with applications, it will suffice to think of such dimensions as a measure of the extent to which space is filled. In fact, our concern here will be almost exclusively with fractal dimensions which vary between 1 and 2. Our focus is on the spatial structure of cities that exist in the plane and although there are many studies of urban structure which stress their three-dimensional form, we will be mainly dealing with cities as they are expressed through two-dimensional maps. However, the fractal dimensions we will develop will depend upon the particular aspect of urban form we are measuring; the boundaries of cities, for example, will have different dimensions from the density of development, while the actual value of the dimensions computed will inevitably depend upon the methods used in their measurement and calculation.

From equation (2.17), it is clear that the number of copies of the initiator generated at any iteration k, N_k, varies inversely with r_k^D, and their product will be constant, that is

$$N_k r_k^D = 1. \tag{2.20}$$

As illustrated in Table 2.1, this relation holds for the straight line when $D = 1$. Where the object in question fills the plane as in the case of a square, then the number of copies generated varies with the square of the scaling factor $1/r_k$ as r_k^{-2}, where $D = 2$. Clearly for a fractal object with dimension between 1 and 2, then equation (2.20) is only satisfied when the value of D ensures it is constant.

However, consider the case where N_k varies as $r_k^{-\delta}$ where δ is not equal to D. Then we can write equation (2.20) as

$$N_k r_k^D = r_k^{-\delta} \, r_k^D,$$
$$= r_k^{D-\delta} = \left(\frac{1}{r_k}\right)^{\delta-D}. \tag{2.21}$$

If δ is less than D, the actual fractal dimension, then N_k will diverge towards infinity. This would be the case where we assumed that the object were a straight line, but in fact it is a Koch curve. On the other hand, if we assumed that δ were greater than D, then equation (2.21) would converge towards zero. Thus the fractal dimension D is the only value which would ensure that equation (2.20) is satisfied. Formally this can be written as

$$\lim_{k \to \infty} N_k r_k^D = r_k^{D-\delta} = \begin{cases} \to \infty & \text{if } \delta < D, \\ 1 & \text{if } \delta = D, \\ \to 0 & \text{if } \delta > D. \end{cases} \tag{2.22}$$

It is possible to visualize the value of δ converging toward D from above or below and only when it is exactly equal to D will equations (2.20) and (2.22) be equal to 1 (Feder, 1988).

We have already introduced the notion that fractals exist which are self-affine in that their scaling ratios $\{r_k\}$ may differ. Such a fractal would be self-similar in that there would be copies of the object at every scale but that these copies would be distorted in terms of the original initiator in some way. There is a straightforward generalization of equation (2.20) for this case. We now have m scaling factors which we call r_{kj} and if we associate a distinct scaling factor with each copy of the object, then the fractal dimension must satisfy

$$\sum_{j=0}^{m} r_{kj}^{D} = 1. \tag{2.23}$$

In this case, we can find D by solving the equation for any level k which is based on the fact that the fractal never changes its scaling factors over the range of levels and scales for which the object is observed (Barnsley, 1988a; Feder, 1988).

We can examine this best by example. In Figure 2.3 and in Plate 2.2, the Koch curve has been regularly distorted in that the two base pieces of the generator have quite different scaling and the two perturbed pieces which are equal in length form a spike rather than a pyramid to the curve. This generates what Mandelbrot (1983) calls a Koch forest. We can easily compute the dimension from this figure, given the scaling factors. Then in the case where $m = 4$ for the Koch forest, equation (2.23) simplifies to

$$0.30^{D} + 0.42^{D} + 0.42^{D} + 0.63^{D} = 1,$$

and the dimension D which solves this equation is 1.750, considerably larger, as expected, than the regular Koch curve whose dimension is 1.262.

2.4 The Basic Mathematical Relations of Fractal Geometry

So far we have assumed that we are measuring the geometric properties of a single object and we have shown how we might do this for strictly

Initiator

Generator

Cascade

Figure 2.3. The self-affine Koch forest.

self-similar fractals. In essence, we compute the fractal dimension by examining the object at different scales, taking the ratio of the number of its repetitions to its scaling factors. There are, however, other ways of looking at the form of such objects and we will use two such ways here. First, we may have a set of objects which we know are of the same type and which are all measured at the same scale. In such a case, we can develop methods for computing the fractal dimension of the set by examining changes in form at the fixed scale of measurement. Second, we may have an object which is constructed or measured at the same scale but whose size changes in some regular way which we might associate with growth or decline. In short, its mass or the number of its parts increases or decreases as the object grows or dies. In one sense these differences in measurement are strongly related to the fact that the object(s) in question changes its size or scale, and it is such changes that are essential in computing its fractal dimension.

We will begin by treating single objects for which we are able to control the scale of measurement as in the cases already introduced for the Koch curve. We will now use the variable r to measure continuous scale and we will drop the explicit reference to iterations of fractal construction. Then generalizing equations (2.17) and (2.18), we get

$$N(r) = Kr^{-D}, \tag{2.24}$$

and

$$L(r) = N(r)r = Kr^{(1-D)}. \tag{2.25}$$

$N(r)$ and $L(r)$ are the number of parts and the length of the object respectively where we are implying that we are dealing with fractal lines, and K is a constant of proportionality. If we have a series of observations of $N(r)$ and $L(r)$ at different scales r, then we can derive the fractal dimension by taking log transforms of each of these equations and performing a regression of these variables in cases where the variation is stochastic, hence statistical not deterministic. Because we will be mainly concerned with regressing length on scale, then the log transform of equation (2.25) yields

$$\log L(r) = \log K + (1-D) \log r, \tag{2.26}$$

where it is clear that the slope of the regression line is $(1-D)$ from which the dimension can be derived directly. We will say much more about this in Chapters 5 and 6 where we will deal with statistical variations, but note here that if we apply equations (2.24) and (2.25) to, say, the Koch curve, then these equations collapse back to those from which they have been generalized.

To derive the dimension from a set of objects all of different size but measured at the same scale r, we now need to define the scale more explicitly and for this we assume that the scaling ratio $1/r$ is applied directly to a size R which is the size of the object in question. Equation (2.25) can be written as

$$L(r) = K \left(\frac{R}{r}\right)^{D} r = KR^{D}r^{(1-D)}. \tag{2.27}$$

When we have a fixed scale, $r^{(1-D)}$ is constant and it is R, the size, which varies. Incorporating the various constants into G, dropping the scale r and subscripting the variables L_i and R_i where i indicates a particular object, equation (2.27) can be written as

$$L_i = GR_i^D. \tag{2.28}$$

The size R_i is clearly related to the area of the object A_i, and if we consider R_i to be equal to the square root of A_i, then

$$R_i = \sqrt{A_i} = A_i^{1/2}.$$

Substituting for R_i in equation (2.28), we obtain a relationship between length and area, the so-called perimeter–area relation,

$$L_i = GA_i^{D/2}. \tag{2.29}$$

A log transform of equation (2.29) gives

$$\log L_i = \log G + \frac{D}{2} \log A_i \tag{2.30}$$

from which it is clear that the slope of any regression line estimated using equation (2.30) is $D/2$. This equation has been widely used to measure fractal dimensions in sets of physical objects such as clouds (Lovejoy, 1982), moon craters (Woronow, 1981) and islands (Goodchild, 1980).

   The third and last method of measuring dimension is based on a single object where the scale change is implied by the object increasing or decreasing in size. Here we will be concerned with the mass of the object which we consider is measured by the number of parts of the object at scale r, $N(r)$. Using R again as the size of the object, equation (2.24) can be written as

$$N(r) = K \left(\frac{R}{r}\right)^D. \tag{2.31}$$

Then at a fixed scale r, the mass or number of parts of the object scales with R as

$$N(R) = ZR^D. \tag{2.32}$$

Note that we now use R instead of r for the index of scale change which is based on the change in the size R of the object. If we have the area of the object $A(R)$, then we can normalize equation (2.32) to obtain a density relation

$$\rho(R) = \frac{N(R)}{A(r)} = Z \frac{R^D}{\pi R^2} \sim R^{D-2}. \tag{2.33}$$

We can obtain the fractal dimension by taking a log transform of equations (2.32) or (2.33) and we will use these equations extensively when we discuss urban growth models in Chapters 7 to 10. Note also that in the sequel we will refer to the measure of mass $N(R)$ as a measure of population size.

   In this section we have examined three ways of computing fractal dimension and in Table 2.2 we summarize these methods in terms of their emphasis on size and scale. In fact we do not have any methods for estimating dimension where there are several objects which vary across several scales.

Table 2.2. Equations associated with measuring fractal dimension

Number of objects	Varying scale	Varying size
One object	(2.24), (2.25)	(2.32), (2.33)
More than one	—	(2.28), (2.29)

In this case, some selection from the three methods introduced here would be necessary. For example, it would be possible to treat every object separately and to estimate a set of fractal dimensions using equations (2.24) and (2.25). If a single fractal dimension were required, then all the scale changes for all the objects could be combined into one set and a single regression carried out. However, in the case of a set of objects where their scale can be varied, then it is likely that the emphasis would be on estimating a set of dimensions and making comparisons between objects. We will develop these ideas further in Chapter 6 when we deal with the fractal dimensions of different land uses in a town.

2.5 More Idealized Geometries: Space-Filling Curves and Fractal Dusts

The last section was something of a digression in that the equations we presented, although derived from the geometry of the Koch curve and of extremely general import throughout this book, will be used mainly for the measurement of fractals using statistical methods. Now we will return to our discussion of methods applicable to exact fractals and provide some more examples to impress the idea that a large number of objects can exist with fractal dimensions between 0 and 2. Perhaps the best examples are those continuous lines which have a Euclidean or topological dimension of 1 but a fractal dimension of 2 and are called space-filling curves, for reasons which will become obvious. We will begin with the curve first introduced by Peano in 1890 (Mandelbrot, 1983) and whose construction is shown in Figure 2.4.

This curve is formed by applying a generator which spans a square whose initiator is a diagonal line across the square. In Figure 2.4, at each level of recursion, the generator replaces the straight line by nine copies of itself, each scaled to one-third the length of the line. To present the curve, we cut off each corner of the right-angled twists in the line to show that the line is continuous. Four generations of the line are shown starting with the originator at $k = 0$. If the recursion is continued beyond $k = 4$, the curve falls below the resolution of the computer screen on which it was generated and for all intents and purposes at the scale of the picture, the curve literally 'fills' the space. However, because it is a fractal, the line has no width, and as we continue to zoom into the picture, the curve continues to generate ever more detail on its path towards infinity. In short, it never fills the

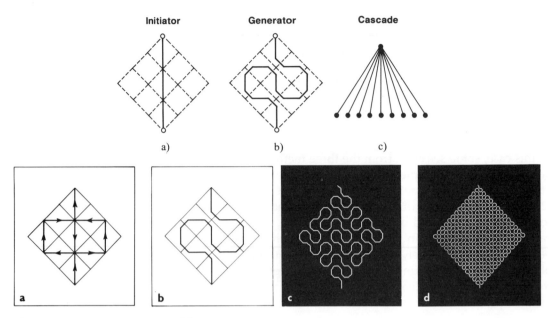

Figure 2.4.   Peano's space-filling curve.

space because we can never reach the limit, thus illustrating the paradox which Bronowski (1973) referred to in the quote which introduces this chapter. In generating the curve at any level k, it is clear that the number of parts N_k are 9^k and the similarity ratio is $(1/3)^k$. From equation (2.19), the fractal dimension is computed as $D = (\log 9)/(\log 3)$, and our intuition that this curve fills all the two-dimensional space available to it is rewarded in that the fractal dimension is indeed 2.

There are several other curves which we can generate which have a fractal dimension equal to 2. If we take a straight line as initiator and generate two parts to the line forming a right angled triangle resting on the initiator (which in turn is the hypotenuse of this triangle shown in Figure 2.5), then

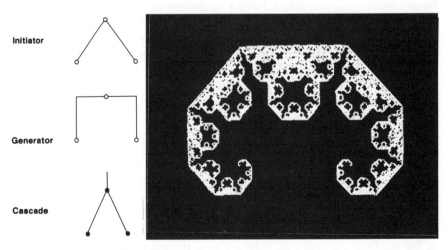

Figure 2.5.   The 'C' curve.

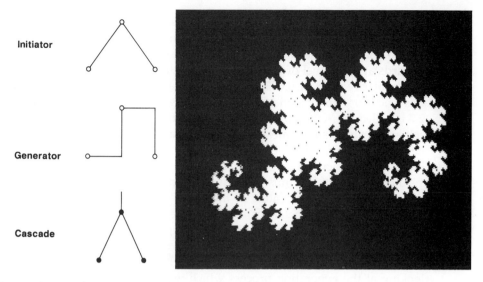

Figure 2.6. The Dragon curve.

we generate a closed curve which is called the 'C' curve. Assuming that the length of each of the two new lines is 1, then the original initiator has a length √2, and the similarity ratio is 1/√2. Using these values in equation (2.19) also gives this curve a fractal dimension of $D = (\log 2)/(\log \sqrt{2}) = 2$. For the C curve, we generate new lines always outwards from the initiator, whereas if we replace the two lines which are generated with one outwards and one inwards as shown in Figure 2.6, the construction which we generate is called the 'dragon' curve which also has a fractal dimension of 2. To further impress this notion of space-filling, examine the double dragon curve in Plate 2.3 which suggests that infinite space can be perfectly tiled and entirely filled with such constructions.

Figures 2.4 to 2.6 illustrate that the actual shape of an object does not necessarily influence the value of its fractal dimension which is, in a sense, obvious in that there is nothing that we have introduced so far which relates dimension to geometric shape. In fact, we can change the fractal dimension by virtually keeping the same shape. Figure 2.7 illustrates how we might

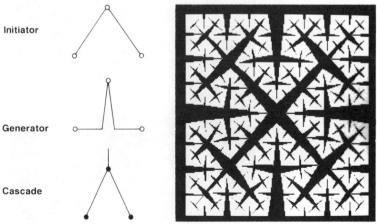

Figure 2.7. The Peano–Cesaro triangle sweep.

sweep out a design in the plane using a generator similar to those used in the C and dragon curves. In this case, the generator is the same right-angled triangle as used in the dragon curve but with both triangles turned inwards at each level of recursion. To actually show the curve, we have set the similarity ratio at 0.673 which is a little less than $1/\sqrt{2}$ (= 0.707) and this leads to a dimension of 1.750. The design we have generated in Figure 2.7 is called by Mandelbrot (1983) the Peano–Cesaro triangle sweep and its self-similarity is sometimes reminiscent of a fern, although as we shall see later, much more realistic designs can be generated as the strictures imposed by exact self-similarity are relaxed.

Another design we must introduce is one which can be interpreted as sculpting out scaled versions of the object in the two-dimensional plane, thus showing that fractals can be generated by taking away rather than adding to the initiator. In Figure 2.8, we begin with an initiator which is a solid equilateral triangle, and take out a scaled copy of the original, positioned centrally in the object at each level of recursion. Another way of looking at the generation process which we will invoke later is to see the scaling as taking three copies of the triangle, and scaling these in such a way as to 'tile' the original triangle. A final way of seeing this which is also shown in Figure 2.8 is as a continuous curve which spans the triangle and it is this which we can use to calculate the fractal dimension. In essence, the scaling is 1/2 and the number of pieces of scaled line or triangle generated at each generation is 3. The fractal dimension of the resulting lattice-like structure, called the Sierpinski gasket, after its originator, is $D = \log(3)/\log(2) = 1.585$. We will return to this construction when we introduce Barnsley's (1988a) IFS approach below.

There is one last construction we must mention before we change tack and examine branching structures, and this is a fractal whose dimension lies between 0 and 1. We refer to such fractals as 'dusts' and the best one to illustrate this is named after the mathematician George Cantor, the 'Cantor Set'. This is based on a straight line initiator which is replaced at each iteration by two copies of itself, but these copies are scaled by 1/3 of the

Figure 2.8. Sierpinski's gasket: sculpting and tiling space.

Plate 2.1 A Koch Island.

Plate 2.2 A Koch Forest.

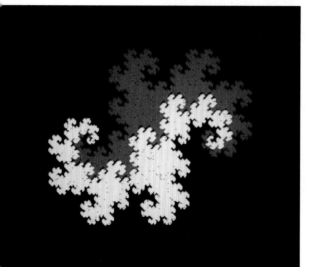

Plate 2.3 Twin Dragon Curves.

Plate 2.4 A Binary Tree in Full Foliage.

Plate 2.5 Tiling the Landscape with Trees.

Plate 2.6 Savannah, a Minimalist Fractal Landscape.

Plate 3.2
(right) Alpine Scene.

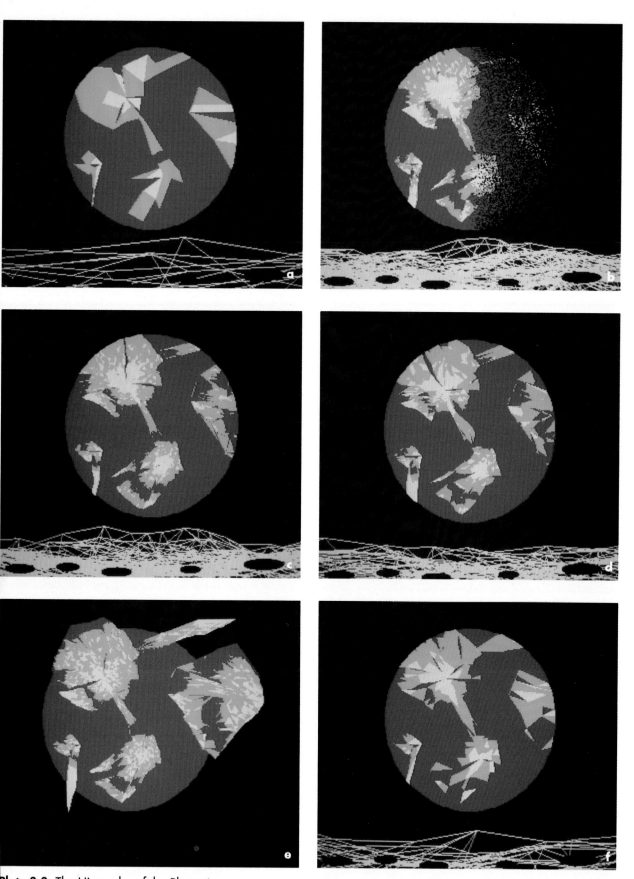

Plate 3.3 The Hierarchy of the Planetrise

The four levels of construction are shown with the two 'tricks' to render 'planetrise' – the circular sculpting and the light source shading – illustrated in the last two subplates.

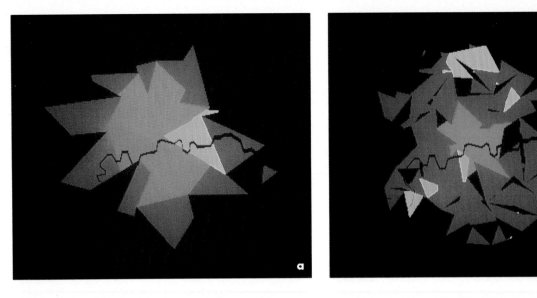

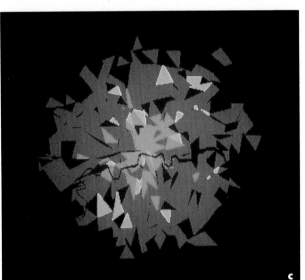

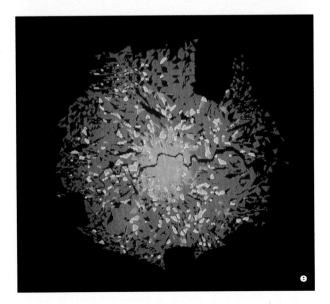

Plate 3.4 The Hierarchy of the Fractal City
Blue is commercial-industrial land use, red is residential, and
green is open space-recreational.

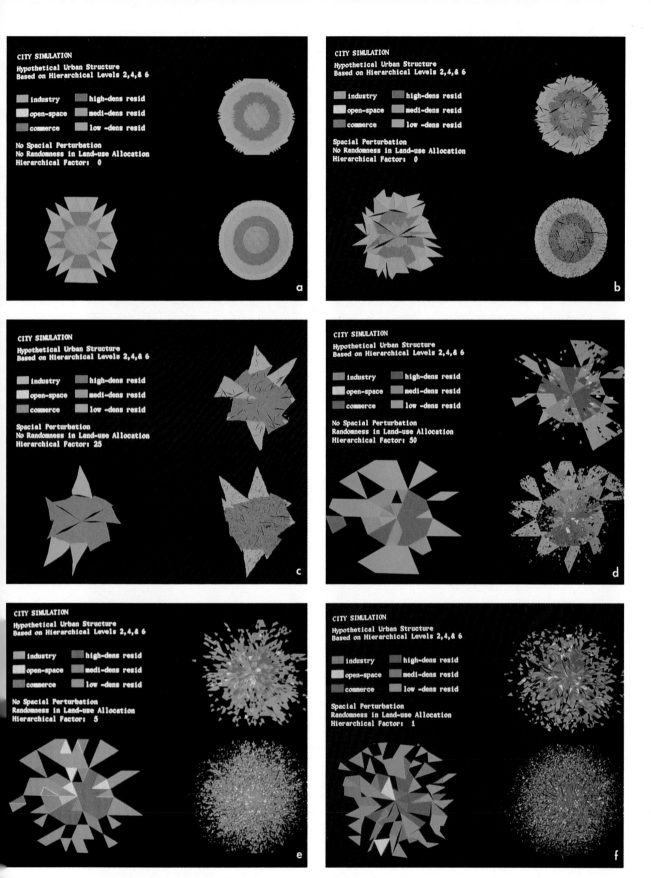

Plate 4.1 A Sampling of the Space of All Cities.

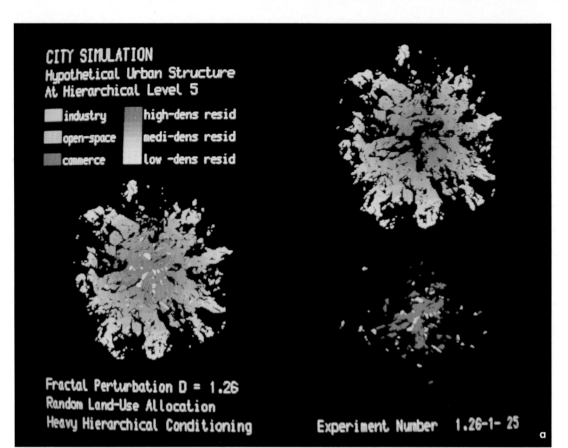

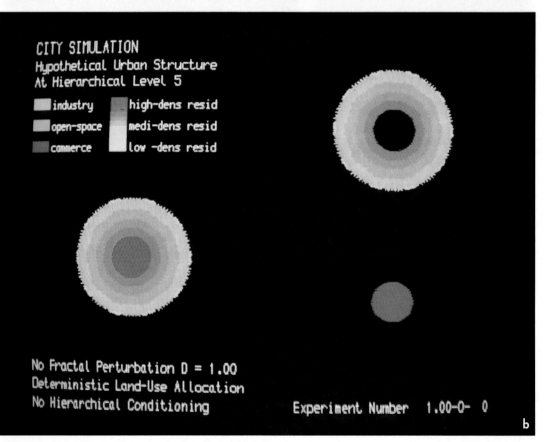

Plate 4.2 'Realistic' Hypothetical Urban Simulations.

Plate 4.3 *(right)* The Graphical Data Base: Age of Housing in London.
Average age of housing: 8 years (white), 26 years (light blue), 48 years (magenta), 78 years (dark blue), 110 years (yellow), 150 years (green), and 175 years (red).

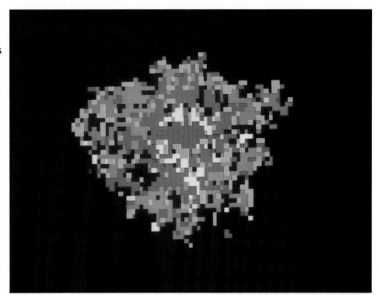

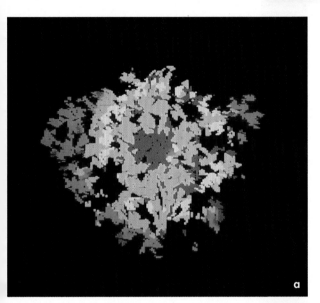

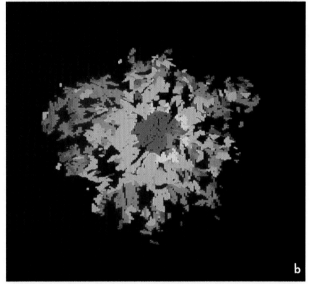

a

b

Plate 4.4 *(above)* Deterministic Simulations of House Type in London.
Converted flats (red), purpose-built flats (yellow), terraced housing (green), and detached/semi-detached housing (blue).

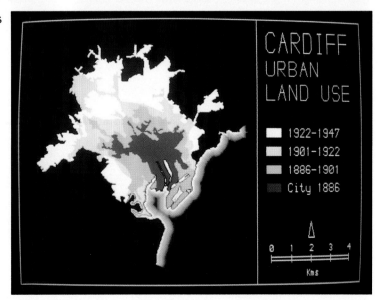

Plate 5.1 *(right)* Urban Growth of Cardiff's Boundary.

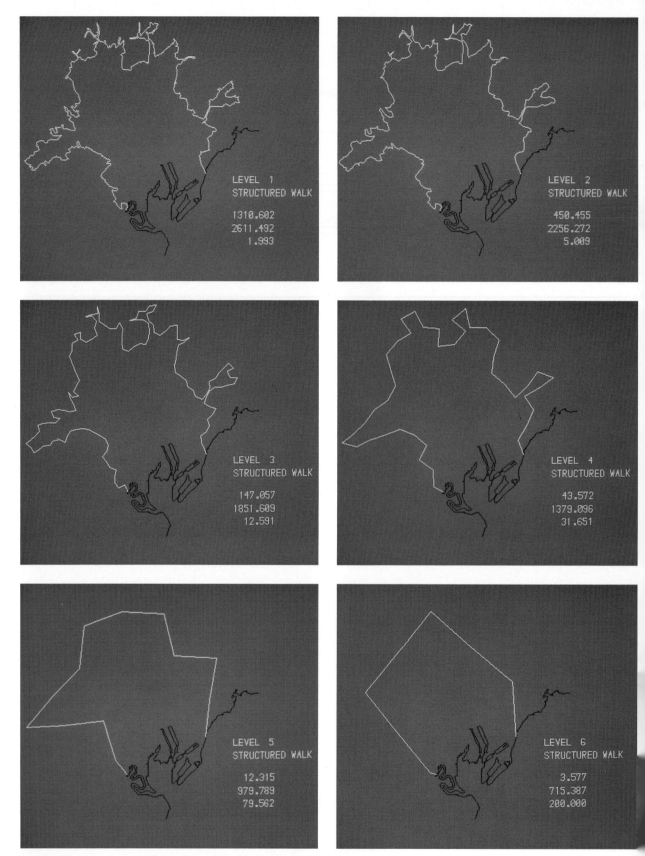

LEVEL 1
STRUCTURED WALK

1310.602
2611.492
1.993

LEVEL 2
STRUCTURED WALK

450.455
2256.272
5.009

LEVEL 3
STRUCTURED WALK

147.057
1851.609
12.591

LEVEL 4
STRUCTURED WALK

43.572
1379.096
31.651

LEVEL 5
STRUCTURED WALK

12.315
979.789
79.562

LEVEL 6
STRUCTURED WALK

3.577
715.387
200.000

Plate 5.2 Structured Walks Along the Urban Boundary.

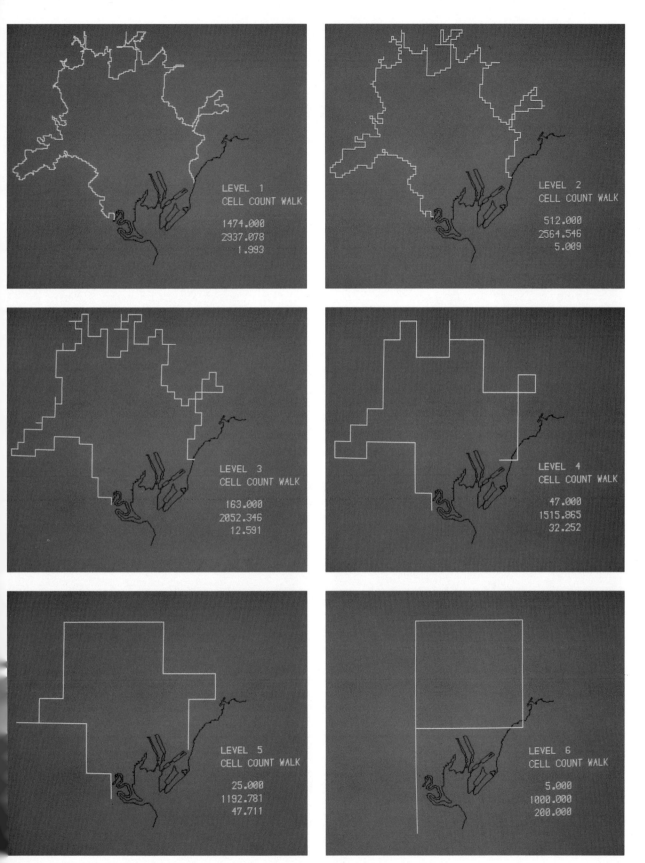

LEVEL 1
CELL COUNT WALK

1474.000
2937.078
1.993

LEVEL 2
CELL COUNT WALK

512.000
2564.546
5.009

LEVEL 3
CELL COUNT WALK

163.000
2052.346
12.591

LEVEL 4
CELL COUNT WALK

47.000
1515.865
32.252

LEVEL 5
CELL COUNT WALK

25.000
1192.781
47.711

LEVEL 6
CELL COUNT WALK

5.000
1000.000
200.000

Plate 5.3 Cell-Counts of the Space Along the Urban Boundary.

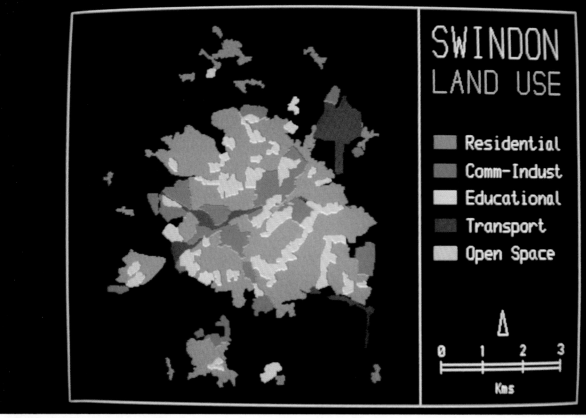

Plate 6.1 Land Use in Swindon.

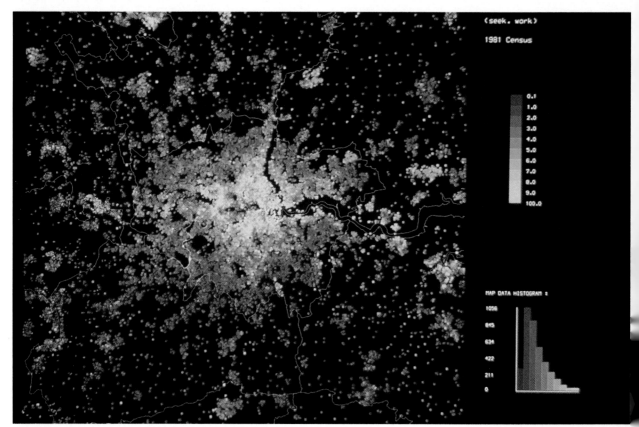

Plate 7.1 Fractal London: Employment Densities.

Plate 7.2 Urban Employment Density in England and Wales.

Plate 7.3 Dendritic Growth from the Diffusion-Limited Aggregation (DLA) Model.
(based on a 500 × 500 lattice with 10 000 particles).

Plate 8.1 Dendritic Growth from the Dielectric Breakdown Model (DBM).
(based on a 150 × 150 lattice with 1856 particles).

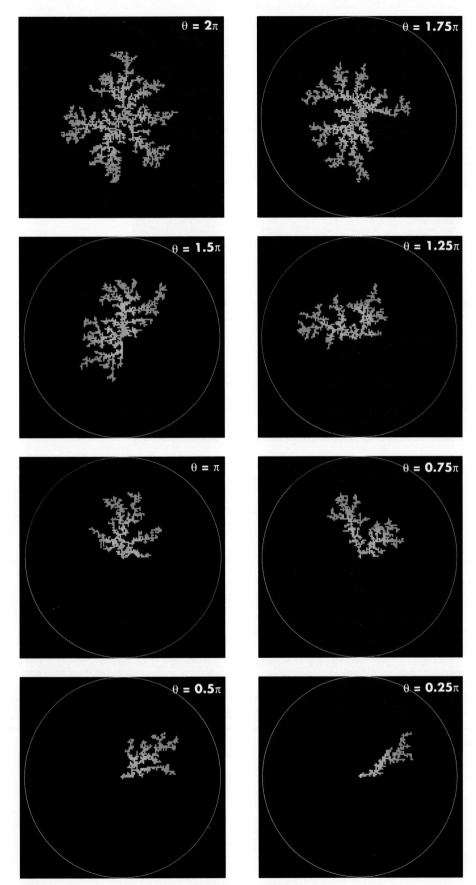

Plate 8.2 Physically Constrained DBM Simulations

Plate 8.3 *(left)* The Baseline Simulation $\eta = 1$.

Plate 8.5 *(below)* The Urban Area of Cardiff.

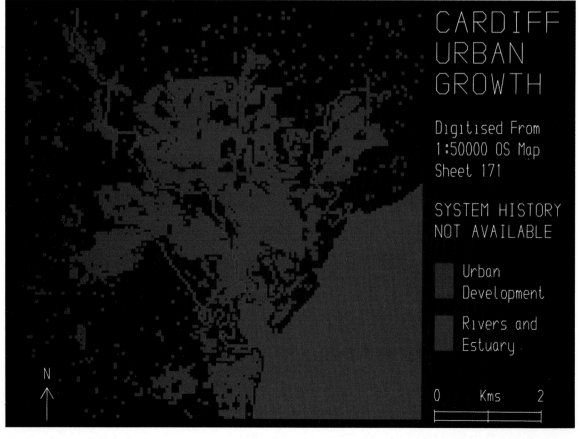

CARDIFF
URBAN
GROWTH

Digitised From
1:50000 OS Map
Sheet 171

SYSTEM HISTORY
NOT AVAILABLE

Urban
Development

Rivers and
Estuary.

N

0   Kms   2

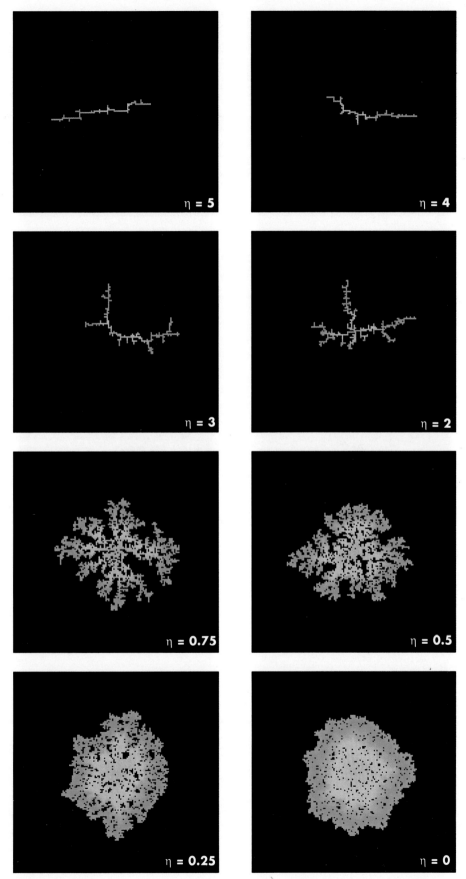

Plate 8.4 Urban Forms Generated by Systematic Distortions to the DBM Field

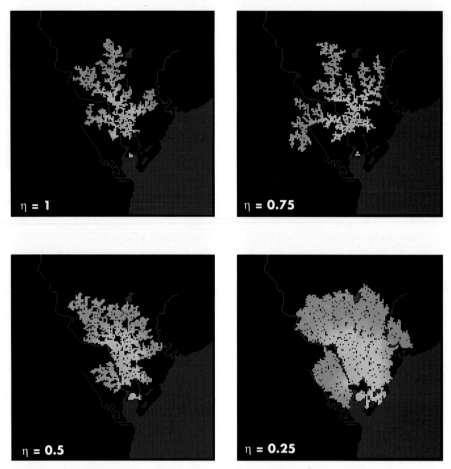

Plate 8.6 Simulating the Urban Growth of Cardiff

previous line. This construction is shown in Figure 2.9 where it is clear that the object is being systematically reduced from the one-dimensional line which is its initiator by removing the middle third of each line. Using equation (2.19), the dimension is $D = \log (2)/\log (3) = 0.631$. In one sense, we can see both the Sierpinski gasket and the Cantor dust as objects which begin with two- and one-dimensional shapes respectively and gradually reduce the dimension of the shape as pieces of it are removed. In this sense, then we might think of both of these as 'dusts'.

Finally in this section we will anticipate later chapters of this book by generalizing these results. In Figure 2.10, we show the sorts of objects which exist across a continuum of dimensions from points to lines to planes to volumes, in Euclidean terms from zero to three dimensions. We also show three typical fractals which exist between zero and one, one and two, and two and three dimensions, these being dusts, trees and surfaces respectively. In fact as we have already implied, we will mainly concentrate upon objects with a fractal dimension between 1 and 2 in this book because our predominant way of representing cities will be through maps. So far in our discussion of fractals we have only dealt with lines and points of the simplest kind, and insofar as we have dealt with trees or dendrites it has been through ideas about hierarchy, not with any more substantial representation of reality. In the next section we will remedy this and then be in a position to introduce a somewhat different approach to fractals which enables us to round off the elementary insights we are attempting to present in this chapter.

2.6 Trees and Hierarchies

We have already noted that the tree or cascade structure used to show how the generator relates to the initiator in deterministic fractals is itself a fractal,

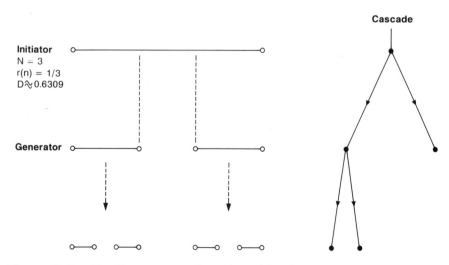

Figure 2.9. The Cantor curve: fractals as 'dusts'.

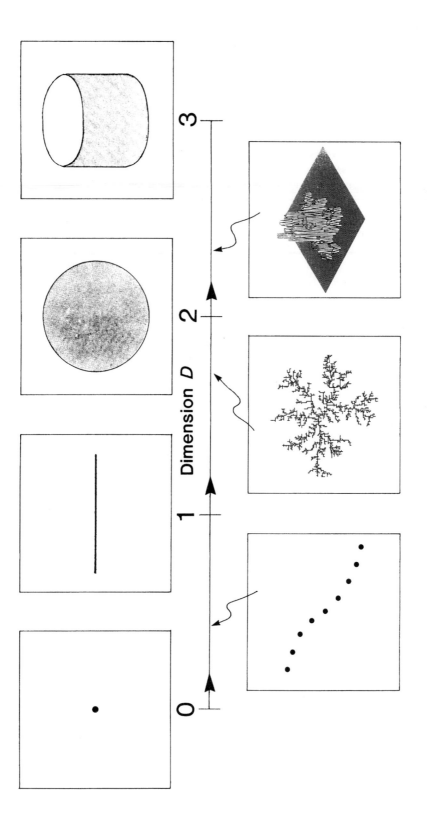

Figure 2.10.   The continuum of fractional dimensions.

for the tree shows how many self-similar copies of the object are generated but not their scaling. In fact we will deal with a much reduced set of tree structures here, and restrict our attention to structures which branch into two copies of the object at each level. In fact, we know that this yields only a subset of all possible trees but it is sufficient for our purposes which is simply to establish the background. There has already been substantial work on the morphology of trees and we will not attempt to summarize this work here. Readers who wish to follow up these ideas are referred to MacDonald (1983) in the biological literature, to Aono and Kunii (1984) in computer graphics, and to Prusinkiewicz and Lindenmayer (1990) for a treatment in terms of fractals.

First we will state some of the obvious relationships governing branching structures of the binary or dichotomous kind. The number of branches of any tree which are generated at a given level of recursion or hierarchy k is given as

$$N_k = \vartheta^k, \tag{2.34}$$

where ϑ is the bifurcation ratio equal to 2 for binary branching, 3 for ternary and so on. The number of branches at any level of the hierarchy is the sum of these numbers over k defined as

$$N_K = \sum_{k=1}^{K} N_k. \tag{2.35}$$

Equations (2.34) and (2.35) can be used to compute the number of elementary operations in any recursive scheme at and down to any level k. With respect to botanical trees, several relationships have been established between branch lengths and widths, angles, their scaling or contraction, and their symmetry, but we will only state one which was first articulated by Leonardo da Vinci in 16th century Italy. This is based on relating the width of any stem in a tree to the two stems which branch from this between levels $k - 1$ and k. Then

$$W_{k-1}^\varsigma = {}_R W_k^\varsigma + {}_L W_k^\varsigma, \tag{2.36}$$

where W is the width at the relevant level, ς is a parameter of the relation and R and L indicate the right and left branches respectively. Leonardo (Stevens, 1974) suggested that the parameter ς in equation (2.36) be equal to 2 and in this case the tree could be called Pythagorean in that the width of the branch stem W_{k-1} would be the hypotenuse of a right angled triangle whose two sides are ${}_R W_k$ and ${}_L W_k$. Examples of such trees are given in the book by Lauwerier (1991). McMahon (1975) suggests that the width of any branch W_k should be proportional to its length as

$$W_k \propto L_k^{3/2}. \tag{2.37}$$

In fact strict Pythagorean trees have the length of their branches identical to their width although this leads to somewhat squat looking trees. As McMahon (1975) and others imply, the parameter ς, which makes the relation in equation (2.37) realistic, is unlikely to be as low as 2 but never more than 3. However, the biggest single factor affecting the shape of trees concerns their branching angles, but these do not affect our computation of fractal dimension which only depends upon the rate at which the branches contract or scale and the number of branches which are associated with each stem or trunk.

Computing the fractal dimension of trees illustrates the existence of several dimensions which depend upon the particular aspect of the tree's form which is measured. Examining the branch tips of a bifurcating binary tree suggests that the canopy of the tree which contains the branch tips is a kind of dust. If the width of the two branches of the stem are less than the width of the stem itself, then the canopy formed is a Cantor set with dimension between 0 and 1. However, this dimension takes no account of the length of the branches. A more obvious dimension is based on the fact that the initiator is a stem and the two branches are scaled copies of the stem as in the C and dragon curves shown earlier in Figures 2.5 and 2.6. Often the branch angles are chosen so that the tree is self-avoiding in that the branch tips do not touch or at least just touch but do not overlap. In Figure 2.11, we show a tree in which the branch angles are chosen so that the tips of the branches just touch one another and the contraction or scaling ratio for each branch is 0.6. The fractal dimension using equation (2.19) is computed as $-\log(2)/\log(0.6) = 1.357$.

In contrast in Figure 2.12, we show two more realistic looking trees. The first is symmetric but with the branches overlapping with a contraction ratio of 0.8, hence a fractal dimension of 3.106 which implies that the overlap more than covers three dimensions, while the second tree is asymmetric with contraction factors of 0.8 and 0.7 for the left and right branches respectively; hence using equation (2.23), the dimension is 2.435 covering more than the plane. This tree has been computed to a depth of 10 branches, thus illustrating how the branches contract to the canopy in contrast to the other tree in this figure which is only plotted to a depth of five branches. Note that in these cases where the branches are not self-avoiding, our equations for fractal dimension gives values greater than 2, thus indicating that our

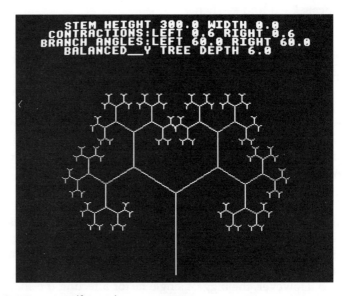

Figure 2.11. A self-avoiding symmetric tree.

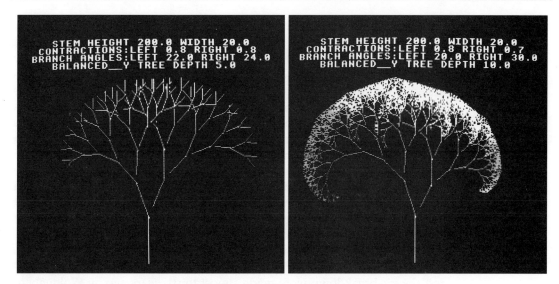

Figure 2.12. Fractal trees with overlapping branches.

pictures of these trees are not entirely adequate in visualizing their geometric form. The full tree is also pictured in Plate 2.4, while its use in 'tiling' space to form landscapes is illustrated in Plates 2.5 and 2.6.

The best example of a tree which fills the plane is provided by the H tree which is shown in Figure 2.13(a). This tree is symmetric, it is self-avoiding in that its branch angles are chosen to be 90° and the rate at which both its branches contract is 0.707. This gives a fractal dimension of 2 which bears out our intuition. A slight variation of this contraction ratio down to 0.7 and a slight decrease in the branch angles from 90° to 85° produces a slightly more realistic structure with a dimension of 1.943, but this remains strictly self-similar. This is also shown as Figure 2.13(b). These forms are

(b)

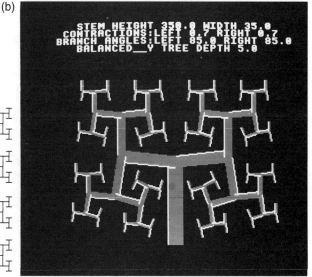

(a)

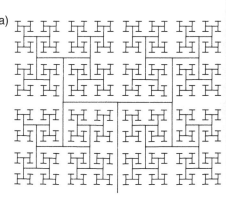

Figure 2.13. 'H' trees as plan forms.

classic space-filling curves. They are reminiscent of traffic systems in residential areas of towns. In fact, one of the features of these binary trees which is brought out by this analogy is that it is possible to visit every branch of the tree without crossing any other branch. As we noted in the first chapter, this form of layout plan was suggested by Clarence Stein as being an ideal layout for a residential housing area in that its residents could walk around the layout without crossing any of the roads. This was adopted quite widely as a model for pedestrian segregation from vehicular traffic and it was widely implemented in the design of residential areas in the British New Towns, illustrated earlier in Figure 1.19. Another feature of such trees is that they are a minimal form of strongly connected graph where every branch is connected directly or indirectly to every other, but which will break into two parts if any branch in the structure is severed.

This model has also been used to show how trees can grow in a constrained space, and the example which best illustrates this is the human lung. Analogies between trees and human lungs as well as rivers, cities and electric breakdown were made almost thirty years ago by Woldenberg (1968) and Woldenberg and Berry (1967). More recently the analogies have been derived and extended to make the tree model more realistic. Figures 2.14(a) and (b) show how bifurcating trees can fill a circular space and be self- avoiding with suitably chosen contraction ratios (Nelson and Manchester, 1988). These trees like the H trees, are reminiscent of views of the tree from directly above, plans of the tree rather than end or side views. In another context, they could be seen as cross sections of the growth of the tree above and below ground showing its roots as well as its foliage in the manner illustrated by Doxiadis (1968). In fact, Nelson and Manchester (1988) use this type of spatial constraint as a model of the growth of the human lung although these models go back to the work of Woldenberg in

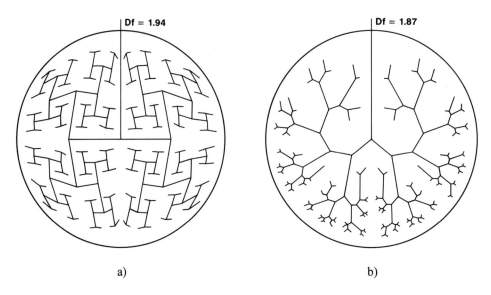

a)   b)

Figure 2.14. Self-avoiding trees with geometric constraints on growth (after Nelson and Manchester, 1988).

the late 1960s. In Figure 2.15(a), we show a plastic cast of the lung made
by Keith Horsfield (see also West and Goldberger (1987)) and in 15(b), the
growth of the lung as a tree structure based initially on an ellipse which
expands into two with increasing fractal dimension. Finally in Figure

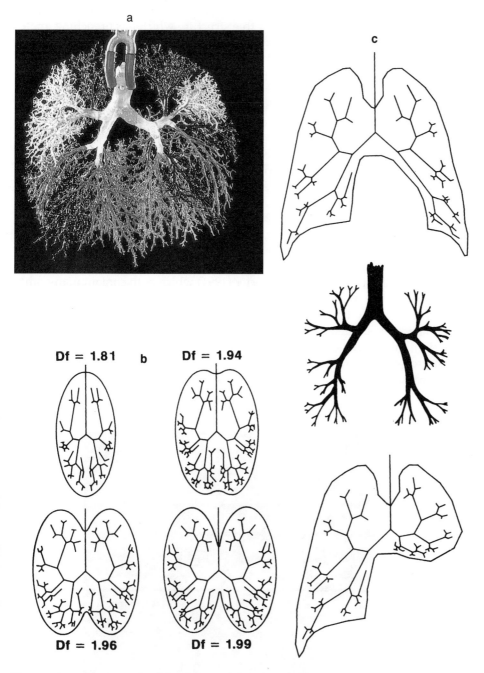

Figure 2.15.   Growth of the human lung: (a) plaster cast (by Horsfield);
(b) idealized growth models; (c) restricted tree growth (both after Nelson
and Manchester, 1988).

2.15(c), we show a stylized representation of a severely restricted lung taken from the models proposed by Nelson and Manchester (1988).

Our last variants of tree fractals indicate what happens to such structures which contract to a point or expand to infinity. If there is no contraction whatsoever in the branches, then the dimension of the binary tree becomes $\log(2)/\log(1/1)$ which is infinite. In Figure 2.16, we show what happens when there is no contraction in a tree structure which has branching angles of 60°. We generate an ever-expanding tessellation of the plane based on regular hexagons, strongly reminiscent of Christaller's (1933, 1966) economic landscapes of central places which we illustrated in Figure 1.23. If we increase the branching angles to 90° then the plane is tiled, as with squares (Figure 1.22). These forms are highly suggestive and have important implications for the hierarchy and form generated by central place theory. We cannot, however, pursue these further here, and the interested reader is referred to the work of Arlinghaus (1985).

To generate fractals with zero dimension, we set one of the branch angles to zero. This means that the stem only ever generates a single branch and whatever the contraction ratio, the dimension is equal to that of a point, zero. We show this in Figure 2.17 where the contraction ratios for the left and right branches are 0 and 0.8 giving a dimension of $\log (1)/\log (1/0.8)$ = 0. In fact this generates yet another fractal – a spiral; readers who wish to explore the meaning of these forms in greater depth should look at books by Mandelbrot (1983) and Lauwerier (1991) which both contain many other examples. We will return to tree shapes again in the last half of the book where we show how such fractals can be grown using geometrically 'constrained' or 'limited' diffusion. But before we conclude our discussion of deterministic fractals, we need to introduce one last approach which gives us greater insights into methods for generating fractals, and in particular, shows us how to generate considerably more realistic shapes.

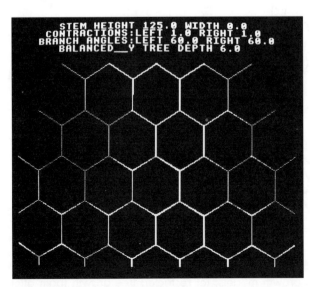

Figure 2.16.   Non-contracting trees: infinite tiling of the plane.

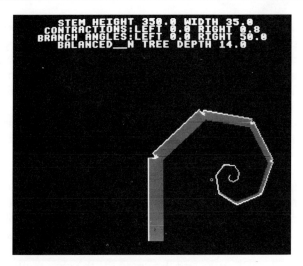

STEM HEIGHT 350.0 WIDTH 35.0
CONTRACTIONS:LEFT 0.0 RIGHT 0.8
BRANCH ANGLES:LEFT 0.0 RIGHT 50.0
BALANCED__N TREE DEPTH 14.0

Figure 2.17. Contraction of a tree into a spiral.

2.7 Fractal Attractors: Generation by Transformation

So far most of the fractals we have generated are strictly self-similar and non-overlapping, although the trees of the last section were based on slight relaxations of these assumptions. Moreover, the way we constructed these fractals was by emphasizing recursion of the generator through many levels of the hierarchy or cascade. There is, however, another way of generating fractals which in one sense is little different from the methods we have used so far, but in another sense exploits the geometric rather than structural properties of the object through its emphasis on the nature of the 'transformations' involved. This method involves treating fractals as a process of transforming and contracting a large object into a smaller one, progressively moving towards the ultimate geometric form of the fractal which is now referred to as a 'fractal attractor'. From what we have said so far in this chapter, we have assumed the existence of fractals without dwelling on the ultimate form of the limiting process which we have taken on trust. The great value of the approach which is based on specifying the nature of transformations is that there are proofs that the limiting forms for a large set of fractals exist and are unique. The mathematical proofs have been developed by Hutchinson (1981) and Barnsley and Demko (1985) amongst others, but the practical application of this fairly esoteric approach is due almost entirely to Barnsley (1988a, b).

As we have indicated, the essence of the approach is to specify the correct set of geometric transformations which enable the object in question to be 'tiled' or formed from copies of the object at successively finer scales. Such transformations do in fact exist in the computer programs used to generate the fractals which we have presented so far in this chapter, although these transformations have not been the particular subject of our interest. The basic idea of Barnsley's (1988a) approach is to approximate the final form of the object which we assume is the given shape by a series of transformations which, when applied to any point on the object, will generate another point on the object but at the same time 'contract' the first point into the second. By applying these transformations successively to the point generated so far, the process will ultimately lead to the shape of the attractor being 'filled in'. The restrictions on permissible transformations imply that they be contractive and that they represent the best possible geometric approximation to the object in question.

If the transformations are badly chosen, then the object's shape will not be generated and the resulting fractal will not be the one that is observed in reality. However, we can first illustrate this approach for strictly self-similar fractals because we can intuitively guess their correct transformations. In fact, we have been doing this throughout this chapter in the computer programs which have been used in their generation. Another feature of the approach is that we must specify the right number of transformations. If some are left out, the ultimate object will in some way be incomplete. The transformations do not have to generate strictly self-similar objects, they can be self-affine and they may tile the object with overlapping copies. In fact the success of the approach is due precisely to this. As we will restrict most of fractals in this book to those with a dimension between 1 and 2, we can illustrate the typical transformation for any pair of coordinates x and y in 2-space in matrix terms as

$$
\begin{bmatrix} x' \\ y' \end{bmatrix} = \begin{bmatrix} a & b \\ c & d \end{bmatrix} \begin{bmatrix} x \\ y \end{bmatrix} + \begin{bmatrix} e \\ f \end{bmatrix},
\tag{2.38}
$$

where x' and y' are the transformed points x and y, based on all three types of transformation – scaling, rotation and translation, where a, b, c and d are the coefficients specifying the scaling and rotation, and e and f are the translations associated with x and y respectively (Barnsley, 1988a, b; Barnsley and Sloan, 1988).

The best way to demonstrate the method is by example. We will show how the Sierpinski gasket discussed earlier in Section 2.5 and illustrated in Figure 2.8 can be generated by suitable transformations. From Figure 2.18, we see three transformations of the big into the little equilateral triangles, and it is clear that successive application of these transformations will yield the Sierpinski gasket shown in Figure 2.8. Moreover, it is easy to specify these transformation because all that is involved are scalings and translations. Now it is also clear that if we merge the three transformations shown in Figure 2.18, we obtain the fractal at the second level of the cascade. Defining the object at level k as F_k, the object at the second level is given as

$$
F_1 = \omega_1(F_0) \cup \omega_2(F_0) \cup \omega_3(F_0)
$$

$$
= \Omega(F_0),
\tag{2.39}
$$

where ω_1, ω_2, ω_3 are the three transformations and Ω a combined transformation operator. If we use equation (2.39) recursively then we obtain at the next level

$$
F_2 = \Omega(F_1) = \Omega[\Omega(F_0)],
\tag{2.40}
$$

and in general for F_k

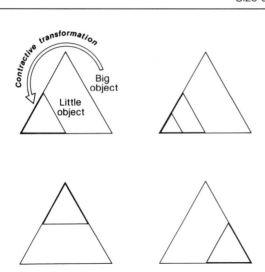

Figure 2.18.   Transforming Sierpinski's gasket.

$$F_k = \Omega(F_{k-1}) = \Omega[\Omega \ \dots \ \Omega(F_0) \ \dots]. \tag{2.41}$$

If the transforms are those in Figure 2.18 which are based on strict self-similarity, then the object is generated in the limit as $F_\infty = \lim_{k \to \infty} F_k$ and the Sierpinski gasket is defined as in Figures 2.8 and 2.18. Barnsley (1988a) summarizes this process of putting the transformations together in the Collage Theorem which ensures that the fractal attractor is generated in the limit.

So far there is little that is radically different from the recursions used in the generation of the previous fractals in this chapter. In the case of the Sierpinski gasket in Figure 2.8 for example, the computer program used to generate this involves a recursion which generates 3^k copies of the initial triangle on the kth level. In Figure 2.8 this yields $3^4 = 81$ copies. Even at this level the ultimate form of the gasket is clear, but if there had been many more transformations which were self-affine and overlapping, then the process of generating these by direct recursion could be very lengthy. This is where the second part of Barnsley's approach becomes important, and we will sketch this in the next section.

2.8 Fractals as Iterated Function Systems

As the recursion of transformations proceeds according to equation (2.41), the generated points move closer and closer to the attractor. At some point the approximation is good enough for the scale of the fractal generated becomes finer than that of the computer screen on which it is viewed or the resolution of the printer on which it is printed. When this scale is reached, further application of the transformations will not add any further detail to the picture. The crucial issue then is to get as close as possible to the best possible approximation to the attractor by generating as few points as possible, for once a point is reached on the attractor, all subsequent transformations of that point will also be on the attractor and the picture will be quickly revealed.

Barnsley (1988a) suggests the following procedure: pick any point on the computer screen, hopefully and ideally in the vicinity of the fractal in that the object is to be plotted on that screen. Then pick a transformation from the set of transformations at random and generate a new point by using this transformation on the old point. Now if this procedure is repeated a sequence of points will be generated which will only move towards the attractor if the transformations are contractive, that is if they scale and distort the object into a smaller copy of the original initiating object. In one sense, we are unlikely to pick objects which have no self-similarity because there would be as many transformations as points in the original picture to generate. The art, of course, is to encode the picture in as few a number of transformations as possible, and for the object to be tiled by these they must contract the original shape. Now assuming that this is the case as in Figure 2.18, a point very near the attractor will be generated with near certainty, say by the 10th iteration, if the original point chosen is 'near' the fractal. Once the point is there, then further applications of the transformations randomly will begin to fill in the form of the attractor and the picture will emerge like a pointillist painting composed of tiny dots.

If only one transformation is chosen from several, the picture will be incomplete. If some of the transformations are more important to the picture than others in terms of the 'amount' of the object they generate, then these transformations should be picked more frequently. Rather than choosing each transformation to apply with equal probability, we can measure the importance of the transformation in proportion to the determinant of the scaling-rotation matrix given in equation (2.38). In short if there are n transformations, then the probability p_j of applying the jth transformation to the point in question can be set as

$$p_j = \frac{|a_j d_j - b_j c_j|}{\sum_{i=0}^{n} |a_i d_i - b_i c_i|}, \tag{2.42}$$

where the coefficients a_j, b_j, c_j and d_j are those associated with the jth transformation specified in equation (2.38). The method is thus operated as follows: each transformation should be chosen in accord with the probabilities computed in equation (2.42) and after about 10 iterations, the sequence of points will be on or very near to the attractor and can thus be plotted on the screen or printed as hard copy. Equation (2.42) is a measure of the area of the fractal associated with the jth transformation. This method of generating fractals is referred to by Barnsley (1988a) as the Iterated Function System (IFS), while the process of randomly generating points but in a structured form is called the 'Chaos Game' (Barnsley, 1988b). In Figure 2.19, we show four stages in generating the Sierpinski gasket given earlier in Figures 2.8 and 2.18. There are three transformations used and the coefficients associated with them are given as $a_1 = a_2 = a_3 = 0.5$, $d_1 = d_2 = d_3 = 0.5$, $e_2 = 1$, $e_3 = f_3 = 0.5$ and $p_1 = p_2 = p_3 = 0.33$ with all other coefficients set to zero, thus showing that scaling and translation are the only transformations used in constructing this fractal.

Figure 2.19.   Generating Sierpinski's gasket using IFS.

The real power of this method cannot be demonstrated with strictly self-similar objects because these can be generated as quickly if not faster in a variety of more direct ways. However where an object is composed of much less obvious self-affine copies of itself, then the method is truly magical. We will demonstrate this for three objects, all tree-like shapes which are much more realistic than those shown in the previous sections of this chapter. First we show a simple twig which involves three transformations of the original object into two which reflect branching and one which reflects the stem. Figure 2.20 illustrates the transformations in terms of the first level of recursion and the final object after some 10,000 iterations. This twig is adapted from Peitgen, Jurgens and Saupe (1992) who show that it does not matter what the actual object is which initiates the process because whatever object it is, it will be scaled down to a point at the resolution of the screen before it is plotted; thus it is only the *transformations* of the point which govern the form of the object which is eventually generated. We might begin with the Taj Mahal or some equally elaborate object but as long as the transformations of the object are those shown in Figure 2.20, a twig will be the ultimate form which we see as an approximation to the fractal attractor.

In Figure 2.21, we show an even more realistic tree, specified as four

Figure 2.20.   Three transformations defining a twig.

transformations to begin with and then as five. These too are adapted from Peitgen, Jurgen and Saupe's (1990) article and their (1992) book and the figure shows how the object can be improved in realism through the addition of a single transformation. However, perhaps the best fractal object created by this approach so far is Barnsley's (1988a, b) fern which is shown in Figure 2.22. This is a remarkable demonstration of how a seemingly complex object can be tiled with only four self-affine overlapping but nevertheless contractive transformations. Demko, Hodge and Naylor (1985) also show how other conventional fractal objects such as dragon and Koch curves can be generated using IFS. The developments of the IFS approach are only just beginning and they are likely to be manyfold. In particular, there are two which are noteworthy. The first relates to showing how very different objects can be transformed into one another. The Koch curve with which we began this chapter consists of four transformations which are structurally identical to those used to generate the Barnsley fern. If the four sets of coefficients {a, b, c, d, e, and f} are compared for each object, then it is possible to interpolate a sequence of values between those for the Koch curve and those for the fern. If the objects associated with these interpolated values are plotted in accordance with the order of interpolation, it is poss-

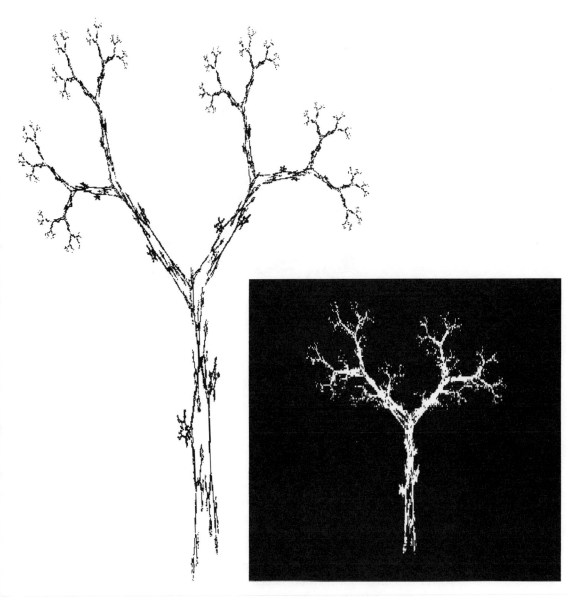

Figure 2.21.   Realistic trees based on four and five transformations.

ible to see the Koch curve transform itself into a fern and vice versa. In fact this 'morphogenesis' can be animated for the interpolated values are like those used by animators in the process of 'in-betweening'; an example is given by Peitgen, Jurgens and Saupe (1992).

A related set of animations are even more powerful in that they consist of transforming a real object such as a tree or fern or Koch curve into an object with the same number of transformations but those with values which specify objects which exist only in mathematical space such as the

Figure 2.22. Barnsley's fern.

Mandelbrot and Julia sets. These are also shown in Peitgen, Jurgens and Saupe (1992) and this is at once a demonstration of the fundamental nature of fractal geometry which links real objects with those which only exist in mathematics as well as real attractors to mathematical attractors which might be the 'strange' attractors appearing in chaos theory. Finally, the power of Barnsley's method is being most widely realized in providing a new approach to image compression. Fractals have been used already for such purposes as in those space-filling curves used to store two-dimensional data in one-dimensional form (Goodchild and Mark, 1987) but Barnsley's approach is more direct. Compressing images by defining IFS codes is immediately apparent in, for example, the fern which only requires four transformations each with six coefficients, making 24 numbers in all to be specified. As Barnsley and Hurd (1993) indicate, the real advantages to such compression are not only the limited data needed but that fractal compression is, in the last analysis, independent of the ultimate resolution of the object. This is a fundamental consequence of thinking and articulating the world in terms of fractals.

2.9 Idealized Models of Urban Growth and Form

This has been a long but necessary chapter, long because it is essential to have at least a rudimentary knowledge of all the key developments in fractal geometry and fractal forms before we begin our applications to urban form, necessary because it puts us into a position to begin speculating on the geometrical properties of city shapes and how we might see them as fractals. In the rest of this book we will be dealing with two basic properties of urban form which involve, on the one hand, boundaries to urban development, and on the other hand, the growth of cities, their size, shape and density as we might perceive them in terms of fractal clusters. We are, however, already in a position to say something about how strictly self-similar fractal forms compare with idealized city shapes which have been suggested down the ages and which we briefly reviewed in Chapter 1. As a conclusion to this chapter, we will present some of these speculations.

The Koch curve was used by Mandelbrot (1967) as an idealized model of a coastline because its fractal dimension was close to that estimated for the west coast of Britain ($D \approx 1.262$), while its geometric properties nicely captured the way a coastline might repeat its form at different scales. In fact, as we will show in Chapter 5, urban boundaries are somewhat like coastlines in terms of the extent to which they fill space, and thus the Koch curve might also be a good model for a city boundary. There is, however, an obvious but perhaps serendipitous comparison we can draw here. Mandelbrot (1983) noted that the slightly distorted H tree such as that shown in Figure 2.13(b) reminded him of the 17th century fortress works of the French Engineer Vauban, and in the same way the Koch island might be likened to the regular fortifications suggested by Renaissance scholars as encompassing ideal cities and actually implemented in many new towns such as Naarden and Palma Nuova (Morris, 1979; Rosenau, 1983). In Figure 2.23, we show a selection of ideal town plans produced during the Renaissance in Europe and echoing the classical ideals of Greek architecture and urban design as portrayed for example by Vitruvius.

The regular sorts of fortification which are such a feature of European towns during these centuries were in fact based on the notion of maximizing the amount of cross-fire which could be directed from the town at an approaching army. At the same time, this increased the amount of wall which had to be defended, and inevitably what was built was some compromise between these conflicting ideas. The town plans shown in Figure 2.23 in fact show fortifications which are built, not on the triangular Koch island which was used to illustrate the meaning of fractals in the early sections of this chapter, but upon regular pentagons, hexagons and octagons. Although these Koch islands only show detailed perturbation of the initiator down one or two levels, it is clear that their fractal dimensions over a couple of orders of scale are close to that of the Koch curve. One last point relating to these ideal towns involves the fact that most organically growing towns prior to the post-industrial age are radially concentric in that the town develops around a seed site, usually a palace, temple or market complex which is linked to other towns and to the surrounding

Figure 2.23. Idealized plans: fortified Renaissance towns and Koch islands (from Morris, 1979).

suburbs by a regular patterns of radial roads. These features are even clear for the ideal towns shown in Figure 2.23.

Our second example also relates to the Koch curve. In Chapter 1, we dealt with the Radburn layout of residential housing in which it was possible to visit any place alongside the branches of roads servicing the area without crossing any of these roads. Such layouts were shown in Figure 1.19 and we discussed their properties in terms of the H tree in an earlier section of this chapter. Arlinghaus and Nysteun (1990) have suggested that fractals such as the Koch forest (Figure 2.3) and the Cesaro–Peano sweep curve (Figure 2.7) might be used as designs which 'maximize' the amount of linear space for mooring boats in a marina. They illustrate the idea using the Cesaro–Peano design which we show in Figure 2.24 where they speculate that the elaborate nature of the mooring is more likely to coincide with the distribution of preferences in the related population than a design based on routine mooring along a waterfront. Moreover, as the amount of boat mooring is also increased dramatically by such space-filling designs, the density of development would be greater and costs per unit of development would likely be lower for each participant in the scheme.

The last example we will introduce here involves an idealized version of the fractal growth model which we will introduce from Chapter 7 on. We have already presented several ways of viewing Sierpinski's gasket and an elaboration on this would be to tile a square initiator with five copies of itself in the manner shown in Figure 2.25. Mandelbrot (1983) refers to

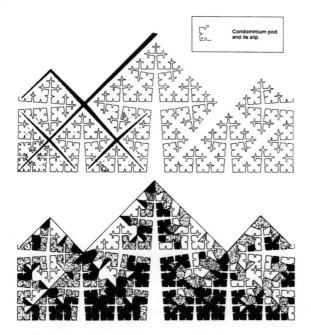

Figure 2.24. Maximizing linear frontage using the Koch forest (from Arlinghaus and Nysteun, 1990).

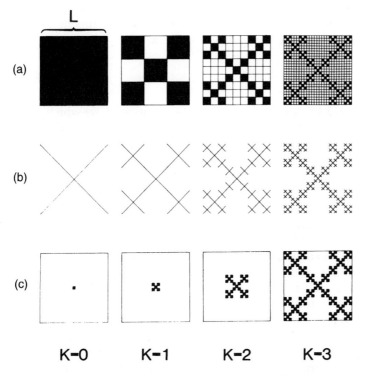

Figure 2.25. Sierpinski's tree: an idealized model of fractal growth.

similar designs as Sierpinski carpets although in this case, the design is a dendritic form rather than that of an object into which holes are punched. We will refer to this then as a Sierpinski tree in the spirit of Mandelbrot. It is easy to see that this tree is formed by tiling the initiator with five copies of itself, each scaled by one third the original size of the initiator. Thus using equation (2.19) the dimension is $D = \log(5)/\log(3) = 1.465$. In Figure 2.25 we show three ways of presenting this idealized tree. In 2.25(a), we show the tree as a strictly self-similar fractal in which we form the attractor by tiling an aggregate unit, a square, by five smaller squares at each level of hierarchy. This is the same way we introduced Sierpinski's gasket; it represents the way we might measure the dimension of this fractal if we were approximating its form at different levels by changing the scale on which we were viewing and measuring it.

However, in Figure 2.25(b), we show the dendrite as a spanning tree at each level of the hierarchy. It is from this figure that we might measure the perimeter of the fractal. Using equation (2.16) with $N_k = 5^k$ and $r_k = r/3^k$, assuming the length of each diagonal of the unit square at $k = 0$ to be $\sqrt{2}$, and that there are four diagonal spans to the perimeter of each square at the appropriate level, then the perimeter of the entire tree at level k would be given as

$$L_k = N_k r_k = 4\sqrt{2}\left(\frac{5}{3}\right)^k. \tag{2.18}$$

The third way to examine the Sierpinski tree is as a growing fractal and this is shown in Figure 2.25(c). In this case, we now have a fixed scale r and a varying yardstick or 'radius' R_k at scale k. Now the mass of the fractal can be measured as its number of parts N_k where this number is growing as the scale k of the tree gets larger. Then

$$N_k = \left(\frac{R_k}{r}\right)^D = R_k^D r^{-D}. \tag{2.43}$$

Equation (2.43) is of the same form as equation (2.31) which is the relationship between mass and linear scale for a growing fractal. In short, this is the relation that we are seeking and which we will exploit from Chapter 7 on when we develop real versions of the Sierpinski tree as the skeleton on which most cities develop.

Noting that the fixed scale r of the growing fractal is $1/27 = 3^{-3}$, then the perimeter can be calculated for each scale k as $(4\sqrt{2}/27)5^k$ where we again use the four diagonal spans as the perimeter of each basic unit whose side is $1/27$ of the unit square. This is a reasonable model of a growing dendrite although its construction is somewhat different from those trees presented in an earlier section. It is easy to use IFS to generate the tree for like the Sierpinski gasket, its only transformations are scaling and translation. There are five transformations and the coefficients are given as $a_i = d_i = 1/3$ for all i; $b_i = c_i = 0$ for all i; $e_1 = f_1 = f_2 = e_3 = 0$; $e_2 = f_3 = e_4 = f_4 = 2/3$; and $e_5 = f_5 = 1/3$. The tree is shown in Figure 2.26 for four stages in its generation.

In the next part of the book, we will begin to apply these ideas to more realistic looking cities than those with which we have concluded here. In this we will link our ideas back to some of those presented in our survey

Figure 2.26.   Generating Sierpinski's tree using IFS.

of urban form in Chapter 1. In particular in the next chapter, we will develop fractal models of cities in the manner in which realistic fractals were first modeled as statistical simulations of self-similar lines and surfaces. We will look once again at the simulation of coastlines and then develop more idealized models based on simple location theory and on principles of hierarchical dependence. To do this, we will develop yet another model of self-similarity, this time of a stochastic, not deterministic, variety, but we will still restrict our models to two-dimensional maps and our fractal dimensions will still range between 1 and 2.

3

Simulating Cities as Fractal Picturescapes

Suppose I want to understand the 'structure' of something. Just what exactly does this mean? It means, of course, that I want to make a simple picture of it, which lets me grasp it as a whole. And it means, too, that as far as possible, I want to paint this picture out of as few elements as possible. The fewer the elements there are, the richer the relationships between them, and the more of the picture lies in the 'structure' of these relationships. (Alexander, 1979, p. 34.)

3.1 The Quest for Visual Realism

The new geometry finds its most obvious expression in the natural world with examples of fractals all around us. Yet as Mandelbrot (1982) himself has argued, fractals are equally applicable to systems other than those portrayed in nature. Any system in which the whole is composed of parts arranged hierarchically in some self-similar order is fractal, and in fact, the most serious candidates may ultimately turn out to be artificial systems ranging from silicon chips to business organizations. Man-made structures such as cities, we will argue, display all the characteristics we have associated so far with fractals. In this spirit then, this chapter pursues two goals. First, we will begin to establish the applicability of fractal methods for describing and modeling cities in terms of the way their form reflects their function, although this will also be our longer term goal throughout subsequent chapters. A second and more immediate goal is to illustrate how fractal geometry combined with state-of-the-art computer graphics, can be used to produce highly realistic but minimalist pictures as Alexander (1979) implies above, pictures which have more than just superficial meaning when applied to city systems.

In a sense, we anticipated this at the end of the previous chapter. But to make real progress, we need to relax our approach to fractals which so far has been mainly based on strictly self-similar forms, completely and precisely determined by their initiators and generating rules. The fractals of Chapter 2 are hardly natural in any case, although as artifacts, they are products of our mathematical imagination, notwithstanding their occasional resemblance to real physical systems. To make progress here therefore, we need to consider fractals whose self-similarity across a range of scales can be described by statistics of randomly distributed variables through various forms of deviation or variance around the mean. These we will refer to as 'statistical or random' fractals whose form can be self-similar or self-affine but only in terms of averages measured across several scales.

Statistical fractals are obviously necessary if we are to generate realistic natural scenes where randomness of form exists within well-articulated structure. The convergence of fractals and computer graphics is important too and we will start our discussion of realism with a little of its history. It is widely recognized that fractal geometry would not have established itself so firmly in so many sciences without the use of computer graphics in generating pictures. Mandelbrot (1983) describes how the mathematics of deterministic fractals remained largely inaccessible to generations of mathematicians because there was no way of illustrating its import in less esoteric and abstract terms. In fact it was Mandelbrot (1975) who first used computer graphics to illustrate ideas about the modeling of natural terrain using Brownian motion. His ideas in this realm were first formed when he noted the coincidence of the frequency distribution of random coin tossing illustrated in Feller's (1950) famous book on probability with typical cross-sections of terrain.

These early graphics were picked up quickly by a number of researchers. Carpenter (1980) used the ideas to generate computer graphic backcloths for flight simulators while Goodchild (1980) showed how these models might represent real terrain. Smith (1982) showed how they were used in the movie *Star Trek II* to generate a living planet, and Fournier, Fussell and Carpenter (1982) generalized this usage further, producing various types of fictional terrain. However, the pictures which accompanied Mandelbrot's (1983) second English edition of his book *The Fractal Geometry of Nature*, particularly those by his colleague Voss (1985), have gained the greatest recognition and have done most to popularize the subject. Stunning pictures of fractal mountainscapes at different fractal dimensions and their aggregation to the terrain and seas of planet-like worlds have been produced. Most recently, these landscapes such as those generated by Musgrave and his colleagues (Musgrave, Kolb and Mace, 1989; Mandelbrot, 1990) have become so realistic that they are hard to tell apart from natural scenes. This suggests that geomorphic and geologic processes of weathering and erosion are bound to generate fractal forms, thus giving further weight to the long-standing notion that 'form follows function'. Moreover, Mandelbrot's (1982) view that "... the basic proof of a stochastic model of nature is in the seeing: numerical comparisons must come second" has gained much credence through such demonstrations.

There have been other powerful demonstrations of fractal geometry using computer graphics and these have revolved around the idea of illustrating the fractal structure of mathematical space. Although this book is not concerned with these types of fractal, much of the glamour of the subject and not a little of its appeal has come from these geometries. In essence, the geometry of mathematical space is usually geometry which shows the properties of the mathematics involved, particularly the solutions to equations. For example, consider the iterative equation $z_{t+1} = z_t^2 + c$ which is the discrete equation for the logistic growth of a variable z such as population. Then if we consider that the solutions to such equations are complex numbers in that they have real and imaginary parts, and if we plot these on

x-y coordinates when z converges to a finite value, then the geometry of the solution is fractal in the following sense. If we start with $c = 0$, then the resulting solutions with different starting values for z_0 based on complex numbers, form what are called 'Julia sets', while the map of real and imaginary values which we get when we start with c as a complex number and $z_0 = 0$, define the 'Mandelbrot set'. When we plot both types of set and color the map systematically, the boundaries between solutions to the equations and the areas where the z_t values diverge towards infinity are fractal; as we zoom in on these boundaries, detail is magnified and shows the same form, however deep we zoom. These are remarkable results from such simple equations whose form can only be revealed directly through the power of computer graphics.

These sets have been beautifully rendered by Peitgen's group from Bremen (Peitgen and Richter, 1986) but on a more fundamental level, formal relationships between mathematical and physical fractals are being pursued through the idea of fractal attractors. We came across this idea in Chapter 2 when we summarized Barnsley's (1988) work. In essence, what can now be shown is that fractals in mathematical space such as Julia sets can be transformed into fractals in physical space. For example, it is easy, using changes in the transformation rules, to show how the Koch island can emerge from the Julia set and vice versa, the Koch island and the Julia set both being attractors in two dimensions. Finally, perhaps with an even greater sense of mystery, the solutions to many chaotic systems have been shown to have an underlying order which is fractal; and the visualization of chaotic solutions has again only been made possible through recent advances in computer graphics (Devaney, 1990).

Computer graphics is fast becoming a new medium for simulation throughout the sciences as well as in the arts and design. Clearly through the desire to simulate the 'fictional realism' of scenes which look realistic but are figments of the designer's imagination, there come useful ways of rendering backcloths in movies and the graphic arts. But the use of graphics to see what has not been seen before, to explore the whole question of scale and limits, and to render scientific predictions in ways in which the data have not been visualized hitherto, are central to the way fractals have been pioneered and are applicable. This is especially true in fields where data are extensive and have hitherto not been easy to visualize, and it is nowhere more appropriate than in the spatial sciences such as those dealing with both natural and artificial, physical and social systems, especially with urban phenomena in the form of cities, our focus here.

Mathematical models of city systems implemented on computers were first developed 30 years or more ago, but the theories of spatial organization and location used therein originated in economic theory from the early 19th century onwards. The typical urban models proposed so far have thus concentrated upon the location of and interaction between economic activities such as employment, population and transportation at the macro-spatial level where cities are divided into large zones such as census tracts (Batty, 1976) or at the micro-level of the individual or firm (Anas, 1982). Models which take the level of analysis down to the physical form of the city or to the relationship between urban activities, land uses and their physical form have rarely been developed. This is possibly because it is the activity level which is the most appropriate for simulation, for it is here that economic theory can be brought to bear on model design, and thus there is the implicit view that the translation of spatial activity into physical land use is a fairly trivial task or at least, does not matter. It is more likely that the dearth of modeling the physical configuration of land use *per se* is largely due to unconscious neglect by those who have found it easier to begin with activity simulation and whose disciplinary biases have constrained their interest in the physical form of cities.

However, a major problem has begun to emerge in conventional urban modeling which relates to the meaning of spatial data and predictions. For a long time it has been known that when model outputs in terms of activities are mapped spatially in aggregate zones or as individual point patterns, their form often looks 'wrong' in some indefinable physical sense. Exceptionally good fits in terms of numerical indicators can be obtained, and such models may manifest robust and causally acceptable structures, but when their predictions are mapped, the whole does not seem to add up to the sum of the parts; systematic biases appear and the patterns often look physically imbalanced. In macro-modeling, such biases can often be corrected, or at least there are strategies which enable under- and over-prediction to be handled consistently, but with models based on individual discrete predictions, these problems are rarely addressed because the outputs are hardly ever mapped spatially. There are thus few checks on whether or not such models generate spatially acceptable predictions. In short, whatever type of model is used, their data and predictions have been difficult to assess spatially for computer graphics in this field is in its infancy.

This problem of visualizing spatial data and urban model predictions has only just begun to be tackled in terms of the development of appropriate computer graphics. It is already clear that a school of thought is fast emerging that the ultimate test of any model is that 'it must look right'. In one sense, this school represents a 'back-to-basics' movement which is not only borne of a dissatisfaction with the structure and focus of contemporary models. It is also based on the fact that as powerful computers are now available which make graphics easy to employ, visual reality would seem to be more important than statistical reality. In this, any models which attempt some physical simulation are likely to produce more reasonable-looking spatial patterns than those which are highly abstracted as points and networks. In fact, in this chapter we will show some examples of urban simulations which look distinctly 'uncity-like', thus demonstrating both the power and limits of simulation and the potential of fractal geometry as an organizing mechanism for such simulation. In one sense, although this entire chapter will be focussed on simulating 'right-looking' cities, it will also show how limited our best known theories and models of urban structure are in simulating the physical structure of land uses and urban activities. Before we can do this, however, we need to continue to relax fractal geometry by presenting the statistical view.

3.2 Randomness and Self-Similarity

In Chapter 2, we introduced several deterministic fractals from the strictly self-similar to self-affine but in each case, their generators produced the same forms or attractors each time they were initiated. Thus there is no uncertainty in the geometry of the resulting structures, and the rules for adding, taking away, displacing and transforming the initiator always produce a form whose ultimate attractor is unique. Such fractals however only exist in the world of mathematics for in nature, there is always chance. Objects may be similar but they are rarely identical, or if they are, their identity is only to the resolution of the measuring device, and there is always uncertainty beyond this. The fact that chance plays so dominant a role in the natural world is underscored by theories of evolution whose basis in selective mutation is now well established (Dawkins, 1986), while in the physical world, the repercussions of quantum theory are still reverberating throughout physical theory. In a less abstract realm, natural scenes composed of terrain, vegetation and particular climatic regimes are subject to all the physical and natural forces which enable change to take place in the landscape. It is clear that for any circumstance, although the processes which act as functions of form might be known, their operation is, to all intents and purposes, beyond our ability to observe, and we must be content in estimating their meaning statistically.

The intensity of the processes involved as well as the degree to which they interact within one another are also complemented by various constraints on the operation of the processes in question. In an urban context, such constraints are physical and artificial, ranging from areas of land upon which urban development is virtually impossible within given technological limits to institutional processes which constrain physical development in diverse ways. In short, processes which form cities operate under a variety of constraints which distort and transform the structure in general, and which thus have to modeled statistically. To demonstrate this we will begin with our basic fractal model, the Koch curve which we portrayed at the end of Chapter 2 as an idealized city form or boundary. We will begin relaxing this strictly self-similar deterministic fractal by introducing some elements of chance into its generation, and it is appropriate that we begin with the curve and its form as an island shown in Figures 2.1 and 2.2 respectively. Peitgen, Jurgens and Saupe (1992) provide similar demonstrations.

To introduce the element of chance, consider the way in which the generator is applied to the initiator in the traditional Koch curve which forms each side of the island shown in Figure 3.1(a). The generator is based on the regular midpoint displacement of the line into a line 4/3 times the length with each of the four segments of the line being 1/4 the length of the original line. The Koch curve is obtained by using this generator with the *same orientation* each time it is applied. However, we can introduce an element of chance by letting this orientation be chosen randomly on either side of the line which, when applied to the island, enables the boundary to be enhanced by adding or subtracting to obtain the new detail. The new island is shown in Figure 3.1(b) where the orientation either side of the line

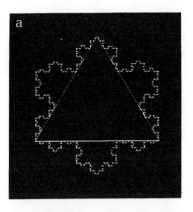

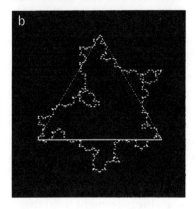

Figure 3.1.   Regular and random Koch islands with identical fractal dimensions.

has been chosen randomly at each iteration of the generation. As Figure 3.1(b) shows, it is quite remarkable how the Koch island becomes irregular by introducing this simple chance effect. It is much closer to a natural coastline than the original island, although as the same number of lines with the same length are generated on each iteration, the fractal dimensions of each figure are the same, that is $D = \log (4)/\log (3) \cong 1.262$. This is perhaps the most remarkable aspect of randomization in generating fractals, and it not only shows that very different looking forms can have the same dimension and virtually identical functions (generators), but that fractal dimension says little about the orientation and overall shape of the ultimate figure. We will leave the reader to ponder this further, for it is an important issue throughout this book. However, before we leave the Koch island, we will show how even more irregular coastlines might be generated.

The generator of the Koch curve contains three parameters which might be manipulated or chosen randomly to form different curves, and we have already seen one way of doing this in Chapter 2 where we altered the midpoint and size of vertical displacement to form the Koch forest shown in Figure 2.3 and Plate 2.2. Thus we can alter not only the height of the displacement but also the position of the perturbation of the line given by the two points which define its location relative to the midpoint. These values, called H, W_1 and W_2 respectively, are shown in Figure 3.2(a). We can now generate Koch islands with the values of H chosen randomly between 0 and say, the length of the initiating line, with the offset values W_1 and W_2 set between 0 and 0.5. In Figure 3.2(b), we show six Koch islands generated in this way where the three parameters are chosen randomly at the beginning of the generation process, but with the orientation chosen randomly at each iteration as in Figure 3.1(b).

The fractal dimensions of the resulting curves are not equal to 1.262, and to compute these, we have used equations (2.25) and (2.26) which are repeated here:

$$L(r) = N(r)r = Kr^{(1-D)}. \tag{2.25}$$

$N(r)$ and $L(r)$ are the number of parts and the length of the line respectively at scale r, and K is a constant of proportionality. The log transform of equation (2.25) yields

$$\log L(r) = \log K + (1-D) \log r, \tag{2.26}$$

where $(1-D)$ is the slope of the regression of $\log L(r)$ on $\log r$ from which the dimension D can be derived directly. For the six islands in Figure 3.2(b) we have calculated the perimeter $L(r)$ over six orders of magnitude and the estimated dimensions and the coefficients of determination associated with these estimates are also shown in this figure. We have not yet formally introduced regression to determine fractal dimensions, and we will postpone further discussion of this until Chapter 5 where we will build on the method first introduced by Richardson (1961).

In fact we will avoid such measurement until then, but from these results it is immediately clear that as the curve becomes more irregular and in this sense fills more of the two-dimensional space available, the fractal dimension increases. The consequent interpretation is that more rugged ria-like coastlines have higher fractal dimensions than smoother lines, and an obvious interpretation is that the value of the fractal dimension has strong implications for the underlying processes of weathering and erosion which lead to such forms. The great appeal of the Koch curve is that its fractal dimension of 1.262 is close to that estimated for the west coast of Britain by Richardson (1961) and Mandelbrot (1967). This is in contrast to the coastline of Australia with a dimension of 1.13 and of South Africa with 1.02. Ria coastlines have higher dimensions, but these are seldom more than 1.5, for above that value, the curve would have to considerably distorted in a rather systematic fashion for it to avoid self-intersection which, of course, is a physical necessity in terms of coastlines.

To illustrate the use of these ideas further in terms of generating realistic curves, we will take a memorable shape and perturb its straightline segments using degrees of perturbation which imply different fractal dimensions. Mainland Australia has been chosen, and it is easily described by the upper left hand shape in Figure 3.3 which consists of 10 straightline segments. Each straightline segment in itself has a dimension of 1, and we can see how close this shape is to the 'real' Australia by simulating different degrees of ruggedness. In Figure 3.3, we show what happens as the degree of ruggedness increases – as the fractal dimension increases in stages from $D \approx 1$ to $D \approx 2$. We must be clear about what we are doing here. If we

(a)

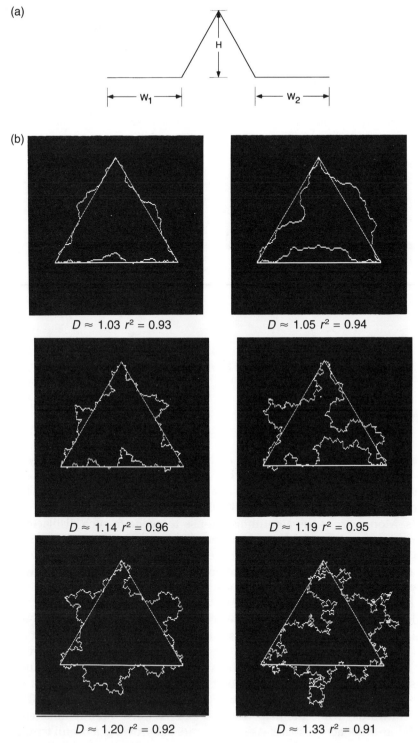

(b)

$D \approx 1.03\ r^2 = 0.93$

$D \approx 1.05\ r^2 = 0.94$

$D \approx 1.14\ r^2 = 0.96$

$D \approx 1.19\ r^2 = 0.95$

$D \approx 1.20\ r^2 = 0.92$

$D \approx 1.33\ r^2 = 0.91$

Figure 3.2. Random Koch islands with different fractal dimensions.

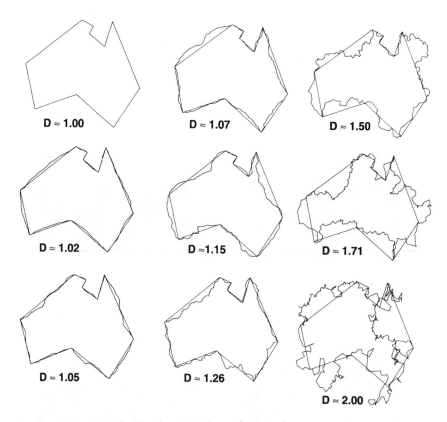

Figure 3.3. Simulating the coastline of Australia.

measured the fractal dimension of each 'Australia' in Figure 3.3, we would get values different from those which we have shown and have used to generate the shape. This is because our overall shape has already been fixed or constrained, and we are just simulating irregularity about each of its parts. Moreover, as the algorithms we use to generate such displacement imply the operation of chance, the values shown are those used to constrain this chance, but do not imply that the level of chance is fixed to those values we input. Nevertheless, the simulations do give us some feel for how the degree of irregularity increases as we increase dimension in the same way we did for the Koch curve in Figure 3.2(b).

Up to $D \approx 1.15$ which is near the accepted dimension of mainland Australia, the simulations clearly increase the realism of the coastline, but after this the coast becomes too rugged. By the time it reaches a ria-like level of 1.5, the only thing in common with Australia is the fact that the simulated coast passes through the eleven points which define the initial map. $D \approx 1.71$ is the dimension of many crystals (and cities as we will see from Chapter 7 onwards) while the map where $D \approx 2$ is much more reminiscent of a random walk across space. As such, Figure 3.3 provides a useful template for assessing approximate fractal dimensions (as Figure 3.2(b) does too). The real point of this example is not simply to show the range of irregularity. It is to emphasize the point that once the degree of irregularity is chosen in terms of a fractal dimension, it is possible to simulate such curves using computer graphics. In fact, Figure 3.3 shows that we are able to simulate more realistic maps of Australia than the straightline map we started with, but the success of the simulation depends intrinsically upon this starting point, that is upon the initiator. For the pictures of planets, mountains and cities we will show in this chapter, all depend upon choosing initiators which are planet-, mountain- or city-like and upon the use of fractal rendering to make them realistic. There are a number of similar applications where fractals have been used to enhance cartographic detail in cases where the shape is too complex to describe in all its available detail, but where it can be approximated using fractal rendering (Dutton, 1981; Hill and Walker, 1982). The classic example is Australia as we have shown, and other examples where this map has been used to illustrate similar ideas are given in Fournier, Fussell and Carpenter (1982) and in Dell'Ocro and Ghiron (1983).

Before we conclude our introduction to statistical fractals generated from the occurrence of random events, we will examine the other classic fractal of Chapter 2, the Sierpinski gasket. Consider Figure 3.4(a) and note that the gasket can be seen as a process whereby an original equilateral triangle is tiled with three copies of itself which cover only three-quarters of the initiator. The number of units used to cover the shape is three and the scaling is $1/2$, in that each side of the original triangle divides into two which form two of the sides of two new triangles. The fractal dimension is thus $D = \log (3)/\log (2) \approx 1.585$. First we will relax the scaling in that instead of choosing the midpoint of each side of the initiator which divides the side into those of two new triangles, we let this value be chosen randomly as any point on the side. This generates the random gasket shown in Figure 3.4(b) whose fractal dimension must be computed using one of the methods such as cell counting introduced in later chapters. The dimension is not important for Figure 3.4(b); this is only one step along the road to a completely random Sierpinski gasket which we will be using as the basis for generating terrain later in this chapter. Imagine now that our initi-

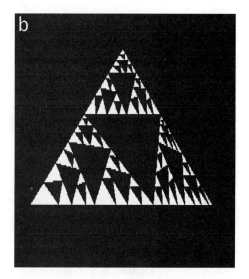

Figure 3.4. The Sierpinski gasket: (a) without, and (b) with random 'midpoint' displacement.

ating triangle is no longer equilateral: it may take on any shape. Then instead of constraining the subdivision of each of the triangle's sides to be somewhere on each of these sides, let this point be chosen randomly somewhere within a circle centered on the midpoints, as in Figure 3.5 which is taken from McGuire (1991). The three new triangles distort the original shape, and further subdivision in the same way continues the distortion. In Figure 3.5, the shape after 10 iterations is shown where the resemblance to terrain is clear. Of course, the Sierpinski gasket is not a particularly good model of a mountain, although the fact that it is a triangle is perhaps close enough for the point to be made. As we did for Australia, we can control the degree of displacement or the fractal dimension in this case by setting the radius of the circle in which the displacement takes place, although we have not pursued this in any formal sense in terms of this example. The way we have generated fractals in this and in the last chapter really depends upon the process of defining a generator which is consistently and persistently applied to an originating or initiating object. At this point, we must step back a little and say something about the possibility that there may be underlying mathematical models of fractals which will help us in

Figure 3.5. Using the random Sierpinski gasket to simulate terrain (from McGuire, 1991).

the quest to generate realistic objects. To this end, we will now introduce Brownian motion, one of the central ideas of this chapter.

3.3 Fractional Brownian Motion

The search for underlying generating functions which give rise to fractal geometries is in some sense a fruitless quest. The generating functions we have used so far can all be specified geometrically, and as Barnsley (1988) has so persuasively shown, a slight change in emphasis based on their treatment as classic transformations yields further insights into their form. In fact, we began our introduction to fractals in Chapter 2 by implying with Mandelbrot (1983) that a shift from continuous functions to discrete represented the obvious way to deal with irregular shapes based on curves which might be continuous everywhere but have no derivatives. Such of course is the Koch curve and its generalization to the coastline. However, the search for an underlying fractal model in one sense throws us back to the very mathematics which fractal geometry has released us from. Not quite perhaps. Although our purpose is not to develop a strict mathematical treatment of fractals in this book, we must indicate that there exist highly formalized models of fractal order which can be approximated by the techniques of continuous mathematics, in particular by infinite series such as Fourier transforms and related functions.

Our starting point in this is 'Brownian motion' or Bm as it is sometimes called. In 1828, the Scottish biologist Robert Brown first made known his observations of the motion of dust particles which appeared to move at whatever scale they were examined. In short, their motion appeared to be fractal. We have almost provided an example of two-dimensional Brownian motion in the last section where our simulation of the coastline of Australia with the dimension near to 2 shows a self-intersecting curve whose lengths and orientations are entirely random. If we were to relax the constraint that the walk should pass through the 11 points of the Australian coastline, then the walk would represent true Brownian motion. However, to get a better sense of this motion, it is worth developing the analysis taking the example of a time-varying phenomena, and then generalizing the analysis to the cases of coastlines and terrain in the two and three dimensions of physical space respectively. Our exposition will closely follow the way the subject is treated in the fractal literature and in this we will closely follow Saupe (1988, 1991) and Voss (1988).

Consider a variable $V(t)$ which is the value of some phenomena at time t and define the change in this variable ΔV as

$$\Delta V = V(t_1) - V(t_0),$$

where the time interval Δt is also defined as

$$\Delta t = t_1 - t_0.$$

It is the change in the variable ΔV which is of major interest in that we will assume that it is this variable which is randomly distributed; thus over any time period Δt, the value of ΔV would be that which is taken from a normal or Gaussian distribution of the variable. However, because the variable is a fractal, it is not possible to determine any limiting value of dV/dt and thus the value of ΔV must be proportional in some way to the length of the time interval Δt. In fact, we assume that it is the variance of the variable called var(ΔV) which is directly proportional to time, that is

$$\text{var}(\Delta V) = \langle [V(t_1) - V(t_0)]^2 \rangle = (t_1 - t_0)\sigma^2. \tag{3.1}$$

Without loss of generality we will assume that the variance σ^2 can be normalized to 1, and thus in the following exposition, we will only include it explicitly where it is important to do so. Thus equation (3.1) can be written as

$$\text{var}(\Delta V) = \Delta t. \tag{3.2}$$

The implication of equations (3.1) and (3.2) is that the variable ΔV is thus proportional to the square root of Δt, that is

$$\Delta V \propto \Delta t^{1/2}. \tag{3.3}$$

This means that the scaling between ΔV and Δt is one where if time changes by four units, then the value of the variable will only increase by two. In short, the relationship over different time scales is self-affine, not strictly self-similar in the language of Chapter 2.

Before we generalize these equations to a wider class of Brownian motion, we will formally examine this scaling. If we assume that the time changes by a factor r, then the appropriate change variables can be written as

$$\Delta V' = V(rt_1) - V(rt_0),$$

and

$$\Delta t' = rt_1 - rt_0 = r\Delta t.$$

Now the variance of $\Delta V'$ can be written as

$$\text{var}(\Delta V') = \Delta t' \, \sigma^2 = r\Delta t\sigma^2$$

$$= r \, \text{var}(\Delta V), \tag{3.4}$$

from which it is clear that the value of the change variable $\Delta V'$ is scaled by the square root of r, that is

$$\Delta V' = r^{1/2}\Delta V \propto (r\Delta t)^{1/2}. \tag{3.5}$$

We can now generalize this formalism to fractional Brownian motion (fBm) where we introduce the exponent H from which, as we will show below, the fractal dimension D can be derived. Following equation (3.1), the variance of ΔV can now be stated as

$$\text{var}(\Delta V) = \Delta t^{2H}\sigma^2, \tag{3.6}$$

where H is the Hurst exponent (named after the researcher who first used this equation in measuring the discharge rate of rivers, see Mandelbrot

(1983)), and σ^2 the variance which we can normalize as 1. The variable ΔV can be written as

$$\Delta V \propto \Delta t^H \sigma, \tag{3.7}$$

and it is easy to show that the scaling of time by r following equation (3.5) is given as

$$\Delta V' = r^H \Delta V \propto r^H \Delta t^H \sigma. \tag{3.8}$$

Thus a change in scale of r units in time leads to a change of r^H in ΔV, and it is clear that the case of pure Brownian motion is given when $H = 1/2$. We will assume that H varies in the range from 0 to 1 in this particular example. The last point we should make is that when equations (3.1) to (3.8) apply to any and every time interval Δt, we say that the variable ΔV shows stationarity.

It is fairly straightforward to determine the fractal dimension of fBm. Let us assume that the variable ΔV is examined over N time periods and that for each equal time interval, $\Delta t = 1/N$. Thus for every change in scale of $1/N$, the variable ΔV changes in proportion to $(1/N)^H$. If we consider that for each time interval of length $1/N$, we place a 'box' of length $1/N$ times $(1/N)^H$ over the change in frequency of the variable, then we have to multiply this by all N boxes to get a total coverage of the change in the variable. Formally, we have the change in ΔV with Δt as

$$\frac{\Delta V}{\Delta t} = \frac{N}{N^{H'}} \tag{3.9}$$

and as there are N time periods, the number of square 'boxes' of size $(1/N)^2$ called $N(\Delta t)$ is given as

$$N(\Delta t) = N \frac{\Delta V}{\Delta t} = N^{2-H}$$

$$= \left(\frac{1}{\Delta t}\right)^{2-H} = \Delta t^{H-2}. \tag{3.10}$$

Now from equation (2.17) which counts the number of equal elements which approximate a fractal line, it is clear that the number of segments is

$$N(\Delta t) = \Delta t^{-D}. \tag{3.11}$$

A comparison of equations (3.10) and (3.11) shows that the exponent in both must be equal; that is

$$N(\Delta t) = \Delta t^{H-2} = \Delta t^{-D}, \tag{3.12}$$

from which it is clear that $D = 2 - H$. We can now write our equations of fractional Brownian motion given above in (3.6) and (3.7) as

$$\mathrm{var}(\Delta V) = \Delta t^{2H} \sigma^2 = \Delta t^{4-2D} \sigma^2, \tag{3.13}$$

$$\Delta V \propto \Delta t^H \sigma = \Delta t^{2-D} \sigma. \tag{3.14}$$

To complete this section, we need to clarify the meaning of different values of the Hurst exponent H and the fractal dimension. Clearly for the case of pure Brownian motion, $H = 1/2$ and thus $D = 1.5$ and in one sense, this represents the baseline. In the case where $H = 1$, then D also equals 1 and this represents a completely smooth function. The change in ΔV is simply a function of time as equation (3.14) indicates. When $H = 0$, then $D = 2$, and this means that at whatever scale the variation in the function is examined, the motion or change is the same. This is characteristic of very spiky-looking functions which 'fill the space available'. We will generalize these ideas to landscapes in the next two sections, but it is worth anticipating what the values of H and D are with respect to terrain. Smoothly varying terrain has both fractal and Hurst dimensions equal to 1, while at the other extreme, very rugged and cavernous terrain has a D near to 2 and a Hurst exponent near to 0. In the next section we will show how these ideas can be developed for simulating landscapes, but if readers wish a more complete exposition, then the chapters by Voss (1988) and by Saupe (1988, 1991) are worth reading as are the relevant sections in Mandelbrot (1983).

3.4 Fractal Planetscapes and Terrain

The equations describing the variance properties of fBm given in (3.1) to (3.14) above only illustrate the properties of these processes and give little insight into the way they might be computed. In fact for pure Brownian motion in the plane this is straightforward and it can be implemented as follows. Defining the variable $V(t)$ now as the total distance traveled so far by a point tracing out a random walk in the plane, we define appropriate units of time; in each equal time interval, we select a pair of x-y coordinates in the plane by drawing random numbers from a Gaussian distribution, appropriately normalized to represent the physical distance-scale properties of the problem. A change in the distance $\Delta \tau(x_{n+1}, y_{n+1})$ can then be computed from $(u^2 + v^2)^{1/2}$ where $u = x_{n+1} - x_n$ and $v = y_{n+1} - y_n$. The total distance traveled at time t_{n+1} is

$$\tau(x_{n+1}, y_{n+1}) = \tau(x_n, y_n) + \Delta \tau(x_{n+1}, y_{n+1}). \tag{3.15}$$

where $n + 1$ acts both as an index of time and space. A plot of such motion is shown in Figure 3.6, while a graph of the change in distance at each time step $\Delta \tau(x_{n+1}, y_{n+1})$ and the total distance traveled $\tau(x_{n+1}, y_{n+1})$ from equation (3.15) is drawn in Figure 3.7. It is clear from these figures that the motion is Brownian, and in particular that changes in the total distance traveled over an arbitrarily chosen time period are proportional in some way to the length of that time period. Detailed measurement of the variation in this function indicates that it is consistent with equations (3.1) and (3.2).

These ideas can easily be generalized to a system with any number of dimensions for fBm in terms of equations (3.13) and (3.14), but their application is somewhat more difficult. There are two broad classes of algorithm which can be used in their implementation, and before we present the original and perhaps most consistent method, we will outline these. The first class of methods is based on *recursive* algorithms, in that its application involves ever more detailed approximation to the limiting fractal function

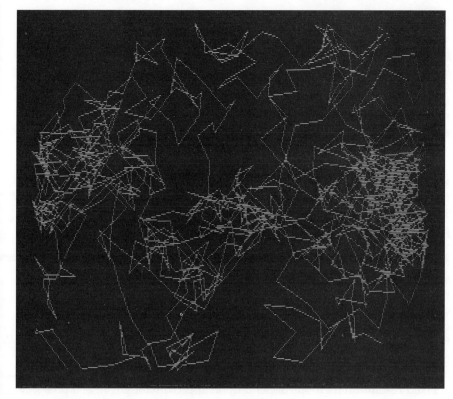

Figure 3.6. Pure Brownian motion in the plane.

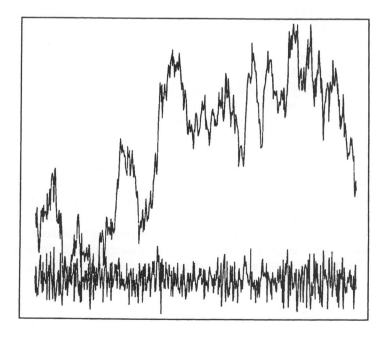

Figure 3.7. Profiles of pure Brownian motion.

and the process of approximation involves algorithms which are iteratively applied at each scale of resolution. In contrast, the second class involves *fixed resolution* algorithms which approximate the function at a prespecified level of detail and thus have to be computed afresh if different levels of detail apply. The computational properties of these algorithms are such that the recursive methods are usually more efficient and enable computation to stop on the basis of what has been computed so far, whereas the second class requires complete computation before the appropriateness of its application can be evaluated.

The best known recursive method is midpoint displacement of the variety we have been using so far in this book and which is best illustrated by the generation of the Koch curve. There are several variants on this process. These involve adding noise and variation after the computation has taken place at each level of resolution in order to resolve the key problem with such methods that the functions generated are not stationary. The second recursive method is more involved although the functions it generates are stationary. This is the random cuts method which is based on the idea of increasing the scale of resolution by taking random cuts across the function, computing its displacement randomly to meet the variance constraints, and continuing this process until a fixed number of cuts are generated. Because the cuts are randomly positioned, it is not possible to ensure that a level of detail is reached by a particular iteration, although the resolution does increase as the method proceeds.

Fixed resolution methods depend upon approximating fBm at a prespecified level of resolution, and these methods are in general based upon approximating the function using various forms of series. The most well-known are based on Fourier transforms, although the general problem with these methods is that they tend to be periodic, in that the functions repeat themselves on a cycle of 2π. Such problems have been dealt with by keeping the transformations well-within the period range, although in general, a major problem remains in that such functions generate intensive demands for computation time. There are also a variety of new methods based on modified midpoint displacement outlined by Mandelbrot (1988), some of which have been implemented by Musgrave, Kolb and Mace (1989). In the sequel, we will not use the fixed resolution methods because the recursive methods are deemed more appropriate for the exploratory ideas developed here. However, there remains the challenge not only to develop new and better methods, but also to provide more definitive comparisons. Useful surveys of the methods and their algorithms are presented by Voss (1988) and Saupe (1988, 1991).

We will begin by outlining how the random cuts method has been applied while in the next section we will deal with midpoint displacement. As indicated earlier, the random cuts method produces functions which exhibit stationarity in their variances. Generalizing fBm to three-dimensional space, for any two-dimensional measure of distance τ_{uv} computed as $(u^2 + v^2)^{1/2}$, the variance must satisfy

$$\langle[z(x+u, y+v) - z(x, y)]^2\rangle = (\tau_{uv})^{2H}\sigma^2, \tag{3.16}$$

where $z(x, y)$ is the elevation of the terrain at coordinate x, y. In this case we can also assume that σ^2 is normalized to unity. The major change when one moves from two to three dimensions, from functions in the plane to those in the volume, is that the fractal dimension is now given as $D = 3 - H$. Note also that the intersection of a plane with the fBm surface yields a profile with a fractal dimension of $D = 2 - H$, and these results can be easily generalized. In the context of terrain, this implies that if the fractal dimension of a coastline is determined, then the dimension of its relevant surface is $D + 1$, while if the dimension of the surface is calculated, then the dimension of the plane which cuts the surface as a coastline is $D - 1$. This can provide a cross check in the computation of such dimensions.

The best way to illustrate the idea of the random cuts method is to consider displacement on a sphere or a circle. On the circle, a randomly chosen line which intersects the circle in two places is chosen, and a displacement consistent with the fractal dimension adopted is made. Another cutting line is then chosen which is independent of the first line, a displacement of appropriate proportions is made and so on. This process continues until a level of accuracy required is reached, but unlike midpoint displacement, this is not known in advance. The process stops when all points defining the circle reach the appropriate level of resolution, but it is likely that more than half of these points will be at a level of detail greater than that specified in the stopping rule. This method was originally used by Voss (1985) for pure Brownian motion, for $H = 1/2$, although in later applications, the method has been generalized to fBm.

The method is beautifully illustrated by Voss's (1985) construction of Mandelbrot's famous planetscape *Planetrise over Labelgraph Hill* which is reproduced on the back cover of Mandelbrot's (1983) book. In another context, we illustrate a much simplified reduction of this in Plate 3.1 (see color section). The method clearly demonstrates how the original sphere is cut and then projected onto the flat plane. This picture was based on the random cuts method simulating pure Brownian motion, but since then, various renditions of similar planetscapes have been made using a modified form of the method consistent with $H \neq 1/2$. Voss (1985) and Mandelbrot (1983) both imply that by zooming in on the planet, it is possible to generate mountain and valley landscapes for the fact that the displacement is based on a sphere means that three-dimensional terrain is actually being simulated. Voss has also produced the terrain for this application, and these too are illustrated in Mandelbrot's (1983) book.

Before looking at these pictures, it is worth noting that little work has been done on calculating the actual fractal dimensions of terrain. This has not yet caught the interest of those concerned with computer graphic simulations, although there has been a good deal of discussion concerning ways to increase the realism of such scenes by varying such dimensions. An exception to this is in the work of Goodchild (1980) who has generated several hypothetical fBm terrains using the cutting plane method and who has explored their geomorphologic properties. Goodchild's hypothetical terrains are shown in Figure 3.8 where it is immediately clear that as the fractal dimension of these scenes increases towards 3, the landscapes become a jumble of spikes like stalagmites and stalactites and bear little resemblance to real surface landscapes (Goodchild, 1982; Goodchild and Mark, 1987). In fact, it is at the lower dimensions that these landscapes look more realistic. Mark and Aronson (1984) have fitted fBm surfaces to 17 sets

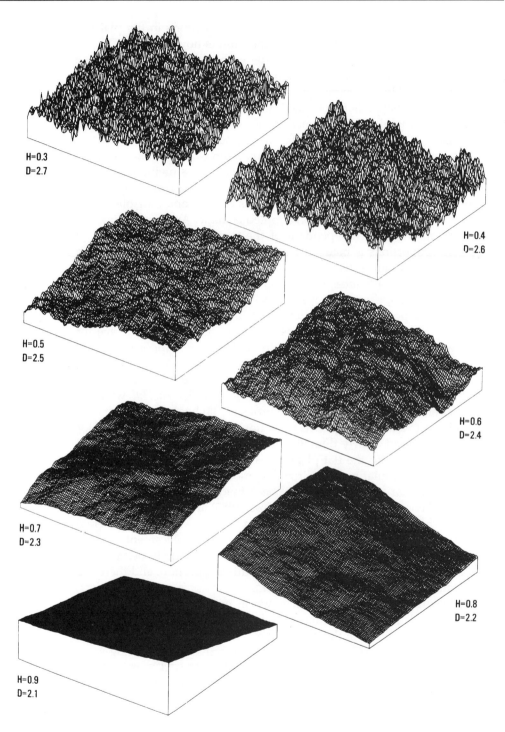

Figure 3.8. Simulated terrain with different fractal dimensions (from Goodchild and Mark, 1987).

of digital elevation data and found that although the fractal function provided rather good fits for spacing intervals less than 0.5 km with a dimension of around 2.25, above this spacing there was a clear break in the slope
of the related variogram, suggesting a dimension of 2.75 for 0.5 to 5 km
spacing. Over 5 km, there was no correlation with the fractal function.

These points have been recognized by those developing simulations of
terrain. Voss (1985, 1988), for example, indicates that several of his landscapes have been made more realistic by scaling elevations to make them
smoother through post-processing of the outputs from the cutting plane
method. Other *ad hoc* techniques have been used. For example, some have
varied fractal dimension directly with respect to elevation, with higher
dimensions at higher elevations. As we have indicated earlier, Musgrave,
Kolb and Mace (1989) have developed such simulations by including
hydraulic erosion and thermal weathering processes directly into such
simulations with striking effect. There is clearly much that can be done to
extend these models, but before we show how they can be applied to city
systems, we will introduce the technique of midpoint displacement which
has been used more widely than the method just described.

3.5 Simulating Brownian Motion by Midpoint Displacement

There are several reasons why the technique of midpoint displacement,
although less consistent than the random cuts method, might be preferred.
First it allows direct control over the level of detail simulated. That is, in
advance, one has some idea of how the landscape might look and this is
important if the goal is simply realistic-looking terrain rather than terrain
which accurately reproduces some reality. It is of course easier to
implement and perhaps easier to analyze, and it relates to the ideas we
have already introduced in our study of fractals. Its basic problem is that
it does not completely produce the required stationary variances; that is,
the variances produced are stationary, but only with respect to those displacements that reflect the hierarchical structure of the way the function
is computed.

To illustrate the process, we will revert to our two-dimensional function
which relates the variable $V(t)$ to time t. To fix ideas, we might think of
this as a line whose coordinates are $V(t)$ and t and to illustrate the method,
we show this line in Figure 3.9. We will first outline the method for the
case of pure Brownian motion using equation (3.1) based on the interval
$\Delta t = t_1 - t_0 = 1$ where $t_1 = 1$ and $t_0 = 0$. First we restate equation (3.1)

$$\text{var}(\Delta V) = \langle [V(t_1) - V(t_0)]^2 \rangle = (t_1 - t_0)\sigma^2, \tag{3.1}$$

where using the unit interval, this becomes

$$\text{var}(\Delta V) = (1 - 0)\sigma^2 = \sigma^2. \tag{3.17}$$

We will now begin the midpoint displacement. In the first step, we choose

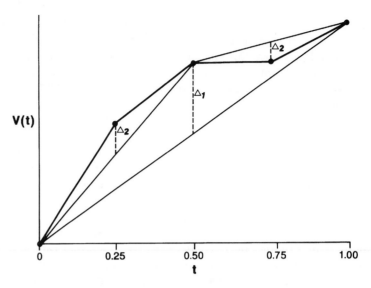

Figure 3.9. Brownian motion as midpoint displacement.

the variance of $V(1/2)$ as the midpoint $1/2$ by adding a variance displacement Δ_1^2 to half the variance of the entire original interval. The variances $\langle[V(1/2) - V(0)]^2\rangle$ and $\langle[V(1/2) - V(1)]^2\rangle$ are equal for one of these, then

$$V(1/2) - V(0) = \frac{1}{2}[V(1) - V(0)] + \Delta_1, \tag{3.18}$$

$$\langle(V(1/2) - V(0))^2\rangle = \frac{1}{4}\langle[V(1) - V(0)]^2\rangle + \Delta_1^2 = \frac{1}{2}\sigma^2$$

$$= \frac{1}{4}\sigma^2 + \Delta_1^2 = \frac{1}{2}\sigma^2. \tag{3.19}$$

It is easy to see that the variance in the displacement and the displacement itself from equation (3.19) are calculated as

$$\Delta_1^2 = \frac{1}{4}\sigma^2 \text{ and } \Delta_1 = \frac{1}{2}\sigma.$$

The second step proceeds in like manner. The variances $\langle[V(1/4) - V(0)]^2\rangle$ and $\langle[V(3/4) - V(1)]^2\rangle$ are equal and taking one of these, the new displacement values Δ_2^2 and Δ_2 are calculated from

$$V(1/4) - V(0) = \frac{1}{2}[V(1/2) - V(0)] + \Delta_2, \tag{3.20}$$

$$\langle[V(1/4) - V(0)]^2\rangle = \frac{1}{4}\langle[V(1/2) - V(0)]^2\rangle + \Delta_2^2 = \frac{1}{4}\sigma^2$$

$$= \frac{1}{8}\sigma^2 + \Delta_2^2 = \frac{1}{4}\sigma^2. \tag{3.21}$$

The displacements are thus

$$\Delta_2^2 = \frac{1}{8}\sigma^2 \text{ and } \Delta_2 = \left(\frac{1}{8}\right)^{1/2}\sigma.$$

Continuing this process and noting the equality of the variance displacements for subdivisions of the intervals at the same level, it is easy to show that on iteration k, the mean squared displacement or variance of the displacement is given as

$$\Delta_k^2 = \frac{1}{2^{k+1}}\, \sigma^2,$$

from which the actual displacement is the square root. The logic of this subdivision is shown in Figure 3.9 where it is clear that equations (3.18) to (3.21) apply to all subdivisions at the appropriate level and not just those intervals that are given above.

This method although applied in its pure form several times (Carpenter, 1980; Fournier, Fussell and Carpenter, 1982), can easily be generalized to fBm. We follow exactly the same steps, but note now that there is an exponent of $2H$ on the time interval associated with the variance. Restating equation (3.6)

$$\text{var}(\Delta V) = \langle [V(t_1) - V(t_0)]^2 \rangle = (t_1 - t_0)^{2H}\sigma^2, \tag{3.6}$$

and using the unit interval as in equation (3.17)

$$\text{var}(\Delta V) = (1 - 0)^{2H}\sigma^2 = \sigma^2, \tag{3.22}$$

we follow an identical sequence to the pure case above. In the first step,

$$V(1/2) - V(0) = \frac{1}{2}[V(1) - V(0)] + \Delta_1, \tag{3.23}$$

$$\langle [V(1/2) - V(0)]^2 \rangle = \frac{1}{4}\langle [(V1) - V(0)]^2 \rangle + \Delta_1^2 = \left(\frac{1}{2}\right)^{2H}\sigma^2$$

$$= \frac{1}{4}\,\sigma^2 + \Delta_1^2 = \left(\frac{1}{2}\right)^{2H}\sigma^2, \tag{3.24}$$

with the displacement calculated as

$$\Delta_1^2 = \left[\frac{1}{4} - \left(\frac{1}{2}\right)^{2H}\right]\sigma^2.$$

The second step proceeds in like manner. The variances $\langle [V(1/4) - V(0)]^2 \rangle$ and $\langle [V(3/4) - V(1)]^2 \rangle$ are equal and the new displacement values Δ_2^2 and Δ_2 are calculated from

$$V(1/4) - V(0) = \frac{1}{2}[V(1/2) - V(0)] + \Delta_2, \tag{3.25}$$

$$\langle [V(1/4) - V(0)]^2 \rangle = \frac{1}{4}\langle [V(1/2) - V(0)]^2 \rangle + \Delta_2^2 = \left(\frac{1}{4}\right)^{2H}\sigma^2$$

$$= \frac{1}{4}\left(\frac{1}{2}\right)^{2H}\sigma^2 + \Delta_2^2 = \left(\frac{1}{4}\right)^{2H}\sigma^2. \tag{3.26}$$

A little rearrangement of equation (3.26) shows that the variance of the displacements is

$$\Delta_2^2 = \frac{\sigma^2}{(2^2)^H}(1 - 2^{2H-2}),$$

and in general

$$\Delta_k^2 = \frac{\sigma^2}{(2^k)^H}(1 - 2^{2H-2}).$$

In Figure 3.10, we show an example of the application of midpoint displacement for the case of a fractal line whose details at successive levels of resolution have been generated using pure Brownian motion (with $H = 1/2$). This illustrates how the profile for each level of resolution provides the initiator for the generation of detail at the next level down.

3.6 Fractal Terrain Using the Midpoint Displacement: the 'Earthrise' Sequence

We have already seen how we might generate fairly realistic terrain by tiling the plane with triangles whose coordinates are chosen randomly but within the logic of hierarchical midpoint displacement. The sequence of

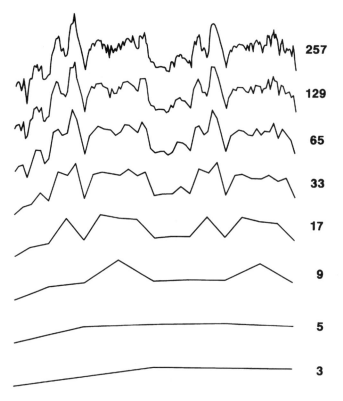

Figure 3.10. Brownian motion computed by midpoint displacement across several scales.

distorting the Sierpinski gasket used by McGuire (1991) presented in Figure 3.5 illustrates a more general approach which we will use in generating landscape and cityscape scenes in the rest of this chapter. A particularly useful demonstration of this method is given as van Dam (1984) which involves replacing each triangle with four, not three, copies of itself is shown in Plate 3.3. There is however a problem in using midpoint displacement in that the nonstationarity of the process sometimes leads to creasing in the landscape (or in the form of whatever object is being rendered). This is due to the fact that at the higher and earlier levels of recursion, the points and lines generated are not subject to any further randomization, thus implying greater degrees of nonstationarity when compared with points which are generated later in the recursion.

We can show this formally in terms of equations (3.17) to (3.26) which we used in the last section to generate fBm. First note that the variances for the intervals [1/4, 0] and [3/4, 1] must be the same, that is

$$\langle [V(1/4) - V(0)]^2 \rangle = \langle [V(3/4) - V(1)]^2 \rangle = \left(\frac{1}{4}\right)^{2H} \sigma^2. \tag{3.27}$$

Now if we add these two variances we would expect them to equal the variance of the interval [1/2, 0] or [1, 0]. Equating these two variances, we get

$$\langle [V(1/2) - V(0)]^2 \rangle = \langle [V(1/4) - V(0)]^2 \rangle + \langle [V(3/4) - V(1)]^2 \rangle$$

which from equations (3.24) and (3.27) implies that

$$\left(\frac{1}{2}\right)^{2H} \sigma^2 = 2 \left(\frac{1}{4}\right)^{2H} \sigma^2, \tag{3.28}$$

which is only the case when $H = 1/2$, the case of pure Brownian motion. This is the main reason why those using the midpoint displacement algorithm usually introduce some form of additional random generator either during the process of iteration or after the output at the required level of resolution has been computed. However, the use of other tessellations in the plane can help resolve this, such as the choice of a square grid as initiator. Mandelbrot (1988) has used nested hexagons to develop the method more recently, although later in this chapter, we will demonstrate the importance of choosing the correct initiator by adopting a square grid for the generation of cityscapes.

We will use the triangular net to first show how it is possible to construct a planetscape and then a mountainous terrain by midpoint displacement for the case of pure Brownian motion. Our method is extremely fast and involves very short computer programs which assume that some overall shape of the object in question is input to the program in the first place. In Figure 3.11, we show how a mountainous landscape can be generated by inputting the basic structure of the landscape in terms of its overall form. In this case, the inputs are large overlapping triangles which are then used in the rendering of fractal detail. Each triangle is rendered separately using the type of triangle displacement shown in Figure 3.11. The colors of the scene are chosen so that the nearer the top of each mountain, the more likely the mountain is to be snow-covered. The technique we use examines

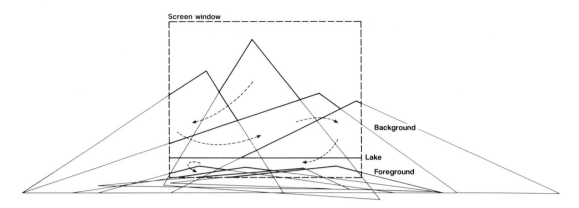

Figure 3.11.   Simulating an Alpine scene using triangular midpoint displacement.

each of the most detailed triangles generated, computes the distance from its centroid to the top of the relevant mountain and then chooses the color randomly but within the limits imposed by the value of this distance. The effect of creasing, however, is quite clear in this picture although this can clearly be used to advantage in that real mountainous terrain often shows this type of creasing due to differences in underlying geological structure.

We have used the same method to copy the Mandelbrot–Voss planetrise picture shown earlier in Plate 3.1. In this case, we use a solid blue circle on which a triangular continental land mass is placed. This land mass is then rendered using triangular midpoint displacement. The colors are chosen in the same way as those determined in the Alpine scene in Plate 3.2. The centroid of the basic land mass is computed and the further away the centroid of each individual triangle at the most detailed level is, the more likely the triangle is to be colored green, the less likely to be colored yellow. This generates reasonably realistic continental land masses. At the same time, islands are spawned from this, for the choice of color is also extended to the generation of blue sea in the peripheral areas of the land masses. However, our pictures are very much in the spirit of Voss's (1985) fractal forgeries in that to generate the planet in the plane, we let the continents overlap the edge of the circle and simply clean them off once the detail of the planet's terrain is complete. This is shown in Figure 3.12(a).

We have also used two other elements to generate the illusion that the picture is a true three-dimensional rendering when it is only two. First we have constructed a lunar-like landscape by triangular displacement and into this we have introduced some oval shaped craters. The colors chosen for this part of the landscape – black and yellow – give high contrast to the picture as the planet is based on blue, yellow and green, typical of the colors of the earth seen from space. Finally we have introduced a light source which, like the sun, is a long distance away from the planet. This means that one side of the planet is dark. In Plate 3.3, we show the planet and its final rendering through four stages of construction. In fact, the picture is sufficiently realistic on the fourth iteration for no further rendering to be necessary, although this is because the scene has been generated on a small computer with a low resolution screen of the order of 320×256 pixels. Note that in both these pictures – the mountainscape and the planet-

(a)

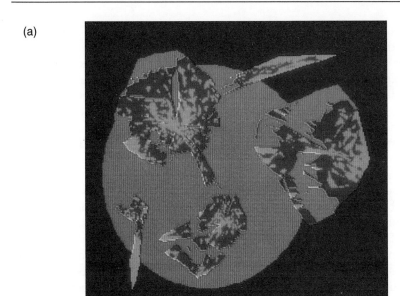

(b)

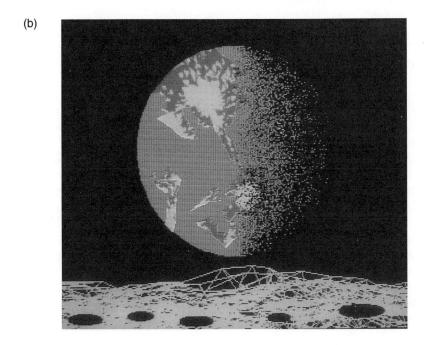

Figure 3.12.   A simple planetrise: (a) construction; (b) final rendering.

scape – only four colors were employed, but even these can still be used to realistic effect.

Saupe (1991) says: "In order to generate a fractal, one does not have to be an expert in some involved theory. More importantly, the complexity of a fractal, when measured in terms of the length of the shortest computer program that can generate it, is very small". This statement can be borne out in the applications which are featured throughout this book, but it is particularly pertinent to the examples of this section. To generate the planetscape in Figure 3.12 and Plate 3.3 requires 165 statements in BASIC with an additional 15 relating to the input data. With some optimization of this code, this can be reduced to around 120 statements. What is so remarkable about fractals is that their realism increases dramatically, perhaps exponentially, as their generation at lower levels proceeds. This is very clear in Plate 3.3 where four levels of successive resolution are illustrated. In running the programs associated with this planetscape, the emergence of realism is almost magical as it is observed on the computer screen, although readers must be warned that such realism is in the eye of the beholder who is viewing the picture from a fixed human scale. What might appear realistic would not be so if its scale where enlarged accordingly. For example, zooming in on the fourth level of recursion which demonstrates fractal detail as in Plate 3.3 and scaling this back up to the base scale of the observer, the detail would then look crude and unrealistic. However, if the fractal generation were to continue to orders of magnitude well below the resolution of the computer screen, scaling back up would give sufficient detail to retain the realism.

3.7 Elementary Models of Urban Structure

When we come to apply these ideas to cities and urban systems generally, we require much more elaborate models than those which lie behind the planetscapes and terrain simulated above. These models are simplistic in the extreme, based on common observations of how landscapes look and even in these contexts, to increase the realism further requires models of erosion and weathering which build on more formal ideas in geomorphology. In developing fractal geometry in city simulation, some rudimentary theory about what activities and land uses are located where, must be used, and this means that theories of location and urban structure which form the basis of urban economics, transportation and human geography, are required. In this section, we will introduce the most elementary of such theories and use the resulting model to determine what activity or land use is to be located in each of our zones or sites of the city, and where in turn these sites are generated, using hierarchical triangular midpoint displacement.

Cities and their activities and land uses clearly manifest forms which are self-similar as we demonstrated in Chapter 1 and loosely alluded to in terms of fractals in Chapter 2. At higher levels of spatial aggregation, for example at the regional level, self-similarity is directly invoked in central place theory (Woldenberg and Berry, 1967). The idea of modeling self-similarity at different scales involves finding an appropriate generating function which can be applied to each scale in a recursive manner. A simple example might be based on central place theory or on theories of the disposition of neighborhoods and district centers within cities: such a rule might involve market area, range of good, population served, the variety of services and goods available at different hierarchical levels and so on. Such a function would be applied first to the largest center, and then follow the rank–size distribution through lower order centers. We are able to use any method which subdivides the original space into regular numbers of subspaces, quadrants, whatever, at each level of the hierarchy and the generation would continue until the lowest order of center is reached. Clearly the recursive rule involves locating lower and lower orders of non-overlapping subdivision. The method we will use will begin with one or four spaces and continually subdivide these by four at lower levels, leading to an hierarchy of locations ordered from 1 to 4, 4 to 16, 16 to 64, and in general for any iteration k, 2^{k-1} to 2^k. We will explain the hierarchical nesting in detail in the next section.

The hierarchy we have just alluded to might equally well be an artifact of the method as it clearly is in the landscape examples given earlier. It does not have to have substantive meaning at each level for it to generate realistic scenes or locations. However, in the examples of cities, we will attempt to give the hierarchy more substantive meaning in terms of location theory and the perception of space at different scales. Central place theory and neighborhood hierarchies have already been mentioned, but there are also hierarchies of traffic routes, public and private services, firms in terms of their spatial organization from regions to the local level and so on, as we implied in Chapter 1. As we also noted there, treating cities as hierarchies is somewhat controversial for a number of studies, notably that by Alexander (1965), argue that hierarchy is too simplistic an ordering device, that activities and land uses in cities are composed of overlapping areas whose order is more lattice- than tree-like. However, this takes us to questions of the rationale for such hierarchies, and we will postpone this until the next section.

We have already introduced the notion that appropriate models of urban activity are to be used to predict the land use/activity type at each level of fractal detail, thus forming a basis for rendering. In this first application, however, we will only use such models to predict land use at the lowest level, not at intermediate levels which would imply that the hierarchy used in simulation has substantive meaning. Thus once a lowest branch in the hierarchy is reached, the model is invoked to enable activity types to be determined. Here we have assumed that there are three key urban activities in one-to- one correspondence to land uses: these are commercial–industrial ($u = 1$), residential–housing ($u = 2$), and open space–recreational ($u = 3$) where the index u defines the particular land use–activity in question. The model for these activities is based on a simple distance relationship to the central business district (CBD) where the profiles of land use type imply that different land uses dominate different concentric rings. These are the so-called von Thunen rings which characterize the organization of land use in strongly monocentric cities. In general these profiles are structured so that commercial–industrial land uses dominate the core and inner areas of the city, residential housing the peripheral areas of the city and the inner suburbs, with open space more randomly configured throughout the city. These patterns have been central to theories of urban structure and location from urban ecology in the mid-1920s to contemporary urban economics which began with Alonso (1964).

The general form of the model predicts a probability $p^u(r)$ which is a function of the distance r from the CBD specific to each land use u. This is given as

$$p^u(r) = a^u + b^u (r - R^u), u = 1, 2, 3, \qquad (3.29)$$

where a^u, b^u and R^u are parameters whose magnitude and sign control the profile of the probability distribution with respect to distance from the CBD. The precise forms of these equations for the simulation which will follow can now be stated. For the commercial–industrial activity $u = 1$, equation (3.29) can be written

$$p^1(r \leq 400) = 1.38 - 0.0074r$$

where the probability declines inversely with distance, and is near to 0 when $r = 186$. When the distance is greater than 400, the probability is set at a threshold value of

$$p^1(r > 400) = 0.002$$

reflecting a minimum threshold on the existence of this activity. It is quite clear, however, if only these equations were to be used, that there would be a break in the profile from $r = 186$ to $r = 400$ where the probability would be 0. To control for this, an additional equation is also applied which is set up as the conditional that

if $p^1(r) < 0.04$, then $p^1(r \leq 400) = 0.04$.

The combined effect of these equations generates the commercial–industrial profile shown in Figure 3.13. Note that the values used are arbitrary and only of relative meaning for they reflect the coordinates for plotting on the particular display used.

Residential land use ($u = 2$) is controlled by a similar set of equations which reflect both positive and inverse distance relations. Then

$$p^2(r \leq 315) = 0.20 + 0.0024 (r - 30)$$

and

$$p^2(r > 315) = 0.88 - 0.0035 (r - 315).$$

The effect of these equations is to generate an increasing function of distance from $p^2(0) = 0.128$ to a maximum of $p^2(315) = 0.88$ which then declines to $p^2(516) = 0$. To ensure a minimum value of residential activity, the conditional is

if $p^2(r) < 0.05$, then $p^2(r) = 0.05$.

Finally for open space $u = 3$, the relationship is simply one of inverse distance

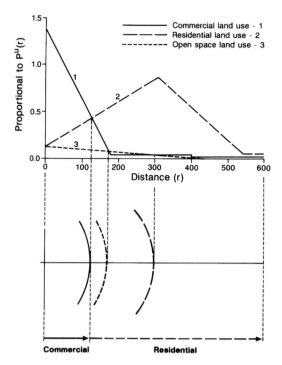

Figure 3.13. Land use profiles and von Thunen rings in the monocentric city.

$$p^3(r) = 0.12 - 0.0002r$$

where the probability declines from $p^3(0) = 0.12$ to $p^3(480) = 0$. To ensure that this function does not predict negative values, the conditional

if $p^3(r) < 0$, then $p^3(r) = 0$

is invoked. These three profiles are shown in Figure 3.13.

Examining these probabilities, it is clear that they are nowhere normalized to exactly sum to 1. We have done this so that when $\Sigma_u \, p^u(r) < 1$, the residual probability is regarded as the probability of vacant land occurring. The overall probability of vacant land occurring is best seen by visually aggregating the profiles in Figure 3.13 and this implies that as distance increases away from the CBD, the probability of vacant land also increases. The other point is that in the vicinity of the CBD, the probabilities sum to greater than 1, that is $\Sigma_u \, p^u(r) > 1$. This does not constitute a problem because the order in which the activities are considered in the simulation means that commercial–industrial are always allocated first, then residential and finally open space. This achieves the following effects.

The probability structure is first set up in the order of importance of these activities. A range of probability is fixed for each activity as: $rN_0 = 1$, $rN_1 = 1000p^1(r)$, $rN_2 = 1000 \, [p^1(r) + p^2(r)]$, and $rN_3 = 1000 \, [p^1(r) + p^2(r) + p^3(r)]$. An activity type is allocated by drawing a random number between 1 and 1000. If the sum of the probabilities is greater than 1, then the commercial–industrial land use takes priority, then the residential and finally open space. In fact when $r = 0$, then $rN_1 = 1000 \times 1.38$ and thus the activity will always be commercial–industrial at the CBD. Only when $r > 50$ will other activities be 'competing' for allocation. However, when $r > 550$, $rN_3 = 6$ and effectively all the activity will be vacant land. In essence, this marks the boundary of the city. These equations thus control many dimensions of urban activity allocation and physical form. The shape of the city can be quite radically altered by changing the parameters a^u, b^u and R^u. The values used were fixed by a process of trial and error simulation as well as being judged consistent with simple urban bid-rent and population density theory which we refer to in later chapters.

We have thus defined a simple model of urban land use location which operates through functions which imply the importance and dominance of each land use at different distances from the CBD. Such a monocentric model is of course a gross simplification. It is not unlike the 'model' we used to render the slopes of the mountainscape in the last section. Nevertheless, it does provide a useful rationale for urban location and much of the theoretical edifice of urban economics and human geography is built upon these basic ideas. However, our focus here is not upon developing the best model but upon using a rudimentary model of urban structure to provide a rationale for 'coloring' the city using triangular midpoint displacement. To this we now turn.

3.8 Fractal Cityscapes: The 'London' Sequence

As we implied above, we will now operationalize the model within the context of triangular midpoint displacement for an urban system with the broad dimensions of a world city such as London or Tokyo. A justification for fractal rendering of the sites of the city at its lowest level is based both on our casual and more formal observations that cities display such irregular patterns. Such patterns are formed from individual sites and parcels whose irregularity is conditioned by a myriad of historical, social and physical characteristics. Such patterns are impossible to describe in detail, and defy conventional modeling over a range of scales, although we do know the general principles and reasons as to how and why such patterns are formed. The patterns do in fact appear to be fractal, and thus a first attempt in unraveling their structure can be based on fractal simulation. This is an important point which we cannot stress too much. This chapter is about using fractals to generate a perceived realism in which traditional urban models might be embedded. This is a much more modest goal than designing a complete fractal model, although our models will become more complete as the chapters unfold.

Here we not only acknowledge that fractals are useful in identifying the basic processes at work in cities, but that they are useful in more superficial ways – for rendering the forms produced by traditional models, thus making their outputs more visually acceptable. Such a goal is important in communicating problems, plans and policies in ways in which decision-makers best understand. As we continue, our focus will begin to change as we move towards models based on better founded urban theory, but we will still retain an emphasis on their visualization using state-of-the-art computer graphics. The method we have developed begins by dividing the urban space, which we define as a circle centered on the CBD, into 10 identical triangular wedges or sectors. Each sector is then subjected in turn to hierarchical subdivision, and once the appropriate level of fractal detail has been reached in any sector, the simulation moves to an adjacent one and begins afresh. The process starts with the due eastern sector and rotates in counterclockwise fashion until all the sectors have been treated. We consider that the use of the triangular lattice rather than a square grid is possibly more appropriate to highly polarized cities where the development has occurred historically from the CBD to the periphery, although the lattice used should make little difference to the simulation.

Let us first define the spatial units or zones in question. The original circular space is subdivided into 10 sectors, each sector referred to as Z_θ where θ is an index reflecting the angular orientation of the sector in question. Within each sector, the zones are referred to by $Z_k(s)$ where k is the zone in question and s is the hierarchical or recursive level. From each branching of the hierarchy, there are K zones, $k = 1, 2, ..., K$. Over the levels of the hierarchy given by recursive levels $s = 1, 2, ..., S$, particular zones are referred to in the sequence $i, j, k, ...$, where i is a typical zone on the $(s - 2)$th level, j is a zone on the $(s - 1)$th, k is a zone on the sth level and so on. The generating rule used to subdivide zones from one level of the hierarchy to the next is given as

$$Z_k(s) = G_k[Z_j(s - 1)], \quad j, k = 1, 2, ... K, s \geq 1, \tag{3.30}$$

where j is the zone being subdivided on level $s - 1$ and G_k is the subdivision operator. A particular sequence of zones can now be generated in the following way. The process is begun by applying the rule in equation (3.30) to the original sector Z_θ

$$Z_i(0) = G_i [Z_\theta], \quad \theta = 2\pi/10, 4\pi/10, ..., 2\pi, i = 1, ..., K. \tag{3.31}$$

Recursion on equation (3.30) using equation (3.31) leads to the sequence

$$Z_n(s) = G_n [G_m [...G_j [G_i [Z_\theta]] ...]]. \tag{3.32}$$

Because K zones are generated from each branch in the hierarchy, it is easy to show that at the sth level down the hierarchy, there a total of K^s zones. There is also need for a stopping rule to end the recursion.

In our case, we are subdividing space to form a triangular mesh. The original segment Z_θ is divided into four triangles in the manner shown in Figure 3.14 where $K = 4$. From this diagram, it is clear that at recursive level $s = 1$, there are four sectors in the original segment, at level $s = 2$, 16; at $s = 3$, 64, and so on. The stopping rule is based on the level of resolution below which further spatial detail is not required. In this case, this is the level of pixel resolution of the display (which is 320×256 pixels). A quick calculation shows that with 10 sectors, when $s = 6$ we are below the level of resolution of the screen, and thus in the sequel we will find that fractal detail can be most clearly articulated at levels $s = 4$ and $s = 5$, not greater. We have chosen G_k to reflect the subdivision of triangular space into four triangles in the manner shown in Figure 3.14. This involves midpoint displacement of each side in a constrained random fashion, the degree of con-

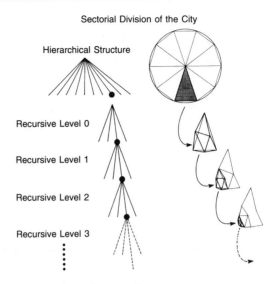

Figure 3.14. Fractal rendering of the monocentric city.

straint reflecting the degree of irregularity, hence the fractal dimension of the resulting surface as described earlier in this chapter. The algorithm used to effect the displacement uses simple trigonometric functions to compute the associated coordinate pairs which define the triangular mesh. The degree of randomness introduced is difficult to quantify in any simple way, but it is reflected in the displacements in Figure 3.14.

The fractal simulations involve a straightforward concatenation of the recursive generating process (in Figure 3.14 and equations (3.30) to (3.32)) with the general model structure (in Figure 3.13 and equation (3.29)). To demonstrate the dependence of pattern and shape on the level of recursion, we have run the model with distances and scale similar to those of Greater London (GLC, 1985) for levels of recursion $1 \leq s \leq 5$. This produces five simulations which are presented in Plate 3.4 where the colors blue, red and green represent commercial–industrial, residential, and open space–recreational land uses respectively. These show quite different patterns. Up to level $s = 2$, the pictures reveal the coarseness of the triangular mesh used to generate shapes of land use activity. Moreover, not enough zones are generated to achieve a reasonable distribution of activity types. However, for $s > 2$, the pattern becomes much more acceptable; but when $s > 5$, which touches the level of pixel resolution, the pattern looks more like a pointillist painting than a city. The most appropriate-looking images are thus generated for $s = 3$ and $s = 5$. This is an important point in the simulation of visual realism, and it also suggests that the probability structure of the underlying model is not invariant to scale, an issue which in some senses is obvious, but one which has rarely been explored in the mainstream of research.

These types of simulation do, however, reveal the inadequacies of conventional urban models in terms of their spatial patterns and visual realism. The images shown in Figure 3.14 are too compact in that one might expect a much greater spread of development unconnected to the main city but indicative of the way development hops around on the edge of a large city.

Despite the preset wedge-sector geometry which provides the template for the city, these patterns do not display the classic corridor effects which characterize the typical radial–concentric city. Compare these, especially the images for $s = 3$, 4 and 5 in Plate 3.4, to those in Chapter 1 – Figures 1.15 and 1.16, and Chapter 7 – Figures 7.2 to 7.5 and Plate 7.1, which illustrate real urban agglomerations. The advantage of fractal simulation thus becomes clear. Spatial effects in models are immediately clarified, and systematic biases can be detected and corrected. Only large-scale simulations can achieve this, and the pictures in Plate 3.6 speak for themselves.

Finally, although the broad shape of our simulations reflect those of London, these simulations are as much 'London' as are the Mandelbrot–Voss planetrise pictures shown earlier which are implied to be the 'Earth' as seen from the 'Moon'. This is a very important issue in fractal graphics for in this case, it suggests the sorts of elements required in order to generate minimal city forms. The whole feel to the images for $s \geq 3$ is that of a large monocentric city like London. In fact, we have cheated slightly by adding the distinctive River Thames to the images after they have been generated. This is a strong perceptual clue to any picture but even without it, the images for $s \geq 3$ reflect a large city like London. In our fully-fledged simulations which we will develop in the next chapter, we will in fact omit the river for in these simulations which will actually be of London; the shape of the city will be encoded in the input data which reflect the built-up area and the Greater London County boundary.

The examples we have ended with in this chapter constitute a good basis for experimentation, in terms of the mechanisms of developing cities in physical terms, of exploring model structures through their causal chains, and of judging visual realism. A particularly important issue is to find out the way parameters might combine with one another to generate realistic and unrealistic morphologies, and the 'London' sequence developed here provides a firm basis for this. In the next chapter, we will extend our hypothetical model by setting up a computer laboratory to generate a variety of experiments in visualizing urban form. This, however, will be but an initial foray into this kind of experimentation, and as such represents a powerful line of inquiry which we will leave for future research. We will also progress our simulations forward by developing more realistic models which we render with fractal midpoint displacement, and the emphasis will turn to explicitly fitting these models to data. The great strength of fractal models which generate picturescapes is that they provide a way of making our theories more real and of communicating more meaning to our analyses. For the first time we can move away from but still retain the logic of our theoretical models which hitherto have usually been regarded as extreme cases; with a little imagination, we can render these more realistically without losing the need for high theory. Fractal rendering represents a powerful way of achieving this, and in the next chapter, we will demonstrate how this is possible in the real as well as in the imaginary world.

4

Laboratories for Visualizing Urban Form

> When I wrote the program, I never thought that it would evolve anything more than a variety of tree-like shapes . . . nothing in my 20 years' experience of programming computers, and nothing in my wildest dreams, prepared me for what actually emerged on the screen. I can't remember exactly when in the sequence it first began to dawn on me that an evolved resemblance to something like an insect was possible. (Dawkins, 1986, p. 59.)

4.1 Experimentation as Visualization

The understanding we have already gained about the systematic irregularity of fractal shapes creates a very strong case for judging the success of models by their visual appearance. For example, it is easy to conjecture that the physical properties of land use in terms of plot size, shape and density display an irregularity which is considered to be fractal. From earlier chapters, we know that cities are self-similar in a variety of ways, central place theory being the clearest demonstration of this principle (Arlinghaus, 1985). Thus the idea that actual city structures might be fractal is appealing, but of more import is the possibility that fractal geometry may well contain the basis for linking activity models to their physical context. However, before we launch into the use of fractal geometry in rendering traditional computer models of cities more realistically, we need to formally consider how we might develop this understanding further through designing a consistent and structured set of experiments for the hypothetical model we introduced in the last chapter. Our 'London' sequence provides us with such a model with a strictly limited number of parameters whose variation will generate different urban forms. Here we will extend this model and in a laboratory-like setting, we will manipulate the values of its parameters so that we might explore the complete set of forms which can be generated. The parameter space which bounds this set we will treat as a mathematical space populated by different forms which can be derived from one another, and we will call this the 'space of all cities'. In this space, we will experiment with city patterns whose forms we will assess and evaluate visually, thus establishing a process of experimentation through visualization and vice versa.

Our experiments will consist of sampling different urban forms from the space of all cities, and simply involve a conventional selection based on different combinations of the limited set of parameter values. The hypothetical models based on our 'London' model from Chapter 3 and which we will explore in the next section, will contain a very limited number of parameters. Such models must reflect the principle of parsimony so that there can be a clear assessment of the effects of different parameter values. Furthermore, throughout this book, we will deal with highly simplified models which in no way approach those operational urban models which are used in the real world by planners and engineers involved in forecasting and designing the future city. Moreover, because our models, although highly structured, are random in that land use is allocated through chance events, we are dealing here with urban forms which portray a general typology of cities rather than anything which is more specific. Indeed in the very title of this book *Fractal Cities*, our emphasis is not upon thinking of some cities as being fractal in contrast to others, which are not, but that all cities display structures and patterns which in certain senses might be fractal, and it is our emphasis on the degree to which their form is fractal which can provide important insights into their functioning.

In the study of form through computer experiments, it is the way certain shapes evolve relative to some baseline which is our essential quest. In one sense, this is the principle which has been used for nearly a century in the study of the evolution of biological forms first exploited by D'Arcy Wentworth Thompson (1917, 1961). His view is cogently illustrated when he says: "In a very large part of morphology, our essential task lies in the comparison of related forms rather than in the precise definition of each; and the *deformation* [his italics] of a complicated figure may be a phenomenon easy of comprehension, though the figure itself has to be left unanalysed and undefined". Thompson's point is of general import to our work here. We can begin as we did at the end of the last chapter with a theoretical model of a city based on the concentric rings of land use around the city's center, the land use being defined according to von Thunen's bid-rent principles which are implied in the land use profiles shown in Figure 3.13. By systematically changing a parameter value, the shape of the city can be deformed or reformed to another, and by systematically charting this deformation, we are engaging in the time-honored tradition of experimentation in which different responses in terms of form are being generated by changing one parameter value at a time. The space in which this occurs is what we have termed the 'space of all cities'.

We have continually alluded to such experimentation in previous chapters. For example, if we have a model whose form is defined in two-dimensional space, in the plane, by various transformations of its x-y coordinates, then as these transformations vary in value, so does the shape which is generated. We noted this in Chapters 2 and 3 where we briefly described how a Koch curve could be related to a Julia set in 2-space using Barnsley's (1988a) IFS method. By interpolating between the transformation values for both objects, we indicated that one object could be slowly transformed into the other. The intermediate forms generated represent the visual trace or trajectory of this process. Whether or not this transition is meaningful will of course depend upon our choice of objects or systems. Here we will not map the complete range of possibilities but simply select some forms which appear to be good bounds to the space in which our family of cities exists. In fact, an extension to our laboratory which we have not yet developed, could be based on a process in which one form actually evolved to another, the decisions concerning the evolution consisting of single small changes to the parameter values being made by the user on the basis of some visual assessment of the appropriateness of the form. The quote from Dawkins (1986) which prefaced this chapter is based on his response to such a process which initially produced tree-like forms, but through judicious selection of changes in parameter values one at a time, ultimately led to insect-like forms. Dawkins' surprise was over the fact that the kinds of parameters which characterized trees, such as branch orders, widths, bifurcation ratios, branch angles and so on, could quickly develop to shapes which were manifestly insect-like. His amazement is no different from that of the transition between a Koch curve and a Julia set as well as the sorts of deformation between biological systems which was first popularized by D'Arcy Thompson (1917, 1961). We will not develop these possibilities further, but there is considerable potential in our field for such evolution through experimentation, and this represents an important area of work for the future.

In Chapter 1, we introduced, albeit informally, many different examples of urban form, far wider than we will explore here. Later in this book, we will eventually develop more fundamental fractal models, and this will give us some scope for generating a massive variety of urban forms, but these we will leave until Chapter 7. However, at this stage, it is worth reiterating the range of forms which are possible with our 'London' model so that the experimental work of the next section can be put in context. There are a series of dichotomies which characterize such forms. First there is the distinction between monocentric and multicentric cities. The monocentric tend to be industrial cities in that their development in terms of commerce and industry has been centered in and around the CBD, and this is contrast to those multicentric cities where there are several dispersed centers which compete with one other. Multicentric cities characterize the presently emerging post-industrial age where the power of the CBD is no greater, if not less, than many peripheral centers. But there are also multicentric cities which have developed as the fusion of several separate industrial cities; these are called 'conurbations' by Geddes (1915, 1949), and 'megalopolis' by Gottmann (1961) and Doxiadis (1968).

Overlying these distinctions is the notion of concentrated to dispersed which is loosely akin with high to low density cities. Centralized and decentralized also follow this classification, and there are more specific terms such as the 'exploded' city and the 'imploded' which represent growing and declining monocentric forms. The classification of form in this way presents an endless array of different characterizations which are all semantically a little different, but in general, cover a range from concentrated to dispersed. Moreover, there are distinctions which overlie these in terms of shape, from linear to concentric, almost mirroring our distinction between one- and two-dimensional forms which we portrayed in Chapter 2, as for example in Figure 2.10. In our experiments which follow, it is essential that we appreciate the bounds which make possible only a restricted set of forms. In essence, the space of all cities which we define only includes monocentric cities which develop around a single pole or CBD. We will see how various cities which are concentrated or dispersed can emerge through changes in the way the chance elements operate on land use allocation; this may suggest some multicentric form, but this is still within the bounds of the monocentric assumption and is caused by chance locations of centers which are not related to the CBD. The way we construct our cities is on the assumption that all development is arrayed concentrically around the CBD, and this rules out the possibility of linear cities emerging. This will only be possible with our more fundamental models which we develop from Chapter 7 on.

Finally, there is the possibility that cities might be classified according to the form of their transport networks, usually in terms of the distinction between radially symmetric nets and 'Manhattan' grids. We will not pursue these types of form either, largely because we are continually conscious that the number of parameters which we can deal with and from which we can derive meaningful conclusions must be severely limited. This is not a book about theories of cities. As Crick (1990) says: "The job of the theorist ... is to suggest experiments", and the experiments we will choose are those which are naturally suggested by simple theories of the monocentric city which still compose much of urban economics. We will be content to explore the role of chance in land use allocation and in the shape which such locational patterns display, rather than being concerned with elaborating new or existing theory. We have resisted extending our approach to multicentric urban systems and to models based on spatial interaction, largely because we view our task here as simply a beginning. Moreover, we are conscious that most urban economic theory has also been developed using the monocentric assumption and thus there is more than enough research to develop in first linking fractal patterns to these theories. It is always tempting to add more and more constraints to the models to reflect how cities actually work. Here, however, our concern is not with developing completely realistic models of cities, but with demonstrating that an approach through fractal geometry leads to important insights into their form and functioning.

To set the context, we will also note the idea that the model-building process is based on the loose cycle of inductive explanation, and deductive prediction. For example, some models such as those based on discrete choice are strongly inductive in their specification and estimation, while spatial interaction models are usually specified *a priori*, and are hence deductive. Proponents of either style of modeling rarely pursue the inductive–deductive cycle in any complete sense, but the argument here suggests that fractal simulation can provide a framework for such a process. Large-scale simulation itself establishes such a framework, but there are few attempts which model the entire cycle. The work of Chapin and Weiss (1968) is an exception in that they attempted to explain urban growth using a linear statistical model and then reproduced that growth as a large-scale random simulation. The ideas of this and the last chapter are very much in this spirit but in attempting to model the entire scientific cycle, a number of corners will be cut and only picked up as items for further research.

Another issue which first emerges in this chapter relates to the variety of computer systems and software used to develop these fractally-rendered models. Our work has only been made possible through advances in computer systems and software, and our demonstrations involve a remarkable mixture of computer and modeling systems and styles. The discrete choice models we use, for example, are estimated using a standard logit package mounted on a mainframe computer, with intermediate processing on a minicomputer which acts as the front end to yet another mainframe on which the spatial mapping is conducted, while the simulations are conducted using a graphics-based micro whose memory is mainly given over to the screen display. In fact, these styles are seen quite clearly in the figures in this chapter and in the various color plates in which the spatial predictions produced for the discrete choice models are presented using standard plotter outputs, in contrast to the simulations which are illustrated in photographs of the raster graphics screen reproduced in the various color plates. Indeed throughout this book, the examples presented have been computed on micros such as PCs and high school computers, Vaxes, Sun workstations, IBM mainframes and so on. Clearly the availability of various machines has influenced what we have used, but it is important not to lose sight of the fact that fractals can be computed using very simple computer programs as Saupe (1991) has noted. Thus the ideas portrayed here should be accessible to a wide variety of readers with different programming skills and with access to very different types of computer.

After extending our hypothetical simulation model, we will take one step back and briefly introduce the model-building process in terms of explanation and simulation, induction and deduction, emphasizing the need to contain both within any complete cycle. We will show how the concept of systems hierarchy, which is so central to fractals, might be exploited through the modeling process, and we will then illustrate how this process can be completed for the fractal simulation of urban structure using the example of residential-housing location in London. The inductive approach we will adopt is based on discrete choice theory, the estimation of a standard multinomial logit model (Hensher and Johnson, 1981) to housing choice, and measurement of its performance using McFadden's (1979) predicted success statistics. We will show how the model is fitted to data which relate choice of house type and location in London to key variables of urban structure based on age and distance. Several models are fitted, some are reestimated and computer maps are used to aid the interpretation process. We are then in a position to begin the fractal simulation of urban structure on the basis of the fitted discrete choice models. The simulations are essentially visual, the data themselves being displayed on the screen and being replaced by predictions of housing types as the simulation proceeds. Two types of simulation are attempted – random and deterministic, and it is shown how it is necessary to develop deterministic procedures to enable the discrete choice models to generate realistic patterns. There are many conclusions to this chapter, and work on both fractal images (Pentland, 1984) and spatial discrete choice models (Lerman, 1985) represent major directions for further research.

4.2 Exploring Urban Forms in the Space of All Cities

The advantage of any computer model of a city is that its parameters can be varied with a view to exploring the effect of such changes on the resulting spatial form. Through visualizing the form using computer graphics, the strength of various relationships which compose urban structure can be assessed, both to improve such models in the laboratory as well as to refine relationships in terms of generating the best fit with reality. In our 'London' model of the last chapter, we could control the distribution and amount of the three land uses generated, by varying their parameters a^u, b^u and R^u. We can also vary the degree of midpoint displacement which is related to the fractal dimension. In fact in this example, if we were to collapse the random allocation of land use to a deterministic one, and use non-random midpoint displacement, we would generate a city in which commercial–industrial land use would entirely dominate the inner suburbs and CBD, and residential the outer suburbs and the periphery, providing a clear example of the von Thunen rings. This is implied in the land use profiles shown in Figure 3.13.

What we will do first is extend our model to encompass other effects. We will increase our land uses by disaggregating the residential sector into three types – high, medium and low density housing, and split the commercial–industrial use into their two separate components. We argued earlier that at different hierarchical levels, various activities might dominate. For example, if we were simulating the growth of an industrial city, then decisions about location depend on the characteristics of a neighborhood. Industrial neighborhoods tend to attract like industries, while residential activity tends to avoid location there, and so on. We will extend our model by allocating land use at each hierarchical level, and using the land use allocation at that level to determine land use allocation at the next. The way this mechanism might work is for a neighborhood to be classed in terms of its dominant land use at the first spatial level of the simulation and then for this dominance to be reflected at the next level of detail down. This involves modification of the probabilities of allocation at that level, these being conditional on the probabilities of land use at the next.

The way we simulate this effect is by modifying equation (3.29) in the following manner:

$$p^u(r_s) = a^u + b^u (r_s - R^u), \quad u = 1, 2, ..., 6, \qquad (4.1)$$

where a^u, b^u and R^u are parameters as before but the distance r_s now reflects the fact that equation (4.1) is applied at each level s of hierarchical simulation. Land use is not actually allocated at level s by the model but at the next level down, $p^u(r_s)$ is used to condition a new probability $P^u(r_{s+1})$ using the following equation:

$$P^u(r_{s+1}) \propto [1 + P^u(r_s)]^{\gamma(u)} p^u(r_{s+1}). \qquad (4.2)$$

$P^u(r_{s+1})$ is the probability used to effect the allocation. In fact the allocation only takes place at the most detailed level of resolution and this probability is in fact that passed down from the previous level which acts on the basic probability given by equation (4.1). $\gamma(u)$ is a parameter greater than 0 which measures the importance of the effects at previous levels. If $\gamma(u)$ is equal to 0, then there is no effect from previous levels and $P^u(r_{s+1}) = p^u(r_{s+1})$. The strength of the influence increases as $\gamma(u)$ increases in value and in the simulations to be shown next we have set $\gamma(u)$ at five values, namely $\gamma(u) = 0, 1, 5, 25$ and 50. Of course equation (4.2) has to be appropriately normalized. We have not made $\gamma(u)$, a^u, b^u or R^u specific to each level because the number of possible combinations of values becomes too large to handle, and in the interest of developing parsimonious but general models, we have begun our experiments with as small a number of parameters as possible.

We will now explore some 20 possible urban forms and the tree of possibilities defining the 'space of all cities' within which different forms exist is shown in Figure 4.1. First we can allocate our land use randomly as in the last section or in deterministic fashion based on the dominant land use predictor at each level and in terms of each basic location. This gives us two choices. As our fractal simulations are based on midpoint displacement of the pure Brownian type with a Hurst exponent $H = 1/2$, then we can either use that level of random displacement of the midpoint or no randomness whatsoever; this also gives us two options. Finally we can use the five values of $\gamma(u)$ and this gives us five possibilities when we keep each value of $\gamma(u)$ the same for each land use u across all hierarchical levels. In total therefore, we have 20 options to simulate. This modified fractal model was simulated on a Sun workstation, and some of its outputs are illustrated in Plate 4.1 (see color section) where the simulations are shown at levels

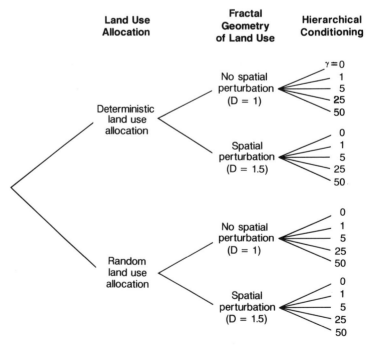

Figure 4.1. The combinatorial map of the space of all cities.

$s = 2$, 4 and 6, thus illustrating once again the extent to which the patterns become more realistic as the scale gets more detailed.

In Plate 4.1, we present six from the 20 simulations to give some flavor of the differences. The deterministic model based on no fractal perturbation, deterministic allocation of land use, and no hierarchical conditioning where $\gamma(u) = 0$, $\forall u$ produces classic von Thunen rings, and as such, represents the theoretical baseline for all our simulations. The CBD and inner areas are dominated by commercial use, while there are three other rings of high, medium and low density housing. Open space and industrial uses do not dominate anywhere, and because any area of the city contains its most dominant land use, these two uses never have a chance of being located. The other feature worth noting is that because there is no fractal perturbation, then the final units for location are identical and perfectly formed triangles. This simulation is illustrated in Plate 4.1(a), and it is just possible to make out the perfect symmetry of the triangles formed by midpoint displacement with no randomness. If we introduce fractal rendering for the same set of parameters, then the von Thunen rings simply appear somewhat cracked due to the fact that the sites are no longer identical in terms of shape and location, although the outputs are still highly reminiscent of von Thunen's theoretical model; this is shown in Plate 4.1(b).

In Plate 4.1(c), we show what happens when heavy hierarchical conditioning is introduced to the model which has fractal rendering but deterministic land use allocation. The heavy conditioning is enabled with $\gamma(u) = 25$ for all six land uses, and the effect is to produce a very strange pattern in which residential land uses dominate everywhere. This is clearly unusual, quite extreme and unlikely to be observed anywhere. Next we show in Plate 4.1(d), the simulation based on no fractal perturbation, hence perfect triangles as sites, randomness in land use allocation, and extreme hierarchical conditioning. Again this produces a slightly more realistic pattern, but one which is sufficiently different from reality to be somewhat unlikely. Note the way the perfect triangles appear at any level here due to the fact that $\gamma(u) = 50$ for all land uses. Reducing the hierarchical factor $\gamma(u)$ to 5 produces more realism as in Plate 4.1(e), while finally in Plate 4.1(f), we show the most realistic simulation we have achieved, based on fractal perturbation, randomness in land use allocation and very slight hierarchical conditioning [$\gamma(u) = 1$, $\forall u$]. This case is interesting in that the simulation at level $s = 4$ is more realistic than $s = 6$ which is, once again, reminiscent of pointillist painting.

The examples we have shown provide a good cross-section of the possible patterns which compose the experiments in our laboratory: we have four examples of hierarchical conditioning and the four possibilities in terms of land use allocation and spatial perturbation. What is quite clear here is that the hierarchical conditioning is far too extreme once it rises much above $\gamma(u) = 1$. Moreover, it is the randomness in land use allocation which seems to provide more of the realism in contrast to fractal perturbation although the fractal perturbation does indicate that the problem of creasing becomes considerably more apparent as hierarchical conditioning is increased. In fact, it is clear that although our model is more realistic than the one we developed in the last section for 'London', it is still fairly unrealistic in its incorporation of hierarchy and of fractal perturbation where the choice is either $H = 1/2$ or non-random midpoint displacement.

Our last foray into this type of fractal modeling partly resolves the problems of the models just outlined in two important ways. We will now introduce control over the fractal dimension in quite explicit terms and we will reduce the range of hierarchical conditioning to screen out the extreme effects such as those shown in Plate 4.1(c) and (d). Thus, the most extreme conditioning in the new model is where $\gamma(u)$ is equivalent to 5 (but on a new scale where this value is given as 25). Another innovation which we find useful is based on replacing the triangular lattice with a square grid. In Figure 4.2, we show this grid and how successive random midpoint

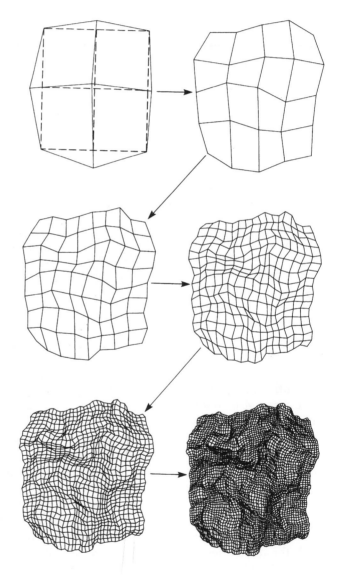

Figure 4.2.   Simulating patterns using midpoint displacement of a square grid.

displacement enables a surface to be produced which appears to have less creasing than the triangular. Moreover, as the grid is based on the unit square, there is no measure of distortion present in the first place and thus this would appear a less arbitrary and less biased form of initiator. We have also increased the land uses in the residential sector to be defined over a continuum of population densities, and this makes the simulations more realistic in that densities are determined as a combination of random allocation and distance from the CBD. In effect, this does not add to the number of land uses *per se*, as the simulation is structured to determine the density of the residential use at the stage when this use is allocated.

We show typical simulations from this model in Plate 4.2(a) and (b). In (a), a fractal dimension of 1.26 has been used, hierarchical conditioning is heavy with a value of 5, and randomness in land use allocation has been used. In fact, this simulation is more realistic than any of those shown in Plate 4.1 and it would appear that our new model provides an ideal basis for computer experimentation. We cannot show all the possibilities here, but in Plate 4.2(b), we show the von Thunen rings case where the fractal dimension is unity (no spatial perturbation), there is no hierarchical conditioning and land use allocation is deterministic. In these examples we have also separated out the residential from other land uses, thus showing how the different patterns stand by themselves. In this way, it would appear that both the residential and commercial land uses, which make up most of the city, have distinctive location patterns which are close to those we might observe in existing cities.

There are many more variants we can generate using this model. Clearly we can let the fractal dimension range from 1 to 2, we can explore a range of hierarchical conditioning from $\gamma = 0$ to $\gamma = 5$, and we can make this parameter specific to each level s and/or each land use u. We can even let these parameters take on values outside the range of 0 to 5. But the models developed here simulate only one type of city, the monocentric, and thus it is important to simulate forms other than those which are unipolar and concentric. This would involve introducing mechanisms which measure the accessibility of any point in the city to any other and it would take us towards the mainstream of urban modeling which is based on spatial inter-action (Batty, 1976). In fact throughout this book, we will steer well clear of these types of models because these are for a very different purpose. Although we continually allude to fitting fractal models to real situations, in the last analysis, our exposition of fractal cities is motivated by our search for the applicability of these ideas, and the insights they might give to the broad domain of urban studies. Indeed from Chapter 7 onwards, we will begin to demonstrate how fractal models give us a very different perspective on studies of urban density, which suggest that much previous research should be reworked. The value, then, of these forays into hypothetical urban form is in the applicability of the fractal idea and the somewhat more superficial idea of visualizing computer models using fractal rendering. We will now turn to more realistic examples, developing a conventional urban model of housing in London and then showing how its predictions can be best evaluated in terms of the spatial forms that they imply.

4.3 Hierarchical Urban Structure

So far the hierarchical structures we have introduced do not relate to any observable characteristics of city systems except in the most superficial way. Clearly for levels $s < 4$ in Plate 4.1, the images generated show the strong influence of the triangular patches making up the hierarchy and are thus not realistic. When levels with $s \geq 4$ are reached, the images no longer display the influence of the triangular method in that the concatenation of triangles at these levels produces the sorts of irregularity characteristic of land use patterns. Thus in one sense, the triangular subdivision process is scale-dependent. However, in fractal simulation, there is still the need to relate the method of construction to substantive characteristics of the system as in other forms of modeling. Indeed, many examples of fractals can only be modelled coherently by defining their intrinsic properties of self-similarity: trees, for example, are self-similar through their mode of reproduction and growth. In geomorphology, the process of weathering and erosion acts in a self-similar fashion. This is clearly true for cities as well and thus hierarchical structure must reflect this.

We can sketch an idealized process of fractal simulation to which we might aspire. We begin by identifying hierarchy in the system of interest based on our perception of self-similarity in description, and we are then able to measure whether or not the phenomenon is fractal and whether or not the fractal dimension is invariant to changes in scale. Each stage of measurement and description leads to further development of the underlying process through which the structure can be generated, and this in turn leads to models which are consistent with fractal structure. Once appropriate models, applicable to different levels of the spatial hierarchy, have been developed, other fractal structures utilizing such hierarchy and incorporating the application of the underlying process through recursion, can be simulated.

This approach is in fact the classic process of observing a phenomenon, deciding whether or not it meets any theoretical preconceptions we have, developing a 'best' model structure, and then using this to enable new and different predictions to be made. Essentially this is the process of induction followed by deduction, or in a different sense, analysis followed by synthesis. We can think of induction as a process of building theory from the bottom up, from specifics to universals, while deduction is a top-down process in which universals are used to predict specifics. The best expression of this complete process is in the fields of design and problem-solving where problems must be understood (through induction and analysis) prior to their solution (through deduction and synthesis). In fact in design, methods for analysis and synthesis exist which are based on searching for hierarchical structure: problems are decomposed in the quest to induce their structure and thence composed in the quest to synthesize a solution from the elements (Alexander, 1964; Johnson, 1984). There are parallels with the process used here to enable appropriate description and explanation prior to fractal simulation.

A simple example which relates to spatial theory is the rank–size distribution of cities. City size distributions display regular properties which are consistent with subdivision of a national or regional space into market areas whose decreasing size reflects the frequency of spatial dependence and the rarity value of spatial goods. Idealized size distributions can be developed by taking a primate city and its national market area, generating two next order cities, then four, and eight, and so on, in the manner we illustrated in Chapter 1 in equations (1.1) to (1.4). This is the type of method used in Central Place Theory, and another interpretation using fractal geometry has been developed by Wong and Fotheringham (1990). In terms of our complete cycle of model-building, we first need to identify the hierarchy of market area, transport routes, population centers etc., thus explaining spatial structure at different levels. This is accomplished inductively in bottom-up fashion, possibly using clustering type methods. The simulation then begins from the top-most level in the hierarchy by subdivision and fractal rendering, generating centers and activities at different scales in such a way that lower levels depend on upper. Although there is a sense in which the simultaneity of dependence is treated by correct bottom-up followed by top-down analysis, in terms of fractal simulation which is arbitrarily structured in hierarchial terms, the dependence is only one way. In fact, this is a problem with many hierarchical descriptions for it is clear that any activity at any position in the hierarchy owes its stability to those activities both above and below. This is the concept of 'niche' and it is something which must be explored in considerable depth in further research on fractal simulation.

In spatial modeling, there are some very well-developed techniques to effect this process of hierarchical explanation and simulation. The logical output of a process of continual subdivision is the elemental space which contains the individual, and thus individual behavior lies at the base of the spatial hierarchy. Such models have been widely developed during the last decade to address problems of discrete choice in the economic domain using standard methods of econometric estimation (Lerman, 1985). These are the models which will be used here, and a particularly attractive feature of them is the fact that they can easily and logically incorporate hierarchical structure: these are the so-called sequential or nested logit models (Hensher and Johnson, 1981).

As yet, very few applications exist of truly spatial discrete choice models, and even fewer have been developed in a spatially-nested form. Nevertheless, these models appear promising as the basis of the recursive generation of activity through the spatial hierarchy. The other class of models which will be considered at a later stage of this research, and which are related to discrete choice models, are spatial interaction-entropy models. It is well-known that such models have highly articulate properties of spatial decomposition (Roy, 1983) and this also makes them attractive to hierarchical simulation. There are a variety of methods for enabling hierarchy to be defined and built into spatial models, such as the standard multivariate cluster-type techniques as well as methods based on more subjective comparisons such as Saaty's (1980) analytic hierarchy process; these could also prove useful to further research.

In the sequel, we will not attempt to address the full process of hierarchical description through the identification and use of hierarchical models but we will follow the broad sequence of inductive, then deductive stages in the modeling process. We will begin by selecting models for individual choice of housing type and location in Greater London which is the urban region we intend to simulate. This first involves a traditional process of formulating, estimating and selecting appropriate discrete choice models. Having accomplished this, we will move onto the simulation in which these discrete choice models are used to predict housing choice at the lowest level of fractal detail generated. In this way, an image of the residential urban structure of Greater London is built up. Hierarchy is still a largely arbitrary affair in these applications, although we will address it in future research. But there are other problems relating to modeling and simulation which emerge and must be dealt with, specifically related to spatial variation. In any case, the logical next step in this work is to develop a 'realistic' version of our hypothetical simulation presented earlier. To this end, we will now sketch the inductive side of this effort, beginning with the theory of discrete choice and its application to residential housing location in Greater London.

4.4 Discrete Choice Models of Urban Structure

To set the context, we must review some fairly standard results but in doing so, we will adapt discrete choice models to our application and thus only select those aspects which are of relevance here. We will first state the multinomial logit model (MNL) in which we can identify the choice by individual i, $i = 1, 2, \ldots, N$, of alternative k, from the set of alternatives $k = 1, 2, \ldots, K$, where there are clearly N individuals in the system making choices from K alternatives. This set of K is referred to as the choice set and in our applications involves types of housing. The MNL model predicts a probability P_{ik} which is the probability of individual i choosing house type k where there are $K = 4$ house types to choose from, and where i implicitly represents the location of the individual in the city. Thus the model is designed to explain choice in terms of location.

First we must associate a utility of choosing alternative k with the individual i. This utility U_{ik} is usually specified as a linear sum of exogenous (input) variables which may be specific to the choice in question or non-specific (generic). In our context, the parameters of these variables are made specific, being referred to as alternative specific constants, but the variables apply to each house type. Then

$$U_{ik} = \sum_m \beta_{km} \, x_{im} + \epsilon_{im}, \, m = 1, 2, \ldots, M,$$

where the first term on the right-hand side of the equation contains strict utility components made up of parameters β_{km} and independent variables x_{im}, and the error term ϵ_{im} reflects differences in tastes, unobservable influences and such like. The MNL model is derived by assuming that the error components $\{\epsilon_{im}\}$ are identically and independently distributed, and by maximizing utility using the traditional economic logic (Hensher and Johnson, 1981; Ben Akiva and Lerman, 1985). This random utility derivation of the MNL model is subject to the normalization

$$\sum_k P_{ik} = 1,$$

and the model is derived as

$$P_k = \frac{\exp\{U_{ik}\}}{\sum_u \exp\{U_{iu}\}} = \frac{\exp\left\{\sum_m \beta_{km} x_{im}\right\}}{\sum_u \exp\left\{\sum_m \beta_{um} x_{im}\right\}}. \tag{4.3}$$

These sorts of models have been widely applied in transport research, but have also been adapted to a variety of spatial contexts (see Wrigley, 1985). We will not dwell on this, but suffice it to say that equation (4.3) is a particularly flexible and adaptable model structure.

For purposes of estimation and prediction we need to express equation (4.3) somewhat differently. First we must choose one alternative, say k, as the base or numeraire, and express equation (4.3) as

$$P_{ik} = \frac{1}{1 + \sum_{u \neq k} \exp\left\{\sum_m (\beta_{um} - \beta_{km}) x_{im}\right\}}. \tag{4.4}$$

We form the ratio of any two probabilities for different choice alternatives u and k using equation (4.3), and this gives

$$\frac{P_{iu}}{P_{ik}} = \frac{\exp\left\{\sum_m \beta_{um} x_{im}\right\}}{\exp\left\{\sum_m \beta_{km} x_{im}\right\}} = \exp\left\{\sum_m (\beta_{um} - \beta_{km}) x_{im}\right\}. \tag{4.5}$$

We can now express P_{iu} in terms of the numeraire P_{ik} using equations (4.4) and (4.5) which simplify to

$$P_{iu} = P_{ik} \exp\left\{\sum_m (\beta_{um} - \beta_{km}) x_{im}\right\}$$

$$= \frac{\exp\left\{\sum_m (\beta_{um} - \beta_{km}) x_{im}\right\}}{1 + \sum_{u \neq k} \exp\left\{\sum_m (\beta_{um} - \beta_{km}) x_{im}\right\}}. \tag{4.6}$$

When $k = u$, equation (4.6) collapses to equation (4.4). In the sequel, equation (4.5) is used in estimation while model predictions are made using equation (4.6).

4.5 Estimation Methods for the Multinomial Logit Model

The logarithm of equation (4.5) is referred to as the log-odds of alternative u versus k, and this is the actual equation which is used in estimation. Then

$$\log \frac{P_{iu}}{P_{ik}} = \sum_m (\beta_{um} - \beta_{km}) \, x_{im} = \sum_m \lambda_{um} \, x_{im}. \qquad (4.7)$$

There is a clear interpretation of the parameters in equation (4.7). If λ_{um} is positive, this implies that the choice of alternative u is more important with respect to the variable x_{im} in question than the choice of alternative k. The reverse is true if λ_{um} is negative, while there is no difference in importance between choices if $\lambda_{um} = 0$.

The model parameters in equation (4.7) are usually estimated using weighted least squares or maximum-likelihood, and here we prefer to use the latter because of the availability of Hensher's BLOGIT computer package (Hensher and Johnson, 1981). To assess goodness of fit we also require the data set of actual choices made which is given as F_{ik} where $F_{ik} = 1$ if i actually chose k, while $F_{ik} = 0$ if this choice was not made. We calibrate the model by maximizing the log-likelihood which is given as

$$\Lambda(\beta) = \sum_i \sum_k F_{ik} \log P_{ik}, \qquad (4.8)$$

and we can also assess the fit as a variation of this likelihood function. A null hypothesis can be set up in which $\beta_{um} = 0$, $\forall \, u,m$ implying no variation across individuals, that is, $P_{ik} = P_k$, $\forall i$. This can be used to compute the null-likelihood from equation (4.8) which is given as

$$\Lambda(0) = \sum_i \sum_k F_{ik} \log P_k = \sum_k N_k \log P_k, \qquad (4.9)$$

where N_k is the actual number of choices of k made by all individuals i. A measure of fit, in some ways similar to the correlation coefficient, is defined as ξ^2. This statistic is defined as

$$\xi^2 = 1 - \frac{\Lambda(\beta)}{\Lambda(0)}, \qquad (4.10)$$

which varies between 0 and 1. The statistic can also be modified to reflect degrees of freedom, while typically good value of ξ^2 range between 0.2 and 0.4. In fact Hensher and Johnson (1981) argue that any model with $\xi^2 > 0.2$ is likely to be acceptable. Other measures of fit and diagnostics for log–linear model equations are discussed in Wrigley and Longley (1984), Wrigley (1985), and Ben Akiva and Lerman (1985).

There is a major difficulty in generating less global goodness of fit measures for discrete choice models. Because the observed data represents discrete choices $\{F_{ik}, F_{ik} = 0 \text{ or } 1\}$ while the predictions are given as probabilities $\{P_{ik}, 0 \le P_{ik} \le 1\}$, comparisons at the individual level are meaningless. Thus some aggregation is always necessary. One scheme suggested by McFadden (1979) involves computing expected choices, that is, the numbers of individuals who originally chose alternative k and are expected to choose alternative u. In fact, in later simulations we will examine individual predictions, but for the applications to London which follow, comparisons between observations and predictions will be confined to success statistics based on expected choices.

To introduce these statistics, first note the structure of the observed choice set $\{F_{ik}\}$. Then by definition,

$$\sum_k F_{ik} = 1, \sum_i F_{ik} = N_k,$$

$$\sum_i \sum_k F_{ik} = \sum_k N_k = N. \qquad (4.11)$$

The first equation in (4.11) implies that any individual can only make one choice, the second is the constraint on the number of choices made for each alternative, while the third simply says that all the number of choices made is the same as the number of individuals N. The analogous structure for the probability set $\{P_{ik}\}$ is

$$\sum_k P_{ik} = 1, \sum_i P_{ik} = \check{N}_k,$$

$$\sum_i \sum_k P_{ik} = \sum_k \check{N}_k = N. \qquad (4.12)$$

Similar interpretations for equations (4.12) exist as for those in (4.11), but note that summation of $\{P_{ik}\}$ with respect to individuals yields predicted numbers of choices $\check{N}_k$ in contrast to actual numbers N_k.

For each individual choice F_{ik} (where $F_{ik} = 1$) there is a probability that the same individual will make a different choice P_{iu}. The number of such choices across all individuals is the number of individuals who originally chose k and are expected to choose u, and this is defined as

$$N_{ku} = \sum_i F_{ik} P_{iu}. \qquad (4.13)$$

$\{N_{ku}\}$ is the so-called predicted success matrix. Using equations (4.11) to (4.13), the matrix has the following properties:

$$\sum_u N_{ku} = \sum_i F_{ik} \sum_u P_{iu} = \check{N}_k \qquad (4.14)$$

and

$$\sum_k N_{ku} = \sum_i \left(\sum_k F_{ik} \right) P_{iu} = \check{N}_u. \qquad (4.15)$$

From these definitions it is clear that

$$\sum_k \sum_u N_{ku} = \sum_k N_k = \sum_u \check{N}_u = N.$$

We can devise a variety of statistics relating to proportions and differences between observed and predicted successes using these aggregations. First we can compute the proportion of correct predictions, noting that N_{kk} gives the number of such correct predictions. Then

$$\eta_k = N_{kk}/N_k, \qquad (4.16)$$

which varies between 0 and 1. Total predictive success occurs when $N_{kk} = N_k$, $\forall k$ and $N_{ku} = 0$, $k \neq u$. For the entire system the equivalent statistic to equation (4.16) is defined as

$$\eta = \sum_k N_{kk}/N. \qquad (4.17)$$

The second index relates to differences between predicted and observed numbers of choices, expressed as proportions or shares. An absolute measure of this index is given by $N_k - \check{N}_k$ while its relative form is defined as

$$\phi_k = (N_k - \check{N}_k)/N, \tag{4.18}$$

which can be positive or negative.

The final index we have computed is called by McFadden (1979) the prediction-success index φ_k. One problem is that if the predicted choices for u were much larger than k, that is if $\check{N}_k \gg N_k$, then the value N_{ku} would be affected accordingly. To account for this, φ_k is defined as

$$\varphi_k = \frac{N_{kk}}{\check{N}_k} - \frac{\check{N}_k}{N},$$

and an overall index φ, appropriately weighted, is defined as

$$\varphi = \sum_k \frac{\check{N}_k}{N}\, \varphi_k = \sum_k \left\{ \frac{N_{kk}}{N} - \left(\frac{\check{N}_k}{N}\right)^2 \right\}. \tag{4.19}$$

The maximum value of φ occurs when $\sum_k N_{kk} = N$, and then

$$\varphi_{\max} = 1 - \sum_k \left(\frac{\check{N}_k}{N}\right)^2. \tag{4.20}$$

A normalized measure is given by $\varphi/\varphi_{\max}$; other applications are given in Wrigley (1985). These indices based on equations (4.13) to (4.20) will be further adapted in the empirical work which follows to aggregations of subsets of individuals located in specific zones; these will be presented below.

4.6 Determinants of Spatial Structure: the Data Base

Conventional descriptions of urban structure tend to be based on disaggregations of urban activities into land use by type and location. One realization of conventional structure was used in the hypothetical 'London' demonstration model presented in the last chapter and its extensions presented earlier in this. In those models, commercial–industrial (work), residential (living) and open space (leisure) activities were treated in a locational framework which emphasized in diverse ways the radial and concentric nature of the contemporary city. It is not possible to take this model further to the applications stage here, largely because we do not have easy access to a comprehensive land use–activity data base. Moreover, we are interested in developing more formally structured discrete choice models which can be embedded within the fractal simulation, thus enabling us to assess the impact of individual spatial choice behavior in the large.

Another consideration which has guided us is not just the absence but the availability of data. We have access to a large-scale housing survey –

the English House Condition Survey (EHCS: DoE, 1978, 1979) – which was conducted in 1976. This was based on a fairly low sample of households in England, something in the order of 1 in 3000, but this represents an easily available, highly disaggregate data source and thus we have chosen to make use of it. Logit models of housing tenure choice have previously been calibrated using this data set (Longley, 1984).

We have chosen housing type as the key variable defining urban structure which is a major category in the EHCS data. Houses are classified into five types: purpose-built flats (apartments), converted flats, terraced (row) houses, detached/semi-detached (single-family) houses, and a miscellaneous group. House type is a particularly clear way of representing urban structure for different areas of the city are often perceived generally in terms of house type: historically, cities have grown reflecting different house types, and house type seems to relate to how far people wish to live from the CBD. Cities are often articulated as spatial patterns with flats near the center, terraced houses occupying the inner suburbs, detached/semi-detached the outer suburbs, each ring reflecting a stage in city growth. Thus density and distance variables are indirectly reflected in house type, and in the case of London, this is particularly relevant in that the city is strongly monocentric, has a well-developed flats market and has been economically buoyant for several centuries. In our applications, we have in fact excluded the miscellaneous category because of the fact that it acts as a residual category and contains less than 2% of the observations available in the data base.

Choice of house type lies at the base of several contemporary theories of urban structure which integrate two important constructs. First, bid-rent theory postulates an implicit trade-off in housing decisions between housing space and type versus proximity to, or distance from, central urban functions; and urban growth and dynamics (as manifest by filtering, suburbanization, urban renewal etc., and as expressed in the age of the stock) exhibit an identifiable correspondence with distinctive dwelling types such as subdivided central city houses, suburban semi-detached homes, purpose-built flats in revitalized inner city neighborhoods and so on. The implication is that dwelling and neighborhood type are clearly related to distance from the CBD and the date at which the land parcel was integrated (or reintegrated) into the contemporary urban development process.

Thus age and distance represent key determinants of urban structure. In designing the models, it was thought important to keep these variables as simple as possible and at the same time, easily measurable. We also considered neighborhood quality at an early stage, but eventually dropped this to keep the model simple; in any case, neighborhood quality was subjectively specified in the EHCS data and thus difficult to predict generally. Age of house in which the household respondent resided was available in the survey, but distance from the CBD was not, and this constitutes a problem. Each individual was not coded by exact location in the data set, but located by Borough, of which there are 33 in Greater London. What we have done in measuring distance is to simply locate a centroid in each Borough and use airline distance from this to a point in the City.

Another consideration involved the fact that when we embed the discrete choice models into the large-scale (fractal) simulation, we require data on age of housing and distance from the CBD at every conceivable point of residential development in Greater London. These data are amongst the easiest to obtain from independent sources. We used an age distribution for housing measured over seven levels which was available from the (then) Greater London Council (GLC) Intelligence Unit Library. Distance is measurable directly from the map, while neighborhood quality, although available from the GLC, did not appear to match that used in the EHCS, and was thus excluded at an early stage of model estimation.

The general form of the models we have estimated, in log-odds form, is

$$\log \frac{P_{iu}}{P_{i1}} = \lambda_{u0} + \lambda_{u1}R_n + \lambda_{u2}Q_i, \ i \in Z_n, \ u = 2, 3, 4. \tag{4.21}$$

The log-odds equation is normalized with respect to the probability of choosing a purpose-built flat, P_{i1} and the other choices involved converted flats ($u = 2$), terraced houses ($u = 3$) and detached/semi-detached homes ($u = 4$). Q_i is the age of the dwelling in which individual i resided and R_n is the distance from the CBD to the centroid of the Borough in which i resides.

In essence, we assume that R_i is unobserved and that equation (4.21) is an appropriate approximation to the underlying discrete choice model analogous to equation (4.21) in which R_i replaces R_n. Equation (4.21) will only be acceptable if R_n is the mean distance, and the sum of the differences around R_n in the Borough cancel. Formally, if $R_i = R_n + \epsilon_i$ where ϵ_i is the 'error' difference between the mean and the actual distance to individual i, the average R_n can be defined in terms of R_i as

$$\sum_{i \in Z_n} R_i/N_n = R_n + \sum_{i \in Z_n} \epsilon_i/N_n. \tag{4.22}$$

Z_n is the spatial definition of the Borough n and N_n is the number of individuals in Z_n. From equation (4.22), the mean will only be equal to R_n if $\Sigma_{i \in Z} \epsilon_i = 0$, that is the errors around the mean are self-canceling in total. We cannot explore the detailed implications of this aggregation further, but it is important to further research. Discrete choice theory is strangely deficient in clear discussion of the spatial aggregation problem, with the exception of important work by Anas (1981, 1982, 1983).

Before we broach questions of model selection and estimation, we will sketch how the model we are working with could be developed in nested fashion, to account not only for the aggregate form of the distance data, but also for more substantive questions related to the sequence of spatial decision-making. Because distance from CBD is only available at Borough level, it might make sense to conceive the house type–residential location process as one in which a choice of neighborhood type is made first on the Borough (Z_n) level in terms of neighborhood quality and distance from the CBD and then the choice of house type made at the individual location with respect to age. Such a model could be written as

$$P_{iqk} = P_{iq} P_{ik|q},$$

where P_{iqk} is the probability of an individual i choosing neighborhood type q and house type k, P_{iq} the probability that the individual chooses neighborhood type q at Borough level and $P_{ik|q}$ the probability the same individual then chooses house type k, having chosen neighborhood type q. Such a sequence could be structured so that the fractal simulation enabled neighborhood type to be chosen at an appropriate level of fractal resolution, house-type at a lower level. Although neighborhood type is predicted here, this could be suppressed if it were regarded as only an intermediate variable of little visual significance. There are many issues to resolve here, but some work along these lines in an industrial location context by Hayashi and Isobe (1985) looks promising, as does the theoretical work of Roy (1983). Nested models of this type need to be pursued in extensions to these applications.

4.7 Model Selection and Estimation

We developed a number of preliminary specifications of the model before we decided upon equation (4.21). We first estimated some models based on housing tenure but then dropped these in favor of house type when our ideas relating to urban structure became clearer. We began with five categories of house type including miscellaneous but dropped this when it appeared non-significant in explanation. We then estimated the house type model with all combinations of up to three exogenous variables: age and distance which we eventually selected, but also neighborhood quality. With three variables, there are seven models in all which can be specified and the global fit of each of these seven is given in Table 4.1.

By far the best of the models, indicated in bold type in Table 4.1, are the two which include the age and distance variables. These models in fact are the only ones which reach the threshold of acceptability in which $\xi^2 > 0.2$ suggested by Hensher and Johnson (1981). The best model also includes neighborhood quality but the percentage increase in fit between the model without this variable and that with is less than 5% and thus neighborhood quality has been omitted. Other reasons relate to the fact that neighborhood quality is difficult to produce in a consistent and comprehensive data base for London, and to the fact that in our fractal simulations we have severe memory limitations, which means we need to hold both input and output

Table 4.1.   Global fits of models incorporating age, distance and neighborhood quality

Independent variables	ξ^2
Age	0.118
Distance	0.089
Neighborhood quality	0.069
Age and distance	**0.207**
Age and neighborhood quality	0.123
Distance and neighborhood quality	0.095
Age, distance and neighborhood quality	**0.218**

Bold type indicates acceptable models within the Hensher–Johnson Limit $\xi^2 > 0.2$.

data in screen memory simultaneously. This limits the number of variables we can deal with and thus neighborhood quality was felt to be dispensable.

We will now examine the discrete choice model estimated for the age–distance variables in equation (4.21). The three fitted equations are given as follows, with the notation: purpose-built flats: $u = 1$, converted flats: $u = 2$, terraced houses: $u = 3$ and detached/semi-detached houses: $u = 4$.

$$\log \frac{P_{i2}}{P_{i1}} = \begin{matrix} -4.862 \\ \{-7.984\}^* \\ (0.609) \end{matrix} + \begin{matrix} 0.034\,R_n \\ \{0.754\} \\ (0.045) \end{matrix} + \begin{matrix} 0.067Q_{i,} \\ \{10.599\}^* \\ (0.006) \end{matrix} \tag{4.23a}$$

$$\log \frac{P_{i3}}{P_{i1}} = \begin{matrix} -3.605 \\ \{-9.818\}^* \\ (0.367) \end{matrix} + \begin{matrix} 0.177R_n \\ \{6.735\}^* \\ (0.026) \end{matrix} + \begin{matrix} 0.052Q_{i,} \\ \{11.439\}^* \\ (0.005) \end{matrix} \tag{4.23b}$$

$$\log \frac{P_{i4}}{P_{i1}} = \begin{matrix} -5.737 \\ \{-12.143\} \\ (0.472) \end{matrix} + \begin{matrix} 0.354R_n \\ \{11.379\}^* \\ (0.031) \end{matrix} + \begin{matrix} 0.046Q_{i,} \\ \{9.102\}^* \\ (0.005) \end{matrix} \tag{4.23c}$$

where $\xi^2 = 0.207$ and $N = 809$. t statistics are shown in curly brackets, significance being denoted by an asterisk; standard errors are shown in parentheses.

Note that the log-odds is essentially the log-likelihood that individual i will select the numerator alternative rather than the denominator alternative. In view of the aggregated nature of the distance data, the ξ^2 of 0.207 indicates a reasonable degree of overall fit, whilst the variable parameters and their corresponding t statistics lend support to our *a priori* expectations. Equations (4.23b) and (4.23c) imply that both terraced and detached/semi-detached are likely to be further from the CBD and to be older than purpose-built flats; and equation (4.23a) suggests that converted flats are likely to be older than their purpose-built counterparts.

These interpretations can only be borne out by a full-scale simulation and the pattern of coefficients suggests that flats of both kinds are nearest to the CBD, while terraced, then detached/semi-detached houses are further away, assuming that terraced are older than detached/semi-detached. As we intend the simulation to be entirely spatial, and spatial structure is not apparent from the model fits presented so far, we need to see how well the models perform spatially at an aggregate level first. The obvious level on which to perform such spatial analysis is similarly aggregate. We will present our analysis visually in the next section where the models' predictive success indices are mapped for the 33 Boroughs.

We have already shown that it is necessary to aggregate individual predicted probabilities so that we can enable some comparison with the observed data. To this end, we introduced McFadden's (1979) predicted success matrix in equations (4.11) to (4.15), and then presented various indices of success in which correct proportions, and differences between observed and predicted choices were computed in equations (4.16) to (4.20). However, it is possible to compute equation (4.13), the numbers of persons originally choosing k and predicted to choose u, for subsets of individuals, in particular individuals residing in certain zones, in this case Boroughs Z_n. In all the indices which follow equation (4.13), N_{ku} is replaced with

$$N_{kun} = \sum_{i \in Z_n} F_{ik}\, P_{iu}, \tag{4.24}$$

where N_{kun} is the number of individuals originally choosing k and predicted to choose u in Borough Z_n.

The proportion of correct predictions defined in equations (4.16) and (4.17) for the whole of Greater London can act as a basis for comparison with their zonal equivalents. These statistics were computed using the model in equation (4.23) as

$$\eta_1 = 0.533,\ \eta_2 = 0.198,\ \eta_3 = 0.433,\ \text{and}\ \eta_4 = 0.397.$$

These indices seem rather low; only in the case of purpose-built flats is there a better than 50% success rate, and converted flats are poorly predicted. The overall percentage of correct predictions from equation (4.17) is computed as $\eta = 0.432$ which is an appropriate average of $\{\eta_k\}$. The spatial (zonal Z_n) equivalents of η_k called η_{kn} are mapped across the 33 Boroughs in Figure 4.3 (note that in all these types of map, the City Borough does not contain any observations and thus is not shaded). These percent-correct predictions show a much wider range of variation. In general, purpose-built flats are better predicted closer to the CBD, while the reverse holds for detached/semi-detached houses. The distribution of converted flats generally shows a low percent prediction with a slight increase towards the CBD while terraced houses show a less distinctive spatial pattern with a slight increase in performance towards the periphery. In fact, Figure 4.3 contains the clearest demonstration we have that individual choice behavior varies spatially. The obvious conclusion is that there are two sets of models, one for inner, the other for outer London, but before we consider these further, we will examine other indices of predictive success.

Indices of the percentage difference between observed and predicted choices given by equation (4.18), $\{\phi_k\}$ have been computed in spatial equivalent form and are mapped in Figure 4.4. The patterns are much less clear than those in Figure 4.3. For purpose-built flats, the largest differences are in the inner suburbs, and the smallest in the center and the west. For converted flats, the pattern is much more random with a slight bias towards higher differences in the inner suburbs. For terraced houses, the inner suburbs show higher levels of under- and over-prediction in the cases of detached/semi-detached houses. These maps are more difficult to interpret than their counterparts in Figure 4.3. What they do show, however, is that there are both sectoral and concentric–geometric spatial biases in the pattern of predictions which can only be accounted for by the addition of new and different explanatory variables (and the possible deletion of one of the existing ones), or the development of models which accept these spatial differences. We will pursue the latter course.

To conclude, it is useful to examine the pattern of overall correct predictions from equation (4.17), computed and mapped spatially, and this is

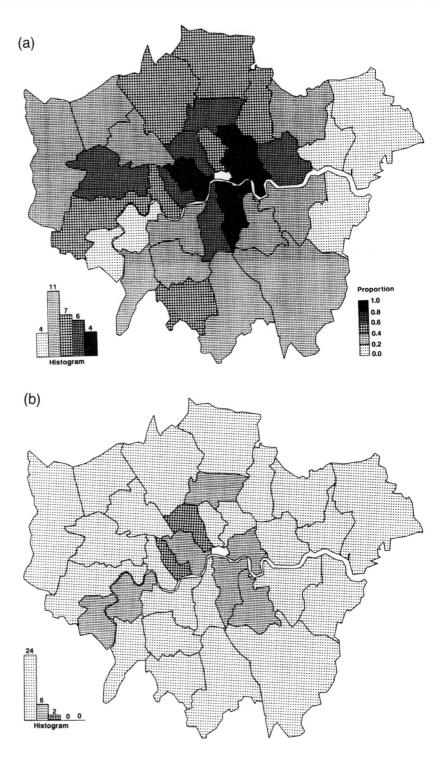

Figure 4.3.   Proportions of correct choices of house types (*cont.*): (a) purpose-built flats; (b) converted flats.

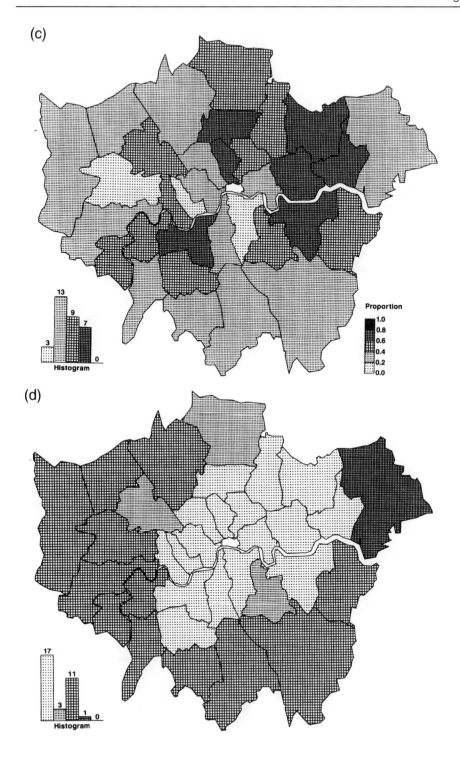

Figure 4.3. Proportions of correct choices of house types: (c) terraced houses; (d) detached/semi-detached houses.

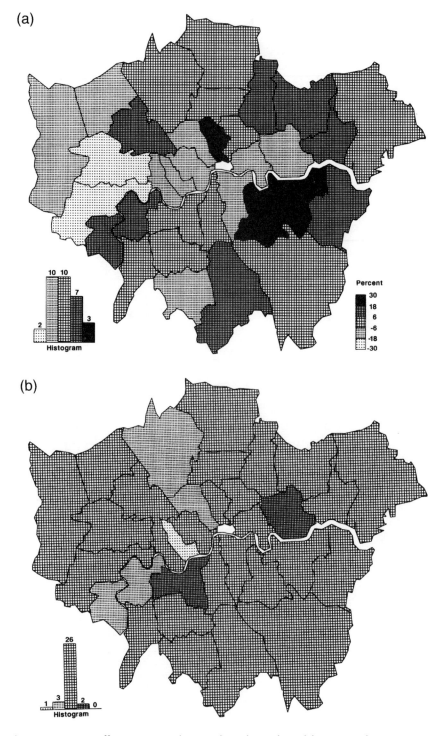

Figure 4.4. Differences in observed and predicted housing choices (*cont.*): (a) purpose-built flats; (b) converted flats.

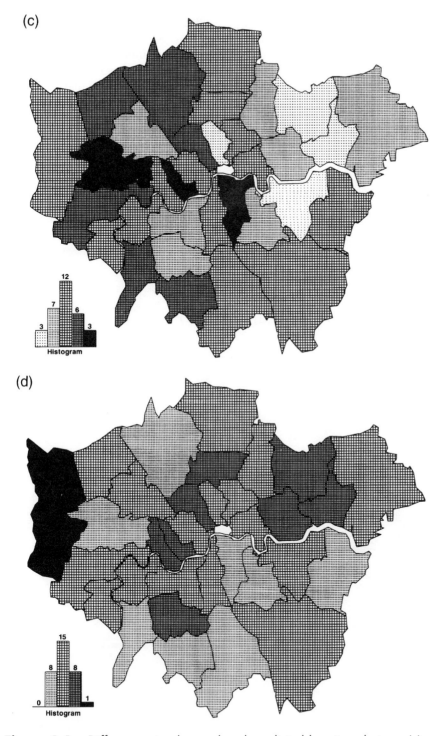

Figure 4.4. Differences in observed and predicted housing choices: (c) terraced houses; (d) detached/semi-detached houses.

presented in Figure 4.5. The best predictions are recorded in and near the center, and in the outermost suburbs. This suggests the need for two separate models of individual choice behavior, one for inner, the other for outer zones. The need for this distinction is even clearer when the normalized success index computed from the spatial equivalents of equations (4.19) and (4.20), and defined as $\varphi_n/\varphi_{n,\,max}$, is examined. This is mapped in Figure 4.6, and shows that the best predictions occur nearest the CBD, the worst in the far western and eastern suburbs. On this basis we decided to reestimate our models based on equation (4.21) for inner and outer London, where inner London is based on the 13 Boroughs which compose the Inner London Education Authority (ILEA).

The sample size of 809 observations was divided into 337 based on the inner Boroughs, the remaining 472 comprising the outer Boroughs. First equation (4.21) for the inner Boroughs was estimated as

$$\log \frac{P_{i2}}{P_{i1}} = \begin{array}{cccc} -5.446 & + & 0.194R_n & + & 0.061Q_i, \\ \{-5.849\} & & \{1.478\} & & \{8.305\}^* \\ (0.931) & & (0.131) & & (0.007) \end{array} \tag{4.25a}$$

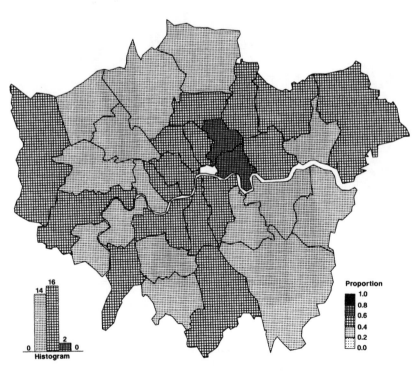

Figure 4.5. Proportions of correct choices for all house types.

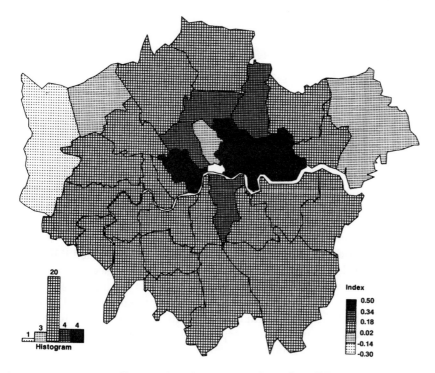

Figure 4.6. Overall normalized success indices for all house types.

$$\log \frac{P_{i3}}{P_{i1}} = \begin{array}{ccccc} -5.106 & + & 0.430R_n & + & 0.050Q_i, \\ \{-7.046\}^* & & \{4.106\}^* & & \{8.722\}^* \\ (0.725) & & (0.105) & & (0.005) \end{array} \tag{4.25b}$$

$$\log \frac{P_{i4}}{P_{i1}} = \begin{array}{ccccc} -7.430 & + & 0.546R_n & + & 0.050Q_i, \\ \{-5.810\} & & \{3.203\}^* & & \{5.767\}^* \\ (1.279) & & (0.171) & & (0.009) \end{array} \tag{4.25c}$$

where $\xi^2 = 0.228$ and $N_{inner} = 337$; t statistics and standard errors denoted as above; and the appropriate equation(s) for the outer Boroughs estimated as

$$\log \frac{P_{i2}}{P_{i1}} = \begin{array}{ccccc} -5.119 & + & 0.030R_n & + & 0.075Q_i, \\ \{-3.307\}^* & & \{0.280\} & & \{6.514\}^* \\ (1.548) & & (0.106) & & (0.012) \end{array} \tag{4.26a}$$

$$\log \frac{P_{i3}}{P_{i1}} = \begin{array}{ccccc} -1.300 & - & 0.009R_n & + & 0.059Q_i, \\ \{-1.754\} & & \{0.170\} & & \{7.450\}^* \\ (0.741) & & (-0.051) & & (0.008) \end{array} \tag{4.26b}$$

$$\log \frac{P_{i4}}{P_{i1}} = \begin{array}{ccc} -3.537 & + & 0.186R_n & + & 0.051Q_{i,} \\ \{-4.740\} & & \{3.816\} & & \{6.538\}^* \\ (0.746) & & (0.049) & & (0.008) \end{array}$$

(4.26c)

where $\xi^2 = 0.106$; $N_{\text{outer}} = 472$. What becomes apparent in terms of the t and ξ^2 statistics is that the inner London model (equations (4.25)) performs very much as the original model (equations (4.23)), whilst the outer London results are rather different. Equation (4.26) reflects a diminished role of the distance variable (two of its associated t statistics are insignificant and one parameter exhibits an unexpected sign) which contributes towards a much lower ξ^2 goodness-of-fit measure.

We might rationalize this in terms of our previous land use theory as follows: whilst difficulties of physical accessibility constrained the physical growth of London up until the First World War, the subsequent innovation of mass transit and the automobile rapidly opened up large tracts of land for development. Because most of this development occurred over very large areas, the form of physical development is much less likely to exhibit a very close and identifiable correspondence with distance from the CBD. Reestimation of our model for outer London without the distance variable yields

$$\log \frac{P_{i2}}{P_{i1}} = \begin{array}{cc} -4.695 & + & 0.075Q_{i,} \\ \{-7.388\}^* & & \{6.490\}^* \\ (0.635) & & (0.011) \end{array}$$

(4.27a)

$$\log \frac{P_{i3}}{P_{i1}} = \begin{array}{cc} -1.399 & + & 0.059Q_{i,} \\ \{-4.990\}^* & & \{7.470\}^* \\ \{0.280\} & & (0.008) \end{array}$$

(4.27b)

$$\log \frac{P_{i4}}{P_{i1}} = \begin{array}{cc} -0.881 & + & 0.048Q_{i,} \\ \{-3.347\}^* & & \{6.241\}^* \\ (0.263) & & (0.008) \end{array}$$

(4.27c)

$\xi^2 = 0.078$ and $N_{\text{outer}} = 372$; t statistics and standard errors denoted as above. The ξ^2 statistic is less than that for equations (4.26) and thus the model has not been used in the simulations which follow. At this point we can conclude our section on estimation. Many avenues remain unexplored but several models have been tested and we will take forward those in equations (4.23), (4.25) and (4.26).

4.8 Fractal Simulation of House Type and Location in London

One of the more obscure reasons for developing such a simplified model based on age and distance can now be made clear. Age is a spatially extensive variable, while distance is a property of space itself. Thus it is possible to display a single map shaded according to age from which distance can also be read, in particular distance to some fixed point from any other. If we had more than a single extensive variable, age and neighborhood quality say, these could not be represented on the same map in easily codable form. Clearly it is useful for ease of interpretation to have a single map of input data, for this can be directly associated with a map of the outputs from the models. In fact, the need to store data in map form is essential, for the fractal simulation was run on a very small microcomputer in which only 8K of memory was available for program and data, 20K of memory being given over to the graphics screen. Although it might be possible to store data on disk, and thus include a larger number of independent spatial variables, the continual reading and writing required would make the operation of the model prohibitively slow. In fact, because the data are spatially extensive, it is essential to store them in screen mode, for the resolution we are working with involves 160×256 pixel points which makes any form other than screen storage extremely problematic. The data on age are stored as a screen map, and airline distance is easy to compute from screen coordinates which in turn are a function of the screen addressing.

The age data were made available by the GLC Intelligence Unit in seven age groups which were coded in grid fashion, and colored in the screen memory according to the age group. The screen map is shown in Plate 4.3 where the colors refer to the age of housing. The following average ages in years define the seven ranges in question, $\rightarrow 8 \rightarrow 26 \rightarrow 48 \rightarrow 78 \rightarrow 110 \rightarrow 150 \rightarrow 175 \rightarrow$, and these are colored white, light blue, magenta, dark blue, yellow, green and red respectively. These represent weighted averages which reflect the distribution of housing in any grid square. Distance from the CBD to Borough centroids is measured in kilometers, the GLC boundary being about 24 km maximum from the City and the ILEA boundary used for the inner London model being about 13 km distant. Note also that the shape of urban development in London is coded into the data through grid squares colored on a black background which does not contain housing. These represent 'vacant' land in the sense used earlier, although in these applications, the model in no way predicts this.

The way the simulation works involves first loading the age map into the screen memory from file. Then the fractal simulation begins in the order used previously in the demonstration model, and when the appropriate level of fractal detail is reached, the program retrieves the color of the centroid of the triangle space reached, from the screen, converts this into an age value, computes distance and uses these variables in the model structure based on equation (4.21) to compute the probability of house type. Thus the simulation works by replacing the regular gridded age map by the irregular fractal land use pattern in a literal sense. This rather innovative technique for input is immediately converted to output and this occurs directly 'before your eyes'. In a sense, it is a version of the WYSIWYG principle ('What You See Is What You Get') which is central to many operations with graphics computers. A note on technical detail is required. The simulation operates on a display with resolution 160×256 pixels in 16 colors. Eight colors are reserved for the age map (seven ages and one vacant land use) and five are used in choosing house type (four types and one vacant land use). The process of replacement is not as clear as it might be because only eight absolute colors are available, hence the replacement of the input map with the output map uses similar colors and is only distinguished in terms of its irregularity.

The process of fractal simulation is essentially the same as that used previously in Chapter 3 in the 'London' sequence. Moreover, we have also used the triangular midpoint displacement technique for fractal rendering which was shown there in Figure 3.14 for the hypothetical demonstrations. The only difference relates to the way the input data are stored and sampled and the way the probability models are developed. Four land use types based on housing, rather than three based on activities, now form the simulated urban structure. The area over which the simulation is operated is fixed and in a sense residential location is already predetermined through the data, and thus it is only house type by location which varies.

We have already noted that two model structures are to be used: that based on the whole of Greater London using equations (4.23) and that based on the distinction between inner and outer London based on equations (4.25) and (4.26). In these simulations, we work at recursive level $s = 5$ which essentially fixes fractal detail at just above the pixel level of the screen. Each simulation takes about three hours and involves examining $10 \times 4^s = 10{,}240$ randomly positioned contiguous triangles which form the network of fractal detail at the lowest level of resolution. In fact, the models are based on 809 data points, and in the area in question there are in excess of three million households, thus the simulation itself is still very much in the nature of a sample-style exercise in which an 'average' individual residing at the lowest level of fractal detail makes a house-type choice which is then assumed to be typical of all individuals at that level and in the space which contains that location.

The other issue involves the conversion of probabilities $\{P_{ik}\}$ into discrete choices. In the demonstration model, a random simulation was adopted in which choice of land use was accomplished according to the probability range fixed by the land use models but ultimately determined using a random number device. The resultant outputs were very satisfactory because the probability profiles were quite distinct, thus enabling fairly clear decisions to be made and characteristic spatial patterns to emerge. Here, however, the probability profiles of the house type models are much less different from one another, and thus to develop clearer spatial patterns, we have also used a deterministic simulation. This simulation is based on choosing a house type according to the rule

$$\text{Type} \leftarrow \max_{k} \{P_{ik}\} \tag{4.28}$$

which simply makes the choice according to that alternative which has the maximum probability for individual i.

We can now show the simulations. We will first discuss the random simulations which are based on equation (4.23), then equations (4.25) and (4.26), but we will not show these visually as they do not generate much imagery of import. The main impression is one of massive variability of house type in spatial terms. There is almost a complete mix of types everywhere for both types of equation, thus implying that the relative evenness and similarity of the probability profiles gives much greater weight to the lower probabilities in each choice situation than would be the case in a real context. Little spatial pattern can thus be discerned and this suggests that random simulations based on discrete choice models are likely to produce too little spatial discrimination if predicted in this way.

The deterministic simulations which involve equation (4.28) are shown in Plate 4.4(a) and (b) for the full, and inner–outer models respectively, where the four colors – red, yellow, green and blue – reflect converted flats, purpose-built flats, terraced houses, and detached/semi-detached houses respectively. Very clear spatial patterns emerge this time which show the characteristic structure of residential land use in London, but there is little difference between the two sets of model. The clearer of the two patterns is Plate 4.4(a) based on the full model, but there is a ring of purpose-built flats between the terraced and detached/semi-detached areas which is unexpected. In Plate 4.4(b), purpose-built flats are closer in towards the CBD. Note that in the simulations the total number of house choices is not scaled in any way to reflect the scale of housing in London; thus this represents an additional prediction from the model. The patterns in general though are very plausible, reflecting flats, terraced and detached/semi-detached houses at increasing distance from the CBD, with the distribution of purpose-built and converted flats clearly characterizing the flat-market in London. One limitation of the deterministic model is that it does not pick up the degree of local variation one might expect, but a more detailed data base might resolve this.

Finally, we have begun to experiment with these simulations. Running the models at $s > 5$ requires a larger processor because the memory required explodes due to the recursion, and so far we have run the model up to $s = 7$, although the increase in time required is exponential. Level of recursion does affect the patterns we get, but generally these help us to improve the ultimate look of the geometry, not the models themselves. Simple policy-predictive runs of the simulations are possible, for the input data are easy to update. One could assume a process of aging and renewal, varying according to simple rules and policies, which would then enable a pseudo-dynamic simulation to be developed. A series of images of the typical house types in London over the next 50 years could be generated in this way. But these are for the future, and in any case, there are many lines of inquiry that have to be followed up before then.

4.9 Extending the Laboratory for Experimentation and Visualization

The ability to display the overall pattern produced by models with an implicit spatial dimension is a clear advantage of the large-scale simulations adopted here. But these need not be generated within a fractal framework. Simulation could proceed by examining each pixel in turn and building up urban structure in this way on a regular spatial grid. Nevertheless, fractals do generate realistic images, and one of the goals of this chapter has been to make abstract models more visually intelligible and acceptable, and for this, the fractal framework seems promising. As such, the technique is one of generating spatial realism, and this clearly depends upon the display devices used. The main problem emerging from this chapter, however, relates to the development of a more consistent modeling strategy which can be effectively incorporated into the hierarchical method used to structure the simulation. We have already indicated what is involved: in essence, the hierarchy guiding the fractal simulation should be based on characteristics of the city, and this clearly relates to the type of explanation and modeling required. Discrete choice models show promise here, but so do sequential and nested approaches involving entropy models (Batty, 1976).

This reasoning leads us to the conclusion that a more fundamental strategy may be actually to explore land-use models which are themselves fractal. Some examples already exist in physical geography: for example, the sorts of terrain model explored by Goodchild (1982) and illustrated in Chapter 3, and image processing techniques such as those developed by Pentland (1984) are suggestive of the types of stochastic model that might underlie the structure of land use. There are difficulties in that some of the patterns are discontinuous, but it is worth exploring how such ideas could be used to link what we already know about land use, central place, and rank-size together in a fractal framework. With respect to discrete choice models, there may even be the possibility of a fractal interpretation of the underlying mechanisms which give rise to various forms of logit and probit models, and there is clearly a possibility that questions of nesting and aggregation might be reconciled with ideas about recursion and hierarchy. In fact, in this chapter, the whole question of the spatial basis of discrete choice models has emerged as problematic, and this suggests that further research on spatial aggregation and discrete choice is worthy as an end in itself, notwithstanding any fractal interpretations which might emerge.

Many other speculations are possible about where such developments will best be focussed. An interesting project would be to examine the extent to which regular, non-random fractal patterns built from cell-space models (Tobler, 1979b; Couclelis, 1985) could be used as first approximations to city patterns, and there is much work now developing in this domain around concepts of cellular automata and artificial life. We also need to consider how such simulations might be made dynamic, especially as there is an obvious dynamic process underlying a model in which age acts as an independent variable. In one sense, our models might already be seen as explaining urban structure in terms of time and space, age and distance, and our earlier comments on possible policy simulations endorse this. In particular, the question of redevelopment is central to residential location, and any dynamic extension to the framework should enable such processes to be captured. We will explore these ideas more fully from Chapter 7 onwards, but we also require a firmer empirical basis to our assertion that urban structure is indeed fractal, in order to inform both description and theory. We will begin our assault on this measurement task in the next two chapters.

5

Urban Boundaries and Edges

The fascination of boundaries lies in their ambivalent role of dividing and connecting at the same time. They mark the transition between different modes of existence. They transmit and control exchange between territories. They are the playground for discovery and conquest ... They are the result of never ending competition and exhibit structure on many scales. (Richter and Peitgen, 1985, p. 571–572.)

5.1 At the Edge of the City

Boundaries, as Richter and Peitgen (1985) so graphically portray, are places which mark the transition between different regimes, different systems, and this is nowhere more so than between the rural and urban worlds at the edge of the city. In one sense, the boundary of the city marks the transition between different epochs, between an older agricultural society and the newer industrial, although the distinction is becoming weaker as contemporary society is beginning to make its transition to a post-industrial era with all its consequences for how cities will be organized. Nevertheless, such zones of transition do reflect the tension between the old and the new, places where more stable, established structures are being continually tested by a newer, ever-changing dynamic. Even in these terms, such boundaries are not likely to be 'smooth' in any sense and as we shall see, their physical form is both irregular but self-similar in that a precise transition between the old and the new can never be definitively marked out.

In defining the physical form of the city, its edge or boundary is the most obvious visual delimiter of its size and shape. Statistical definitions of cities rely upon the definition of boundaries, although such definitions are never comprehensive; there are so many possible ways of cutting the continuum of development from urban to rural that the general idea of a boundary remains a conceptual notion which is only given physical form through narrow definitions. Urban boundaries, however, are not simply linear constructs which mark off one side of the continuum from the other but they imply area, and thus shape (Batty, 1991). As we have argued in earlier chapters, although cities can be visualized across many dimensions, they are usually best pictured in the plane as two-dimensional phenomena and thus their boundaries immediately imply some measure of area. In this sense, the boundary is clearly something more than a one-dimensional line for whenever we examine such an edge, we conceptualize an area.

There are many notions as to what constitutes the boundary of the city, several of which we will be using in this book. In Chapters 3 and 4, we defined cities in terms of concentric rings of different land uses about their CBDs based on von Thunen's original division of land use along a spectrum from highly urban to rural; in contemporary terms, this continuum begins with high density commercial at the core of the city and evolves to low density agricultural uses such as market gardening at the periphery. We also referred extensively in Chapter 4 to the notion of inner and outer suburban areas, while the idea of the suburban fringe as the zone of transition between urban and rural can be extended to the quasi-urban area at the rural edge of the city sometimes called exurbia. In later chapters, we will have recourse to extend our definition of the city to its wider hinterland or field, that area which contains all the development which in one way or another is associated with the city. Definitional problems abound, too, for in the age of the world city, activities may exist everywhere on the globe which are in some sense dependent upon the city in question. Finally, we will make our definitions of the extent of the city much more precise from Chapter 7 on when we begin to introduce the idea that population density must be the delimiter of form and that density itself rather than the shape of land use or physical development, is the true measure of whether or not cities are fractal.

In this chapter and the next, we will begin to define and measure the form of the city in analogy to the way we discussed the definition of a fractal line in Chapters 2 and 3. There we argued that fractal lines are something more than the one-dimensional Euclidean line but something less than the two-dimensional plane; the coastline is the example *par excellence*. In fact, it is likely that the fractal dimension of our urban boundaries will be closer to 1 than to 2 for we will not consider cities which are entirely composed of boundaries, in which the boundary itself twists and turns to fill the two-dimensional space. This point in itself is somewhat controversial, for it is possible to define cities which are entirely composed of boundaries if the level of spatial resolution is chosen accordingly. Moreover, there are recent theories of the post-industrial city which are predicated on the idea that everything significant in the modern city is at the edge: 'Edge Cities' as they have been called (Garreau, 1991), thus giving some meaning to our own notion that the most interesting aspects of urban phenomena depend upon what is happening on their boundaries.

However, urban boundaries or edges can be very different from coastlines in the following sense. Whereas our interest in coastlines is often only over a fixed stretch of the line, our interest in urban boundaries is likely to be over their entirety in that to define a city by its boundary, there is usually some measure of closure to the line. The boundary thus marks out an envelope. In fact, if we examine coastlines in their entirety too, we must consider the same sorts of closed line. It is nonetheless a comment on the rudimentary development of fractal geometry that there are virtually no discussions so far of the implications for measurement posed by objects with closed, in contrast to open, boundaries. We will in fact extend our discussion into these realms, but to anticipate the outcome, much remains to be done. In this chapter we will define the problem of the closed boundary away by adopting artificial closure, and only in the next will we broach the matter directly.

In Chapter 2, we identified four ways in which we might define objects of interest and measure their scale-dependence, hence their fractal dimension. We noted that we could derive the fractal dimension of a single object by measuring the same object at different scales or by varying the extent or size of the object over which the dimension might be computed. In essence, we will be adopting the first method here, that is taking a given city and examining its physical properties at different scales in contrast to the second method where we change the size of the given object; this we will develop from Chapter 7 on. We can also derive the fractal dimension of a set of objects by examining the size distribution of the objects in question, and we will do this for individual land use parcels in Chapter 6 which will extend the ideas of this chapter. If we have a set of objects, we could also change each of their scales and simply combine all the scale-dependent results and use the methods of this chapter to compute a fractal dimension for the entire set. But for a set of objects, the most appropriate methods are those which involve examining their size, not scale. In short, what we will introduce in this chapter are methods such as those we presented in Chapter 2 for deterministic fractals such as the Koch curve and we will apply these to a single city, deriving its fractal dimensions from the lines which compose its boundary.

Here we will use the town of Cardiff, which is the capital city of Wales, as our example. Cardiff has a very distinct urban edge, and our problems of defining its boundary are considerably less than in many other possible examples. However, the boundary is a closed line, and without any knowledge of fractal geometry, it seems intuitively obvious that such a line implies an object with a dimension somewhat greater than one. Any layman would probably associate the closed line with an area and argue that the purpose of the line was simply to mark out the area. Common sense would thus imply that resulting object was in the plane rather than the line. However, as we shall see, the measurement of the fractal dimension of these closed lines yields values which are much closer to one than two, and which are quite close to the theoretical Koch coastline where $D \approx 1.262$. What these findings will impress is that the concept of fractal dimension is completely dependent upon what is being measured, or rather what physical properties of an object are being selected for measure, and that there are likely to be many different types and values of fractal dimension. We will, of course, elaborate this important point throughout the rest of this book.

We will first discuss the way geographical boundaries might be represented before we move to outline the formal methods which we use to derive the fractal dimension of a line. These methods are those which we have already presented in Chapter 2 but they will be repeated again here for we will adapt them somewhat differently to this context. We illustrate the basic method for the case of Cardiff's urban edge (in 1949) and this serves to point up some problems of measurement and statistical method. We then go on to outline the way these methods might be used to compute the changing dimension of a growing city, using data from the growth of Cardiff from the late 19th century to the middle of the 20th. To generate the relevant dimensions, we will use four different methods of approximating a fractal line, namely, the structured walk, equipaced polygon, a hybrid of both these, and the so-called cell-count which is a simplification of the well-known box-counting method (Voss, 1988). Finally, we will draw these results together so that we might extend them to measuring the boundaries of different land uses in Chapter 6.

5.2 Cartographic Representation and Generalization of Geographical Boundaries

As we demonstrated in Chapters 2 and 3, the most celebrated example of a fractal is a coastline. Although the development of fractal geometry only really took off after Mandelbrot's famous paper in *Science* in 1967 where he posed the conundrum of length in terms of 'How long is the coast of Britain?', it was Richardson (1961) who first articulated the problem in these familiar terms. Richardson demonstrated quite unequivocally that the length of a coastline depended upon the yardstick or scale with which its length was measured. As we illustrated for the Koch curve, he showed that as the scale became finer, more and more detail could be picked up by the measuring instrument, thus implying no bounds on its length. Although Richardson did not formalize the concept of fractal dimension, which was left to Mandelbrot (1967), he did derive the familiar log–linear relationship between length and scale, and in estimating this, demonstrated that the fractal dimension of coastlines ranged from around 1.02 for South Africa, 1.13 for Australia to 1.25 for the western shore of Britain.

As we also noted in Chapter 2, this conundrum has been remarked upon for at least a hundred years, and it is likely that it was known in some form to Renaissance geometers and thus probably to the Greeks. In the 1960s with the development of mathematical geography, Nysteun (1966) in a seminal paper, not only identified the problem and suggested a solution through the definition of length contingent upon the scale used, but he also pointed to the work of the Polish mathematician Steinhaus (1954, 1960) and geographer Perkal (1958a, 1958b) who had both reflected upon the paradox. Perkal in fact drew attention to the work of the Viennese geographer Penck (1894) who was familiar with the problem in the late 19th century. However, the problem was simply noted, and apart from some attempts at its resolution with respect to associating length with explicit scale, there were no attempts until Mandelbrot (1967) to pose it in a wider framework. It would, in fact, have been remarkable had not the problem been posed in countless guises throughout history, but it probably had to await the arrival of computer graphics, hence fractals, before its universal import could be appreciated.

What is fascinating is that the problem has never been restricted simply to physical systems. Nysteun (1966) described the conundrum of length in discussing the boundary of the town of Ann Arbor, Michigan; Perkal (1958b) illustrated the same for the boundary of the town of Wroclaw in Poland, while Richardson (1961) himself used political frontiers as examples of fractal curves. In fact, he derived the fractal dimension of the frontier between Spain and Portugal as 1.14 and of the German land frontier in 1899 as 1.15. Although Mandelbrot (1983) developed his new geometry mainly with natural examples in mind, he is strident in maintaining that the geometry is applicable to artificial systems. He says in discussing the amount of circuitry which can be packed onto a chip: "This and a few other case studies help demonstrate that in the final analysis, fractal methods can serve to analyze any 'system', whether natural or artificial, that decomposes into parts in a self-similar fashion, and such that the properties of the parts are less important than the rules of the articulation".

That urban boundaries are fractal in some sense might already seem self-evident, although we still have to demonstrate the point. There is, however, another issue which dominates the definition of boundaries for geographical systems, and this involves the concept of 'generalization' as it appears in cartography. Generalization is the process of aggregating cartographic features which encompass a map, from one scale to another, and as such, the various methods developed have often alluded to the problem posed by the conundrum of length where cartographic lines are involved. In fact, cartographers have made considerable progress in the search for methods for selectively aggregating and filtering geometric detail as lines are generalized from smaller to larger scales, and have, perhaps unwittingly sometimes, invoked the geometry of fractals (Lam and Quattrochi, 1992).

In exploring the extent to which any boundary or line might be dependent on scale, the process of generalization is likely to detect such variations and thus its development is important to the measurement of fractal dimension in cartographic lines. Buttenfield (1985) has conceptualized it as encompassing four related procedures and processes: first, simplification, such as in the removal of unwanted detail and the smoothing of features; second, symbolization, in which line character is graphically encoded according to geographical and perceptual conventions; third, classification, in which cartographic information is aggregated and/or partitioned into categories; and fourth, induction, in which the creative logical assumptions which are made during generalization are applied. As such, it is clear that the depiction of cartographic information is the end result of a variety of codification conventions mediated by a human judgmental process. This is no less the case in the generation of computer-digitized data bases than in traditional cartographic line-drawing (Jenks, 1981).

There are many types of method for line generalization. Buttenfield (1985) develops a comprehensive classification and critique of such algorithms including various random and systematic point weeding routines to simplify detail, the fitting of various mathematical functions to lines, the epsilon neighborhood concept based on linking line length to scale (Perkal, 1958a, 1958b), and the use of both angular and band-width tolerancing to dispense with successive points which fall outside a prespecified angular and/or band-width threshold (Peucker, 1975). She concludes that the choice of method used can depend upon the often-conflicting emphases that different studies have placed upon geographical and perceptual accuracy.

The measurement of shapes through boundaries has a long history in natural science too and has also been absorbed into the locational analysis tradition of human geography (see Haggett, Cliff and Frey, 1977). Many of the earliest shape indices were based upon simple length, breadth and area relations. This was primarily because the constraints associated with time-consuming manual measurement restricted the assessment of line structure to simple indices of variation at selected points and to the monotonicity of line segments about a base line anchoring the end points of the line. These efforts were nevertheless well-motivated, since even fairly crude measurements and classifications of form can enhance urban analysis. There are numerous examples of such use. At an extreme, Thomson (1977) develops simple areal density measures in order to classify the functional relationship between transport infrastructure and urban form, while closer to the ideas to be developed here, Benguigui and Daoud (1991) have undertaken a detailed empirical analysis of the relationship between the form of the Paris suburban railway system and the distribution of the urban population. As we demonstrated in Chapter 1, many of our conceptions of the city, ancient and modern, are rooted in the idea that the geometry of the city in terms of simple indices of shape can, in some way, be tied to its functioning, and that to change or control its functioning involves manipulating its geometry. In this sense, form follows function and our ultimate aim in this book is to demonstrate how the new geometry of fractals can inform this quest. In this chapter, we will begin by linking the shape of cities to their boundaries.

In the present context, we suggest that most of these methods involving techniques of generalizing lines or measuring simple geometric properties of shapes are flawed in at least two fundamental ways. First, in a geographical sense, most are heavily reliant upon the *a priori* definition of the scale, starting points and ending points of constituent line features for the synthesis of total line structure. Second, in a perceptual sense, many algorithms fail to preserve the qualitative visual character of a line in terms of its shape when it is generalized (Muller, 1986). Seen in the context of the emergent relationship between measurement and simulation of urban form, this produces two grave shortcomings. First, it is not possible to specify *a priori* those features which we expect to characterize urban boundaries, since their inductive generalization remains one of the primary goals of the measurement exercise. Second, if we are to derive visually acceptable space partitioning rules for land use simulations then our measurement parameters must maintain perceptual accuracy in any of the lines which they are used to generate. In this chapter, we will contend that use of fractal techniques can provide a consistent and feasible route beyond this impasse, since first by using very few parameters, the line can be measured as a total entity rather than as a piecemeal amalgam of constituent features; and second, the line's visual character is preserved by using the concept of self-similarity and by sensitive assessment of the range of scales over which the fractal property holds.

Before we launch into the measurement task, it is important to reflect upon the notion of exact or statistical self-similarity resulting from a single, or small number of processes. Clearly this notion becomes increasingly strained as we make the transition from physical to social systems where, for example, urban edges clearly evolve under a wide range of simultaneous physical and social processes. At a theoretical level, many of the more abstract spatial theories anticipate self-similarity, with central place theory being perhaps the best example (Arlinghaus, 1985). At a procedural level, we might consider that at worst, the differences in the nature of self-similarity between physical and social systems are of degree rather than of kind. In such circumstances, there would be no rationale why fractal measurement should not proceed in a similar manner to applications in disciplines as diverse as particle science, mineralogy and music (Dearnley, 1985; Kaye, 1978; Mark and Aronson, 1984; Dodge and Bahn, 1986).

All such analyses depend critically upon isolating the most appropriate range of scales over which any statistical property of fractals holds. For example, it is likely to be the case that geographical features will revert to man-made Euclidean dimensions at certain fine scales. Additionally, and in all such instances, the cartographer is the arbiter, and to some extent the architect, of the final depiction of the map feature, and any summary measure must ultimately be viewed in part as the outcome of a human judgmental process. In summary then, the measurement and generalization of cartographic lines using fractals is likely to have a number of advantages over other forms of representation (Muller, 1987) and there are grounds to anticipate that empirical evaluation of the fractal dimension ". . .may be the most important parameter of an irregular cartographic feature, just as the arithmetic mean and other measures of central tendency are often used as the most characteristic parameters of a sample" (Goodchild and Mark, 1987). The rest of this chapter will be focussed on demonstrating how such dimensions emerge as a natural consequence of the process of generalization.

5.3 The Basic Scaling Relations for a Fractal Line

The two basic relations for a fractal line associate the number of parts into which the line can be divided, and its length, to some measure of its scale. These relations have already been stated in equations (2.24) and (2.25) respectively and we will proceed in analogy to these. First, consider an irregular line of unspecified length R between two fixed points. Define a scale of resolution r_0, such that when this line is approximated by a sequence of contiguous segments or chords each of length r_0, this yields N_0 such chords. Now determine a new scale of resolution r_1 which is one-half r_0, that is, $r_1 = r_0/2$. Applying this scale r_1 to the line yields N_1 chords. If the line is fractal, then it is clear that ". . .halving the interval always gives more than twice the number of steps, since more and more of the self-similar detail is picked up" (Mark, 1984). Formally this means that

$$\frac{N_1}{N_0} > 2 \text{ and } \frac{r_0}{r_1} = 2. \tag{5.1}$$

This is illustrated for three different scales in Figure 5.1. Using equation (2.25), the lengths of the approximated curves or perimeters, in each case, are given as $L_1 = N_1 r_1$ and $L_0 = N_0 r_0$ and from the assumptions implied in equation (5.1), it is easy to show that $L_1 > L_0$. This provides the formal justification that the length of the line increases without bound, as the chord size (or scale) r converges towards zero.

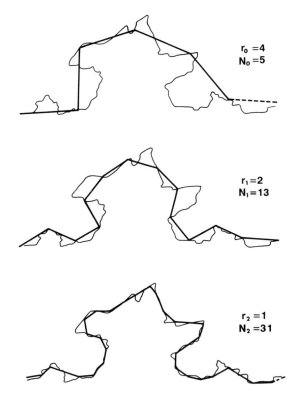

Figure 5.1. Approximating an irregular line and measuring perimeter length at three adjacent scales.

The relationship in (5.1) can be formally equated if it is assumed that the ratio of the number of chord sizes at any two scales is always in constant relation to the ratio of the lengths of the chords. Then

$$\frac{N_1}{N_0} = \left(\frac{r_0}{r_1}\right)^D, \tag{5.2}$$

where D is defined as the fractal dimension. If halving the scale gives exactly twice the number of chords, then equation (5.2) implies that $D = 1$, and that the line would be straight. If halving the scale gives four times the number of chords, the line would enclose the space and the fractal dimension would be 2. Equation (5.2) can be rearranged as

$$N_1 = (N_0 r_0^D) \, r_1^{-D} = \alpha r_1^{-D}. \tag{5.3}$$

where the term in brackets $(N_0 r_0^D)$ acts as the base constant α in predicting the number of chords N_1 from any interval of size r_1 relative to this base.

From equations (5.2) and (5.3), a number of methods for determining D emerge. Equation (5.2) suggests that D can be calculated if only two scales are available (Goodchild, 1980). Rearranging equation (5.2) gives

$$D = \log \frac{N_1}{N_0} \bigg/ \log \frac{r_0}{r_1}. \tag{5.4}$$

However, most analyses not only involve a determination of the value of

D but also of whether or not the phenomenon in question is fractal, and thus more than two scales are required. Generalizing equation (5.3) as in equation (2.25) gives

$$N(r) = \alpha r^{-D} \tag{5.5}$$

where $N(r)$ is the number of chords associated with any r. Using logarithms, we can linearize equation (5.5) as

$$\log N(r) = \log \alpha - D \log r. \tag{5.6}$$

Equation (5.6) can be used as a basis for regression by using estimates of N and r from several scales. The related formula involving the length of the curve or perimeter L analogous to equation (2.25) is derived from equation (5.5) as

$$L = Nr = \alpha r^{(1-D)}. \tag{5.7}$$

Equation (5.7) can also be linearized by taking logarithms,

$$\log L = \log \alpha + \beta \log r \tag{5.8}$$

where $\beta = (1 - D)$. It is clear that the intercepts α in equations (5.6) and (5.8) are identical and the slopes are related to the fractal dimension D in the manner shown. In later sections, we will use equation (5.8) rather than equation (5.6), for equation (5.8) will enable us to check the range of scales used more effectively.

The original method used by Richardson (1961) to measure the length of coastlines and frontiers involved manually walking a pair of dividers along the boundaries at different scales and then determining D from equation (5.8). To enable the entire perimeter to be traversed, the last chord length which always finishes at the last coordinate point is generally a fraction of the step size, and the step sizes used at each scale usually reflect orders of magnitude in geometric relationship; that is $r_n = a^{-n} r_0$, $a > 1$, which enables each step size to be equally weighted and spaced in the log–log regression. In Richardson's (1961) research, about six orders of magnitude or scale were used which is regarded as sufficient to determine a least-squares regression line. Computer simulations of Richardson's manual method are now well established. Kaye (1978, 1989a) refers to the method as a 'structured walk' around the perimeter of an object, and he calls the log–log scatter plot of perimeter lengths versus scale intervals a 'Richardson plot'; this provides a useful visual test of whether or not the phenomenon is fractal. The structured walk method is easy to implement on a computer, and here we have used the algorithm developed by Shelberg, Moellering and Lam (1982) which involves approximating the boundary of an object consisting of line segments between digitized coordinates, with different sized chord lengths.

There are two variants involving this method. First, the number of chords and perimeter lengths will depend upon the starting-point along the curve. To reduce the arbitrariness of this variation, several workers have suggested the structured walk be started at several different points, and averages of the results then formed (Kent and Wong, 1982). For example, Kaye, Leblanc and Abbot (1985) start the walk at five different points along the curves, but there is no reason why, in principle, the walk should not be started at each of the digitized points which define the base curve. In the illustrative example which we will develop in the next section using the digitized points of Cardiff's urban boundary in 1949, we will initiate successive walks from each of the 1558 digitized points which define the urban edge, the walks proceeding in both directions towards the endpoints of the boundary. This variation on the basic method is inevitably time-consuming in computational terms.

The second variant involves starting the structured walk at different divider lengths and generating sequences of predictions from these different lengths. The range of scales over which the perimeter lengths were computed varied from about half the average chord length associated with the digitized data, to over the maximum distance between any two coordinate points on the perimeter. The average chord length is computed as follows. First, the distances between each adjacent pair of (x,y) coordinates, i and $i + 1$, are computed using the standard triangle equality

$$d_{i,i+1} = [(x_i - x_{i+1})^2 + (y_i - y_{i+1})^2]^{1/2}, \; i = 1, \ldots, n - 1,$$ (5.9)

and then the perimeter L of the base-level curve which has been digitized at resolution r can be summed as

$$L(r) = \sum_{i=1}^{n-1} d_{i,i+1}.$$ (5.10)

The average chord length $\bar{d}$ of the original curve is therefore

$$\bar{d} = \frac{L(r)}{n - 1},$$ (5.11)

and a lower bound for the chord length used to start the approximation, as suggested by Shelberg, Moellering and Lam (1982), is taken as approximately $\bar{d}$. The maximum distance between any pair of coordinates, which in fine particle science is referred to as Feret's diameter by Kaye (1978, 1989a), is given as

$$F = \max_{i,i+1} (d_{i,i+1}),$$ (5.12)

and Kaye (1978), amongst others, suggests that an appropriate upper bound for chord length approximation is $\approx F/2$. The intermediate chord lengths between these lower and upper limits should be ordered a geometrical sequence so as to ensure more equal weighting in the regressions.

5.4 Estimating the Fractal Dimension: the Urban Boundary of Cardiff

We have now presented sufficient method to derive our first example of a fractal dimension for a city. In order to illustrate the procedure, we have digitized the 1158 points composing the boundary of the town of Cardiff in 1949 which we show in Figure 5.2. This figure provides an excellent example of the problems of measurement which we confront. As such it represents a visual trace akin to the sorts of photographs physicists use to search for the existence of elementary particles, but with an important difference. The points which are defined in Figure 5.2 represent a series of subjective judgements as to the level of detail needed to represent the boundary at this elemental level. As the irregularity of the boundary varies over its length, then more points in general are defined where more detail is observed. It could be argued that we should represent this elemental level at the same level of detail everywhere and this of course would occur if, for example, a grid or other regular tessellation of the plane were used to detect the boundary. However, such a grid would have much redundancy if it were to detect the finest level of detail and therefore we have proceeded on the assumption that it is important to present as much detail as possible at the elemental level. As we shall see, some of the methods we use to derive fractal dimension will be based on regular tessellations of the plane but the problem of measuring 'objective' statistics such as fractal dimensions in subjectively specified data sets will continue to concern us throughout this book and we will return to it again in the sequel.

The boundary marking the extent of the urban area of Cardiff was defined from the 1:25,000 Ordnance Survey map published in 1949. The usual problems of definition were encountered in determining the edge of the urban area, and several rules of thumb were invoked. Typically, allotments and other urban fringe land-uses were excluded, villages linked to the urban area by ribbon development were included, man-made alter-

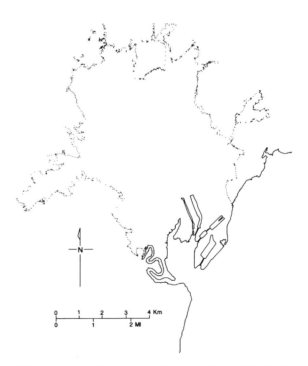

Figure 5.2. The density of point digitization of the 1949 Cardiff urban edge.

ations to rivers and coast were included, but large landed estates which subsequently become part of the urban fabric were included only if development had surrounded them. The entire definition process emphasized the obvious problems that urban processes and constraints operate at different scales, and this casts some doubt on the fractal concept of self-similarity in this context; but perhaps no more doubt than exists in other areas of the physical sciences where fractal concepts have been shown to apply only over restricted scales. Once the boundary had been defined, it was digitized to within 1 mm resolution; the coastline contained some 900 points, whereas the urban boundary was based on 1558 points. Figure 5.2 is thus a fair representation of the land which by 1949 had become 'irreversibly urban' in character, and is consistent with other official standards for defining 'urbanity' (OPCS, 1984).

Figure 5.3 shows the digitized outlines as well as a coarse approximation to the boundary produced by the structured walk method, which is about 30 times the scale of the original data. The approximating polygon touches the original boundary at those points on the base curve which are retained for the approximation, and all of the chords are of equal length except for the end (residual) chord distance(s). The perimeter of the digitized boundary determined from equations (5.9) and (5.10) gives $L = 3104.456$ units, with the average chord length $\bar{d} = 1.993$ from the equation (5.11), and the Feret diameter $F = 432.935$ from equation (5.12). These measures are useful to keep in mind when we discuss the relative merits of different fractal measurement methods. We will deal first with the structured walk method. For a given chord length used to start the sequence of predictions of perimeter lengths, a complete series of 10 chord lengths are used in the

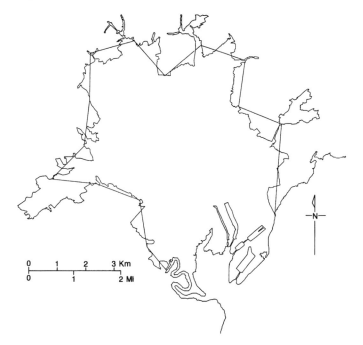

Figure 5.3. A typical scale approximation to the digitized urban edge of Cardiff.

approximations, starting from the finest level of scale now given by r_0 and moving to coarser scales r_n. The sequence of chord lengths is computed from $r_n = 2^n \nabla$, $n = 0, 1, \ldots, 9$, where ∇ is the start length which is always a function of $\bar{d}$, the average chord length. Thus, for example, where $\nabla = \bar{d}/2$ which is the lower bound recommended by Shelberg, Moellering and Lam (1982), the sequence of chord lengths used are in the following ratios: $\frac{1}{2}$, 1, 2, 4, 8, 16, 32, 64, 128, 256. In this case, $r_0 \approx 1$ and $r_9 \approx 510$ which is much larger than Kaye's (1978) upper bound of $F/2$. To provide some feel for this range of approximations, we have plotted the approximated boundaries of Cardiff for r_n, $n = 0, 1, \ldots, 8$, in Figure 5.4. With r_9, the boundary is approximated by only one chord which is clearly inappropriate. Indeed, even with r_7 and r_8, the approximations are too coarse to be of much use. This is clear from Figure 5.4 which shows that this kind of visual test is essential in selecting an appropriate range of measurements for use in the subsequent regressions.

We will illustrate the issue of ascertaining the most appropriate scale

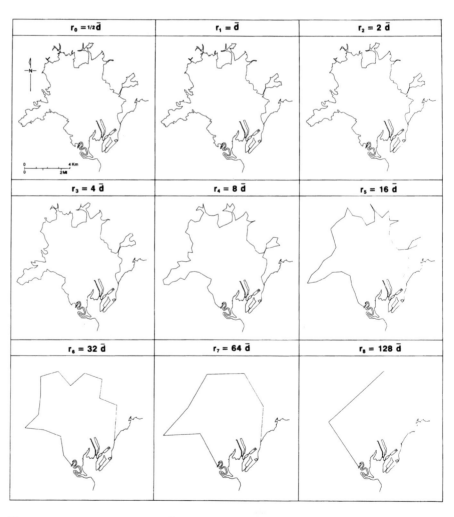

Figure 5.4. A sequence of scale approximations to the urban edge.

range for measuring fractal dimension by selecting 10 different starting values of the chord length ∇, and generating ten sets of measurements for each of these starting values. The values of ∇ chosen are $\nabla = 0.4\bar{d}$, $0.5\bar{d}$, $0.6\bar{d}$, $0.8\bar{d}$, $\bar{d}$, $1.5\bar{d}$, $2\bar{d}$, $3\bar{d}$, $4\bar{d}$ and $5\bar{d}$. From the sequences generated, it is clear that several of the chosen measurements are the same between series, but each of the regressions developed below involves different sets of measures. A visual comparison of each of the ten sequences generated is also contained in the Richardson plots in Figure 5.5 which show the ten measures of log L versus log r for each of the ten starting values of ∇. These plots are all on the same scale for comparative purposes and also show the values of $\bar{d}/2$, $\bar{d}$, $F/2$ and F.

Before we present the results of the regressions, we need to consider how we can systematically narrow the range of results we are able to generate, and to this end, we have devised five criteria. First, we have used the range $0.4\bar{d} \le r \le F/2$ to select those observations which are appropriate. Second, we have used the Richardson plots to identify outliers for exclusion. In particular, when $r > F$, then the algorithm always gives the same perimeter length because it always closes the single chord on the last coordinate point. Such points show up horizontally on the Richardson plots and must be excluded. Third, the scale approximation must be acceptable visually. An examination of Figure 5.4 suggests that approximations with ten chords or less are not satisfactory in representing the overall shape, and thus must be excluded. Fourth, we suggest that the r^2 measure of fit (coefficient of determination) should always be better than 0.95, and fifth, the standardized variation in average perimeter length for each chord r should not be greater than 10% of the mean value. This also enables poor approximations to be excluded.

For each of the 10 starting values of ∇ in the structured walk, we have performed regressions on all 10 points shown in the Richardson plots in Figure 5.5, on the first nine, the first eight, seven, six, then five, below which it is not appropriate to carry out such least-squares fitting. The absolute values of the slopes of the regression lines $|\beta| = |(1 - D)|$ are shown in Table 5.1 along with the r^2 values, but as Shelberg, Moellering and Lam (1982) indicate, such r^2 values should be used in a descriptive rather than an inferential sense. In Table 5.1, the figures which are in bold type involve regressions in which the observations meet all the five criteria mentioned above, and this narrows the range considerably. Note that the fractal dimension is given by adding 1 to the absolute slopes in Table 5.1, that is, $D = 1 + |\beta|$.

For the structured walk method, there is still a large variation in fractal dimension from $1.155 \le D \le 1.289$, and from Table 5.1 it is quite clear that as finer and finer scales come to dominate the regression, so the value of D decreases. This implies that there is greater irregularity at coarser scales, but it also indicates that where the scale is below the level of resolution of the digitized boundary, that is, where $r < \bar{d}$, then no further detail is picked up and the boundary must be considered Euclidean. This is the case for the first four starting values (first four rows) in Table 5.1, and if these are excluded from consideration, the range of D is from 1.234 to 1.289. In fact, the rule of thumb suggested by Shelberg, Moellering and Lam (1982) that

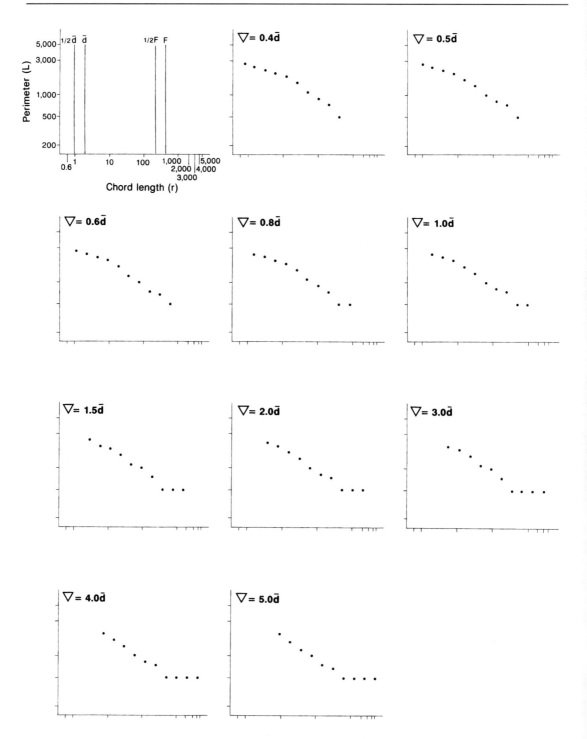

Figure 5.5.   Richardson plots based on ten structured walks.

Table 5.1. Logarithmic regression of perimeter on scale associated with the Richardson plots in Figure 5.5

Starting values ∇^1	Number of observations[2]					
	10	9	8	7	6	5
$0.4\bar{d}$	0.269	0.244	0.231	0.207	**0.177**	**0.155**
	0.953	0.959	0.947	0.944	**0.961**	**0.969**
$0.5\bar{d}$	0.278	0.258	**0.255**	**0.236**	0.211	0.180
	0.969	0.975	**0.963**	**0.956**	0.956	0.975
$0.6\bar{d}$	0.279	0.263	0.254	**0.236**	0.216	0.185
	0.975	0.975	0.964	**0.963**	0.953	0.966
$0.8\bar{d}$	0.292	0.291	0.266	0.254	**0.231**	0.198
	0.976	0.966	0.973	0.962	**0.957**	0.974
$\bar{d}$	0.291	0.297	0.276	0.278	**0.261**	0.234
	0.982	0.977	0.983	0.975	**0.967**	0.963
$1.5\bar{d}$	0.293	0.309	0.308	0.280	**0.261**	0.254
	0.975	0.980	0.971	0.980	**0.980**	0.963
$2.0\bar{d}$	0.282	0.304	0.315	0.293	0.303	**0.289**
	0.969	0.984	0.982	0.989	0.987	**0.979**
$3.0\bar{d}$	0.274	0.303	0.327	0.331	0.301	**0.282**
	0.945	0.972	0.984	0.977	0.986	**0.985**
$4.0\bar{d}$	0.254	0.284	0.313	0.331	0.306	0.328
	0.924	0.958	0.981	0.983	0.989	0.996
$5.0\bar{d}$	0.245	0.276	0.308	0.331	0.321	0.329
	0.915	0.953	0.984	0.996	0.997	0.996

[1]Starting values in each sequence of the structured walks.
[2]Number of observations of perimeter–chord lengths used in regressions. The first value in each row–column is slope $|\beta|$; the second value in parentheses is r^2.

∇ should begin at about $\bar{d}/2$ should be reevaluated in future work so that the variation around $\bar{d}$ can be considered.

5.5 Form and Process: Cardiff's Changing Urban Edge

Boundaries which partition complex systems from their environment and from one another reflect properties and processes which can be inferred from their morphology, as Richter and Peitgen (1985) imply in the quote introducing this chapter. For example, transport and building technologies, social controls over development as well as physical constraints determine the boundary investigated in the previous section, just as the shape and form of the coastlines referred to in Chapters 2 and 3 reflect the action of a variety of geophysical processes. If we were able to observe the change in boundaries through time, then this should give us some clue to the various processes at work, and in this section, we will explore this issue with respect to what the changing boundary of Cardiff over a 50 year period implies for the urban growth of that city.

Thus far, we have seen how perimeter–scale relations may be displayed as a Richardson plots as in Figure 5.5, and we have used such plots in order to detect the range of scales over which it is appropriate to extract information from a data base digitized to a given level of resolution. If a fractal dimension is stable over many scales and the scatter of points about a simple regression line is well-behaved (that is, close fitting), we can infer that the morphology is consistent with a single set of processes operating at every scale. In the case of an urban boundary, which evolves as a concatenation of a variety of processes, it is more plausible to anticipate that a multitude of processes leads to the emergence of a particular fractal dimension. In fact, measurements of the fractal dimensions of boundaries, particularly coastlines (Kent and Wong, 1982; Mandelbrot, 1967; Nakano, 1983, 1984; Richardson, 1961) and fine particles (Flook, 1978; Kaye, Leblanc and Abbot, 1985; Orford and Whalley, 1983), have suggested that such phenomena may be 'multifractal', that is, with different (in this case usually lower) fractal dimensions at smaller scales. This is intuitively plausible in that we might anticipate that different processes operate at different scales, especially where man-made and natural processes combine (Kaye, 1984; 1989a). The importance of the fractal dimension thus lies in identification of the range of scales over which processes operate and the different scales at which such properties manifest themselves over time. It also enables changes in the morphological effects of self-similarity to be explored.

Here we will develop the example used above in order to examine how the irregularity of the boundary of an urban area changes at different scales and through time. We will seek to use these measurements to infer changes in the processes which condition urban growth in time and space. Reexamining some of the graphs in Figure 5.5 reveals evidence of a slight curvilinear trend about the points in the Richardson plots, suggesting that a multifractal (rather than conventional straight line, or log–linear) formulation of the perimeter–step length/scale relationship may have been appropriate in this instance. In focussing upon temporal changes in detailed morphology, we have therefore increased the precision with which the boundaries for this substantive analysis were digitally measured. We will consider the urban boundaries of Cardiff in 1886, 1901 and 1922, but in order to avoid ambiguity of interpretation we will not compare our results with the 1949 digitized perimeter, since this data set was not digitized at a directly comparable level of resolution. We do, however, show the four boundaries overlying one another in Plate 5.1 (see color section) which shows the town's urban expansion, its extent and the changing irregularity of the urban edge over time.

Just as the form of a coastline evolves as the outcome of a range of simultaneous physical circumstances, so the morphology of the city is the outcome of a multitude of physical and social processes as we have already implied (Batty, 1992). These include the technology of building, patterns of land tenure, the size of building plots, the demand for residential space, the mobility of the population, and the efficiency and availability of transport technology. These processes manifest themselves at different scales, for example, building technologies at smaller, transport at larger scales. It is a reasonable assumption that these processes are reflected in the boundary of the city, hence in its degree of irregularity and fractal dimension (Perkal, 1958a, 1958b).

Accordingly, we will advance three hypotheses concerning changes in the fractal dimension of these urban boundaries. First, we consider that the boundary is multifractal across a range of scales; second, that as there is greater control over physical development at smaller scales, the fractal dimension is likely to decrease with scale; and third, that the fractal dimension at smaller scales should decrease over time as greater controls over building technology and land development have been instituted. At larger scales, it is less clear how the fractal dimension changes although increasing mobility and accessibility imply it too will decrease through time. We will test these hypotheses by determining the fractal dimensions of the urban boundary of Cardiff in 1886, 1901 and 1922. These times have been chosen because of the rapid urban growth of the city from a population of 80,000 to 230,000 during this period. This period also marked the development of the tramway system which began in 1872 and was complete by 1914, and it was the period when the predominant style of late Victorian worker housing gave way to more spacious suburban housing. The landed estates which dominated the form of development in Cardiff in the mid-19th century were no longer significant and the period represented the pinnacle of industrial prosperity in Cardiff which was ended by World War I (Daunton, 1977).

The urban boundaries defined from 1:10,560 scale Ordnance Survey maps in 1886, 1901 and 1922, which were digitized to 1 mm accuracy, are displayed Figure 5.6, and overlayed in Plate 5.1. Considerable control was exercised in digitizing to ensure the same level of detail was picked up

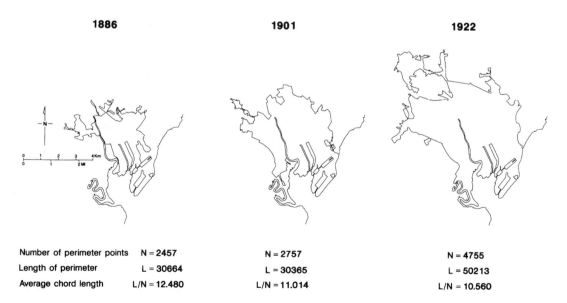

	1886	**1901**	**1922**
Number of perimeter points	N = 2457	N = 2757	N = 4755
Length of perimeter	L = 30664	L = 30365	L = 50213
Average chord length	L/N = 12.480	L/N = 11.014	L/N = 10.560

Figure 5.6.   The urban edge of Cardiff in 1886, 1901, 1992.

from each map, thus minimizing the possibility that the fractal dimension becomes an artifact of the mapping process. Computing these dimensions involves the same procedure as was outlined above in the previous section: first the length of the perimeter of each boundary is calculated by simulating a traverse of the curve at different scales, and second, these perimeter estimates are related to their associated scales using a curve fitting procedure which yields the fractal dimension. The perimeter L is measured using a simulation of Richardson's method of walking a pair of dividers around the curve, the step length of the dividers r being a measure of scale (Richardson, 1961; Shelberg, Moellering and Lam, 1982). Details of the way in which the algorithm operates will be given below in the next section.

The two variants in the method described in Section 5.3 above have both been invoked. First, successive measurements are started at every digitized point on the curve and the perimeter taken as an average of each walk to remove any dependence on starting values. The method is extremely time-consuming, each pass of the method taking 65 minutes of CPU time for a curve involving 4755 digitized points (the 1922 boundary), running on a computer operating at 2 MIPS. Second, the scales used in each walk varied from a step length r_0 computed as the average of the chords linking the digitized points, to a scale which gave not less than eight chords, below which any approximation to the boundary was deemed unacceptable in accordance with the criteria developed at the end of Section 5.4. Thirty changes in scale were used and each scale was related to the lowest step length r_0 by $r_n = 2^n \nabla$, $n = 0, 1, \ldots, 30$, where ∇ is the parameter controlling the geometric scaling related to $\bar{d}$ in equation (5.11). As in Section 5.4, these scales ensure equal weighting of values in the log–log regressions based on the log–log plots of perimeter against scale. These are shown in Figure 5.7 for each boundary.

As we have seen in Chapter 3, geophysical boundaries are characterized by a wide variation in the value of D (Burrough, 1981), but for coastlines, the value of D is likely to be less than 1.3 as first shown by Richardson (1961) and confirmed many times since (Kent and Wong, 1982; Mandelbrot, 1984; Shelberg, Moellering and Lam, 1982). The slope α and intercept β are once again determined by a linear regression of $\log L$ on $\log r$ as in equation (5.8). Richardson plots describing the scaled perimeter measurements for the three time periods in Figure 5.7 form the basic data for the regressions and the results of fitting straight lines through these scatters are given in Table 5.2. The fractal dimensions D decrease as hypothesized with the largest falling in the period 1886–1901. However, both Figure 5.7 and Table 5.2 reveal that the phenomena are multifractal. It is impossible to identify clear breaks in the slopes of the plots and thus approximating the plots by several linear functions would be arbitrary. It would appear that the fractal dimension itself is a function of scale, and thus we have postulated that the scaling coefficient β is determined as

$$\beta = \lambda + \phi r. \tag{5.13}$$

Substituting (5.13) into (5.8) gives

$$\log L = \log \alpha + \lambda \log r + \phi r \log r, \tag{5.14}$$

from which it is clear that

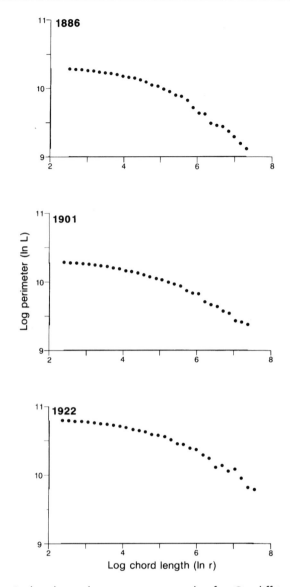

Figure 5.7. Richardson plots over many scales for Cardiff in 1886, 1901 and 1992.

Table 5.2. Scaling constants and fractal dimensions from equation (5.8)

Data set	Log α	$D = 1 - \beta$	Goodness-of-fit (r^2)
1886	11.080	1.239	0.914
1901	10.866	1.184	0.927
1922	11.393	1.185	0.907

Table 5.3.   Scaling constants and fractal dimensions from equation (5.14)

Data set	Log α	$D = 1 - \lambda$ (when $r = 0$)	$\phi \times 10^{-5}$	Goodness-of-fit (r^2)
1886	10.719	1.141	5.865	0.983
1901	10.622	1.117	3.947	0.985
1922	11.114	1.109	3.901	0.984

$$D = 1 - \lambda - \phi r. \tag{5.15}$$

As the scale $r \rightarrow 0$, $D \rightarrow 1 - \lambda$. Thus the term $\phi r \log r$ in equation (5.14) acts as a dispersion factor which increases the fractal dimension as the scale increases. If $\phi = 0$, then this factor which introduces the non-linearity into the plots is redundant and equation (5.14) collapses back to equation (5.8). The model is thus consistent with increasing fractal dimension with scale.

Regressions based on equation (5.14) are shown in Table 5.3 and the performance of each model measured by r^2 dramatically improves in comparison with equation (5.8) and Table 5.2. Changes in the fractal dimensions based on equation (5.15) are plotted in Figure 5.8 from which it is quite clear that the smallest scale dimension where $r = 0$, declines over time in the manner hypothesized. The effect of scale given by ϕ also decreases over time, and in both cases, the greatest decreases in λ and ϕ occur between 1886 and 1901 when the greatest changes in transport technology – new docks and tramways – were developed. These results are consistent with

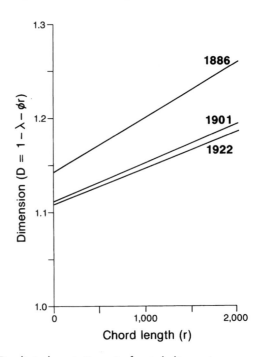

Figure 5.8.   Predicted variations in fractal dimension over scale for the 1886, 1901 and 1992 data sets.

the three hypotheses originally stated, although the decrease in the irregu-larity of Cardiff's urban boundary between 1886 and 1922 cannot be specifi-cally attributed to changes in any single process of development. However, the traditional image of urban growth becoming more irregular as tentacles of development occur around transport lines is not borne out by this analy-sis. It would appear that greater social and physical controls over develop-ment in the late 19th and early 20th century city, together with increased accessibility due to improvements in transport, have combined to gradually reduce the irregularity of urban areas such as Cardiff. These results will only apply to West European cities and similar analyses of North American and other world cities are required. It is also tempting to speculate that these results reflect the general notion of man's increasing control over environment, but such a conclusion should be avoided because there is greater variation in the dimensions produced by different methods than by different temporal data sets on the same city (Batty and Longley, 1987).

These empirical findings suggest that it is necessary to postulate fractal models based on processes which operate at different scales and which thus generate multifractal geometries. Nakano (1983) has indicated how this is possible for a coastline, and Suzuki (1984) has demonstrated how such geo-metries can emerge theoretically over time. These ideas involve the notion of transient self-similarity and transfer the analysis to models of varying self-similarity with respect to morphology and scale. In fact, since the mid-1980s, there has been increasing concern for the concept of multifractals and the notion that all physical objects are likely to imply a multitude of fractal dimensions has become accepted as the basic notions of what consti-tutes a fractal have been relaxed and broadened through empirical examples (Feder, 1988; Stanley and Ostrowsky, 1986). In this context, it may now be possible to examine detailed changes in the form of a city, developing an incremental model of urban change in which changes in shape through the boundary are associated with different processes, differ-ent degrees of irregularity, different fractal dimensions, all persisting through time, a theme we will return to in Chapters 7 and 8. For the moment, however, it is sufficient to note that fractal dimensions of urban boundaries are a function of scale. Other published data such as that per-taining to coastlines, fine particle morphologies, indeed a host of other related examples throughout the physical and natural sciences (Kaye, 1989a), should be reexamined in the light of this argument.

5.6 Fractal Measurement Methods Compared I: the Structured Walk

Thus far, we have described how fractal dimensions are calculated for 'real world' or 'empirical' irregular curves, and this has been developed using the analogy between automated computation and the manual process of obtaining scaled measurements through dividers. The process of changing the divider span with which a base curve is measured is, in fact, just one way of adjusting the scale or resolution at which that curve is measured. In this and the following sections, we will first review the process by which the divider-based measurement algorithm works, and will assess the accuracy and computational burden associated with its use. We will then describe three other methods of measuring fractal irregularity and will discuss the relative merits of each with reference to the basic structured walk method. We will evaluate each of these methods using the examples introduced in Sections 5.4 and 5.5 above.

In his original application, Richardson (1961) manually 'walked' a pair of dividers along a mapped boundary, and obtained scale-dependent measurements by systematically increasing the divider span. Shelberg, Moellering and Lam (1982) were among the first to automate this procedure with an algorithm designed to approximate a digitized curve using a pre-specified range of chord lengths. In Section 5.4, we described how the initial (base) scale length for each curve was computed by first calculating the distances between each adjacent pair of (x,y) coordinates i and $i + 1$ using equation (5.9). Successive scale changes were then incremented using a geometrical progression of chord lengths. In our later examples, we specified criteria to define the maximum and minimum chord lengths to be used in the measurement process, and interpolated 30 scale changes across the scale range bounded by these two extremes.

The walk at any given scale begins by calculating the distance $d_{s,i}$ from a starting point (x_s, y_s) to the second coordinate pair (x_i, y_i) using equation (5.9). If this distance is less than the chord length r, the next coordinate pair (x_{i+1}, y_{i+1}) is selected, the distance $d_{s,i+1}$ is computed and the test against chord length r is made again. This process continues until the distance $d_{s,i+k} > r$ and when this is achieved, a new point (x_{s+1}, y_{s+1}) is interpolated onto the line segment which joins points (x_{i+k-1}, y_{i+k-1}) and (x_{i+k}, y_{i+k}). The walk then recommences from this interpolated point and proceeds through painstaking use of trigonometry to span the curve with chords of exactly length r. As the end of the curve is approached, the distance between the last interpolated point and the end point will invariably be less than r; in this instance, a fraction of the chord length r is computed in order to close the interpolated curve. Measured perimeter lengths (L) at any scale (r) can be obtained from any starting point on the digitized base curve; if the walk begins other than at either the end points, the interpolation proceeds along the curve in both directions and the final recorded length is the sum of these computed values. As stated previously, the empirical measurements recorded in the Cardiff example comprise the average of the lengths measured from every possible starting point on the curve, repeated, of course, for every scale change.

The rudiments of this procedure are given visual expression in Figure 5.9(a) and (b) and in Plate 5.2. The displays in Plate 5.2 are of the 1949 urban edge and were produced using an interactive version of the structured walk algorithm. In this algorithm, the user specifies the initial and final chord lengths (the former as a percentage of mean chord length on the base curve, the latter as an absolute value), the starting point on the base curve, and the number of generalizations (levels) that are to be produced using the walk algorithm. Screen annotation for each level records (from the bottom line to the top) the chord length to be interpolated onto the base curve, the

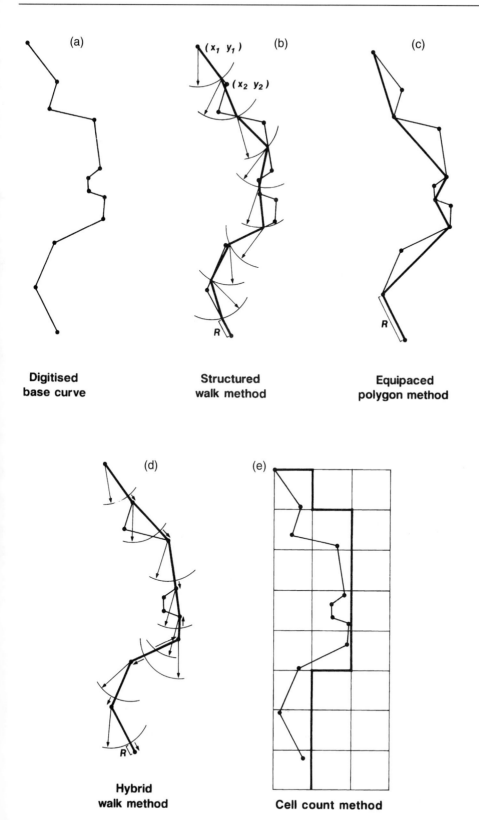

Figure 5.9. The mechanisms underlying the four measurement methods.

measured perimeter of the curve at this scale, and the number of (complete or partial) traverses that are necessary to close the curve on its end points. The sequence of displays allows the user to gain a visual appreciation of the manner in which measured perimeter lengths (and number of chords) decrease as scale increases, and could also assist a decision on the level of fractal detail most appropriate to the storage and display of a given digitized data set.

We have recorded the computer time required to make repeated measurements of the 1949 urban boundary information used in Section 5.4 as well as the 1886, 1901 and 1922 data used in Section 5.5. Scaled measurements for each of the four data series are shown together in Figure 5.10, and the range of scales common to all four analyses are highlighted here. The rate of increase in CPU time in relation to increased numbers of digitized points is shown in Figure 5.11. In order to compare the methods, we have fitted both of the functional forms (5.8) and (5.14), and the results for this basic structured walk are shown alongside the CPU times in Table 5.4. One of our earlier substantive findings was that a 'transient dimension' model (in which fractal dimension is itself a function of scale) was appropriate to the measurement of urban boundaries and these results are presented in summary form in Table 5.4, together with the computer processing times

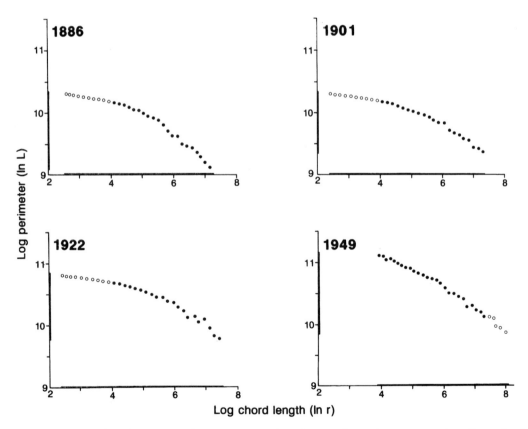

Figure 5.10.   Richardson plots of perimeter–scale relations from the structured walk method. •: observation falling within scale range common to all four temporal data bases, 1886, 1901, 1922 and 1949.

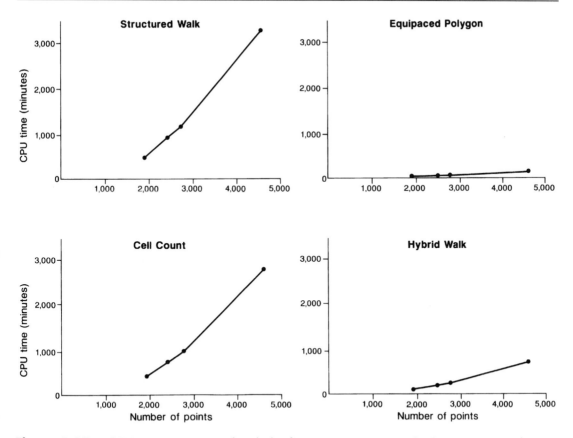

Figure 5.11. CPU usage associated with the four measurement methods.

Table 5.4. The structured walk method: computational costs and statistical performances

Data set	CPU usage Day:h:min	Log–linear form equation (5.8)			Transient dimension model equation (5.14)			
		Log α	D	r^2	Log α	$1 - \lambda$	$\phi \times 10^{-5}$	r^2
1886	0:15:23	11.080	1.239	0.914	10.719	1.141	5.865	0.983
1901	0:19:11	10.886	1.184	0.927	10.622	1.117	3.947	0.985
1922	2:07:10	11.393	1.186	0.907	11.114	1.109	3.901	0.984
1949	0:07:49	12.150	1.267	0.975	11.883	1.211	1.202	0.991

associated with each of the analyses. The r^2 values show that the transient dimension model produces a consistently better statistical fit than the standard log–linear form for every one of the four time slices under analysis.

The Richardson plots shown in Figure 5.10 illustrate that the structured walk method produced estimates which correspond closely to this functional form, with the clearest continuous trend being discernible for the smaller step lengths. Although the positioning of the points does become slightly more erratic for the largest step lengths, there is no evidence of any sudden 'flattening' of the curve, which would have indicated that the scales were too coarse to pick up further fractal detail. This cohesion of the larger scale points about the best fitting functional form is the result of the averaging of each scale observation through measurements from every single possible starting point. Finally, Figure 5.11 shows that the structured walk method is consistently associated with the highest CPU usage of the four methods to be described here. This is a consequence of the precise trigonometric interpolation of points upon the base curve. It might be conjectured that this precision obviates the need to average out the measured perimeter lengths by using every conceivable starting point, although the decay in the trend in the points at larger scale steps suggests this is not necessarily the case.

5.7 Fractal Measurement Methods Compared II: Equipaced Polygon, Hybrid Walk and Cell-Count Methods

The structured walk method provides a precise means of calculating the fractal dimensionality of vectorized boundary data. As we have seen in Chapter 2, fractal measurement and compression provides a general and powerful means of storing coordinate information. It can be used on information stored in both vectorized and rasterized formats, and its use in association with these different data structures can make alternative measurement methods more appropriate. Moreover, data processing requirements for large data sets can make computer processing time an important consideration in devising measurement algorithms. Three such alternative measurement procedures are the equipaced polygon, hybrid walk and cell-count methods. In this section, we will describe their computation and evaluate the comparative performance of each using the Cardiff urban edge data. Repeated averaging of measurements is carried out as earlier, and similar ranges of scale changes are also used.

The equipaced polygon method was first suggested by Kaye (1978, 1989a) and elaborated in Kaye and Clark (1985) as a measurement method in which there is no need to compute new base-level points. The first perimeter length for the sequence of scale changes is computed by summing the distance between adjacent coordinates; the second perimeter length represents the summed distance between every second coordinate; the third sums the distance between every fourth coordinate; and so the progression continues, weeding out all but every 8th, 16th, 32nd, ... point. This geometric point weeding series is contrived so as to give observations a more equal spacing in the Richardson plots, and hence a more equal weighting in the regression analysis. In terms of the Richardson plots and regression analysis, the chord length r which is to be paired with an associated measured perimeter length is given by the average chord length spanning the points at the corresponding level of the point weeding sequence. This is illustrated in Figure 5.9(c).

Formally then, a direction is established from a given starting point on the base-level curve (x_i, y_i) and a chord is constructed to a digitized point (x_{i+k}, y_{i+k}) which is k steps away from (x_i, y_i); k is thus an index of scale. The distance $d_{i,i+k}$ is computed using equation (5.9), and then the next chord involving the point (x_{i+2k}, y_{i+2k}) is constructed from (x_{i+k}, y_{i+k}). Eventually the endpoint of the base-level curve is approached, and the level k curve is closed on this endpoint when the remaining number of base points is less than step length k (this is equivalent to the 'remainder' as described for the structured walk). Computations in both directions from the starting point are added to determine the perimeter and mean chord lengths.

The Richardson plots from the Cardiff data which are associated with this method are shown in Figure 5.12 and the results of regression analysis in Table 5.5. At an intuitive level, one might anticipate that this method yields results of a slightly more arbitrary nature, because exact perimeter lengths will be dependent upon the evenness with which the base curve has been digitized. For example, points are unlikely to have been 'forced' on long straight sections, so these sections are unlikely to contain chord end points; moreover, the entire shape of a measured curve is likely to change if the base curve contains major irregularities or fissures (for exam-

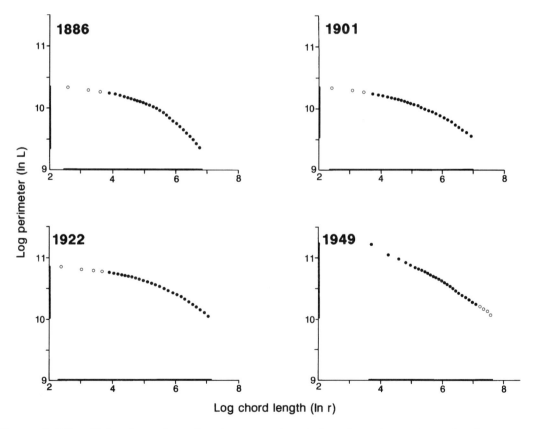

Figure 5.12. Richardson plots of perimeter–scale relations from the equipaced polygon method. ●: observation falling within scale range common to all four temporal data bases, 1886, 1901, 1922 and 1949.

Table 5.5. The equipaced polygon method: computational costs and statistical performances

Data set	CPU usage Day:h:min	Log–linear form equation (5.8)			Transient dimension model equation (5.14)			
		$\log \alpha$	D	r^2	$\log \alpha$	$1 - \lambda$	$\phi \times 10^{-5}$	r^2
1886	0:00:36	11.176	1.236	0.875	10.589	1.086	11.200	0.995
1901	0:00:45	10.923	1.178	0.917	10.594	1.094	5.920	0.994
1922	0:02:09	11.420	1.172	0.902	11.078	1.085	5.187	0.992
1949	0:00:20	12.342	1.293	0.992	12.132	1.250	1.211	0.998

ple, lines bounding suburban communities connected to the main urban area by ribbon development) which will be detected abruptly at a shift between two scale changes. The equipaced polygon method was particularly susceptible to such phenomena, since the measured curve could suddenly dislocate when the point weeding criteria missed some fissured points for the first time. Figure 5.13 shows an example of this susceptibility

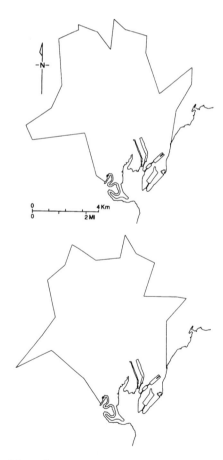

Figure 5.13. Sudden changes in approximation at two adjacent scales using the equipaced polygon method.

at two adjacent scales. In fact, the Richardson plots show that this effect is removed by the averaging process, and the points actually follow a clearer trend than the structured walk plots. The regression results compare directly with the structured walk results, both in terms of measured fractal dimensions and the statistical fits of the two competing functional form specifications. The biggest apparent difference between the two methods seems to be CPU usage as seen in comparing Tables 5.4 and 5.5, in that the equipaced polygon method used less than 5% of the resources required for the structured walk in a fully averaged run. However, intermediate polygon plots are more erratic than those for the structured walk when full averaging does not take place.

The second alternative method is the hybrid walk which was suggested by Clark (1986) as a method which retains some favorable characteristics of both the structured walk and the equipaced polygon methods. It is based directly upon the same prespecified geometric chord length series as the structured walk, which makes it less vulnerable than the equipaced polygon method to the spacing of points on the base curve. However, it is similar to the equipaced polygon method in that no new points are interpolated onto the base curve; rather, each chord is either extended or contracted to coincide with the nearest digitized point, which is then used as the origin from which the next chord is sought. Removal of the time-consuming trigonometric interpolations thus serves to speed up the computations. It is based on the same lowest level of resolution r_0 as the previous two methods and entails similar treatment of the 'remainder' distance as the end of the curve is approached. This is illustrated in Figure 5.9(d).

Formally, the method proceeds in the same way as the structured walk, except that when a point (x_{i+k}, y_{i+k}) is reached where $d_{s,i+k} > r$, no new point is interpolated using the Shelberg–Moellering–Lam algorithm. If $|d_{s,i+k} - r|$ $\leq |d_{s,i+k-1} - r|$, then point (x_{i+k}, y_{i+k}) is selected; if not, then the point (x_{i+k-1}, y_{i+k-1}) is selected, because this point is the closest to the point at which chord length r intersects the base curve. The Richardson plots associated with this method illustrated in Figure 5.14 show a similar pattern to those of the structured walk method in Figure 5.4. The analytical results given in Table 5.6 are also comparable with the first two methods, although the method is unable to discriminate between the log–linear forms of the 1901 and 1922 series. The graphs of CPU usage in Figure 5.11 show that only comparatively modest savings are made compared to the structured walk method, and the equipaced polygon method remains the least demanding by far in this respect.

The final method that we will consider is the cell-count method. This method is more akin to a rasterized conception of the digitized base curve and has been suggested by a number of authors (Dearnley, 1985; Goodchild 1980; Morse et al., 1985). In effect, the computer algorithm imposes a square lattice for a range of different spacings on the base curve. The spacings of the different lattices introduce the sequence of scale changes over which the irregularity of the base curve is to be measured. At each scale (grid spacing), the cell-count algorithm simply enumerates all of the cells that the base-level curve passes through. Counts are made at each scale change for grids originating at each point on the base curve: these are averaged to produce the final observations for each scale change in the now familiar

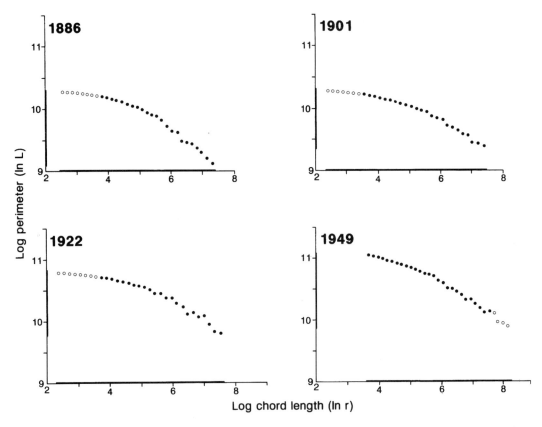

Figure 5.14. Richardson plots of perimeter–scale relations from the hybrid walk method. •: observation falling within scale range common to all four temporal data bases, 1886, 1901, 1922 and 1949.

Table 5.6. The hybrid walk method: computational costs and statistical performances

Data set	CPU usage Day:h:min	Log–linear form equation (5.8)			Transient dimension model equation (5.14)			
		Log α	D	r^2	Log α	$1 - \lambda$	$\phi \times 10^{-5}$	r^2
1886	0:12:34	11.119	1.248	0.913	10.715	1.137	7.256	0.987
1901	0:15:52	10.895	1.190	0.929	10.633	1.117	4.560	0.990
1922	1:21:56	11.412	1.190	0.906	11.111	1.106	4.567	0.989
1949	0:06:52	12.416	1.308	0.989	12.197	1.262	1.001	0.996

way. Strictly speaking, each grid scale should be defined with respect to the start and endpoints on the base-level curve, although for reasons of convenience and comparability, the empirical results reported and depicted below are based on the same 31 scales used for the structured and hybrid walk methods. This is illustrated in Figure 5.9(e). This cell-counting procedure is related but not identical to box-counting, and its associated dimension, the box dimension (Voss, 1988). Falconer (1990), however, includes all four of the techniques introduced here under the broader heading of box-counting to distinguish these from spectral methods for computing dimension which we alluded to in Chapter 3.

Formally, from a given starting point (x_s, y_s) with a selected cell size r and direction of traverse, the next coordinate (x_i, y_i) on the base curve is alighted upon. A test is made to see if this point lies within the same cell by considering whether $|x_s - x_i| \geq r$ or $|y_s - y_i| \geq r$. If either of these conditions hold, a new point is established where the coordinate in question is updated in the direction of greatest increase. Thus if $|x_s - x_i| \leq |y_s - y_i|$, $x_{s+1} = x_s + r$ and $y_{s+1} = y_s$, whilst if the converse holds, $x_{s+1} = x_s$ and $y_{s+1} = y_s + r$. If the increase along both the x and y axes is less than the grid size r, then a new coordinate point (x_{i+1}, y_{i+1}) is selected and the tests are made once again. Each time the direction is updated, a cell has been crossed and is thus counted. Unlike the previous methods, when the end point of the curve is approached, the cell approximation simply finishes when the cell in which the end point exists has been identified.

The way in which this procedure works is illustrated in Plate 5.3 where the aggregation shows that the intricate form of the line is lost at an early stage in the cell-count process. It is for this reason that the method has been advocated as a computationally inexpensive first approximation to measurement. Figure 5.11 shows that the cell-count method is closest to the equipaced polygon method in its meager CPU requirements. Although the Richardson plots shown in Figure 5.15 exhibit generally smooth trends, there is some evidence of the 'bottoming out' of the curves at the coarsest scales. This indicates that the method does not detect fractal detail at these scales, despite the averaging that has taken place. Although the choice of starting point makes little or no difference to the results when the base curve is being traversed in very small increments, Figure 5.16 shows that this is not invariably the case for large step increments which only crudely approximate the curve. Such measurements are highly sensitive to the lengths of the residual steps which are left at a fairly coarse resolution using the cell-count method. This is illustrated in Figure 5.16 where the outline initiated at coordinate 456 (Figure 5.16(a)) is very different from that initiated at coordinate 1234 (Figure 5.16(b)). Largely because of this, the fractal dimensions and statistical fits shown in Table 5.7 bear less direct comparison with the other methods than has been the case in the previous sections.

5.8 Beyond Lines to Areas

The algorithms described in this chapter have been used to investigate a wide range of physical phenomena (Burrough, 1984), but rarely has the irregularity of artificial boundaries been investigated. The preceding sections have illustrated that fractal measurement provides a plausible and flexible means of detecting the structure and character of cartographic boundaries, while our substantive example suggests that the processes which structure urban form and urban edges might be investigated with

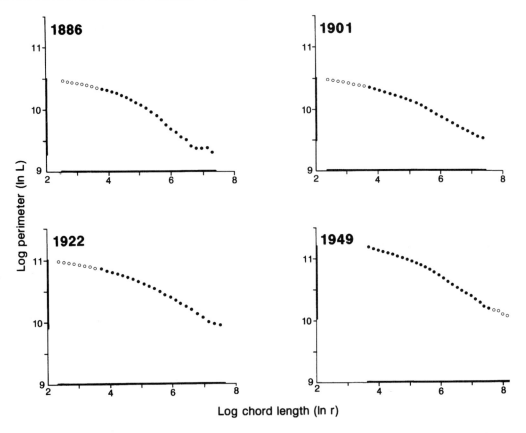

Figure 5.15. Richardson plots of perimeter–scale relations from the cell-count method. ●: observation falling within scale range common to all four temporal data bases, 1886, 1901, 1922 and 1949.

respect to the manifest fractal irregularity which characterizes different cities in time and space. This latter objective might be accomplished by having regard to what urban theory suggests about the concatenation of processes, but also by recognizing different types of irregularity at different scales and over different ranges of the same phenomenon. Historical variations in fractal dimension are indeed likely, for the development of cities has been influenced by processes whose form and scale has changed over time. Whilst fractal methods can be used to generate 'semi-realistic' tessellations of the plane in order to facilitate routine spatial forecasting as we demonstrated in Chapter 4, such measurements are likely to be more useful in developing appropriate physical theory for cities. We will return to this issue of reconciling form with function in later chapters.

Describing the fractal form of cities from cartographic lines which mark their edge is perhaps the most simplistic approach we can take to linking form to function. Although it is clear that planned cities are likely to have dimensions which are integer in contrast to the organically growing cities whose irregularity gives fractional dimension, urban boundaries simply provide the envelopes for urban form and as such give little clue as to how much of the two-dimensional space is filled by the city. Envelopes do not

(a)

(b)

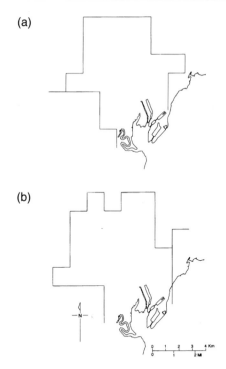

Figure 5.16. Variations in shape approximation using different starting points for the cell-count method.

Table 5.7. The cell-count method: computational costs and statistical performances

Data set	CPU usage Day:h:min	Log–linear form equation (5.8)			Transient dimension model equation (5.14)			
		Log α	D	r^2	Log α	$1 - \lambda$	$\phi \times 10^{-5}$	r^2
1886	0:03:04	11.326	1.267	0.953	11.109	1.207	3.525	0.973
1901	0:03:51	11.079	1.200	0.967	10.919	1.156	2.592	0.989
1922	0:11:30	11.617	1.209	0.957	11.426	1.156	2.686	0.988
1949	0:01:37	12.288	1.274	0.985	12.144	1.244	0.646	0.990

pick up the detailed texture and irregular fabric of urban development and thus offer little by way of linking dimension to the density of development. We will in fact explore these notions from Chapter 7 onwards where we will switch our focus away from boundaries to cellular development where the focus will be upon density, occupancy and area rather than upon lines and edges.

In Chapter 10, we will return once again to questions of the urban boundary, but then we will explore the way boundary length and area are related across different sizes of city, in this way seeking to model the relation between area and perimeter and deriving fractal dimensions which pertain to different size classes of city. Here, however, we will continue to explore the fractal form of single cities, and to this end, we will examine the pattern of land uses which occur within the urban envelope, seeking to generate the fractal dimension and properties of sets of different land use. The notion that boundaries and edges do not exist in their own right but simply serve to define space by marking off different regimes from one another, while closing some from others, is central. In the next chapter we will examine the patterns of several sets of land uses in a small English town, measuring their boundaries and computing their fractal dimensions, but with the explicit intention of exploring the extent to which we can relate boundaries to areas through the area–perimeter relations which enable the dimension of *sets of objects* rather than a *single object* to be computed. However, in providing an unambiguous link between boundaries of entire cities and their areas, we will have to wait until the last chapter before we tie together these ideas formally and empirically. In the meantime, we will disaggregate not aggregate our spatial focus, exploring land use inside the city rather than relations between cities of different sizes.

The Morphology of Urban Land Use

Nature uses only the longest threads to weave her patterns, so each small piece of her fabric reveals the organization of the entire tapestry. (Feynman, 1965, p. 34.)

6.1 Inside the Fabric of the City

As soon as we turn our attention to the geometrical composition of a city's land use, the urban boundaries with which we have been working, reveal themselves to be both crude and simplistic descriptors of urban form. Inside these envelopes lies a rich mix of heterogeneous activities and uses which are often easier to distinguish from one another than 'urban' is from 'rural' but which belie a level of complexity that threatens to destroy the most sustained attempt to classify their geometry. New problems of boundary definition arise where different land uses, clearly embodying different processes of development, have common edges, and thus the problem becomes one of knowing how to distinguish different processes from a geometry which shows itself in only one form. The problem of defining fractal objects which are spatially adjacent or contiguous to one another becomes central, and thus introduces the tantalizing specter of fractal objects which are clearly different geometrically at one level but when aggregated to the next, compose higher-order objects which have their own integrity and unity. It is in this sense then that the tapestry which Richard Feynman (1965) refers to above is woven from threads which reveal themselves at the lowest level. This chapter will be concerned with identifying how these threads which we defined as entire boundaries to urban development in the last chapter, compose the fabric of the city at the more detailed level of its land use.

So far in our analyses, we have focussed upon the difficulties inherent in measuring geographical boundaries to satisfactory levels of precision, and we have also addressed the difficulties in obtaining objective and consistent definitions of categories of urban land use. We have produced some limited evidence to suggest that the ambiguities inherent in defining 'irreversibly urban' phenomena and the subjective nature of boundary encoding are not in themselves sufficient to impede us in observing temporal trends in the changing fractal dimension of urban boundaries. In the spirit of fractal measurement primarily in the natural sciences, in the last chapter we developed and extensively tested four different algorithms for measuring irregularity, drawing conclusions as to the strengths and weaknesses of these alternative procedures. In this chapter, we will use these methods to explore the fractal nature of the more detailed urban fabric. This amounts to a broad conceptual treatment and a thorough technical exposition, yet there is an important sense in which our analysis remains a simplistic treatment of geographical tessellations and land use categories. That is, whilst measurement in science can, in many circumstances, be considered to concern physically and geographically isolated structures, this assumption clearly becomes strained where the subjects of our measurements constitute juxtaposed contiguous areal units, which are embedded within an overall geographical matrix.

Viewed from this more holistic perspective, we might expect measurements of line character to reflect predominantly the processes that have molded the form of each pair of adjacent land parcels, or have embodied both sets of processes in more or less equal amount. We are not aware of fractal measurement that explicitly acknowledges the role of boundaries as mediators between adjacent categories, for in the mainstream, such phenomena are considered to be the edges of geographical isolates. From this new standpoint, the coastlines in Chapters 2 and 3 should also reflect characteristics of both adjacent media, that is, the lithology and structural geomorphology of the land mass, and the erosional and/or depositional characteristics of the water body (Kaproff, 1986; Turcotte, 1992). In a system of contiguous land use areas that compose an urban settlement, the boundary to each use will similarly always consist of parts of the boundary of other uses. In this chapter we will begin to address this issue and in so doing, will raise, but not resolve, some severe conceptual problems for the first time.

We will begin by providing a brief summary of the fractal relations we seek to define, in particular the area–perimeter relations which are central to this chapter as well as the perimeter–scale relations which we discussed extensively in the last. We will also present two formulations of scale dependence which we will apply to each of these relations. The application of these methods to land use boundaries in the English town of Swindon is then introduced by first describing the characteristics of the urban area in question. Fractal dimensions based on area–perimeter relations across scales are estimated, and these same dimensions are next derived by examining scale changes within the digital representation of the perimeters themselves. Finally, individual dimensions of each of the land use parcels can be classified on the basis of their fractal dimension. The analysis contains some inevitable ambiguities, but it is clear that careful measurement is required in all such applications, and thus we see this exposition as charting the ground rules for fractal measurement in this domain. Moreover, the sensitivity of the analysis to measurement differences casts considerable doubt on many of the results from applications of fractal geometry presented to date in a variety of other fields.

6.2 Area–Perimeter Relations and Scale Dependence

As we indicated at the end of Chapter 5, in moving to a more detailed level of spatial resolution, we now require methods which will not only compute the fractal dimension of a single object, but of many objects, in this case land uses composing distinct sets. To do this, we must supplement the perimeter–scale relations given in Chapter 2 as equations (2.24) and (2.25), and in Chapter 5 as (5.5) and (5.7) with the relationship between perimeter and its area. This area–perimeter relation was derived in Chapter 2 as equation (2.29) and we will begin by discussing its relevance to the application posed here. In this section, we will also repeat, for the reader's convenience, the perimeter–scale relations which we used in the last chapter.

In Euclidean geometry, a measure of size in a given dimension will scale directly with a measure in another, for example in an adjacent dimension, and this scaling will be some product of the dimensions themselves. Consider area A and volume V based on two and three dimensions respectively. Area has a size calculated as the square of the line measure L, that is L^2, while volume has a size L^3. If it is required to derive area from volume, it is clear that this can be done as $A \propto V^{2/3}$. In the same way, if it is required to derive the line L (which we will henceforth term more familiarly the perimeter) from area A, the relation is

$$L \propto A^{1/2}. \tag{6.1}$$

All relationships such as those implied by equation (6.1) show that size in one dimension can be scaled directly by knowing the dimension of the object in a higher or lower dimension. For example, if $A = \pi r^2$, the area of a circle with radius r, $L \propto r$ and so on for variety of regular forms. These types of relation appear widely in the natural sciences where they form an essential part of the study of relative growth or allometry (Gould, 1966). If the relationship between a line and an area is as postulated in equation (6.1), this is the condition of isometry. If the power of A were greater than $1/2$, this would be positive allometry, if less, this would be negative allometry.

Let us now define the area at a given scale k as A^k. If area is regarded as a measuring device for the perimeter, when the scale is increased to $k + 1$, it is clear that

$$\frac{L_{k+1}}{L_k} > \left(\frac{A_{k+1}}{A_k}\right)^{1/2}, \tag{6.2}$$

because more and more scaled detail concerning the boundary will be picked up. In fact, the equivalent to the coastline conundrum is that in the limit as $k \to \infty$, the ratio of areas in equation (6.2) will converge but the ratio of the perimeters will continue to increase. From equation (6.1), it is clear that to derive L from A, area must be rescaled by a parameter which is greater than 1 but less than 2. That is

$$L \propto (A^{1/2})^D = A^{D/2}, \tag{6.3}$$

where $1 < D < 2$. If $D = 2$, then perimeter would scale up as area which would imply that the area be defined as a space-filling curve, a physically impossible realization for the kinds of geographical systems that we will consider here. If $D = 1$, perimeter would not scale more than the basic unit of measurement, the line, which would imply that no scale effects were present as area increased. The coefficient D is, of course, the fractal dimension. In this context, it again serves as an empirical measure of how much the curve in question departs from a straight line, thus indicating how 'crinkled' or tortuous the boundary across the space is. The relation in equation (6.3) is known as the *area–perimeter relation* and the nature of its scaling clearly implies a way of estimating the value of D (Lovejoy, 1982).

In measuring the boundary of single objects, we have restricted our attention to a single geometrical relation, namely that between a scale defined by a unit r and a measured perimeter L. The general form of this relation was given earlier in equations (2.25) and (5.7) and indexing it now by its scale r, it is

$$L(r) = N(r)r = \alpha r^{(1-D)}, \tag{6.4}$$

where $N(r)$ is the number of chords at scale r which approximate the perimeter $L(r)$. We thus have two relationships for the perimeter $L(r)$, one in terms of area as in equation (6.3), and one in terms of scale as in equation (6.4). Combining these gives

$$L(r) \propto A^{D/2} \propto r^{(1-D)}. \tag{6.5}$$

It is tempting to try to equate these by considering how A relates to the scale r. However, it is not possible to do this in general for it is only meaningful in special cases where the geometry is known or assumed.

Besides the area–perimeter and perimeter–scale relations, there is a third which could be used to estimate the fractal dimension D. This is the number–area rule known as Korcak's law (Mandelbrot, 1983). It relates the number of or fraction of areas $Fr(A)$ with an area greater than A, to the area itself as

$$Fr(A) \propto A^{-D/2}. \tag{6.6}$$

Here the characteristic length is again taken as the square root of area A and used in a generalization of the number–scale relation in equation (2.24). We will not use equation (6.6) in any of our analyses for it requires a much larger number of objects, in this case land use parcels, than the level of resolution of the application we have chosen permits. Nevertheless, there may be circumstances amongst the kinds of geographical applications which we will describe where it might be useful (Kent and Wong, 1982).

Both the area–perimeter and perimeter–scale relations in equations (6.3) to (6.5) are intrinsically linear in their parameters D and can thus be estimated by regression techniques after suitable logarithmic transformation. However, the data for these estimations are quite different. For the area–perimeter relation, it would in theory be possible to measure the area and perimeter of an irregular object at different scales and perform the regression on these measurements: but the relation is more suited to estimation using a series of areas and perimeters associated with a set of objects, all of different sizes. If the relationship holds over many scales, more scaling detail will be picked up in larger objects than in smaller ones. In the case of the perimeter–scale equation, we will use the techniques of Chapter 5 which involve measuring the same object at different scales. In this chapter, we will explore the consequences of these two methods and note some of the conceptual difficulties resulting from their comparison. In the rest of this section, however, we will concern ourselves solely with their estimation as well as techniques for measuring the effects of scale.

First we will write the area–perimeter relation in equation (6.3) as

$$L = \gamma A^{f(D)}, \tag{6.7}$$

where γ is a constant of proportionality and $f(D)$ is some power function involving the fractal dimension D, in this case $f(D) = D/2$. Taking logs of equation (6.7) gives

$$\log L = \log \gamma + f(D) \log A, \tag{6.8}$$

where in the case of equation (6.3), $\log \gamma$ is the intercept and $f(D) = D/2$, the slope of the regression line of the log of perimeter on the log of area. Clearly the slope $f(D)$ can take different functional forms from which D can always be derived, given an estimate of the slope. The perimeter–scale relation in equation (6.4) can also be generalized as

$$L(r) = \alpha r^{g(D)}, \tag{6.9}$$

where α is the constant of proportionality and $g(D)$ a function which in equation (6.4) is $(1 - D)$. Taking logs of equation (6.8) gives

$$\log L(r) = \log \alpha + g(D) \log r, \tag{6.10}$$

where $\log \alpha$ is the intercept and $g(D) = (1 - D)$, the slope of the associated regression line. Note that equations (6.9) and (6.10) are generalized versions of the perimeter–scale relations given in Chapter 5.

The conventional fractal model based on the use of equation (6.3) in (6.7) or equation (6.4) in (6.9), has a linear form implying that D is scale-invariant. However, as we have seen in Chapter 5, in some contexts it can be hypothesized that dimension itself might vary with scale or area and in this case, the linear form would be more complex. A second model based on the notion that fractal dimension does vary systematically with scale was used in Chapter 5 and these variants will also be tested here. In the case of the area–perimeter relation, the fractal dimension D can be hypothesized to be $f(D) = (\zeta + \eta A^{1/2})/2$ which when used in equation (6.8) gives

$$\log L = \log \gamma + \frac{\zeta}{2} \log A + \frac{\eta}{2} A^{1/2} \log A. \tag{6.11}$$

In equation (6.11), the coefficient $\zeta/2$ has an analogous role to $D/2$ in equation (6.3) as applied to (6.7). The third term on the right-hand side of equation (6.11) is a dispersion factor which measures the non-linearity of the area–perimeter relation. It is clear that as $\eta \to 0$, $\zeta \to D$ and equation (6.11) collapses back to the logarithmic transformation of equation (6.3) or strictly (6.7) with $f(D) = D/2$.

For the case of the perimeter–scale relation in equation (6.10), we have already seen in Chapter 5 that when $g(D)$ is a function of scale $\lambda + \phi r$, then

$$\log L(r) = \log \alpha + \gamma \log r + \phi r \log r, \qquad (6.12)$$

where the fractal dimension D is given by

$$D = 1 - \lambda - \phi r, \qquad (6.13)$$

In equation (6.13), as the scale $r \to 0$, $D \to 1 - \lambda$. The term $\phi r \log r$ in (6.12) also acts as a dispersion factor which increases the fractal dimension as the scale increases and is a kind of weighted entropy, modulating the effect of the fractal dimension. In the sequel, these 'transient dimension' models based on the systematic variation of dimension with area or scale will be referred to as the 'modified models' in contrast to the 'conventional models' of equations (6.3) and (6.4) where dimension is scale-invariant.

Estimating D for the two models using the area–perimeter relations in equation (6.8) with $f(D) = D/2$ and in equation (6.11) is straightforward. For each land parcel, the area and perimeter can be easily measured and form the dependent and independent variables respectively. The number of parcels in the study obviously affects the fit of the regression, and it may be necessary to identify and exclude outliers. However, the variation in scale within the observations forming the data set is only influenced by the prior selection of land parcels, not by any peculiarity of the area–perimeter measurement. In contrast, the perimeter–scale relations in equation (6.10) with $g(D) = 1 - D$ and in equation (6.12) depend upon the choice of scale and the measurement of the perimeter associated with that scale for each individual object. In some of the applications we present below, we will adapt this procedure to form aggregate perimeters from more than one land parcel. Furthermore, we will make these perimeter–scale measurements using each of the four measurement methods outlined previously in Sections 5.6 and 5.7 of Chapter 5.

6.3 Areas and Perimeters: the Fractal Geometry of Urban Land Use

Swindon, the town chosen for our expository analysis, is located in south central England about 70 miles west of London. The town is quite compact and not affected in its form by the presence of any rapidly growing nearby towns. It has a reasonably buoyant economy which in the 1960s was due to its designation as an expanded town, taking overspill population from Greater London. More recently, its favored location in an expanding area of southern England has led to the location of new service and high technology industries in and around the town itself. Figure 6.1 and Plate 6.1 shows the pattern of land use composing the town in 1981 from which it is clear that as the town has grown, it has absorbed villages in its immediate periphery. This fairly aggregated land use map was compiled using diverse data sources: remotely sensed data and local authority map records used by Rickaby (1987) as part of his studies into the energy requirements of small towns. The five land uses – residential, commercial–industrial, educational, transport and open space – shown in Figure 6.1 constitute the basic

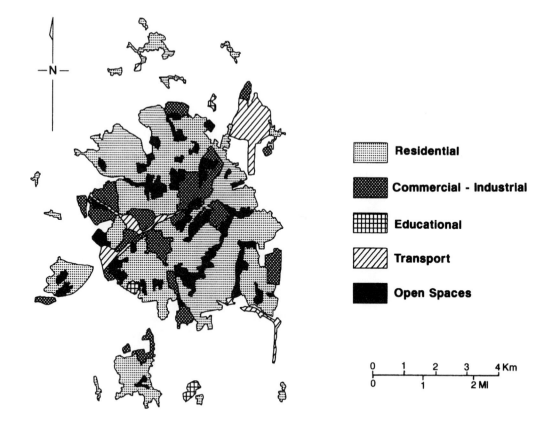

Figure 6.1. Urban land use in Swindon, 1981.

data for this study. The map was digitized using locally available software (Bracken, Holdstock and Martin, 1987) and the land parcels were extracted in polygon form using conventional digital cartographic techniques.

Figure 6.2 shows the polygons which represent the land parcels, drawn to scale and classified according to the five land uses but not arranged in any particular order. Observing how these parcels fit together to form the overall map, the conundrum raised in the introduction to this chapter relating to contiguous boundaries between different uses is immediately apparent. For example, the largest land parcel of all is part of the set of residential land uses shown in Figure 6.2. In one sense, this parcel can be considered as a skeleton for the entire town, but it is clear that about half its boundary is common with other land uses; this raises the conceptual difficulty of making comparisons of the irregularity and form of this boundary with that of adjacent land uses. For the moment, we will assume that the different parcels can be treated separately, and we will pursue the estimation in this manner before commenting further on the problem below.

Some characteristics of the digital representation of the five land uses are presented in Table 6.1. There is considerable variation in the set of land uses, and it is clear that no generalizations can be made about educational land use which comprises only three parcels; and there are limits to how far one can make inferences about the transport land use which comprises

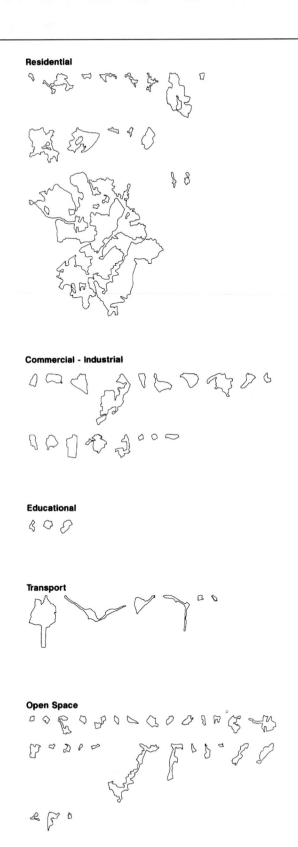

Figure 6.2. Land parcels separated into distinct land uses.

Table 6.1. Characteristics of digitized urban land use in Swindon

Land use	Number of parcels	Number of digitized points N	Number of common points	Percent of common points
Residential	16	2989	1534	51.4
Commercial–industrial	18	1030	626	60.8
Educational	3	109	17	15.6
Transport	6	510	261	51.2
Open space	29	1421	1286	90.5
All land uses	72	6059	3724	61.5

Land use	Mean no. of points per parcel	Average chord length $\bar{d}$	Length of perimeter $L(r) = N(r)r$	Feret's diameter F
Residential	186.8	0.785	2344.9	119.5
Commercial–industrial	57.2	0.837	861.8	42.4
Educational	36.3	0.727	78.5	11.5
Transport	85.0	0.821	417.7	52.8
Open space	49.0	0.776	1106.2	52.9
All land uses	84.2	0.795	4816.3	119.5

only six parcels. However, examining the average chord length of these data which ranges from 0.727 to 0.837 base level units, indicates that the base level digitization is fairly independent of land use type. The number of digitized points given in Table 6.1 for each land use and for the total involves the double counting of common boundaries referred to above in that the points which are common to any pair of land uses are included in each land use.

Of the 6059 points which comprise the total of points in each of the distinct land uses, there are only 2335 points which are not common to adjacent land use boundaries. The remaining 3724 points which are common to various pairs of land uses are in fact counted twice (for each land use in each pair) and thus there are 1862 points which are common in the data set. In total, there are 4197 distinct points in the set, 43% of these being common to adjacent land uses. In terms of the individual uses, 51% of the points defining the residential parcels are common to other uses, while over 90% of the points referring to open space are part of the boundaries of other land uses. These percentages, shown in Table 6.1, give some indication of the position of the land uses within the town. For example, most of the open space is enclosed within the town itself, not on its edge, while educational land use is mainly on the town's edge. In Table 6.1, the perimeter length refers to the sum of all the perimeters relating to a given land use while the Feret diameter represents the maximum spanning distance found amongst the parcels of any given land use, as defined previously in equation (5.12). It is clear from this and from Figure 6.2 that there is some considerable variation among land use parcels with respect to size.

We are now in a position to estimate the first set of fractal dimensions based on the area–perimeter relation, In Figure 6.3, the log–log plots of perimeter against area are presented as scatter diagrams for each of the five sets of land uses in turn, and then for all five land uses comprising the 72 land parcels in the town. These plots demonstrate strong relationships

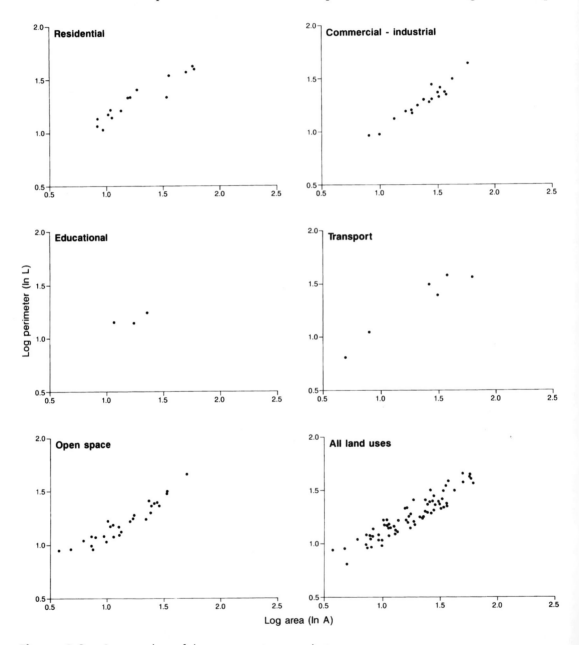

Figure 6.3. Scatter plots of the area–perimeter relations.

between perimeter and area, and it is difficult to detect any significant non-linearity in their form. To these data we have fitted the conventional perimeter–area model based on using equation (6.3) in (6.7) which we can write in the form of equation (6.8) as

$$\log L = \log \gamma_1 + \frac{D}{2} \log A. \tag{6.14}$$

The modified perimeter–area model given earlier in its logarithmic form in equation (6.11) we will repeat for convenience as

$$\log L = \log \gamma_2 + \frac{\zeta}{2} \log A + \frac{\eta}{2} A^{1/2} \log A. \tag{6.15}$$

but note that we now distinguish the intercept terms in equations (6.14) and (6.15) as γ_1 and γ_2 respectively.

The results of these regressions are presented in Table 6.2. With the exception of educational land use where there are only three observations, the adjusted r^2 statistics for both sets of models are acceptable. There are no obvious outliers, for example, whose removal might improve these statistics. The modified model gives a slight improvement over the conventional one, but this is not significant. The fractal dimensions in the conventional model are as postulated, that is, $1 < D < 2$, with the exception of the educational land use which we must exclude from serious analysis. Interpretations of the parameter ζ in the modified model are problematic because of the size of η. As $\eta \rightarrow 0$, it is hypothesized that $\zeta \rightarrow D$ but none of these results suggest any refined interpretation comparable to the 'transient dimension' perimeter–scale specification explored in Chapter 5. The conventional model is the only one acceptable here and excluding education, the analysis suggests that the commercial–industrial ($D \approx 1.478$) and transport land uses ($D \approx 1.447$) have more tortuous boundaries than those of residential ($D \approx 1.331$) and open space ($D \approx 1.243$). The dimension associated with all the land uses ($D \approx 1.296$) is clearly an average. All these results are consistent with other estimates using aerial data produced by applications of the area–perimeter method (Lovejoy, 1982; Woronow, 1981) but the correlations are not as good. Nevertheless this provides a backcloth and comparison to the perimeter–scale analyses which now follow.

Table 6.2. Parameters associated with the area–perimeter relation

Land use	Conventional model equation (6.14)		Modified model equation (6.15)		
	D	r^2	ζ	η	r^2
Residential	1.331	0.924	0.499	0.229	0.924
Commercial–industrial	1.478	0.923	0.307	0.361	0.926
Educational	0.569	0.111	−15.426	5.461	Not computed
Transport	1.447	0.913	3.996	−0.845	0.950
Open space	1.243	0.892	−0.710	0.693	0.925
All land uses	1.296	0.880	0.339	0.301	0.892

6.4 Perimeters and Scale: Constructing Long Threads from Land Use Parcel Boundaries

Before we introduce the analysis based on perimeter–scale relations, it is worth discussing the degree of irregularity associated with different land use patterns as we perceive it in *a priori* terms. In examining the five land uses, we might argue that open space is more likely to be defined according to the boundaries imposed by natural terrain in contrast to more artificially determined land uses such as the commercial–industrial and transport uses. Residential land use is likely to have a degree of irregularity in its form somewhere between these extremes as might educational use. With respect to the area–perimeter relations, this *a priori* ranking of open space/ residential/educational/commercial–industrial/transport from higher to lower degrees of irregularity is not borne out at all by the fractal dimensions. Indeed, Table 6.2 implies somewhat the reverse but the r^2 coefficients are lower than anticipated, and it is possible that area–perimeter relations do not capture scale effects to the same precision as do methods based on perimeter–scale equations.

However, to be consistent with the area–perimeter analysis, it is necessary to devise a way of determining single fractal dimensions for each set of land parcels according to land use types. In a later section, we will look at the variation in fractal dimension across land parcels and types, but here we will begin by defining a global (or total) perimeter for each land use set. Were we to simply calculate a single total perimeter for each land use based on all its parcels, and regress these against scale, this would be similar to our previous analysis as scale would be a proxy for area. What we have done in fact is to calculate a total perimeter for each land use by stringing together the individual land parcel perimeters in the arbitrary order in which the parcels and their coordinate points have been digitized. We have also derived a total of total perimeters in the same way which contains all the points relevant to each land parcel.

In Figure 6.4, we show these total perimeters for each of the five land uses. These are not drawn to the common scales of the parcels contained in Figures 6.1 or 6.2, but are scaled up or down to be roughly comparable in area when displayed on a graphics device. It should be quite straightforward to identify the land parcels from their classification in Figure 6.2. The total perimeters are in fact derived by centering the first digitized point of each land parcel on a common point and producing a string of coordinates in the order in which each land use was digitized. The educational and transport land uses with the fewest land parcels show this most clearly in Figure 6.4. We have not included the total of total perimeters because it is not possible to produce a clear and clean plot due to the continual overlapping of boundaries: we will, however, use this total of totals in the subsequent analysis.

From these base level perimeters, aggregations across the given range of scales yield new perimeters which provide the data for estimating the parameters of the perimeter–scale relation. Two issues are important. First, the order and orientation of the land parcels forming the total perimeter

Figure 6.4. Aggregate perimeters for the five land uses.

could be crucial, and second the aggregations should not be as great as to pick up the aggregate shape of these composite perimeters which is clearly quite arbitrary. Order and orientation have been varied and this makes little difference to the subsequent results, but the aggregate shape problem does affect the estimated dimension. In fact, this leads to a reestimation of the perimeter–scale relations using a reduced set of aggregations to be reported in the next section.

As in Chapter 5, the number and scale of the aggregations for each of these perimeters (which provides the set of observations for the log–log regressions) is fixed so that each observation is of equal weight in the estimation. The limits of aggregation for the four measurement methods based on the structured walk, hybrid walk and cell-count are first calculated as follows. The average chord length $\bar{d}$ in these data sets is computed from equation (5.11) and the maximum spanning distance or Feret diameter F from equation (5.12). Note that we assume there are N points in the digitized base level curve, which is thus made up of $N-1$ straightline segments or chords. The sequence of aggregations where $\bar{d}$ represents the first chord size and F represents the last, and where m is the number of aggregations, is given by

$$F = \omega^{(m-1)} \bar{d}. \tag{6.16}$$

In fact, in this instance the starting point is set as the minimum, not average, chord size, and this can be represented as a fraction ψ of $\bar{d}$. Therefore, equation (6.16) becomes

$$\psi F = \omega^{(m-1)} \psi \bar{d}. \tag{6.17}$$

The weight ω scales one chord size to the next in the sequence of aggregations and this is computed from equations (6.16) or (6.17) as

$$\omega = \exp\left(\frac{\log F - \log \bar{d}}{m - 1}\right). \tag{6.18}$$

This method of aggregating perimeters can only be applied to the structured walk, hybrid walk and cell-count methods of perimeter approximation, for the equipaced polygon method does not involve distances between points, only the order of points in the base level data set. A similar method of weighting is used, however, involving numbers of base level chords, not length based on distances. As the number of base level chords used to form a new chord increases, the actual length of the new chord increases and this is akin to aggregation to larger distance scales. Then if the number of original points needed to approximate the coarsest acceptable perimeter is N_{max} and the minimum number N_{min}, the sequence of chord sizes in the sequence of aggregations is given as

$$N_{max} = \omega^{(m-1)} N_{min}, \tag{6.19}$$

from which ω is determined in the same way as previously; that is, as

$$\omega = \exp\left(\frac{\log N_{max} - \log N_{min}}{m - 1}\right). \tag{6.20}$$

In fact, N_{min} is always 2, and N_{max} is set as $N/6$, thus implying that the number of chords defining the most aggregate perimeter is 6; this would make the top level of aggregation consistent with the maximum spanning distance F.

In fact, the algorithm used to aggregate the original chords on each iteration into new perimeters employs ω in equation (6.20) only as a guide. Clearly the number of chords must be integral, not real, thus equation (6.19) involves truncation or addition to create integer numbers. The number of aggregated chords on each iteration $k + 1$ is given as $N_{k+1} = \text{int}(\omega N_k)$. However, if N_{k+1} is equal to N_k, then N_{k+1} is increased by one chord length, that is $N_{k+1} = N_k + 1$. In the application of these algorithms, we have set m as 100 in each case. In fact, for the equipaced polygon method, although this also applies, the actual number of aggregations made is always less than 100 because of the discrete conditional nature of the aggregation.

The observations produced by applying each of these four methods to the five total perimeters and the total of totals are shown as Richardson plots in Figures 6.5 to 6.8. Before the associated regressions are discussed there are several points to note. First there are quite clear upper scale effects caused by aggregation to too high a level. These are seen as departures from the trend of each graph and as obvious twists and turns in the tails of some of the plots. Second, these plots show strong evidence of nonlinearity suggesting, as in Section 5.5, that the modified model, where fractal dimen-

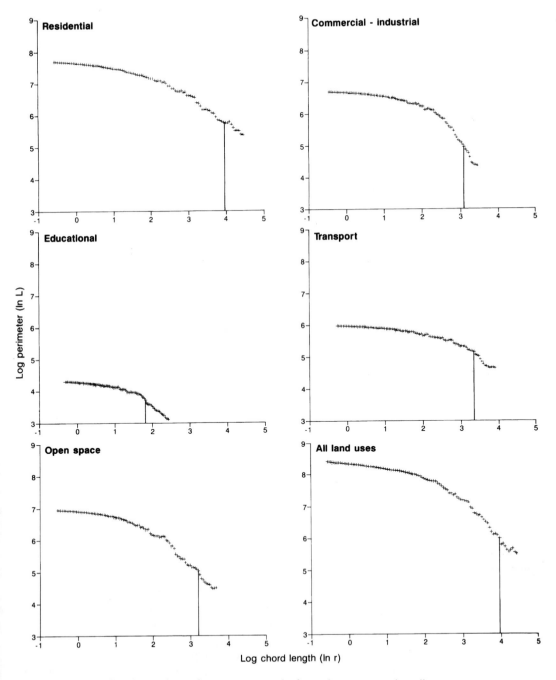

Figure 6.5. Richardson plots of perimeter–scale from the structured walk.

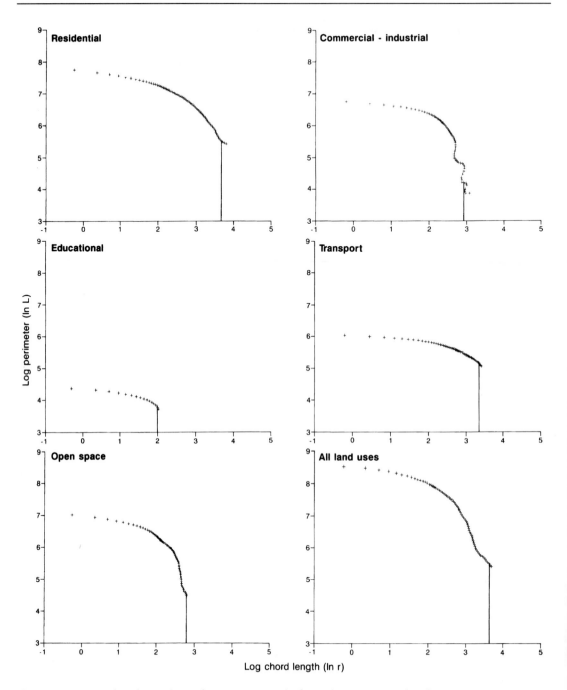

Figure 6.6. Richardson plots of perimeter–scale from the equipaced polygons.

sion varies with scale, is more applicable than the conventional model. Third, and in the context of our evaluation of these different algorithms in Sections 5.6 and 5.7, the equipaced polygon method gives cause for concern in that the algorithm attempting equal weighting does not perform well in establishing equal spacing of observations or in meeting the fixed number ($m = 100$) of aggregations. There are clear twists in the tails of the associated

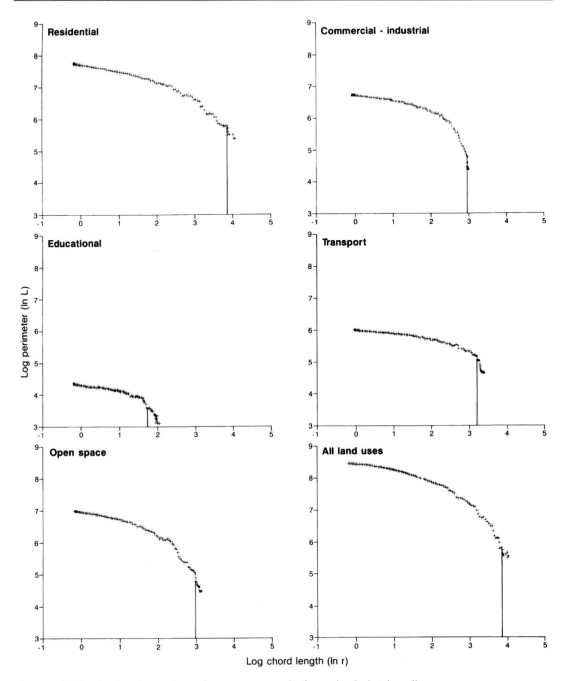

Figure 6.7. Richardson plots of perimeter–scale from the hybrid walk.

plots at the higher levels of aggregation. Finally, the aggregation in the case of educational land use to over 100 levels, is problematic in that there are only 109 digitized points in the total perimeter set as shown in Table 6.1.

We will present the fractal dimensions derived from the conventional and modified models for all the plots shown in Figures 6.5 to 6.8, notwithstanding the fact that the equipaced polygon method and educational land use are, in the sense just described, likely to yield unreliable results. In

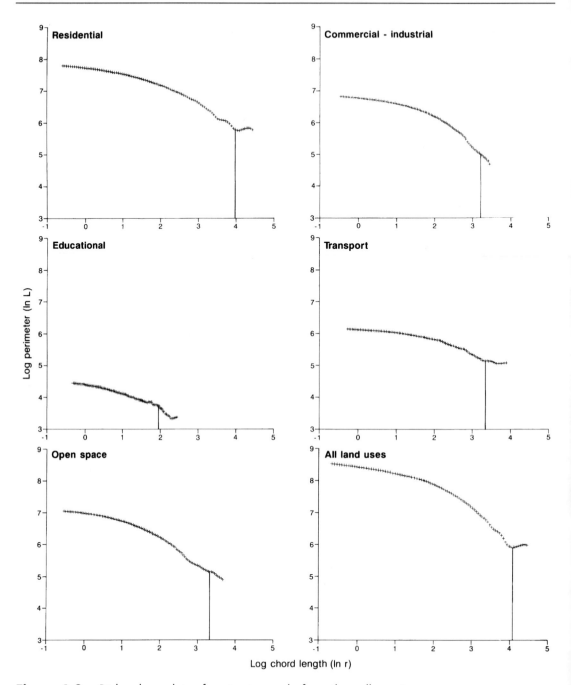

Figure 6.8.   Richardson plots of perimeter–scale from the cell-count.

Table 6.3, we show the fractal dimension D, computed from the slope of the regression line $g(D) = 1 - D$ as in equation (6.4) applied to equations (6.9) and (6.10) which involves the conventional model; and we also show the performance of the model in terms of the r^2 statistics. In Table 6.4, we show the same for the modified model as given in equation (6.12). In this table, we first give the fractal dimension D derived from the coefficient λ

Table 6.3. Fractal dimensions based on the conventional model[1,2]

Method	Residential	Commercial–industrial	Educational	Transport	Open space	All land use
Structured walk	1.450 0.903	1.508 0.773	1.396 0.842	1.289 0.836	1.593 0.880	1.570 0.867
Equipaced polygon	1.694 0.853	2.066 0.619	1.274 0.827	1.300 0.811	1.957 0.687	2.021 0.795
Hybrid walk	1.496 0.904	1.566 0.757	1.442 0.799	1.314 0.803	1.666 0.860	1.619 0.862
Cell-count	1.447 0.939	1.499 0.872	1.402 0.946	1.294 0.920	1.543 0.937	1.571 0.909

[1] The structured walk, hybrid walk and cell-count methods are based on $m = 100$ aggregations for each land use. The equipaced polygon method has $m = 72, 68, 17, 53, 65$ and 75 for the five land uses and all land use applications, respectively. These m values also pertain to the modified model results in Table 6.4.
[2] Each cell shows the fractal dimension $D = 1 - g(D)$ with the r^2 statistic beneath.

Table 6.4. Fractal dimensions based on the modified model[1]

Method	Residential	Commercial–industrial	Educational	Transport	Open space	All land use
Structured walk	1.272 −0.004 0.981	1.076 −0.212 0.995	1.058 −0.041 0.991	1.096 −0.006 0.992	1.292 −0.012 0.980	1.291 −0.006 0.981
Equipaced polygon	1.187 −0.011 0.997	0.559 −0.061 0.941	1.006 −0.036 0.988	1.045 −0.007 0.999	0.716 −0.064 0.956	1.176 −0.020 0.974
Hybrid walk	1.249 −0.006 0.994	0.956 −0.036 0.977	0.925 −0.082 0.978	1.041 −0.011 0.974	1.157 −0.027 0.996	1.225 −0.010 0.996
Cell-count	1.333 −0.002 0.972	1.204 −0.014 0.993	1.223 −0.021 0.991	1.190 −0.003 0.968	1.375 −0.007 0.976	1.374 −0.004 0.967

[1] Each cell shows the fractal dimension $D = 1 - \lambda$, the dispersion coefficient ϕ, and the r^2 statistic beneath.

as $1 - \lambda$, and then we give the dispersion coefficient ϕ, noting of course that as $\phi \to 0$, $D \to 1 - \lambda$.

It is immediately clear from Tables 6.3 and 6.4 that the modified model in which dimension is a function of scale gives by far the best performance over all methods and land uses. Yet the equipaced polygon and hybrid walk methods produce strange results for the modified model in that fractal dimensions are less than 1 in four cases. In the case of the conventional model, these methods also appear to give D values higher than anticipated. With respect to the ranking of D values from Table 6.3, there is, however, a fairly consistent order over all methods in which open space, all land uses, and commercial–industrial have higher fractal dimensions than residential which in turn is higher than educational and transport.

A more disordered set of ranks is associated with the modified model although there are some similarities with the conventional model results, and in any case, the dispersion coefficients pick up the nonlinearity in the relations, hence influencing the value of D. In this respect, the dispersion coefficients are quite low for most land uses. To summarize then, if the equipaced polygon and hybrid methods which seem to pick up inappropriate larger scale effects, are ignored, the structured walk and cell-count methods produce a ranking of fractal dimensions across all land uses (with the exception of educational) which accord to our *a priori* expectations. At this stage, it is even possible to say that variations in dimension and coefficients between land uses are clearly wider than between methods, and this implies that the choice of method is less significant than the division into standard types of land use. However, the really important point at issue here is the presence of unwanted and arbitrary scale effects in the data. It is quite clear from Figures 6.5 to 6.8 that we must remove the highest aggregations from all these plots. In doing so, we also immediately remove some of the non-linearity from the data, thus hopefully improving the conventional model estimates as well as resolving some of the anomalous dimensions evident in Tables 6.3 and 6.4.

6.5 Refining the Perimeter–Scale Relations for the Aggregated Land Use Boundaries

The range of aggregations with respect to the structured walk, cell-count and hybrid walk methods given in equations (6.17) and (6.18) begins with the first and last chord lengths set as low as 70% of the average distance $\bar{d}$ and Feret diameter F for residential land use, to as high as 99% of $\bar{d}$ and F for the educational land use. As we have seen in Chapter 5, Shelberg, Moellering and Lam (1982) recommend that the starting points should be no lower than $\bar{d}/2$ while Kaye (1978) recommends the end point be no higher than $F/2$. The lower limits based on $\psi\bar{d}$ we have used do not pose any problem, but the upper limits based on the Feret diameter ψF yield approximations to the total perimeters with as few as two chords and only as many as five in number. As a general rule it is most unlikely that an approximation to the boundary of any irregular object can be made in less than six chords and in the case where we have up to 30 land parcels forming an aggregated perimeter, it could be argued that we should never go below 180 chords. Below this level we unwittingly include scale effects which pick up the arbitrariness of the 'constructed' perimeters; these are also sensitive to order and orientation of the land parcel strings. In these terms, it would appear that we should take an upper limit no greater than 20% of Feret's diameter, that is $\psi = 0.2$.

Examining the Richardson plots in Figures 6.5 to 6.8, it is quite straightforward to determine cut-off limits at their upper tails which would remove those observations clearly sensitive to these unwarranted scale effects. We have defined cut-off limits in these figures, showing the number of obser-

Table 6.5. Reestimation of the fractal dimensions for the conventional model[1,2]

Method	Residential	Commercial–industrial	Educational	Transport	Open space	All land use
Structured walk	1.403	1.389	1.229	1.210	1.499	1.486
	0.892	0.786	0.910	0.897	0.869	0.864
Equipaced polygon	1.663	1.747	1.244	1.273	1.916	1.993
	0.850	0.624	0.860	0.823	0.689	0.787
Hybrid walk	1.458	1.477	1.291	1.239	1.573	1.559
	0.911	0.793	0.853	0.895	0.877	0.869
Cell-count	1.422	1.452	1.329	1.263	1.516	1.541
	0.925	0.870	0.980	0.892	0.924	0.891

[1] Format of this table is as Table 6.3.
[2] The number of observations used for each regression is indicated in Figures 6.5 to 6.8.

vations each set has been reduced to. This varies for the case of the structured walk from between 9% and 22% of the original data set, and to as little as between 5% and 10% in the case of the equipaced polygon methods. From Figures 6.5 to 6.8, it is clear that we could impose even harsher constraints on the range of observations used, but although this would probably improve the results still further, relevant scale effects would probably be removed too.

Tables 6.5 and 6.6 show the reestimations of the two models using the four methods applied to each land use and the total of all land uses. There are marginal increases in the performance of the conventional model as comparisons between Tables 6.3 and 6.5 indicate. There is increased consistency between the methods with respect to the dimensions estimated with

Table 6.6. Reestimation of the fractal dimensions for the modified model[1,2]

Method	Residential	Commercial–industrial	Educational	Transport	Open space	All land uses
Structured walk	1.213	1.050	1.070	1.094	1.203	1.203
	−0.006	−0.023	−0.035	−0.006	−0.019	−0.008
	0.990	0.996	0.986	0.993	0.986	0.991
Equipaced polygon	1.162	0.700	1.030	1.048	0.074	1.117
	−0.011	−0.051	−0.031	−0.007	−0.062	−0.022
	0.999	0.921	0.996	0.999	0.952	0.980
Hybrid walk	1.237	1.017	1.024	1.093	1.176	1.216
	−0.007	−0.031	−0.057	−0.007	−0.026	−0.010
	0.994	0.988	0.961	0.994	0.995	0.997
Cell-count	1.261	1.166	1.249	1.110	1.303	1.285
	−0.005	−0.017	−0.015	−0.007	−0.012	−0.007
	0.992	0.997	0.991	0.996	0.984	0.991

[1] Format of this table is as Table 6.4.
[2] The number of observations used for each regression is indicated in Figures 6.5 to 6.8.

the exception of the equipaced polygon method. This is the most volatile of all the methods with the structured walk being the most consistent in terms of the original estimation and the reestimation. With respect to the ranking of land uses by dimension, an even clearer pattern emerges. Those with the higher fractal dimensions are open space and all land uses, followed by commercial–industrial and residential, with much lower dimensions for educational and transport uses. This bears out the *a priori* analysis even more strongly but it must be noted that the performance of the conventional model is barely adequate.

The modified model results shown in Table 6.6 are even better than those of Table 6.4. The ranking pattern is more variable than that of the conventional model with the commercial–industrial, educational and open space land uses having the highest degree of non-linearity as measured by the dispersion coefficient. The equipaced polygon method, somewhat ironically perhaps, has by no means the worst performance, but it still generates coefficients out of line with the other methods. As with the conventional model, the structured walk provides the most consistent results over each land use, and together with the cell-count method gives the best performance.

It is now worth summarizing all these results with respect to the fractal dimensions produced. In Figure 6.9, an attempt has been made to capture the variations in dimension produced across all methods and land uses in a single diagram. Each of the diagrams shows this variation with respect to the area–perimeter, conventional perimeter–scale and modified perimeter–scale methods, the latter two being shown with respect to their original estimation and reestimation. It is quite clear from these plots that the equipaced polygon method is the most problematic and should be excluded. Yet the structure of these results does show that there are greater differences between land uses than between methods, and this bears out the original hypothesis that such differences can be detected and possibly explained with respect to the processes governing the formation and evolution of different land use activities. We will say more about this in our conclusion but before we explore the variations between land parcels, we have averaged the dimensions produced in the last three sections, and these are shown, together with those of the subsequent section, in Table 6.7.

It is clear that the area–perimeter method produces quite different results from the perimeter–scale methods but that the patterns produced by these latter methods are more robust and consistent with our *a priori* theorizing. For the conventional model, the order of magnitude values of the fractal dimensions vary from $D \approx 1.5$ for open space and all land uses to $D \approx 1.4$ for residential and commercial–industrial to $D \approx 1.3$ for educational and transport. With respect to the modified model, $D \approx 1.2$ (in its limit) for open space, all land use, and residential, while for the other three land uses, $1.0 \leq D \leq 1.1$. This implies that these three – commercial–industrial, transport and educational land uses – present greater non-linearity; that is, their fractal dimensions vary more strongly with scale. These results mask the wide variation in dimension between land use parcels within any land use type, and do not in any way address the equality of fractal dimension over common boundaries between different land uses. In one sense of course, the purpose of this chapter is to ultimately focus on these questions and thus, we will address some of these in the next section.

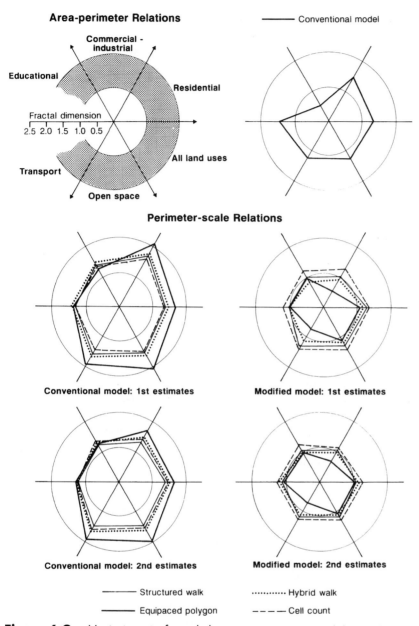

Figure 6.9. Variations in fractal dimensions across models, methods and land uses.

6.6 Fractal Dimensions of Individual Land Parcels

Figure 6.2 shows that there are 72 distinct land use parcels although in the previous analysis, the inner boundaries of some residential land parcels where such boundaries existed as 'holes' in the urban fabric, were added to the aggregate perimeters. There are eight such inner boundaries, all relating to residential land use as shown in Figure 6.2, and in the subsequent

Table 6.7. Fractal dimensions 'averaged' over methods of aggregation

Models/methods[1]	Residential	Commercial–industrial	Educational	Transport	Open space	All land uses
Conventional model: area–perimeter	1.33	1.47	0.56	1.45	1.24	1.29
Conventional model: PS 1st estimates	1.46	1.52	1.41	1.29	1.59	1.58
Conventional model: PS 2nd estimates	1.42	1.43	1.28	1.23	1.51	1.52
Modified model: PS 1st estimates	1.28	1.07	1.06	1.10	1.27	1.29
Modified model: PS 2nd estimates	1.23	1.07	1.10	1.10	1.22	1.23
Conventional model: average land parcels	1.15	1.10	1.09	1.11	1.13	1.13
Modified model: average land parcels	1.08	1.05	1.05	1.06	1.08	1.07

[1] PS: Perimeter–Scale.

analysis, they are treated as separate land parcels, thus augmenting the number of parcels treated to 80. First, all four aggregation methods – the structured and hybrid walks, the equipaced polygon and the cell-count – were applied to each of the 80 parcels, with the number of aggregations structured in geometric form as implied by equations (6.16)–(6.20), but with ω fixed and m varying accordingly.

In the case of the equipaced polygon method, the aggregation of 16 perimeters out of the 80 possible yielded too few observations for any subsequent regression. The other methods produced Richardson plots that were generally more linear than those shown in Figures 6.5 to 6.8, and therefore it was decided to fit the conventional model to all sets of observations generated. The r^2 values ranged from 0.833 to 0.999 in the case of applying the equipaced polygon method, but it was the structured walk that produced the most consistent plots in contrast to the hybrid and cell-count methods which were more volatile across the land parcels. Some methods produced dimensions for individual land parcels outside the range $1 < D < 2$. It was therefore decided to pursue more detailed analysis and model fitting using a narrower range of observations taken from the structured walk method only. In fact, the emphasis in this section is on the variation between land parcels, not on the variation between methods, hence our choice of the most robust method to generate the perimeter–scale data.

The application of both the conventional and modified models is shown in Figure 6.10 with respect to their fractal dimensions and associated r^2 statistics. The results for each land parcel are shown in the arbitrary order of Figure 6.2 according to the way the parcels were digitized but ordered within land use types as given previously. All fractal dimensions for the

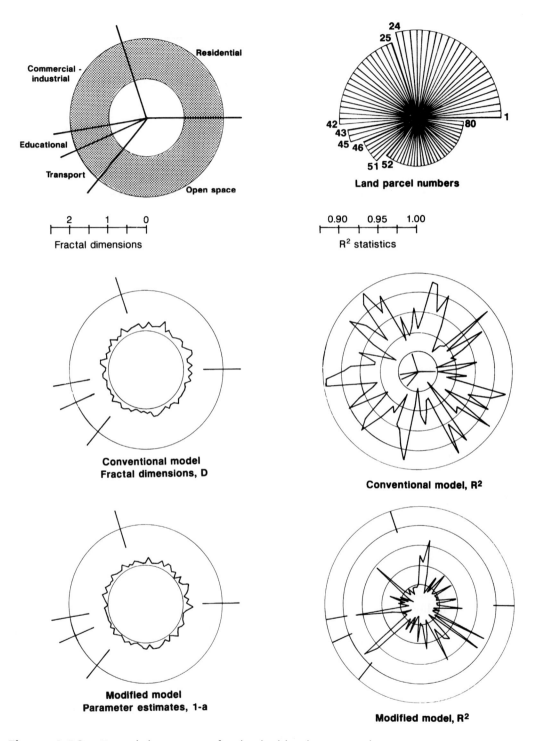

Figure 6.10. Fractal dimensions of individual land use parcels.

conventional model are in the postulated range from $1 < D < 2$. For the largest land parcels, the dimensions appear higher than for the rest, but a regression of the number of digitized points of all parcels on their conventional model dimensions yields an r^2 value of only 0.156. With respect to the five sets of land uses, these r^2 values were more variable, rising to 0.686 in the case of commercial–industrial. But in general, there does not appear to be a strong bias to higher dimensions for those land use parcels with the highest number of perimeter coordinates. Figure 6.10 also shows that the parameters of the modified non-linear model are consistent with the range of $1 < D < 2$, and the level of dispersion reflecting each parcel's non-linearity over scale, is fairly modest in every case.

One way of summarizing these parameters and statistics is by computing means and standard deviations. Table 6.8 presents these results for both models. The parameters and dimensions in this table are in their original form as predicted from the use of equations (6.10) and (6.12), that is, where the coefficient of the conventional model is $g(D) = 1 - D$, and those for the modified model λ and ϕ where $\lambda \rightarrow (1 - D)$ as the dispersion parameter $\phi \rightarrow 0$. Table 6.8 presents the variation in size of the land parcels for each land use and over the whole set in terms of their mean number of coordinates. The distribution of these coordinates with respect to the number of land parcels is skewed with a much greater proportion of parcels below their mean size. In the case of the residential parcels, this distribution is highly skewed, largely because of the existence of the one large parcel which provides the skeletal structure of the town.

The variation in parameter values and performance of the models, however, is much less than the variation in the features of the land parcels themselves. Figure 6.10 makes this apparent, while these results are averaged for each land use over all parcels in Table 6.8. With respect to the conventional model, the r^2 values only range from 0.934 in the case of residential parcels down to 0.919 for transport and the range for each land use over the land parcels is also quite narrow. The fractal dimensions D also show a pattern over the land uses which is consistent with the aggregated perimeter–scale results but is considerably clearer. The ranking of land uses from largest to smallest D is ordered from residential ($D \approx 1.152$), open space (1.132), transport (1.113), commercial–industrial (1.105), and educational (1.091) with an average over all land uses of 1.129. These values are considerably smaller than those shown previously, yet they are more in line with the examples developed in Chapter 5. In fact, the largest residential parcel (see Figure 6.2) is just one of five parcels which has a dimension greater than 1.2. From these results it is clear that the much higher dimensions produced by the aggregated perimeter–scale relations are due to the method of aggregating individual perimeters into strings of coordinates. It would appear that the aggregation picks up arbitrary scale effects which are central to the method itself and not the order or orientation of the individual parcels in the process of forming these composite perimeters.

The modified model results also shown in Table 6.8 have a wider range of variation around their mean estimates than those of the conventional model. In terms of the parameter λ, the residential, open space and all land use parcels have a dimension higher than those of transport, commercial–industrial and educational, in that order, although these values are over a

Table 6.8. 'Average' dimensions and statistics for the individual land parcels[1]

Land use	Zones	No. of coords	Mean coords	σ_c	$1 - D_1$
All land parcels	80	6059	75.7	177.4	−0.129
Residential	24	2989	124.5	317.2	−0.152
Commercial–industrial	18	1030	57.2	33.3	−0.105
Educational	3	109	36.3	6.65	−0.091
Transport	6	510	85.0	65.8	−0.113
Open space	29	1421	49.0	38.9	−0.132

Land use	σ_{D1}	r^2	σ_{r1}	$\lambda = 1 - D_2$	σ_{D2}
All land parcels	0.057	0.927	3.3	−0.071	0.051
Residential	0.063	0.934	3.3	−0.079	0.063
Commercial–Industrial	0.061	0.920	3.1	−0.050	0.042
Educational	0.035	0.921	4.3	−0.047	0.005
Transport	0.040	0.920	2.2	−0.065	0.028
Open space	0.046	0.928	3.6	−0.077	0.048

Land use	ϕ	σ_+	r^2	σ_{r2}
All land parcels	−0.024	0.021	0.969	2.3
All land parcels	−0.029	0.022	0.972	1.8
Residental	−0.018	0.011	0.979	1.6
Commercial–industrial				
Educational	−0.022	0.018	0.952	3.1
Transport	−0.006	0.001	0.960	3.9
Open space	−0.030	0.025	0.966	2.3

[1] The standard deviations are defined as: σ_c of the coordinates, σ_{D1} of the slope parameter $(1 - D_1)$ in the conventional model, σ_{D2} of the parameter λ in the modified model, σ_ϕ of the parameter ϕ in the modified model and σ_r (σ_{r1} and σ_{r2}) of the r^2 fits of the appropriate model to the land parcel data.

narrower range. The values of the dispersion factors also confirm this order and the r^2 estimates, although slightly better than those of the conventional model, are not as high as those produced by the aggregate perimeter–scale relations. Nevertheless, the non-linear model is an improvement over the linear and in general, these results for the individual parcels are better than anticipated.

6.7 The Problem of Measurement

The analysis presented here is suggestive rather than definitive and it reveals some basic problems of observation and measurement which are generic to all empirical science. In the development of fractal geometry, these problems have only just been broached and they will hold the center stage for a long time yet. In terms of developing a morphology of urban land use based on fractal geometry, it would appear that residential and open space land uses have a greater degree of irregularity than commercial–industrial, educational and transport. There is a logic here which we spelt out before we began the analysis in that for land uses which are larger in scale, there is likely to be less effort put into the geometric control of land under development. Yet there remains considerable uncertainty over the processes in operation. We have, however, shown that in general, scale effects vary with scale itself, and this is likely to be the result of multiple processes changing their relative importance through the range of scales. This argument is consistent with our treatment in Chapter 5 of cartographic lines as bounding geographical phenomena which are ostensibly isolated.

We have added to Table 6.7 the results of the last section where the whole range of models and methods applied throughout this chapter are displayed in suitably 'averaged' form. This shows up the arbitrariness of the analysis, with dimensions varying from as large as 1.6 to as low as 1.1. In previous work, the methods themselves have been subject to considerable variation but here despite some association of dimension values with land uses, the main variation concerns the way area, perimeter and scale are defined and measured, and the emphasis on area–perimeter or perimeter–scale relations. Questions of scale are never very clear in much fractal analysis, despite the fact that fractals are defined by scale-invariance. The area–perimeter method assumes that objects of varying sizes show the effects of varying scale itself (Woronow, 1981).

In short, a small residential development will not pick up the aggregate scale effects which can be detected by a large scale development, so runs the logic. However, this will depend on the base level of resolution in the first place, but there has seldom been much discussion of this in the field to date. The method of aggregating perimeters used in the composite perimeter–scale analyses of land uses is also suspect, because of arbitrary scale effects which can be produced, despite careful control over the process of aggregation. Lastly, the individual land parcel analysis using conventional perimeter–scale, not aggregated relations, suffers from its very inability to aggregate parcels, other than by arbitrary statistics such as simple averages.

What is clearly required in future work is a close examination of these approaches in terms of scale effects. We have paid great attention to problems of defining scale limits and ranges here but on reflection, our analysis should probably have employed a much narrower range of scales. However, from the Richardson plots in Figures 6.5 to 6.8, the reader can get some sense of how the dimensions might change if narrower ranges were to be used.

New methods are urgently required which are more robust than those used here, and we have now convinced ourselves that in perimeter–scale analysis, the hybrid walk and equipaced polygon methods should be abandoned in favor of methods such as the structured walk and cell-count whose properties of aggregation are better understood. But the final conclusion to these last two chapters relates to more substantive questions. Although we have tackled both individual and aggregate analysis here, much finer analysis of the fractal dimension of parts of perimeter boundaries is required. Further classification of the fractal shapes of land parcels will not emerge until the common boundary problem is directly broached. This must involve a detailed examination of how such boundaries are formed and how they evolve over time. By explaining the development process, more satisfactory explanations can be given of the way land uses 'stick' to each other to form the whole town. Only by extending the analysis along these lines can conclusive results about the ways in which urban morphologies are structured and evolve, be demonstrated.

Although we will not concern ourselves any further with conceptual problems of physical definition and practical problems of measurement, at least in terms of urban boundaries and edges, we will in fact begin to examine the ways in which entire morphologies of towns evolve, but at a more aggregate level. Our focus will move away from cities composed of edges and boundaries to cities composed of activities, mainly development in general and population in particular, which fill space. In the next two chapters, we will also retreat back to examining single fractal objects as complete cities, but this time with respect to the way they evolve and grow. We will, however, continue to examine the way the land parcels which compose the fabric of the city 'stick' to one another, and once again, we will trace the way the smaller threads of urban development can be woven into complete mosaics whose form is similar across many scales.

Urban Growth and Form

To terms of magnitude, and of direction, must we refer all our conceptions of Form. For the form of an object is defined when we know its magnitude, actual or relative, in various directions; and Growth involves the same conceptions of magnitude and direction, related to the further concept, or 'dimension', of Time. (Thompson, 1917, 1961, p. 15.)

7.1 Cities in Evolution

The fractal patterns we have presented so far are largely based on superficial pictures of urban form, and go little way to suggesting how such structures might emerge. All we have done is to show that the geometry of cities with respect to their boundaries, and the size and distribution of their land uses, are consistent with fractal laws, but as yet, we have hardly even implied how such patterns come into existence. This will be our quest in this and the next chapter where we will seek to show how the fractal structures illustrated in earlier chapters emerge as cities grow and evolve. In the terminology of modeling and simulation, our focus will move from describing static structures which exist and are observed at a cross-section in time, to developing theories and models for simulating dynamic structures which grow and change through time.

The way we have generated fractal structures so far in this book is by choosing some initiating object, regular or not, such as a line or a triangle, and then systematically computing its geometric form at finer and finer scales according to some scaling principle embodying self-similarity or affinity. This is the way we generated the Koch curve in Chapter 2, the large city forms based on London in Chapters 3 and 4, and the simulated boundaries of Cardiff and Swindon in Chapters 5 and 6. But of course cities do not grow in such stylized ways. Like all natural growth, they evolve through the cumulative addition and deletion of basic units, cells or particles. In the case of cities, such units may be individuals, households, firms, transportation links and so on, represented in terms of the immediate space they occupy, and cities thus grow through successive accumulation at these basic scales. Those patterns which might exist at higher scales, and which indicate self-similar scaling, thus emerge almost magically from the growth process itself.

In short, contained within the growth process are codes which determine how the organization of these basic units of urban development might repeat their form and function across many scales above that at which the city actually develops. How this is achieved is almost akin to the secret of life itself and the fractal codes which are embodied in the growth process might be likened to those composing DNA and RNA (Dawkins, 1986; Levy, 1992). In one sense, however, there is perhaps less mystery than might first appear; when development is planned at any scale, the individuals and agencies involved almost subconsciously take account of economies of agglomeration, the need for similar facilities and functions of different orders at different scales which must serve associated market areas efficiently, and the provision of various transportation linkages which combine to meet principles of least cost and minimum effort. In this chapter, we will in fact suggest a model of urban growth which is consistent with all of these notions.

The physical units which we have used to describe the city so far have been largely in terms of lines or edges and the areas these seek to define, either implicitly in terms of the boundaries of entire urban areas, or explicitly in terms of the zones which compose various land uses. Moreover, we have associated edges with areas, at least in Chapter 6, and we have purposively blurred the distinction between them. If we now consider what constitutes an elemental unit of development such as the occupancy space surrounding a single individual, then the areas and the edges associated with this occupancy can to all intents and purposes be considered the same, at least from the scales at which we typically view urban phenomena. For example, if we assume that each individual in a city has the same occupancy based on their immediate use of space, then the number of edges or boundary lines will be proportional to the number of units of development at the given scale. In this sense then, edges and areas are simply manifestations of the same pattern. In this chapter as in the last, we will find that edges and areas and the way we can count these represent different sides of the same 'fractal coin', and can both be used to unravel the growth processes which give rise to such patterns.

We will begin by sketching a more basic theory of the fractal city based on scaling relations than we have done so far, although this will largely be a restatement and synthesis of relations already introduced. In particular, we will show that fractal patterns, whether static or growing, can be identified by fixing size and varying their scale, or by fixing scale and varying their size, and that the fractal dimensions of such structures are equivalent. We then assemble some preliminary evidence for the existence of the fractal city by an examination of static and dynamic urban patterns, but this simply forces us to begin the search for better explanations of why such patterns evolve. This we start to do in this chapter by introducing a model of fractal growth consistent with our observations so far.

The model, first developed by Witten and Sander (1981) and referred to as the Diffusion-Limited Aggregation (DLA) model, generates highly ramified tree-like clusters of particles or populations with self-similarity about a fixed point. The extent to which such clusters fill their space is measured by their fractal dimension which in turn is estimated from the scaling relations linking population counts and density to various radii within the clusters. We suggest that this model provides a suitable baseline for simulation models of urban growth and form which manifest similar scaling properties. A typical DLA simulation is presented and a variety of measures of its structure and dynamics are developed. These measures link to those which we initially present for several city systems in this chapter, but we tailor them specifically to the urban growth and form of Taunton, a small town in South West England. Important differences and similarities with the DLA model are elicited from this analysis and this leads to a generalization of the model which is developed in detail in the next chapter.

7.2 The Basic Scaling Relations of the Fractal City

In Chapter 2, we made an important distinction between geometric objects whose properties might be studied by varying their scale, and those same objects whose properties could be revealed by varying their size. In short, their geometry might be explored, first by fixing size and varying scale, and then by fixing scale and varying size. This is a distinction which is echoed throughout this book, but it is of central importance to the development of a theory of the fractal city. In Chapter 2, we also suggested that this distinction might be extended to the treatment of sets of objects as well as single objects, although we will not take this any further here. Later, in Chapter 10, we will discuss the generalization of these ideas to systems of cities. We are now, however, in a position to demonstrate that these two related approaches to fractal measurement are equivalent. This will form the basic theory which we synthesize in this section in preparation for its application to measuring and modeling urban growth in the rest of the chapter.

As previously, we will use the variables N, L and A to define the number of parts composing an object, the total length of these parts, and their total area at a given scale r. We will also assume that the size of the object is proportional to R which as we can anticipate, might be a measure of radius although could be any linear measure appropriate to its context of measurement. In Chapter 2, we defined number $N(r)$ and length $L(r)$ relations for varying scale r in equations (2.24) and (2.25) and we will restate these as

$$N(r) = \alpha r^{-D}, \tag{7.1}$$

and

$$L(r) = N(r)r = \alpha r^{1-D}. \tag{7.2}$$

The total area $A(r)$ of the $N(r)$ parts of the object can be calculated as

$$A(r) = L(r)r = \alpha r^{2-D} \tag{7.3}$$

and the density $\rho(r)$ is given as

$$\rho(r) = \frac{A(r)}{A(R)} \propto \alpha r^{2-D}, \tag{7.4}$$

where $A(R)$ is the area of the object which we assume is constant whatever the scale of resolution. As the scale becomes finer, the number of parts of the object and the total length increase without bound, but the area and the density (which are proportional to one another) decrease to zero; that is as $r \rightarrow 0$, $N(r) \rightarrow \infty$, $L(r) \rightarrow \infty$ and $A(r) \rightarrow 0$, $\rho(r) \rightarrow 0$. This of course is based on the assumption that the dimension D lies between 1 and 2, something we will now take for granted unless we state otherwise.

Although we have directly demonstrated the meaning of the basic scaling relations in equations (7.1) to (7.2) for urban boundaries and edges, we should note that equation (7.1) is now being used to determine the number of parts into which a plane area such as a city of area $A(R)$ with radius R might be divided. Equation (7.2) gives the total length of these parts, (7.3) the total area, and (7.4) the density. We will illustrate these ideas, once we have completely elaborated them, for the Sierpinski carpet which we used as a model of urban growth in Chapter 2. For the moment, however, let us simply note that if the object has a diameter $2R$, then the scale can be given as $r = 2R/n$ where the scale gets finer as n increases integrally. All the above equations could be rewritten in these terms, but we will only present the number–scale relation in equation (7.1) which becomes

$$N(n) = N(r) = \alpha r^{-D} = \alpha \left(\frac{2R}{n}\right)^{-D}$$

$$= \upsilon n^D, \tag{7.5}$$

where υ is a suitably defined constant. Equation (7.5) is perhaps a more intuitively satisfying representation for it relates the number of parts at the ever finer scale given by n directly to the fractal dimension D. Without loss of generality, we can assume that the diameter $2R$ can be set as 1 and then $\upsilon = \alpha$. There is one other feature to note in relation to equation (7.1) and that is that this scaling relation gives the number of parts into which an object is successively subdivided as the scale becomes finer. The distribution thus created reflects the hierarchical process of subdivision and is thus clearly related to the rank-size rule of central place theory noted in Chapter 1; this is also equivalent to Korcak's rule which we introduced in Chapter 6. In the sequel, we will explore this further when we relate it to the number of 'empty' parts or 'free space' as Frankhauser and Sadler (1991) calls it, which is the complement of the number of parts into which the fractal is divided.

Let us now change tack and consider the same object at fixed scale r so that we might explore what happens to its geometry as its size, which is proportional to R, changes. Consider the number of parts into which the object is divided based on equation (7.5) and without loss of generality, assume that $N(n)$ is the number of parts into which the original object is first divided. If we keep the scale fixed and simply increase the size of the object by R, then the number of parts increases in direct proportion. Using equations (7.1) and (7.5), the number of parts for the new resized object is given as

$$N(R) = \upsilon(Rn)^D = \upsilon n^D R^D \tag{7.6}$$
$$= \varphi R^D$$

where we note that n is fixed and that $\varphi = \upsilon n^D$. Clearly the number of parts increases as the power D of the object's size R. Following equations (7.2) and (7.3), it is easy to show that the total length and area of the growing object are both proportional to area; that is

$$A(R) \propto L(R) \propto N(R). \tag{7.7}$$

However, the density relation is different and important. Assuming that the total size of the space within which the object is contained is given by

$$\hat{A}(R) \propto R^2, \tag{7.8}$$

then the density $\rho(R)$ is given as

$$\rho(R) = \frac{A(R)}{\hat{A}(R)} \propto \frac{\varphi R^D}{R^2}$$

$$= \xi \, R^{D-2}. \tag{7.9}$$

As $R \to \infty$, then $\rho(R) \to 0$ as is consistent with the density scaling of the object in equation (7.4). Equations (7.6) and (7.9) are formally equivalent to equations (2.32) and (2.33) which we derived using a similar argument in Chapter 2.

The perimeter–area relation which we used in Chapter 6 can be easily derived from the fractal growth relation in equation (7.6) by noting that $R = \hat{A}(R)^{1/2}$. However, frequently the perimeter $L(R)$ is likely to scale differently from both the total area $\hat{A}(R)$ and the actual area $A(R)$. Let us call the actual scaling dimension $\check{D}$ in contrast to D, and then the perimeter–total area relation equivalent to equations (2.29) and (6.3) which we used in Chapter 6 to compute the fractal dimensions for different sets of land uses, is

$$L(R) \propto \hat{A}(R)^{\check{D}/2} \propto R^{\check{D}}, \tag{7.10}$$

which is simply equation (7.6) in another form, but now distinguishing $\check{D}$ from D. We can write many such relations in the manner of equation (7.10) for different perimeter dimensions, but a useful form given by Frankhauser and Sadler (1991) is similar to (7.10) but using $A(R)$ as in (7.7). Then it is possible to derive $\hat{A}(R)$ in (7.8) from (7.7) as $A(R)^{2/D}$ $(= (R^D)^{2/D})$, and using this, equation (7.10) becomes

$$L(R) \propto A(R)^{\check{D}/D}. \tag{7.11}$$

Equation (7.11) is considerably more general than equation (7.10) in that when $\check{D} = D$, the actual area relation in (7.6) and (7.7) is derived; when $D = 2$, the total area relation in (7.10) is derived while when $\check{D} = 1$ and $D = 2$, the relation for a circle or other plane Euclidean figure results. Moreover, this relation is particularly useful when it is already clear that perimeter and number scaling differ and when different methods are available for computing $\check{D}$ and D independently.

We can illustrate our theory of the fractal city most clearly using the Sierpinski carpet which we first presented in Chapter 2 as a preliminary example of the scaling laws of urban growth. Figure 7.1 shows an elaboration of this fractal at two levels of magnification, the first for $k = 1$ where $r = 1/3$ and the second for $k = 2$ where $r = 1/9$. Here we will show that the dimension of this deterministic fractal is the same whichever way its

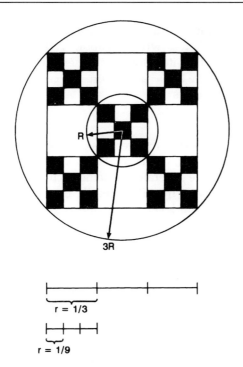

Figure 7.1. Scale and size in the Sierpinski carpet.

scale and size is examined and that the approaches elaborated in equations (7.1) to (7.5), and in (7.6) to (7.9), yield identical results. First using equation (7.1), $N(1/3) = \alpha(1/3)^{-D}$ and $N(1/9) = \alpha(1/9)^{-D}$. Taking the ratio of these two numbers and counting the actual parts at these two scales in Figure 7.1 gives

$$5 = \frac{25}{5} = \frac{N(1/9)}{N(1/3)} = \frac{\alpha(1/9)^D}{\alpha(1/3)^D} = 3^D,$$

from which it is immediately clear that $D = \log(5)/\log(3)$. Now taking the other approach and using equation (7.6), the size of the unit square carpet is given as $N(R) = \varphi R^D$ while the whole carpet at the next level is grown to radius $3R$ and is thus $N(3R) = \varphi(3R)^D$. Forming the ratio and counting parts gives

$$5 = \frac{25}{5} = \frac{N(3R)}{N(R)} = \frac{\varphi 3^D R^D}{\varphi R^D} = 3^D,$$

from which it is quite clear that the dimension has the same value as that given by the scaling method. Use of the perimeter–area relation in equation (7.10) (and (7.11) gives the same, that is

$$5 = \frac{25}{5} = \frac{L(3R)}{L(R)} = \left(\frac{(3R)^2}{R^2}\right)^{D/2} = 3^D.$$

Perhaps, as a brief digression from the main argument of this chapter, but as an important pointer to the future development of the fractal geometry of urban structure, it is worth examining what Frankhauser (1990, 1992) calls the 'free space' generated in the construction of a regular fractal such as the Sierpinski carpet. Let us write equation (7.1) in the form of (7.5) but now note that on the first iteration $k = 1$, there are n subdivisions, on the second where $k = 2$ there are n^2 and so on. We can thus drop the index (n) from (7.5) and write this as

$$N_k = v(n^k)^D, \tag{7.12}$$

where equation (7.12) models the Sierpinski carpet when $v = 1$. Now on the first iteration of the carpet, of the total $n^2 = 9$ parts into which the carpet is divided, $N_1 = 5 = 3^D$ are generated as being occupied or developed leaving $N_\tau = n^2 - N_1 = 4$ empty or free. It can easily be shown that the number of 'free spaces' Nf_k at the kth level of iteration is given by

$$Nf_k = N_\tau N_{k-1} = (n^2 - n^D)(n^{k-1})^D = (n^{2-D} - 1)N_k, \tag{7.13}$$

which, for the Sierpinski carpet, generates a hierarchy of four spaces at the first level, 20 at the next, then 100 and so on down the cascade. In contrast to equation (7.12) which gives the number of successive subdivisions, the series created by equation (7.13) actually generates spaces which continue to exist as 'holes' within the fabric of the fractal and can thus be observed as a hierarchy. Frankhauser (1990, 1992) demonstrates that this is likely to be a promising line of inquiry in observing the free space in regular as well as irregular town forms, a concept that we are not emphasizing in this book but which could become important in further research.

7.3 Preliminary Evidence for a Theory of the Fractal City

Even though it is clear that there are considerable problems in defining what constitutes 'urban development', there is wide agreement that cities do not fill the space in which they exist in any compact sense. Most cities in fact spread out in the plane and hardly touch the third dimension. They are peppered with undeveloped land, not only the result of physical constraints on what can and cannot be built, but caused by the very processes of development at the micro level which take place slowly and incrementally, with little coordination at this basic scale in terms of physical contiguity. As such we can take as a working assumption that their fractal dimension lies between 1 and 2, and that the sorts of process characteristic of the way we generated the Sierpinski carpet represent a first approximation to simulating urban structure. We will refine this considerably as we proceed, but as such, it provides a useful starting point.

The fractal dimension of cities displayed by their patterns of development in the plane can be calculated from either of the two sets of scaling relations outlined in the previous section. Any of the four scaling relations based on $N(r)$, $L(r)$, $A(r)$ and $\rho(r)$ in equations (7.1) to (7.4) can be used as can $N(R)$ and $\rho(R)$ based on equations (7.6) and (7.9), and the perimeter–area relations in equations (7.10) or (7.11). If the fractal was a perfect magnification or

dilation at each scale as in the case of Sierpinski's carpet, then only one
observation for a fixed scale or size would be necessary to compute the
fractal dimension; for example, using equation (7.12) for the carpet gives v
= 1, hence $D = \log(N_k)/(k \log(n))$ where k is the level of generation, n the
original scale factor and N_k the number of parts at the observed scale. However, it is possible to compute first approximations to the dimension (for
cases where the growth process is unknown but clearly not perfectly self-
similar or affine), from two sets of observations associated with two scales
or two sizes. In this case, any constants of proportionality cancel, leaving
the dimension the only unknown. For example, for scales r_1 and r_2, the ratio
$N(r_1)/N(r_2)$ from equation (7.1) can be transformed to give the value of D,
as can all the other scale and size relations for L, A and ρ. However, the
more usual method is to fit these intrinsically linear relations directly to
several sets of observations through their logarithmic transformations
which yield equations whose parameters can be estimated by regression.

We will use both the 'grid' or 'cell-counting' method implied in the varying scale relations and the 'radius' method implied by varying size, which
are both illustrated in Figure 7.1 for the Sierpinski carpet. In fact although
we will position our grid systematically above the CBD and also fix the
radius from this center, this does not imply that these methods need be so
used. Later in this chapter, we will argue that it is essential to position
such grids and radii in as many positions as possible across the object, thus
computing 'average' dimensions. Although we will use the varying scale
relation for static structures, and the varying size relation for growing structures, no restriction is implied by this use. As we illustrated for the Sierpinski carpet, both approaches give equivalent results for a perfect fractal,
although we will show a mild preference here and in subsequent chapters
for the use of the size relations in equations (7.6) and (7.9) for the case of
fractal growth.

We have already illustrated the kinds of urban growth patterns which
we intend to measure and model in this chapter. In Chapters 3 and 4, we
developed simulations of land use for hypothetical and real cities using
dimensions and data for London, and we will review the fractal dimension
of this city in some of the examples of this section. To really impress the
extensive evidence for fractal urban growth, however, in Plate 7.1 (see color
section) we illustrate the employment density of London. This was produced for us by Bracken based on his interpolation algorithms applied to
the 1981 Population Census from which he is able to generate data at 200 m
grid square level (Bracken, 1993). The spectrum from yellow to red matches
high to low densities. More dramatic evidence of the fractal nature of urban
development and its applicability across scales is shown in Plate 7.2 where
the same data are mapped for England and Wales, thus implicitly generalizing fractal growth to the entire hierarchy of cities, something which we will
explore later in Chapter 10. We could repeat these types of example for
different urban activities and at different scales, time and again, and we
could complement this display of data with that taken from remotely
sensed imagery which shows the same. But our concern here is with
measurement and simulation which requires a somewhat more abstracted
picture of urban development to which we now return.

Our first foray in the computation of fractal dimensions for urban growth involves four large cities – London, New York, Paris and Tokyo – taken from Doxiadis's (1968) book *Ekistics*. We have used the cell-counting method for equation (7.1) in these cases to compute the values of D for the patterns shown in Figure 7.2. These cities are represented at the same basic scale, although it is immediately clear that in the case of Tokyo, the city fills much less than the physical space available to it due to the presence of Tokyo Bay. Furthermore, it is clear that what we count or color as urban development, and how far out from the CBD we take the cell-count or grid will both affect the computed values of the dimension. Here we have computed these values of D as 1.774, 1.710, 1.862 and 1.312 for London, New York, Paris and Tokyo respectively. Apart from the clearly lower value for Tokyo which we might expect because of the Bay, we will refrain from commenting on these except to note that all these values are what we might expect from casual observation of Figure 7.2. As we shall see, there can be such substantial differences in the values of D due to the different definitions of development and the use of different methods, that we will not provide any comment on the likely values for such structures until we have introduced our models in this and later chapters.

Our next examples relate to growing structures, and for these we have used London and Berlin. The growth of London from 1820 to 1962 provides a classic picture of fractal growth, and is superbly illustrated in both Abercrombie's (1945) *Greater London Plan 1944* and in Doxiadis's (1968) *Ekistics* from which we have compiled Figure 7.3. We have used the ratio of two successive scales based on equation (7.1) for each of the eight stages of growth, and from this, we report dimension values of 1.322, 1.585, 1.415, 1.700, 1.737, 1.765, 1.791 and 1.774 for the years 1820, 1840, 1860, 1880, 1900, 1914, 1939 and 1962. The increase in values during this time is quite consistent with our analysis of the growth of Cardiff in Chapter 5 where we argued that as cities grow, they come to fill their space more efficiently and compactly (or at least homogeneously) due to better coordination of development and increased control over physical form due to better technology. This evidence is also borne out by Frankhauser's (1990, 1991, 1994) results for Berlin, three stages of growth of which are shown in Figure 7.4. The values computed here are 1.43, 1.54 and 1.69 for the years 1875, 1920 and 1945. A comparison of Figures 7.2 to 7.4, however, also reveals how subtle changes in definition begin to creep into the representation of patterns of development, thus affecting the values computed in unanticipated and uncontrolled ways.

The last examples we will develop here are for cities in the North Eastern United States, namely Albany, Buffalo and Syracuse in New York, Cleveland and Columbus in Ohio, and Pittsburgh in Pennsylvania. We have exceptionally detailed and innovative data sets for these cities based on 100 m grid square lattices ranging from a 1042 × 552 grid for Buffalo to a 1102 × 1201 grid for Albany. These have been derived from the 1990 digitized line files (TIGER files) available for all areas in the US down to block group features and compose those cells within which some segment of residential street exists. As an example, the pattern for Buffalo is shown in Figure 7.5 where it is clear that like Tokyo, a large portion of the space within which the city might have grown lies across the international frontier with Canada, adjacent to the downtown, where there has been hardly any

London

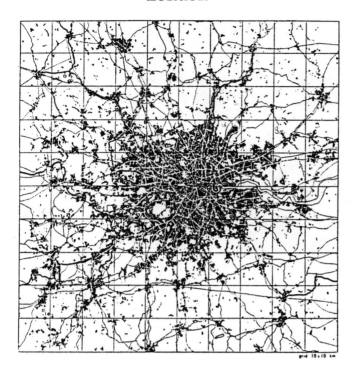

Paris

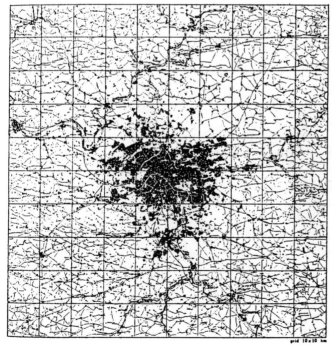

Figure 7.2.   Fractal patterns of urban development: London, Paris, New York and Tokyo (from Doxiadis, 1968).

New York

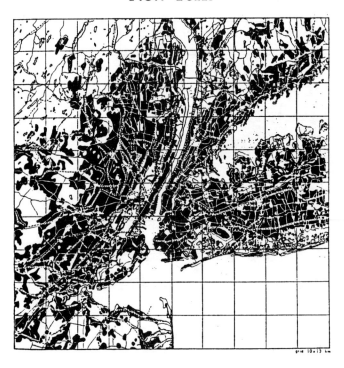

Tokyo

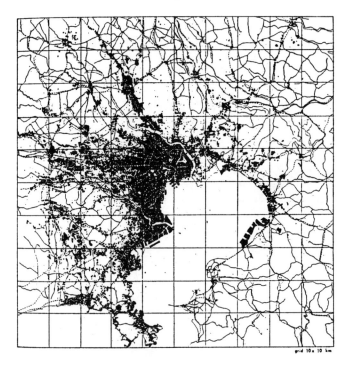

Figure 7.2. Continued.

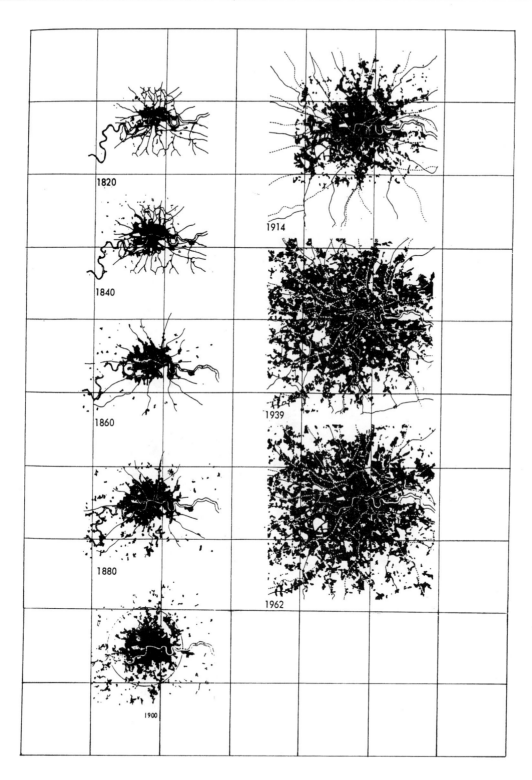

Figure 7.3. The growth of London (from Abercrombie, 1945; Doxiadis, 1968).

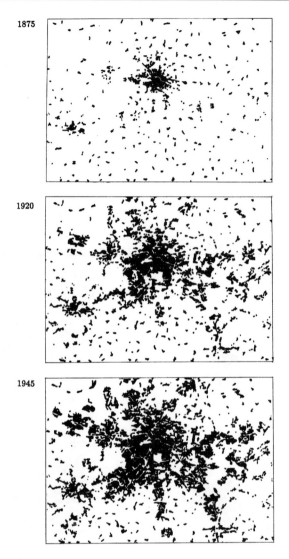

1875

1920

1945

Figure 7.4.   The growth of Berlin (from Frankhauser, 1994).

development at all. We do not in fact have any data for the Canadian side of the border, but this is unlikely to affect the value of the dimension very much. We have estimated fractal dimensions for these six cities in various ways; these are reported elsewhere (Batty and Xie, 1993), but here we do report the use of a radial method of analysis which involves the density relation in equation (7.9). In the case of a lattice, this density can be written as

$$\rho(R) = \frac{A(R)}{\hat{A}(R)} \sim \frac{\pi R^D}{\pi R^2} = R^{D-2}. \tag{7.14}$$

From equation (7.14), we can approximate the dimension directly for any density $\rho(R)$ at distance R from the CBD as

Figure 7.5. The pattern of development in Buffalo, NY.

$$D(R) \sim 2 + \frac{\log \rho(R)}{\log R}. \tag{7.15}$$

We can in fact produce a continually varying dimension $D(R)$ as R increases which we will refer to later as the 'fractal signature' of the urban area. However, at this point, a suitable value for equation (7.15) would be the mean density given as $\rho(\bar{R})$ at radius $\bar{R}$, which gives values of $D = 1.494$, 1.729, 1.438, 1.732, 1.808 and 1.775 for Albany, Buffalo, Syracuse, Cleveland, Columbus and Pittsburgh respectively.

Frankhauser (1992, 1994) has also computed measures for several cities around the world using both the radius and traditional box-counting methods. His results together with those we have just presented, those for the towns of Cardiff and Taunton and the city of Seoul which we compute in this and later chapters, and Smith's (1991) result for Guatemala City, are presented in Table 7.1. It is immediately clear that there are considerable variations in the values computed due to the definitions and methods used and although it is difficult to draw definitive comparisons, there are some points worthy of note. First all the dimensions lie between 1 and 2 as we might expect. Second, most of these values are greater than 1.5, most lying

Table 7.1. The preliminary evidence for fractal cities

Settlement name	Dimension D	Settlement name	Dimension D
Urban development patterns		*Urban growth patterns*	
Albany 1990 (Chap 7)	1.494	London 1820 (Dox/Ab)	1.322
Beijing 1981 (Fra)	1.93	London 1840 (Dox/Ab)	1.585
Berlin 1980 (Fra)	1.73	London 1860 (Dox/Ab)	1.415
Boston 1981 (Fra)	1.69	London 1880 (Dox/Ab)	1.700
Budapest 1981 (Fra)	1.72	London 1900 (Dox/Ab)	1.737
Buffalo 1990 (Chap 7)	1.729	London 1914 (Dox/Ab)	1.765
Cardiff 1981 (Chap 8)	1.586	London 1939 (Dox/Ab)	1.791
Cleveland 1990 (Chap 7)	1.732	London 1962 (Dox/Ab)	1.774
Columbus 1990 (Chap 7)	1.808		
Essen 1981 (Fra)	1.81	Berlin 1875 (Fra)	1.43
Guatemala 1990 (Sm)	1.702	Berlin 1920 (Fra)	1.54
London 1962 (Dox)	1.774	Berlin 1945 (Fra)	1.69
London 1981 (Fra)	1.72		
Los Angeles 1981 (Fra)	1.93	*Transport networks*	
Melbourne 1981 (Fra)	1.85		
Mexico City 1981 (Fra)	1.76	Suburban Rail	
Moscow 1981 (Fra)	1.60	Lyon I 1987 (T & M)	1.88
New York 1960 (Dox)	1.710	Lyon II 1987 (T & M)	1.655
Paris 1960 (Dox)	1.862	Lyon III 1987 (T & M)	1.64
Paris 1981 (Fra)	1.66	Paris 1989 (B & D)	1.466
Pittsburgh 1981 (Fra)	1.59	Stuttgart 1988 (Fra)	1.58
Pittsburgh 1990 (Chap 7)	1.775		
Potsdam 1945 (Fra)	1.88	*Public bus*	
Rome 1981 (Fra)	1.69	Lyon I 1987 (T & M)	1.45
Seoul 1981 (Chap 9)	1.682	Lyon II 1987 (T & M)	1.00
Stuttgart 1981 (Fra)	1.41	Lyon III 1987 (T & M)	1.09
Sydney 1981 (Fra)	1.82		
Syracuse 1990 (Chap 7)	1.438	*Drainage utilities*	
Taipei 1981 (Fra)	1.39	Lyon I 1987 (T & M)	1.79
Taunton 1981 (Chap 7)	1.636	Lyon II 1987 (T & M)	1.30
Tokyo 1960 (Dox)	1.312	Lyon III 1987 (T & M)	1.21

References: B & D – from Benguigui and Daoud (1991); Dox – from Doxiadis (1968); Fra – from Frankhauser (1988, 1990, 1992, 1994); T & M – from Thibault and Marchand (1987); Dox/Ab – from a compilation of data from Doxiadis (1968) and Abercrombie (1945); Sm – from Smith (1991).

Notes: All results are reported to the number of decimal places published and in the case of several different estimates, in particular from Frankhauser and our own work here, the lower estimates of dimension are given.

between 1.6 and 1.8 with a mean of about 1.7. As we shall see, the model we suggest in the next section also generates dimensions with a value around 1.7. Before we conclude our experimental evidence, however, it is also worth noting that urban transport networks can be regarded as ramified fractal structures as we indicated in Chapter 2. The same type of scaling equations can be used to measure their fractal dimension by simply counting links in the networks identified through a grid say, as numbers $N(R)$ or $N(r)$. Thibault and Marchand (1987) computed the dimensions of three different local urban networks – suburban rail, public bus, and drainage utilities – in three different areas of Lyon and their results are also reported in Table 7.1. Benguigui and Daoud (1991) have done much the same for the metro and suburban rail networks of Paris giving a typical dimension of 1.466, while Frankhauser (1990) has calculated the value of D for Stuttgart's rail system as 1.580. The networks for Stuttgart and Paris are shown in Figure 7.6. where either equations (7.1) or have (7.6) could be used to effect the computation. These network results are also summarized in Table 7.1.

To impose some order on this casual evidence, we need to explore how we might model urban structures which show these types of pattern. The Sierpinski carpet is hardly a model but simply a geometrical generating principle, and does not show how the carpet evolves in terms of its basic unit of development. In fact, a remarkable model of fractal growth which might apply to systems as diverse as crystals and cities, cells and galaxies has recently been fashioned in the physics of far-from-equilibrium structures, building on basic ideas of diffusion and transition. It is to this that we will now turn here and in subsequent chapters before returning towards

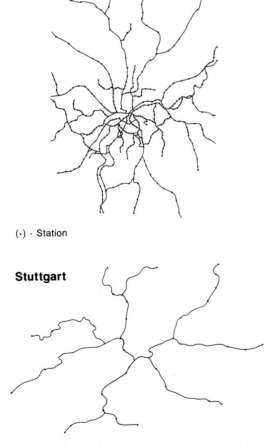

Paris

(·) - Station

Stuttgart

Figure 7.6.   Rail networks as fractal patterns: Paris and Stuttgart (from Benguigui and Daoud, 1991; Frankhauser, 1994).

the end of this book to problems of generalizing scale and size relations to systems of cities.

7.4 A Scaling Model of Urban Growth

So far, our analysis of the fractal city has been largely empirical with few implications for the way urban development processes might generate fractal forms. However, a remarkable product of this new concern for structures which scale physically has been a series of models in which simple random growth, constrained by the geometry of the system in which the growth is occurring, generates highly ordered fractal structures. The most complete examples of this new approach to modeling morphologies have developed in the physics of critical phenomena, particularly involving the aggregation and growth of fine particles. Since the early 1980s, computer simulation models have been used to generate forms visually similar to a variety of particle clusters which also manifest spatial self-similarity across a wide range of scales, and whose structure is subject to scaling laws consistent with ideas in fractal geometry. The clearest, most articulate examples can be generated by a process of diffusion about a seed particle, such diffusion taking place on a regular lattice which embodies the seed.

These models first suggested by Witten and Sander (1981, 1983) are collectively known as Diffusion-Limited Aggregation (DLA) models. The structures generated are familiar tree-like forms or dendrites, grown from the seed, manifesting self-similarity of form across several scales, and whose properties of scaling suggest that they are fractals. The great power of these techniques is that they link growth to specific geometrical forms. They can be easily generalized to other forms such as those with the characteristics of percolation clusters; and more importantly, they are consistent with the sorts of scaling found in the physics of critical phenomena, particularly in structures which are far-from-equilibrium (Feder, 1988). These ideas have excited so much interest in the last decade since they were first proposed, that the physicist Leo Kadanoff (1986) has been prompted to say: "*Physical Review Letters* complains that every third submission seems to concern fractals in some way or another". There are several books and proceedings which summarize this emergent field; readers are referred to an early volume by Stanley and Ostrowsky (1986) and a more recent one by Bunde and Havlin (1991).

To develop the model, we will proceed using the time-honored method of analogy (Wilson, 1969). Anticipating our conclusions, there is no perfect correspondence between theoretical DLA simulations and any of the empirical urban structures we have examined so far in this book (see Table 7.1) which we might use as a basis for comparison. Nevertheless, the similarities are strong, and give us confidence that this approach has great potential in urban simulation which we will explore further in Chapter 8. However, what the approach does suggest is that traditional ways of measuring urban structure, particularly urban population densities, are particularly limited. The DLA approach suggests we must define and measure densities much more accurately, having recourse not simply to general urban concepts such as the density of developed areas, but to the actual geometry of location: populations measured at point locations, not over areas or volumes. This has important implications for previous and existing quantitative models and measures of urban population density which we will elaborate in detail in Chapter 9.

The model is conceived as follows: imagine the simplest process in which a city might grow from some central point or site. Through time, the city grows by new individuals locating next to or near individuals who have already clustered about the central point. If the city were to grow irreversibly and individuals were to occupy every available space adjacent to the growing cluster, the area of the city would expand in proportion to the square of the radius of the cluster. However, it is most unlikely that all available space would be occupied as the city grows. Other land uses are required, some space always remains vacant due to physical obstacles to development and so on. In real cities, the population is never stable for individuals move within the city and occupied sites become unoccupied. For the moment, we will assume that once an individual locates, the location remains occupied; this type of irreversibility is still consistent with a process in which individuals can move within the city, although it assumes that physical locations, once occupied, remain so.

The essential variables describing this growth are $N(R)$, which is the cumulative number of occupied sites (proportional to population), and $\hat{A}(R)$, the total area of all sites occupied and unoccupied at radius R from the center. These are related to radius R through the size relations in equations (7.6) and (7.7) which we can rewrite without constants of proportionality as

$$N(R) \sim R^D, \tag{7.16}$$

and

$$\hat{A}(R) \sim R^E, \tag{7.17}$$

where D is the parameter or fractal dimension which scales population with distance and E the parameter which scales area with distance, that is, the Euclidean dimension. We have explicitly assumed E to be the dimension of area, that is $E = 2$, although we will continue to refer to this dimension as E to enable our equations to be generalized.

In analogy to equation (7.9), the density $\rho(R)$ can now be defined from (7.16) and (7.17) as

$$\rho(R) = \frac{N(R)}{\hat{A}(R)} \sim R^{D-E}. \tag{7.18}$$

The change in population and area, the first derivatives of equations (7.16) and (7.17) with respect to R, are given as

$$\frac{dN(R)}{dR} \sim R^{D-1} \tag{7.19}$$

and

$$\frac{d\hat{A}(R)}{dR} \sim R^{E-1}, \tag{7.20}$$

and the ratio of these equations also defines the density at the margin as

$$\frac{dN(R)}{dR} \bigg/ \frac{d\hat{A}(R)}{dR} = \frac{dN(R)}{d\hat{A}(R)} \sim R^{D-E}. \tag{7.21}$$

Finally, the change in density with respect to distance is given as

$$\frac{d\rho(R)}{dR} \sim R^{D-E-1}, \tag{7.22}$$

and higher derivatives of equation (7.22) can be taken if required.

These relationships in equations (7.16) to (7.22) are only of substantive interest if values are specified for D and E. First, the physical dimension E could relate to a line, area or volume. In fact, earlier we assumed $E = 2$, but it is possible to develop the analysis for urban systems with $E = 3$ if the population were to be modelled in three dimensions. From our earlier argument, we also assumed $1 < D < 2$, that is, that the population does not occupy the entire space $\hat{A}(R)$ which would imply $D = 2$ and a uniform density, nor that the population simply varies with R which would imply a linear city with $D = 1$. Thus assuming $E = 2$, we will use the following four relations:

$$N(R) \sim R^{\beta_1} = R^D, \tag{7.23}$$

$$\frac{dN(R)}{dR} \sim R^{\beta_2} = R^{D-1}, \tag{7.24}$$

$$\rho(R) \sim R^{\beta_3} = R^{D-2}, \tag{7.25}$$

$$\frac{dN(R)}{d\hat{A}(R)} \sim R^{\beta_4} = R^{D-2}. \tag{7.26}$$

If we assume that $1 < D < 2$, then β_1 and β_2 in equations (7.23) and (7.24) are positive, while the exponent on density, β_3 in equation (7.25), is negative, hence consistent with traditional urban density theory and observation (Clark, 1951; Mills, 1970). β_4 the exponent on marginal density, is also negative and in theory should equal β_3. These β parameters can be estimated using ordinary least squares regression on the logarithmic transforms of equations (7.23) to (7.26) and represent different ways of calculating the scaling parameter D. A fifth estimate of D could be derived from equation (7.22) where the parameter is $D - 3$. However, the relationship is negative and cannot be found by logarithmic regression. We have thus excluded this from our subsequent analysis.

The above relationships describe how the population of a city or particles in a cluster fill space, and as we have argued, it is reasonable to assume that the density of the city or cluster falls at increasing radial distance R from the center. This is of course borne out by casual observation which suggests D cannot be as large as 2 but is certainly greater than 1. There is another way, however, of considering how population fills space. Let us assume that populations can be linked by a continuous line. If every population point on a lattice were occupied, there are well-known curves which link all such points and seem to fill space as we demonstrated in Chapter 2. However, it is always possible to find a continuous curve which links less than all points on a lattice (assuming some are unoccupied). Such a curve is clearly longer than the diameter of the city but not as long as the space-filling curve linking every lattice point such as the Peano curve illustrated in Figure 2.4. It is well-known that such a curve has a fractal dimension greater than the line ($D = 1$) but less than the area ($D = 2$) and as such, it is a measure of the extent to which space is filled.

Scaling relations such as these have been used throughout the development of social physics, and in this sense, we have always worked with fractals where their parameters have been dimensions; but the new framework provides links between these relationships and the underlying geometry of the system which has hitherto eluded us. We have already noted the consistency between urban density theory and densities as given by equations (7.25) and (7.26), but considerable work has also been done on relationships between population and area. From equations (7.16) and (7.17), it is clear that area can be derived from population through the perimeter–scale relation given in equations (7.10) and (7.11). These types of relationship are allometric, and have been extensively studied with respect to the growth of cities (Dutton, 1973; Nordbeck, 1971; Woldenberg, 1973). In the development of urban allometry, there has been little attempt to link these scaling coefficients to urban form, and most of the analysis has been with respect to the growth of different cities through time, not individual cities across space. Nevertheless, there are connections here between fractal geometry and urban allometry which we will explore in detail in Chapters 9 and 10.

There is also a connection between the fractal dimension D in this context and the exponents in gravitational and potential models of spatial interaction (Stewart and Warntz, 1958). From the approach developed here, we would argue that the value of the exponent in such gravity models is a consequence of the form of the system, rather than any noise in the data (Curry, 1972). In Chapter 9, we give greater substance to these notions, but we do not follow the idea through in this book, notwithstanding its important implications for the entire class of urban models based on spatial interaction (Batty, 1976). It is worth noting, however, that the ideas developed here might represent a new variety of social physics, a 'postmodern' social physics as some commentators have already referred to it (Woolley, 1988). In this blend of physics, growth and form are inextricably linked.

7.5 The Process of Diffusion-Limited Aggregation

The above scaling relations can be estimated for any spatial system of individual objects in which central points can be identified; as such, these relationships are independent of any particular spatial form. Here however, we will introduce a particular spatial form resulting from a growth process of constrained diffusion – diffusion-limited aggregation – which will represent our baseline model through which we will make comparisons with observable urban growth. It is necessary now that we introduce the DLA model. To this end, we will follow the terminology of the field and hope the reader will bear with our indulgence in referring to the irreducible objects of the system as particles.

Consider a bounded circular region with a single seed particle fixed at its center. New particles are launched from points far away from the seed, on a circular boundary which is at least three times the radius of the cluster grown so far. These particles are launched from random points on this boundary one at a time. When a launch occurs, the particle begins a random walk, usually on a regular lattice, often square, which is centered over the seed particle, the particle moving only one lattice step at a time. Two states can occur: if the particle moves outside the boundary circle, it is 'killed' or abandoned; if it approaches the cluster and is within a neighborhood, usually one lattice step, of an already fixed particle, it sticks to the particle, its walk is terminated, and the cluster is extended. If either of these cases occur, another particle is launched, and the process of 'walking' on the lattice begins again. The process only terminates once a size threshold is reached such as that based on a fixed cluster size in terms of the number of particles, or once a maximum cluster radius or cluster span is attained.

The form which results is dendritic with tentacles extending from the seed particle, growth proceeding in a tree-like fashion. It is not immediately obvious why this is so, but a little thought reveals that when a particle sticks to another, the probability of more particles sticking in that neighborhood is much increased. Ribbons of particles begin to form around the center of the cluster, making it ever more likely that new particles will stick to the tips of existing dendrites which effectively screen the fissures between the emerging tentacles from receiving further particles (Sander, 1987). The resulting form (which can be seen below in abstract in Figure 7.7 and in simulation in Figure 7.8 and Plate 7.3) is clearly fractal in that the dendrites making up the cluster appear similar at every scale.

The association between particle clusters and fractal geometry goes back to a paper by Forrest and Witten (1979) but the original model was suggested by Witten and Sander (1981, 1983). Its subsequent application and estimation to different particle clusters was motivated by its clear visual similarity to many naturally occurring forms. The diffusion process itself has high generality in that it is consistent with the Laplace equation which applies to many physical systems. Other models such as those simulating such phenomena as dielectric breakdown (Niemeyer, Pietronero and Wiesmann, 1984; Satpathy, 1986) which we will develop in the next chapter, and viscous fingering (Nittmann, Daccord and Stanley, 1985) are also consistent with DLA. As already indicated, there have been extensive explorations of the DLA model. Meakin (1983a, b, 1986a, b) has explored a variety of simulations with dimensions ranging from $E = 2$ to $E = 6$ and particle systems of varying sizes. Changes to the probabilities of sticking have been investigated as well as constraints on the direction of the random walks, all illustrating the robustness of the model.

Apart from the highly characteristic form generated by the model, several independent researchers have concluded that $D \approx 1.71$ for the DLA model. This dimension hardly changes when the sticking probability is relaxed, although there is still considerable argument concerning the universality of this scaling exponent (Meakin, 1986c). There is some recent work which suggests that the shape of the underlying lattice has an effect on the simulation (Meakin, 1985; Turkevich and Scher, 1985). Attempts at generating a mean field theory for the model by Muthukumar (1983) have led to a prediction that $D = (E^2 + 1)/(E + 1)$ which for a two-dimensional system gives $D = 5/3 = 1.66$ and for a three-dimensional system, $D = 5/2 = 2.5$; these are both consistent with simulations. But as yet, there is no general consensus concerning these issues. The most complete reviews of this enormous body of work are contained in recent books by Jullien and Botet (1987), Vicsek (1989), Pietronero (1989), and Bunde and Havlin (1991).

At this stage, we must attempt a preliminary justification for the choice of DLA as a baseline model for our urban simulations. As we have pointed out in earlier chapters, many rapidly growing cities during the 19th and 20th centuries appear to be structured along transportation routes radiating from the central business district, for example, Paris and Stuttgart shown earlier in Figure 7.6. Similar dendrites incorporating the same pattern are associated with smaller commercial centers within the city, which are also structured in a fairly clear hierarchy based on several orders of transport route. There is a problem in saying much more than this because of the way in which urban form is traditionally characterized and measured. Much of urban morphology is predicated in terms of land use patterns and physical structures which do not map easily onto the density and distribution of population.

The patterns shown for London, New York, Paris, Tokyo, Berlin and Buffalo in Figures 7.2 to 7.5 and Plates 7.1 and 7.2 bear this out in that they do not correspond to the way the population of these same cities has been measured in previous estimates of their density (as reviewed, for example, by Berry and Horton, 1970). Urban population densities are usually defined across census tracts rather than in terms of the actual physical location of the population. Indeed, there is some speculation in urban allometry that urban populations should be conceptualized in three, not two, dimensions (Dutton, 1973), but there has been no investigation of how such densities are reflected in the geometry of urban form. Thus, it is not surprising that the sorts of form characteristic of DLA are not manifest in the data on which urban population density models have been developed. In short, a clearer view of how processes of growth give rise to particular urban geometries such as those seen in DLA, would provide a new approach to measuring urban densities; and although it is still very much an open question as to whether the dendritic structures of DLA are highly correlated with the geometrical characteristics of urban growth, the modest verifications we have presented so far can only be strengthened through better data.

The other major issue relates to the process by which DLA occurs. Clearly urban growth is based on a kind of diffusion which leads to cities growing at their edges. But the process of random wandering necessary to DLA cannot be given any physical meaning in the behavior patterns of individuals locating in cities. The random walking might be thought of as a proxy for the process of spatial search which does not normally take place physically, but this analogy cannot be forced too far. Moreover, cities are not irreversible in the sense in which DLA clusters are. There is substantial mobility among any urban population due to life style changes, economic competition and such like which change occupancies in the physical stock of buildings in any city. We fully recognize these issues, although we consider it necessary to begin with the simplest DLA model, and only in later chapters will we adapt this to the peculiarities of urban growth. The only work in an explicitly geographical context which we are aware of other than that summarized earlier in this chapter, is by Lovejoy, Schertzer and Ladoy (1986) in their study of the global coverage of the Earth's weather by meteorological stations for which they estimated a fractal dimension of $D \approx 1.75$.

7.6 The Statistical Measurement of DLA Clusters

In estimating the dimension of any structure which can be described as a cluster of particles around a central seed such as DLA clusters, we will assume that there are a total of N particles, each of which occupies a unique location on a regular lattice. Note now that we are defining the distance from any particle l to any other particle k as r. The range l, k is 1, 2, ..., l, k, ..., N, where these index numbers are consistently ordered around the central seed site on the lattice l, $k = 1$. A particle k at distance r from l is given as

$$n_{lk}(r) = \begin{cases} 1 \text{ if a particle occupies the lattice point,} \\ 0 \text{ if the lattice point is unoccupied.} \end{cases}$$

We will now present two sets of measures: first those based on a location around the seed site $k = 1$, and second, those based on locations around every occupied site which are formed as averages. We refer to the first as one-point measures, the second set as two-point.

For the one-point measures, the number of particles at a given distance r from the seed site is given as $n_1(r)$ or $n(r)$

$$n(r) = n_1(r) = \sum_l n_{l1}(r), \tag{7.27}$$

where the summation in equation (7.27) is over all those particles l which are at distance r (or in distance band r) from the site $k = 1$. Note that we can suppress the index $k = 1$ in subsequent notation because all the one-point measures introduced are relative to this seed site. The cumulative number of particles at all distances up to radius R is given as

$$N(R) = \sum_{r=1}^{R} n(r), \tag{7.28}$$

and the number of particles at distance R (or in band R) is

$$\Delta N(R) = N(R) - N(R-1) = n(R), \tag{7.29}$$

noting that $N(0)$ is not defined. $N(R)$ and $\Delta N(R)$ are the discrete equivalents of equations (7.16) and (7.19) where we assume the distance bands $r = 1$, 2, ..., R are equal in all cases.

To measure density, we must count all lattice points, occupied or unoccupied around each point $n_{l1}(r)$ associated with r, and these are defined as $s(r)$. The total number of such points up to distance R is given as

$$S(R) = \sum_{r=1}^{R} s(r), \tag{7.30}$$

and the density of particles associated with all distances up to R is thus

$$\rho(R) = \frac{N(R)}{S(R)} = \frac{\sum_{r=1}^{R} n(r)}{\sum_{r=1}^{R} s(r)}. \tag{7.31}$$

Two measures of the change in density can be computed. First from equation (7.31)

$$\Delta\rho(R) = \rho(R) - \rho(R-1) = \frac{N(R)}{S(R)} - \frac{N(R-1)}{S(R-1)}, \tag{7.32}$$

and second,

$$Q(R) = \frac{\Delta N(R)}{\Delta S(R)} = \frac{\sum_{r=1}^{R} n(r) - \sum_{r=1}^{R-1} n(r)}{\sum_{r=1}^{R} s(r) - \sum_{r=1}^{R-1} s(r)} = \frac{n(R)}{s(R)}, \tag{7.33}$$

from equations (7.29) and (7.30). Equation (7.31), the cumulative (average) density, is equivalent to equation (7.18), equation (7.32) to equation (7.22), and equation (7.33) to (7.21). As noted previously, we will not use equation (7.32), and in the subsequent analysis, equations (7.28), (7.29), (7.31) and (7.33) will be used as approximations to equations (7.23) to (7.26) in that order.

So far, these measures are all specified in terms of the radius R about a central point, the seed point at the center of the lattice. It is possible, indeed appropriate due to the self-similarity of DLA clusters, to compute the measures as averages around all N particles in the system. In analogy to equation (7.27), we first compute the number of particles $n_k(r)$ at distance r from *any* lattice point k as

$$n_k(r) = \sum_{l} n_{lk}(r). \tag{7.34}$$

The average of all particles at distance r from one another is then given as

$$\bar{n}(r) = \frac{\sum_{k=1}^{N} n_k(r)}{N} = \frac{\sum_{k=1}^{N} \sum_{l} n_{lk}(r)}{N}. \tag{7.35}$$

The cumulative two-point average of particles up to distance R and the change in particles between distances or distance bands are defined respectively as

$$\overline{N}(R) = \sum_{r=1}^{R} \bar{n}(r) \tag{7.36}$$

and

$$\Delta\overline{N}(R) = \overline{N}(R) - \overline{N}(R-1) = \bar{n}(R). \tag{7.37}$$

Density measures can now be formed, noting that the number of lattice points l for each distance r is independent of k and l. In analogy to equation (7.30), the two-point cumulative density is given as

$$\bar{\rho}(R) = \frac{\overline{N}(R)}{S(R)} = \frac{\displaystyle\sum_{r=1}^{R}\sum_{k=1}^{N}\sum_{l} n_{lk}(r)}{N\displaystyle\sum_{r=1}^{R} s(r)}. \tag{7.38}$$

Density change can be computed as

$$\Delta\bar{\rho}(R) = \bar{\rho}(R) - \bar{\rho}(R-1) = \frac{\overline{N}(R)}{S(R)} - \frac{\overline{N}(R-1)}{S(R-1)}, \tag{7.39}$$

and the marginal change in density as

$$\overline{Q}(R) = \frac{\Delta\overline{N}(R)}{\Delta S(R)} = \frac{\bar{n}(R)}{s(R)} = \sum_{k=1}^{N} \frac{\displaystyle\sum_{l} n_{lk}(r)}{s(r)} \bigg/ N. \tag{7.40}$$

As in the case of the one-point measures, the two-point measures in equations (7.36), (7.37), (7.38) and (7.40) will be used as approximations to equations (7.23) to (7.26) in that order.

The two-point measures defined between equations (7.34) and (7.40) clearly take account of any self-similarity in the physical structure, but in the case of all these measures, it is necessary to be extremely careful concerning the radial distances over which they are computed. Much of the subsequent analysis is concerned with these issues for in all cases, the measures are only appropriate for those parts of the system which are fully developed, and in any cluster, this will be somewhat less than the total cluster itself. Lastly, Witten and Sander (1981, 1983) and Meakin (1983a, b) amongst many who have worked with these models, argue that the two-point measures are considerably more appropriate than the one-point, and they suggest that the two-point density measure $\overline{Q}(R)$ is the best to use in estimating D. In the sequel, we will use all the measures presented, thus demonstrating the sensitivity of the estimation to the measures themselves as well as to different ranges of distance.

7.7 Space–Time Histories and Accounts

The DLA model has an extremely straightforward growth dynamics. Particles are launched one at a time and no more than one particle can be randomly walking on the lattice at any one point in time. Therefore a complete history of the system's growth dynamics is represented by the order in which the particles stick to the cluster along with their location on the lattice. We must now formulate the model with respect to time t as well as space r for several reasons. First, in comparison with real systems, it may be necessary to calibrate the model so that the theoretical growth process can be tailored to an actual process if a development history of an urban area is available. Second, it is necessary to explore the stability of the cluster over time with respect to the stability of its dimension D and the spatial properties of successive particle locations. Third and perhaps of greatest importance here, we need to measure the growth profiles of the cluster with regard to its fully developed parts; thus the dynamics of the growth process will enable us to define the appropriate sub-cluster from the whole.

We will now extend our spatial notation where we refer to any distance by r, and up to a given radial distance by R, to an index of any time by t, and up to a given time by T. Assume that space is recorded by $r = 1, 2,$ ..., R_b where the units of space are distance bands and R_b is the boundary of the system, and that time is given by $t = 1, 2, ..., T_e$ where the units of time are periods and T_e is the last period in the growth process. Strictly speaking, each particle has a unique location in time and space for no more than one lattice point is ever occupied and no more than one particle ever circulates in the system at any point in time. However, in the subsequent analysis, we will require these distance and time bands to be defined.

The basic unit of account is now the number of particles in distance band r and time period t, $n(r, t)$. We are able to analyze this number over time or space or both, Thus

$$n(t) = \sum_{r=1}^{R_b} n(r, t) \tag{7.41}$$

and

$$n(r) = \sum_{t=1}^{T_e} n(r, t), \tag{7.42}$$

where $n(r)$ is defined as in (7.27). Note that an equivalent unit of account $\bar{n}(r, t)$ could be defined based on two-point averages but this is less meaningful with respect to the actual growth of the cluster. Equations (7.41) and (7.42) when summed over t or r respectively add to give the total particles in the system, that is

$$N = \sum_{t=1}^{T_e} n(t) = \sum_{r=1}^{R_b} n(r)$$

$$= \sum_{t=1}^{T_e} \sum_{r=1}^{R_b} n(r, t). \tag{7.43}$$

Equations (7.41) to (7.43) define a simple but complete set of space–time accounts.

It is necessary, however, to examine how the system converges towards the marginal and total sums in equations (7.41) to (7.43). Cumulative variables are thus defined as

$$n(R, t) = \sum_{r=1}^{R} n(r, t) \tag{7.44}$$

and

$$n(r, T) = \sum_{t=1}^{T} n(r, t). \tag{7.45}$$

Equations (7.44) and (7.45) are equal to (7.41) and (7.42) when $R = R_b$ and $T = T_e$ respectively. A total accumulation over time and space defined in analogy to equation (7.43) is

$$n(R, T) = \sum_{t=1}^{T} n(R, t) = \sum_{r=1}^{R} n(r, T)$$

$$= \sum_{t=1}^{T} \sum_{r=1}^{R} n(r, t). \tag{7.46}$$

The other variable of interest which serves to integrate these accounts with the previous one-point measures is defined as

$$N(R) = \sum_{r=1}^{R} n(r) = \sum_{t=1}^{T_e} n(R, t), \tag{7.47}$$

and the analogous cumulative total over time is given as

$$N(T) = \sum_{t=1}^{T} n(t) = \sum_{r=1}^{R_b} n(r, T). \tag{7.48}$$

As $R \to R_b$ and $T \to T_e$, equations (7.47) and (7.48) converge to the total number of particles in the system, N, defined by equation (7.43).

For DLA simulations, we already have a clear idea how the growth process develops with respect to time and space due to the fact that in general, particles launched later in time, are added to tips of dendrites on the periphery of the cluster; in short, there is a strong correlation between time of launch and location of particles with respect to distance from the central seed in the cluster. Examining the distribution of particles $n(r, t)$ across space r for each time t, or across t for each distance band r, reveals wave-like phenomena with most particles locating on the edge of the cluster grown so far in the latest time period. The cumulative distributions $n(R, t)$ and $n(r, T)$ also show cumulative waves across space and time as will be clearly illustrated in a later section when an example of the DLA model is presented. The build-up of waves of growth generated from $n(R, t)$ where R is accumulated over space, but plotted at different times t, and generated from $n(r, T)$ where T varies across time, but is plotted for different distance bands r, is easy to show. We can also plot $n(R, T)$ through time from equation (7.46), but across space and vice versa. In the sequel, we will plot these variables on size–distance graphs for each individual time *t* and accumulated time *T* so that we can examine the spatial similarities through time, and define appropriate thresholds for the one- and two-point measurements of the cluster.

7.8 Theoretical Simulations: I. Statics

Before we explore the statistical and spatial properties of a typical DLA simulation, we must present the method of simulation in more detail. As we indicated in an earlier section, a seed is first planted at a point on the lattice and a cluster is built up around this seed by launching particles at some distance far away from the edge of the cluster. Each particle makes a random walk on the lattice until it reaches a lattice point adjacent to one already occupied by a particle where it 'sticks', or until it leaves the system by crossing its boundary where it is deemed to have disappeared or been destroyed. Although there is some debate about the anisotropy introduced by the geometry of the underlying lattice as we noted earlier, lattices based on a square grid have mainly been used, and we will adopt this convention here.

To reduce the computation time required, particles are launched from a circular orbit which is set at the maximum radius of the cluster plus five lattice steps. Particles are deemed to have been destroyed once they enter the region outside the bounding circle which is set at least three times the maximum cluster radius. As the cluster builds up, its maximum radius, the launch circle and the bounding circle continually increase, and with these conventions, clusters can be grown to any size: the only limits are computer time and memory. The geometry of the method is illustrated in Figure 7.7 which shows how these assumptions are incorporated into the spatial development of the cluster. This mechanism, first proposed by Meakin (1983b), enables modest clusters up to 10^4 or so particles to be grown in

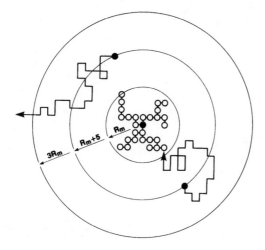

Figure 7.7. The mechanism of diffusion-limited aggregation.

about 10 hours CPU time using a MicroVax. However, if bigger clusters need to be grown on workstations, it is necessary to develop faster methods based on off-lattice random walks when far away from the cluster, with a transition to lattice walks in the neighborhood of the cluster. Differences in form are not apparent and clusters up to 10^5 particles have been grown successfully (Meakin, 1986b). Clusters of larger magnitude can be grown, but these require high performance machines.

Here we will illustrate the operation of a typical DLA model but we must note that definitive results concerning the fractal dimension D of such models depend upon averaging the dimensions associated with many runs. Different clusters are produced for each run due to the random walk mechanism of the model, and thus on average, $D \approx 1.71 + 0.03$ where the value 0.03 represents the standard error (Jullien and Botet, 1987). This standard error is fairly low, but suggests that for the majority of runs, D should be within the range 1.68 to 1.74. The DLA simulation discussed here is shown in Figure 7.8 where the gray tones give some idea of the sequence in which particles are added to the cluster, and it is also illustrated in Plate 7.3. This aggregate consists of $N = 10,000$, clustered around a seed particle which is located at the center of a 500×500 square lattice.

Some properties of this simulation are shown in Table 7.2 which also includes similar properties of urban growth for the town of Taunton; these will be used later as a basis for comparison. To enable analysis to proceed, the various measures of cluster size and spread must be normalized with respect to the number of points in the lattice. Such normalization involves computing indices relating to the size of the cluster and its radius. The maximum radius of the cluster R_m, computed as the largest distance from any particle to the seed, can be used to compute the effective area of the cluster (πR_m^2) if all lattice points were occupied. The actual area is given by

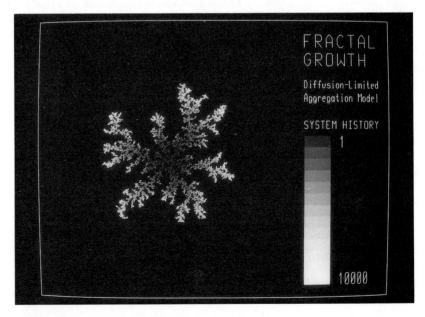

Figure 7.8.   A typical DLA simulation.

Table 7.2. Spatial properties of the theoretical and real systems

System characteristics	DLA simulation	Taunton
Dimension of lattice	500×500	150×150
Lattice points	250,000	22,500
Points occupied, N	10,000	3179
Maximum radius, R_m	248.244	62,936
Total effective area, πR_m^2	193,600.700	12,443.850
Average density, $N/\pi R_m^2$	0.052	0.256
Mean radius,[1] $\bar{R}$	124.620	33.184
Standard deviation, σ	56.075	14.189
$\bar{R}/R_m$	0.502	0.527
σ/R_m	0.226	0.225
$\sigma/\bar{R}$	0.450	0.428
Length of boundary, B	19,855	3994
Maximum circumference, $2\pi R_m$	1559.762	395.442
Tortuosity index, $B/2\pi R_m$	12.729	10.100
Number of boundary points, N_b	10,000	2709
Density of boundary, N_b/N	1.000	0.852
Interior points, N_i	0	470
Density of interior, N_i/N	0	0.148
Nearest neighbors, N_n	23,938	13,804
Average neighbors, N_n/N	2.394	4.342

[1] Mean radius $\bar{R} = \{[\Sigma_i r_i \Sigma_l n_{l1}(r_i)]/N$, where r_i now represents the distance from the seed particle $k = 1$ to the distance band i which contains particles l associated with r.

N (assuming each point occupies a unit square), thus the density here is only about 5% of the total effective area. This is an extremely sparse structure; indeed, all the occupied lattice points are on the boundary of the cluster and there are no interior points (occupied points entirely surrounded by other occupied points) whatsoever. The length of the boundary is 12.7 times the circumference of the effective area $(2\pi R_m)$ which represents a good measure of the tortuosity of the structure. The sparsity is also indicated by the fact that on average, there are only about 2.4 nearest neighbors to each lattice point. We will return to this table in a later section when we come to examine the properties of the urban area composing the town of Taunton.

For both this and the subsequent application to Taunton, we will examine the spatial distribution of development using the four relationships given earlier in equations (7.23) to (7.26). We first use the one-point $N(R)$ from equation (7.28), $n(R)$ from equation (7.29), $\rho(R)$ from (7.31) and $Q(R)$ from (7.33) as approximations to $N(R), dN(R), \rho(R)$ and $dN(R)/d\hat{A}(R)$ in equations (7.23) to (7.26) using 50 distance bands each of width $R_b/50$. The computed absolute values of these variables and their logarithmic transformations are shown in Figures 7.9 and 7.10 respectively. Note that each distance band is the same width, thus no approximation to dR is required.

From equations (7.23) to (7.26), $N(R)$ should increase at an increasing rate, $dN(R)$ should increase at a decreasing rate, the density $\rho(R)$ should decrease at a decreasing rate as should $dN(R)/d\hat{A}(R)$. Figure 7.9 indicates this for $\rho(R)$ and $dN(R)/d\hat{A}(R)$, but $N(R)$ behaves like a logistic function, while $dN(R)$ is

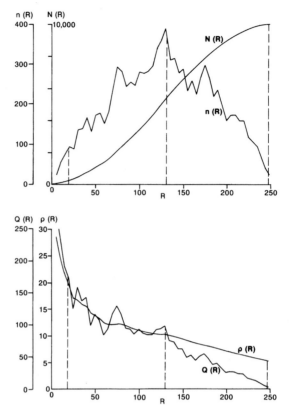

Figure 7.9. Absolute one-point relationships for the DLA simulation.

almost parabolic. These functions should all be linear when plotted logarithmically as in Figure 7.10, but the graphs indicate very sharp changes in slope and direction in the neighborhood of $R \approx 125$. All this is an indication that the cluster is well developed up to this distance from the central seed; at greater distances the development is increasingly incomplete due to the termination of the growth process. Thus it is standard practice in fitting these relationships to data to exclude longer distances which reflect the incomplete peripheral regions of the cluster, and sometimes to exclude short distances which can also be subject to volatile fluctuations in occupancy.

Therefore, we have generated the parameters from the following equations which have been fitted using ordinary least squares regression:

$$\log N(R) = \alpha_1 + \beta_1 \log R,$$

$$\log n(R) = \alpha_2 + \beta_2 \log R,$$

$$\log \rho(R) = \alpha_3 + \beta_3 \log R, \tag{7.49}$$

$$\log Q(R) = \alpha_4 + \beta_4 \log R.$$

Initially, we fitted these equations to all 50 distance bands, reestimated their parameters using an upper cut-off after the 26th band, and then produced a final estimation of the equations excluding the first three distance bands. These thresholds/cut-offs are indicated in Figures 7.9 and 7.10.

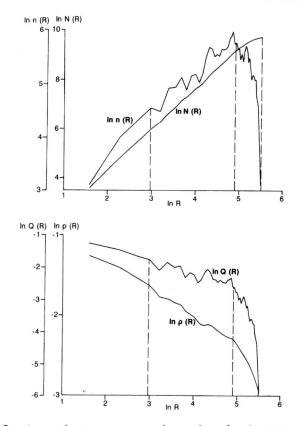

Figure 7.10. Logarithmic one-point relationships for the DLA simulation.

Estimates of the various parameters β_1, β_2, β_3 and β_4 in terms of their fractal dimensions are shown on the first rows of each estimate in Table 7.3, with their standard errors on the second rows, and their adjusted r^2 values on the third. For these one-point estimates, β_1 and β_3 are related by

Table 7.3. One-point estimates of the scaling equations for the DLA simulation

Distance bands	$D = \beta_1$	$D = 1 + \beta_2$	$D = 2 + \beta_3$	$D = 2 + \beta_4$
1–50	1.574	1.267	1.574	1.174
	0.017	0.100	0.017	0.095
	0.994	0.111	0.924	0.602
1–26	1.665	1.777	1.665	1.638
	0.006	0.032	0.006	0.029
	1.000	0.959	0.992	0.856
4–26	1.659	1.739	1.659	1.686
	0.009	0.049	0.009	0.050
	0.999	0.908	0.985	0.632

Note: the first line of results for each distance band gives the fractal dimension, the second line the standard error, and the third the adjusted coefficient of determination r^2. These definitions are used for all subsequent tables of this type in this and the next chapter.

$\beta_3 = \beta_1 - 2$ and thus there are only three, not four independent estimates in this table. The initial estimation over all 50 distance bands reveals volatile r^2 values and considerable inconsistency between the β estimates. Cutting off the cluster at the 26th band improves these results dramatically. The standard errors are considerably lower, and all r^2 are greater than 0.850. The fractal dimension of 1.665 from β_1 is close to the value of 1.71 produced in averaging many DLA simulations and it is even closer to Muthukumar's (1983) field theory prediction of $(E^2 + 1)/(E + 1) = 1.666$. Excluding the shorter distance range does not change these estimates very much and it is encouraging that all three independent estimates of D from β_1, β_2 and β_4 for distance ranges 1–26 and 4–26 lie between 1.638 and 1.777.

It is widely argued in the literature that two-point measures are considerably better than one-point, for these measures capture the dilation symmetry or self-similarity implicit in Figure 7.8. Using $\overline{N}(R)$, $\bar{n}(R)$, $\bar{p}(R)$ and $\overline{Q}(R)$ from equations (7.36), (7.37), (7.38) and (7.40) respectively as the dependent variables in equations (7.49) provides another set of estimates of the fractal dimension D. First these variables are plotted against distance in absolute and logarithmic form in Figures 7.11 and 7.12. The graphs are considerably smoother than those in Figures 7.9 and 7.10 due to the extensive averaging for every particle related to every other. In fact the two-point averages required about three hours CPU time on a MicroVax and these cannot easily be generated alongside the DLA simulation. Moreover

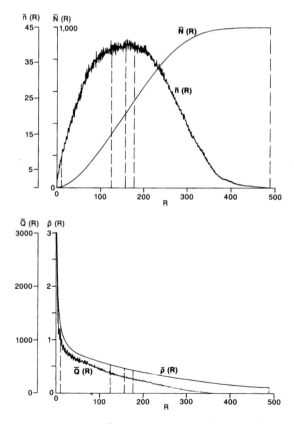

Figure 7.11. Absolute two-point relationships for the DLA simulation.

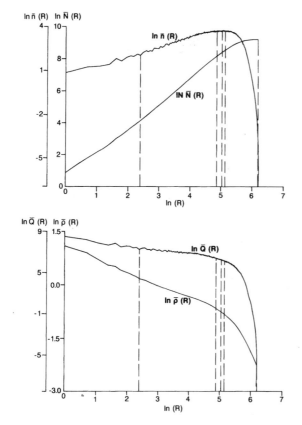

Figure 7.12.   Logarithmic two-point relationships for the DLA simulation.

the set of distances now relates to all possible distances between every lattice point, there being $R = 1, 2, \ldots, 488$ in contrast to the one-point measures where we have assumed that 50 distance bands is a good approximation to the variation in the cluster up to $R_b = 248$. It is considerably more difficult to detect distance thresholds from these plots because of their smoothness. Thus we have selected five possible ranges for estimation purposes. The initial range uses all 488 distances but this is reduced to 174, 11–174, 11–157 and 11–123, the last three also excluding the first 10 bands.

Estimates of the β parameters and the associated fractal dimensions are shown in Table 7.4. As expected, these coefficients are quite inconsistent as estimated over the whole range of distances, but as the ranges are reduced, the coefficients converge quite remarkably to give fractal dimensions between 1.640 and 1.677. The standard errors shown in this table and the correlations are also much improved as the range is reduced, with the final estimates based on the range 11–123 giving near perfect correlations. From the analysis, it would appear that the fractal dimension is nearer 1.66 than 1.71, and this is borne out in several other simulations we have generated. However, we have not attempted anything like the number of simulations reported by Witten and Sander (1983) and Meakin (1983b) amongst others, although it is interesting that since the DLA model was proposed, the certainty with which researchers have held to the universality of $D \approx 1.71$, has become much weaker. The precise value of D, however, whether it be

Table 7.4. Two-point estimates of the scaling equations for the DLA simulation

Distance bands	$D = \beta_1$	$D = 1 + \beta_2$	$D = 2 + \beta_3$	$D = 2 + \beta_4$
1–488	1.338	0.161	1.367	0.179
	0.011	0.081	0.012	0.079
	0.966	0.178	0.852	0.519
1–174	1.586	1.588	1.644	1.588
	0.004	0.008	0.002	0.008
	0.999	0.972	0.992	0.945
11–174	1.619	1.545	1.641	1.545
	0.003	0.011	0.004	0.011
	0.999	0.941	0.983	0.917
11–157	1.631	1.575	1.654	1.575
	0.003	0.010	0.003	0.010
	1.000	0.954	0.988	0.920
11–123	1.652	1.640	1.677	1.641
	0.002	0.009	0.002	0.009
	1.000	0.978	0.997	0.933

1.66 or 1.71 is not important *per se*. What is important is that DLA generates self-similar forms which provide a baseline for comparison with real growth, and it also provides a vehicle for adapting such models to more realistic simulations of urban growth and form.

7.9 Theoretical Simulations: II. Dynamics

As already indicated, we will not examine the temporal dynamics in the DLA model in complete detail for we are unlikely to have substantial histories of urban growth on which to base our comparisons. But we are able to use the model dynamics to explore the extent to which the cluster is complete at any stage of its development. This issue has already been broached in selecting distance thresholds for the estimation of fractal dimensions as reported above. Thus there are two aspects of the growth process which we will focus upon: first the question of spatial development with respect to the form of the cluster, and second, measurement of the statistical properties of the cluster at different time periods. We will deal with these in turn.

We have arbitrarily divided the growth process into 10 (= T_e) time periods and have allocated $N/T_e = 1000$ particles to each time period. In short, we will associate the first 1000 particles with $t = 1$, the second thousand with $t = 2$ and so on. With respect to the temporal accounts presented earlier, for each time period t

$$n(t) = \sum_{r=1}^{R_b} n(r, t) = 1000 \tag{7.50}$$

and

$$N = \sum_{t=1}^{T_e} \sum_{r=1}^{R_b} n(r, t) = \sum_{t=1}^{T_e} n(t) = 10,000. \tag{7.51}$$

The location of each of the N particles on the lattice with respect to each time period t in which the location takes place, is shown in Figure 7.13. This is a dramatic example of the model's growth dynamics which indicates quite clearly how the ultimate form of the cluster is established. The first and perhaps second time periods determine the basic skeleton of the form with subsequent evolution largely representing the addition of particles to the already established dendrites. Growth takes place mainly on the cluster tips. We have computed the correlation (r^2) between the location of particles represented in terms of radial distance from the seed, and the time of development: this value is 0.79 for a linear comparison and it rises to 0.90 if a non-linear relationship between time and space is postulated. These are very high values giving a clear indication that the dendritic structure is extremely effective in screening undeveloped areas from further development. Figure 7.13 also presents a classic example of the fact that the overall form of the cluster cannot easily be inferred from its parts. Finally, speculation that the underlying lattice on which the cluster is based introduces anisotropy which biases the form to a diamond shape (Meakin, 1986c), is seen clearly in the growth of the cluster in later time periods.

The wave-like spread of the cluster is clearly observed in Figure 7.13, but the high correlation between space and time must be qualified in that some particles are still locating at short distances from the seed as late as the final time period. For example in the fifth time period, particles are locating in the 11th distance band from the center while in the last (10th) time period, particles are locating as close in as the 18th distance band when over 90% of the cluster has been developed. It is these effects which make it essential to consider a fairly tight distance threshold over which to measure the cluster's properties, as was used in the previous section.

It is also possible to demonstrate the wave-like growth of the system in a manner akin to the cumulative and individual growth of population given by $N(R)$ and $n(R)$ respectively. In Figure 7.14, we have plotted the cumulative total $n(R, t)$ for increasing R in terms of each 10 time periods. This is essentially the growth pictured in Figure 7.13 collapsed to one-dimensional form. The individual profiles $n(r, t)$ are also plotted and these show the overlapping nature of the waves which occur when all the particles in Figure 7.13 are collapsed to form Figure 7.8. Figure 7.14 also shows the cumulative total $n(R, T)$ over R for cumulative time $T = 1, 2, \ldots$. Note that the graph of $n(R, T_e)$ is that of $N(R)$ shown in Figure 7.9. The composition of the aggregate of individual change $n(R)$, given as $n(r, T)$ where $T = 1, 2,$ $\ldots$ is also shown revealing how wave upon wave of growth builds up the overall cluster.

We can estimate the stability of the cluster through time by computing the fractal dimension associated with $n(R, t)$ and $n(R, T)$ in Figure 7.14, using the graphs of $n(r, t)$ and $n(R, T)$ to indicate appropriate distance thresholds over which the regressions can be run. Both these variables $n(R, t)$ and $n(R, T)$ should be proportional to R^D if the cluster is fractal in its

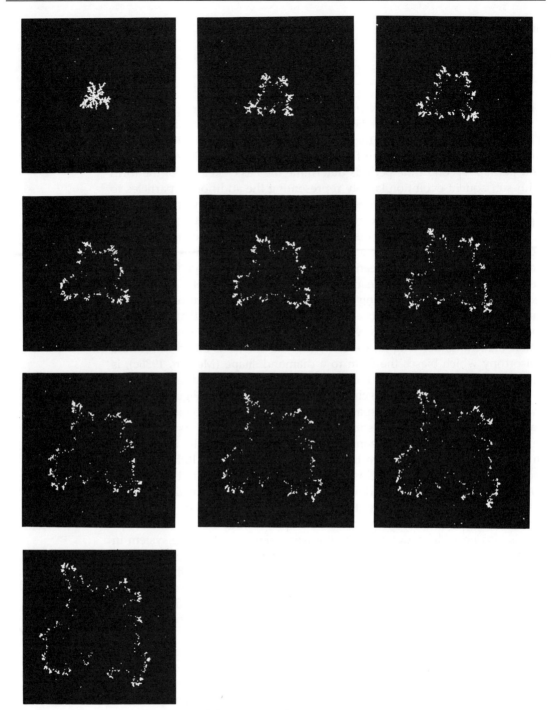

Figure 7.13.   Spatial dynamics of the DLA simulation.

parts. Appropriate distance thresholds have been set by inspecting changes in the profiles of $n(R, t)$ and $n(R, T)$ in Figure 7.14. The fractal dimensions associated with these cumulative populations are shown in Figure 7.15. For $n(R, t)$, the fractal dimensions are fairly volatile ranging from 1.351 to 1.966

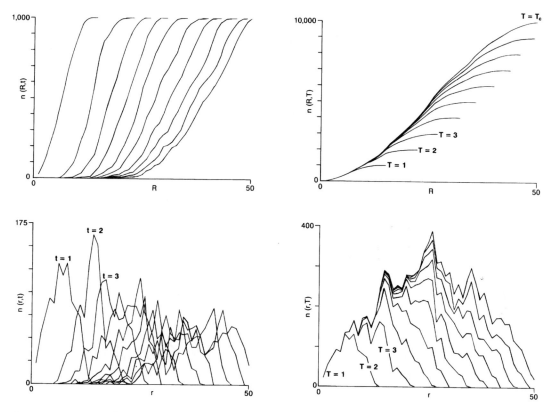

Figure 7.14. Diffusion waves characterizing the DLA simulation.

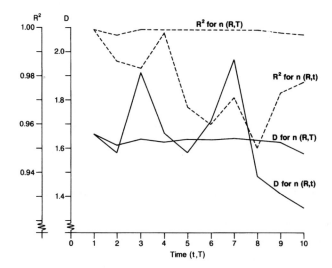

Figure 7.15. Time-dependent fractal dimensions and r^2 statistics for the evolving DLA cluster.

with r^2 values ranging from 0.950 to 0.999. When these same regressions are carried out on the cumulative population which is also accumulating over time periods $n(R, T)$, the dimensions estimated are much more characteristic of the dimensions given in Tables 7.3 and 7.4. These dimensions vary from 1.600 to 1.664 with the dimension falling slightly in later time periods. The r^2 values are very high, only varying from 0.997 to 0.999.

What is important for analysis is the great variation in fractal dimension for the time-period-specific accumulation. Whereas the first time period development shown in Figure 7.13 looks fractal with $D = 1.664$, later ones do not. Remarkably though, once put together to form the whole cluster as shown in Figure 7.8, these patterns appear fractal over many scales: an intriguing demonstration that the whole is greater than the sum of the parts, that overall pattern emerges from ordered partitions of this system which display no such form. This type of analysis is of considerable significance for any adaptation of the model which might attempt to incorporate some reversibility. The early development of the cluster appears to have an enormous influence on the ultimate form, and it is this early development which would be first subject to further change. If these earlier parts of the cluster were to change, the whole cluster might suddenly become non-fractal in form. Indeed, this type of experiment is worth attempting without thinking of any reversible DLA process so that the dependence of the overall cluster on its parts can be explored more thoroughly.

7.10 An Empirical Test: The Urban Growth of Taunton

In developing DLA and related models of urban systems, it is first essential to see how close the baseline model is to reality. Comparisons with the various examples displayed in the third section of this chapter have been in mind throughout the development of the model and as Table 7.1 clearly shows, there is a strong tendency for the observed fractal dimensions of all our examples, hence perhaps all cities, to lie between 1.5 and 1.9 with a mean around the value of the theoretical model of DLA. However, the model in its current form does not account for any specific constraints on its development, other than those posed by the geometry of the dendrites which screen areas from further growth. Accordingly, to progress the empirical analysis quite carefully, we have selected an urban area whose development has not been strongly affected by its underlying geomorphology or by large-scale man-made constraints: the town of Taunton in Somerset, South West England (population $\approx$ 49,000 in 1981) meets these criteria quite well.

The urban form was digitized on a 50 m grid imposed on the 1:10,000 scale Ordnance Survey maps which were last revised in 1981. This scale was not fine enough to pick up individual locations, but it was sufficient as a first attempt in that it involved making hard decisions about the exclusions of small areas of open space, and of course, non-population-related land uses. It is clear, however, that the underlying form of the population distribution in detailed spatial terms is still largely unknown, although detailed scrutiny of the 1:10,000 scale does reveal considerably greater variety in geometry than has been picked up in the measurements illustrated here.

The digitized map of urban Taunton is shown in Figure 7.16. Although this does not reveal clear dendritic structure, this is as much due to the scale of digitization as to the fact that no dendritic structure might exist. There are 3179 developed cells contained within a rectangular grid of 110×118 cells. These cells were then located on a square 150×150 lattice with the center positioned on the ruined castle, the first known center of settlement. The physical characteristics of the town have been given previously in Table 7.2 where direct comparisons can be made with the DLA simulation. The density of cells or lattice points is much higher than the DLA simulation: nearly 26% of all points in the total effective area are occupied in contrast to only 5% in the DLA simulation. However, it is remarkable that 85% of the 3179 cell points are on the boundary, only 15% being classed as interior points. The index of tortuosity is 10.100 in comparison with 12.729 for the DLA simulation, but there are nearly twice as many nearest neighbors for each occupied point in Taunton in comparison with the DLA example (4.342 compared with 2.394). One fascinating similarity involves the mean radius $\bar{R}$ which is 52% of the maximum radius in Taunton, 50% in the DLA, while the ratio of the standard deviation to this mean is 0.225 in both cases. Although Taunton is more compact than the DLA cluster, several of its basic dimensions are comparable as Table 7.2 shows.

Measurement of the four relationships given in equations (7.23) to (7.26) proceeded in the same way for Taunton as in the DLA simulation. The measures $N(R)$, $n(R)$, $\rho(R)$ and $Q(R)$ were computed and graphed over 50 distance bands as shown in Figure 7.17. Figure 7.18 illustrates their logarithmic transformation and a comparison of the equivalent Figures 7.9 and 7.10 in the DLA simulation reveals a strong similarity. The major difference is the clear discontinuity in these relations within short distances of the center

Figure 7.16.   Urban development in Taunton at 1981.

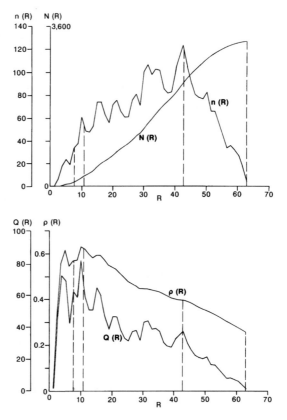

Figure 7.17. Absolute one-point relationships for Taunton.

of the town, which is strong evidence of reversibility in that it is consistent with the crater effect observed in population profiles around the Central Business District in many western cities. This is clearly seen in the density variables $\rho(R)$ and $Q(R)$ and their logarithmic transformation in Figures 7.17 and 7.18.

In estimating the parameters of equations (7.49) using the Taunton data, the need to restrict the distance range by defining cut-off points is also clear from these figures. We have defined four ranges beginning with all 50 distance bands, restricting these to the first 34, then excluding the first six bands and finally the first eight. The β parameters and fractal dimensions are given in Table 7.5. There is considerably more volatility in these estimates than in the case of DLA, with probably the best results reflected in the narrower ranges 6–34 and 8–34. Fractal dimensions vary between 1.573 and 1.716 for the 6–34 range and between 1.484 and 1.515 for the 8–34 range. Standard errors and r^2 statistics in Table 7.5 are also more variable than for the DLA model but there is some evidence here that the dimension D is a little lower than for the DLA simulation, notwithstanding the fact that the town is more compact.

Measurement of the two-point variables also proceeded in the same manner as that reported earlier. The graphs of $\overline{N}(R)$, $\bar{n}(R)$, $\bar{\rho}(R)$ and $\overline{Q}(R)$ against distance shown as absolutes and logarithmic transformations in Figures 7.19 and 7.20 are again very similar to those for the DLA simulation in

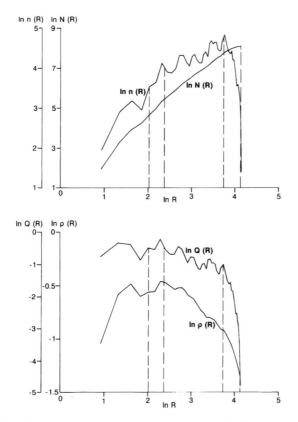

Figure 7.18. Logarithmic one-point relationships for Taunton.

Table 7.5. One-point estimates of the scaling equations for Taunton

Distance bands	$D = \beta_1$	$D = 1 + \beta_2$	$D = 2 + \beta_3$	$D = 2 + \beta_4$
1–50	1.766	1.309	1.766	1.254
	0.032	0.121	0.032	0.118
	0.984	0.104	0.522	0.446
1–34	1.893	1.787	1.893	1.727
	0.034	0.051	0.034	0.047
	0.990	0.882	0.217	0.523
6–34	1.716	1.573	1.716	1.536
	0.022	0.057	0.022	0.056
	0.996	0.784	0.861	0.703
8–34	1.647	1.515	1.647	1.484
	0.013	0.069	0.013	0.069
	0.998	0.680	0.967	0.678

Figures 7.11 and 7.12. These graphs are smoother than the one-point measures and they do not show any crater effect at small distances within the density profiles. In some respects, the distance thresholds are easier to define than for the one-point measures. We begin with all 125 distances, reduce these to the first 43, cut out the first five values, and finally work

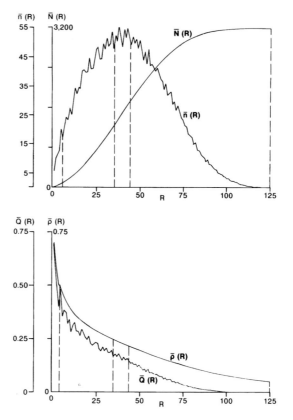

Figure 7.19. Absolute two-point relationships for Taunton.

with the range 6–35. The β parameters and fractal dimensions are shown in Table 7.6. In contrast to Table 7.5, the fractal dimensions increase in value as the ranges are restricted, the best values being those in the 6–35 range where D varies between 1.430 and 1.638. The standard errors are better than those for the one-point averages as are the r^2 statistics shown in Table 7.6. In fact, the values in the ranges 1–43 and 6–43 are not radically different from those in the 6–35 range, and as in the one-point analysis, the fractal dimensions would appear to be lower than those for the DLA simulation.

What is clear from this analysis is that urban density in Taunton is associated with a more compact urban form than that produced by DLA. Growth in Taunton is structured around four or five main tentacles emanating from the center which is fairly similar to the DLA simulation. But the fingers of growth are much wider in Taunton, and it is not possible to say anything about self-similarity in this example because of the level at which urban growth was digitized. Nevertheless this analysis is suggestive and encouraging enough to prompt us to search further and to develop finer measurement techniques for detecting the geometry of urban form.

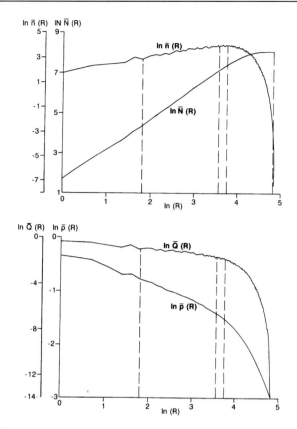

Figure 7.20.   Logarithmic two-point relationships for Taunton.

Table 7.6.   Two-point estimates of the scaling equations for Taunton

Distance bands	$D = \beta_1$	$D = 1 + \beta_2$	$D = 2 + \beta_3$	$D = 2 + \beta_4$
1–125	1.284	0.017	1.353	0.021
	0.022	0.181	0.025	0.179
	0.964	0.187	0.843	0.494
1–43	1.539	1.584	1.683	1.584
	0.005	0.015	0.007	0.015
	1.000	0.972	0.981	0.947
6–43	1.588	1.525	1.616	1.526
	0.005	0.022	0.006	0.022
	1.000	0.941	0.989	0.929
6–35	1.574	1.570	1.638	1.571
	0.004	0.025	0.005	0.025
	1.000	0.948	0.993	0.912

7.11 Extending the Growth Model

We could have chosen other particle simulation models which give more compact clusters than the DLA model. There are a number of variants which are being actively explored, based not only upon particle–cluster aggregation, but cluster–cluster aggregation, ballistic aggregation, percolation and so on. In fact, there are different ways of formulating the DLA model in terms of probability fields which involve rather different methods of simulation. Nittman and Stanley (1986), for example, develop models governed by parameters which explicitly control the compactness of the resulting form in which dendritic forms can be simulated as particular cases. In fact, in the next chapter, we will generalize the DLA model to deal explicitly with the relation between fractal dimension and compactness, adopting Niemeyer, Pietronero and Wiesmann's (1984) dielectric breakdown model (DBM) which will enable us to generate cities of many different shapes and degrees of compactness.

There are several extensions to our baseline model which have already been developed (Jullien and Botet, 1987). Lowering the sticking probabilities can increase the compactness, while constraints on the direction of the random walk have a strong influence on the resulting form. Many of these forms are not fractal, but there is increasing doubt that the Witten–Sander DLA model is fractal over as many orders of scale as has been assumed, and recently large-scale off-lattice simulations suggest the existence of somewhat different forms (Meakin, 1986c). In any case, the concept of fractal dimension itself should not be interpreted too narrowly. Strictly speaking, this dimension only exists as a mathematical limit (Feder, 1988), and its real importance is in the identification of appropriate length scales and self-similarities which provide useful but contingent characterizations dependent upon context.

A related use of the DLA model as the baseline for urban simulation involves the focus upon urban form. The geometry of urban form has largely remained separate from empirical and theoretical models of urban structure as we anticipated in Chapter 1. In the case of discrete urban models, form is represented as areas defined by points or centroids, while in urban density theory, form is largely assumed away in assumptions concerning monocentricity. Consequently in measuring urban densities, there has been little thought given to the underlying geometry of urban structure. Our focus on fractal models changes this substantially. Very hard questions about the space which individuals occupy have to be resolved for inappropriate definitions of density will hinder the development of any models in which growth processes and geometrical form are inextricably linked. In Chapter 9, we will look at the underlying patterns of urban growth and extend both the empirical observations and theoretical models of this and the next chapter to mainstream urban density theory.

The DLA model is one of the simplest formulations of irreversible cluster growth. We know that the assumption of irreversibility (that is, once particles stick, they never move) is incorrect with respect to urban structure. Densities of large cities increase over time, whereas growth by DLA leads to lower average densities as the aggregate grows. The difference is largely accountable in terms of reversibility, as seen in the fall in central city densities and the flattening of density gradients over time (Bussiere, 1972a; Parr, 1985a). There is little work as yet on DLA models which incorporate reversibility, but extending such models is not difficult in principle, given that a complete history of particle aggregation is always available. The real issue is to extend such models in ways which appear close to what we know about urban growth and decline without losing the underlying simplicity in their growth processes and the resulting geometry. To this end, we will now extend our DLA model to fully-fledged computer simulations in which we can fine-tune growing clusters to mimic the characteristics of 'real cities'.

Generating and Growing the Fractal City

Mandelbrot has attracted the attention of scientists on the ubiquity of fractal shapes among natural objects. This was an important and fruitful contribution. What is still missing in general is an understanding of how fractal shapes arise. (Ruelle, 1991, p. 178.)

8.1 Simulating Growth

Fractals have caught our imagination because the geometric patterns that they weave seem superficially simple, but on further scrutiny reveal infinite complexity through their self-similarity. Our fascination with them thus revolves around the mystery of explaining the myriad of processes which give rise to such patterns, and as David Ruelle (1991) suggests above, our concern for their geometry is only just giving way to a serious study of the dynamics of this pattern creation. Most of our knowledge of fractals so far is based upon methods for describing their geometry in the manner we began to illustrate in Chapter 2, and as yet, our knowledge of the way fractal structures emerge and evolve – their dynamics – is rudimentary. In this book, our use of fractal geometry in modeling city systems, and the limitations and potential which it displays is little different from many other domains in which this geometry is being developed. However, the DLA model which we developed in Chapter 7 and its generalization which we will seek in this chapter probably still represents the most promising approach to fractal dynamics (Orbach, 1986).

The ideal approach to a fractal dynamics of cities would be based on detailed histories of the development process in which the location of each behaving unit and its characteristics are recorded in time and space. As we noted in the last chapter, such histories are rarely available, certainly not from secondary data. The best we can hope for without engaging in massive primary survey, are time-series assembled from isolated observations of the system development at cross-sections in time, ideally on a regular time scale but unlikely at intervals finer than five years. In short, all we have are snapshots of development through time from which we can only infer the system's underlying dynamic. The pictures of London and Berlin, for example in Figures 7.3 and 7.4, provide the most detailed dynamics we have available in the empirical work reported in this book. Thus for the most part, we are forced back to grounding and validating our models of fractal processes in terms of the ultimate development of the system at a single point in time; this was how we compared Taunton against the DLA model and how we will compare the town of Cardiff with the dielectric break-down model (DBM) which is the subject of this chapter.

Yet despite these limitations posed by data, we can turn our attention away from comparisons of ultimate outcomes from static models of urban development patterns, to more detailed simulations of the growth process. As we illustrated in Chapter 7, the DLA model provides a rich dynamics with many similarities to the way urban development takes place. Indeed, one of the themes implicit in our notion of the fractal city is that the models we are proposing are not necessarily immediately applicable to real cities *per se* but enable us to work toward a general theory of cities. As such, fractal geometry changes the way we think about and observe the development of cities. There are, of course, many ways in which we might fine-tune our fractal models to real examples and we will demonstrate some of these in this chapter. But unlike more mainstream simulation models useful in urban analysis and planning, our approach separates models from their applications far more strictly than the norm. The example which we use here – based on Cardiff – simply provides the geometric container or the physical space within which we are able to grow a fractal cluster using DLA or DBM. In this sense then, our applications will emphasize the way in which the real geometry of the system interacts with a standard fractal dynamics to provide a simulation which best mirrors the reality.

In the more mainstream modeling of city systems, there is much less emphasis on the geometry of the system and how this molds and constrains development, and thus more concern for fine-tuning the dynamics of the simulation to the particular reality. Of course it is possible to fine-tune fractal models in this way, and in related work, we have explored how this might be done by altering the way particles aggregate and diffuse in DLA (Fotheringham, Batty and Longley, 1989). But here our focus will be upon showing how realistic urban systems can be simulated by growing 'pure' fractal clusters, but within geometrically 'impure' physical systems where the constraints and local conditions of the geometry are specified exogenously. It is these exogenous factors which we would not expect a fractal model to be able to replicate. An example is in order. If a fractal cluster growing in an unrestricted space according to a DLA interpretation of urban dynamics were to meet some physical barrier such as a mountain range which would distort its growth, ways of breaching the barrier might be necessary. Such breaches would clearly have to be input from outside the model. Although the model might be able to simulate the build-up of pressure against such a barrier which in turn might imply a need for some decision to breach it, the ultimate decision would have to be made outside the model and input as data to the process. It might be possible to link the model to another submodel of such decision-making, for example in the case of the mountain, a model which would predict what roads, bridges, tunnels and so on might be built. But these factors are outside the remit of the models we are working with here, and thus effective simulation of urban systems using fractal dynamics can only come through a judicious manipulation of fractal growth processes with the geometry of the real system under study.

The model we developed in the last chapter was able to generate fractal structures whose self-similarity was dendritic or tree-like (Feder, 1988). These structures are far-from-equilibrium and, like cities, display a high degree of order. Such systems are the result of irreversible growth which keeps the structure intact; growth does not turn to decline, and thus the dynamics of development remain simple. As we have noted, such irreversibility is not the case for urban development, but the existence of models which link growth to form in such a simple way, yet generate richly ordered structures, is attractive as an analogy for city growth. Such parsimony provides a useful benchmark or baseline model which accounts for a substantial amount of all development, whilst enabling us to relax its assumptions slowly, one by one, in adding more realistic detail.

The model we will explore here generates a variety of urban forms of the dendritic type whose actual structures range from the linear to the concentric. Their units of development or 'particles' as we will continue to refer to them (Jullien and Botet, 1987), locate around a core or seed site such as the CBD. This DLA model which generates ramified dendritic structures around the seed site, is based on a simple process of diffusion which is limited by contact with the growing cluster of particles. It mirrors how a city might grow around a CBD with particles diffusing from a distant source which controls the amount of growth the city could attract, eventually reaching the growing city and sticking irreversibly once contact had been made. Its fractal dynamic is based on diffusion by random walk. Walkers are released one by one, at a far distance from the cluster, and then wander randomly on a lattice, one lattice step at a time, eventually walking away from the system and being 'killed' or towards the seed site, thus adding to the growing cluster. The emergence of a tree-like structure is a result of the fact that the particular places where the particles stick to the cluster are randomly formed. As branches begin to grow, these reinforce the structure. It is clear that the dendrite which is formed is the result of noise in the system, for, if the process of working towards the cluster was not random, an amorphous mass with little order would form. Thus it is noise or randomness which causes structure of the most articulate and ordered kind, a surprising conclusion perhaps, but one which is also emerging in the study of evolution and adaptation (Allen, 1982; Levy, 1992; Lewin, 1992; Waldrop, 1992).

The structure generated is fractal in the following sense: the mass of the dendrite created is less than the mass of the space that it occupies. Imagine a circular space in which the cluster is grown around the center of the circle. The dendrite occupies 'more' space than the line across the circle (its diameter say) but 'less' space than the entire circle itself. The line has dimension $E = 1$, the circle $E = 2$, and it is intuitively attractive to think of the dendrite as having a fractal dimension D between 1 and 2. In this chapter we will reformulate the model as a diffusion process in a potential field, using the logic of the dielectric breakdown model (DBM). This is done to show how the model is able to generate a continuum of forms by systematic distortion of the potential field. The fractal case is the 'pure' case where there is no distortion of the field and where we refer to this as the 'baseline' model. We will introduce a parameter to control the distortion and show how forms can be generated which are reminiscent of ideal linear cities with D (and E) = 1 to radial–concentric cities with D (and E) = 2, the forms in-between embodying a continuum of city shapes with fractional dimension. Moreover, it is absolutely essential to formulate and solve this DLA model mathematically if an efficient means for generating these forms is to be developed.

We will first explore the relationship between DLA and DBM (which we will call the continuum model) and then show how we can solve the model. We will show how the fractal dimension can be measured with respect to the distributions of particles and their densities, introducing conventional but slow, then approximate but fast methods of estimation. A typical solution of the model based on a 300×300 lattice is presented in terms of its spatial properties and its fractal dimensions are estimated using the procedures outlined in Chapter 7. As the model is based on random site selection, it is necessary to see how its forms vary with respect to this randomness, and the stability of its form and dimension is then evaluated over several runs of the model, showing how robust the procedures are. A circular space has been assumed, but in comparison with real city systems, such circularity is unrealistic. Therefore the effect of 'taking out' larger and larger sectors of the circle, and the resultant model forms, are presented, demonstrating how both dimension and form are affected. We are then in a position to see how a variety of such forms can be generated by varying the control parameter on the potential field of the model, thus illustrating how a continuum can be simulated. Finally, we will show how the model might be used to mimic reality using data pertaining to urban development in the medium-sized town of Cardiff.

8.2 Diffusion-Limited Aggregation and Dielectric Breakdown

In diffusion-limited aggregation, a source of diffusion is assumed at a distance far enough from the seed to have no effect upon the isotropy of the plane around the growing cluster. The source is modeled on a distant circle where particles are released one at a time, to begin a random walk on a lattice, usually square with unit spacing, progressing in any of the four adjacent directions on the grid. If the walker goes outside another circle defining the 'sphere of influence' of the cluster, its walk is terminated and another walker is released from the source. If the walker remains on the lattice, it will eventually touch a lattice point adjacent to the cluster where it sticks irreversibly. Another walker is then released. Because the sticking point is essentially random, initial perturbations from a compact cluster are exaggerated and branches form. Walkers are more likely to reach the tips of these branches than the crevasses in between, the tips effectively screening the crevasses from potential growth. A useful explanation of this process is given by Sander (1987).

As we illustrated in Chapter 7, the emerging dendritic cluster does not fill the space, but it is not as sparse as a line of particles running across the space. In short, the number of particles, $N(R)$, at a distance R from the seed scales according to a fractional power law, $N(R) \approx R^D$, where D is the fractal dimension and $1 < D < 2$. Witten and Sander (1983) argue that $D = 1.70 \pm 0.02$ and this has been confirmed by many other simulations and real experiments since then (Jullien and Botet, 1987). It is argued that D is a universal scaling constant for such structures, although as we noted in the last chapter, there are other theorists such as Muthukumar (1983) who argues that $D = (E^2 + 1)/(E + 1)$, where E is the dimension of the space: when $E = 2$, $D = 1.66$. No way has yet been found to predict D theoretically. In the previous chapter, we showed that D was nearer 1.66 than 1.70, but there is recent speculation and some evidence that D depends on the size of the lattice and the number of particles constituting the cluster as well as the methods used to estimate this parameter (Meakin and Tolman, 1989). Meakin (1986b) who has produced extensive simulations of DLA also argues that the geometry of the underlying lattice has an effect on the shape of the growing cluster (Meakin, 1986c).

Although the usual model of DLA is based on algorithms which simulate the random walk, the original statement of the model by Witten and Sander (1983) was presented in more formal terms as follows. On a square lattice whose coordinates are given as (x, y), the probability of a walker visiting point (x, y) at time t, given by $u(x, y, t)$ is

$$u(x, y, t) = \tfrac{1}{4} [u(x + 1, y, t - 1) + u(x - 1, y, t - 1)$$
$$+ u(x, y + 1, t - 1) + u(x, y - 1, t - 1)]. \tag{8.1}$$

Rearranging equation (8.1), we get

$$[u(x + 1, y, t - 1) - 2u(x, y, t) + u(x - 1, y, t - 1)]$$
$$+ [u(x, y + 1, t - 1) - 2u(x, y, t) + u(x, y - 1, t - 1)] = 0. \tag{8.2}$$

Equation (8.2) is a discrete approximation to the continuum limit of the Laplace equation

$$\frac{\partial u(x, y, t)}{\partial t} = \frac{\partial^2 u(x, y, t)}{\partial x^2} + \frac{\partial^2 u(x, y, t)}{\partial y^2} = 0, \tag{8.3}$$

which can be more generally stated as

$$\frac{\partial u(x, y, t)}{\partial t} = \wp \nabla^2 u(x, y, t), \tag{8.4}$$

where $\wp$ is the diffusion constant. Note that we can assume that equations (8.3) or (8.4) are equal to zero (or a constant) because the source of diffusion is far away, the walk of each particle is slow, and the emission of particles is uniform. It is also clear that the growth velocity $v(x, y, t)$ of any site is

$$v(x, y, t) = \nabla u(x, y, t), \tag{8.5}$$

and that growth is subject to the following boundary conditions. On the interface between the edge of the cluster and the lattice, that is, for those particles forming the boundary of the cluster, there is zero probability of reaching these sites, $u(x, y, t) = 0$. This simply rules out the already developed cluster from reoccupation. At the distant source, the probability of reach is 1, that is $u(x, y, t) = 1$, for this is the source of the walkers. The model can then be solved from equation (8.4) subject to these two boundary conditions. Further details are given in the review paper by Witten (1986).

The DLA model provides a remarkable analog for a range of physical diffusion problems such as the diffusion of viscous fluids and dielectric breakdown, and there is very clear evidence that the model is applicable to these real physical processes (Ball, 1986). For viscous fluids, the applicability of DLA was first noted by Paterson (1984) for a process in which a fluid with low viscosity replaces one with high viscosity through permeation. Here $u(x, y, t)$ is the velocity potential, the equation of fluid flow $v(x, y, t)$ embodies Darcy's law, and the Laplace equation is the incompressibility condition. A variety of such simulations are noted in the paper by Nittmann, Daccord and Stanley (1985). However, the most useful model for generating a continuum of forms is the dielectric breakdown model (DBM) first presented by Niemeyer, Pietronero and Wiesmann (1984) which we refer to here as the continuum model.

In this model, the probability field $u(x, y, t)$ of the DLA model is now a potential electric field, $\phi(x, y, t)$. The central seed site is the point of discharge in the field; its potential $\phi(x, y, t) = 0$, and the breakdown occurs in the direction of the highest potential in the field, $\phi(x, y, t) = 1$, which is the uniform attractor at a distance far from the source. The model thus simulates the breakdown of the field and produces dendritic structures characteristic of, for example, lightning amongst other forms. The probability that any site adjacent to the discharge pattern created so far will form the next point of discharge, is analogous to the flow modeled by equation (8.5), that is

$$p(x, y, t) = \frac{\dfrac{\partial \phi(x, y, t)}{\partial x} + \dfrac{\partial \phi(x, y, t)}{\partial y}}{\sum \left(\dfrac{\partial \phi(x, y, t)}{\partial x} + \dfrac{\partial \phi(x, y, t)}{\partial y} \right)} \tag{8.6}$$

where the summation is over all candidate sites adjacent to the pattern of discharge. The partial derivatives in equation (8.6) reduce to $\phi(x, y, t)$ for all the candidate sites, because the potential at the interface is zero. This is the boundary condition equivalent to that on the edge of the cluster generated by the DLA model.

The DBM model is thus solved from Laplace's equation as

$$\nabla^2 \phi(x, y, t) = 0, \tag{8.7}$$

subject to the boundary conditions $\phi(x, y, t) = 0$ at the interface between the discharge and the field, and $\phi(x, y, t) = 1$ for those potential points which are at distance $r > R_\tau$, where $r = [(x - x_c)^2 + (y - y_c)^2]^{\frac{1}{2}}$, and R_τ is a distance threshold. x_c and y_c represent the coordinates of the central point of discharge. This model is formally equivalent to the DLA model sketched previously. It leads to fractal structures which are simply-connected dendrites which in turn form the patterns of discharge. Moreover, the Laplace equation in equation (8.7) ensures that the field is non-local and the boundary condition at the edge of the cluster or discharge ensures that this field continually adapts to the increasing discharge.

The most innovative feature of DBM, however, relates to the way in which the field, $\phi(x, y, t)$, can be systematically distorted. Niemeyer, Pietronero and Wiesmann (1984) show that different forms of discharge can be predicted if the probability of discharge in equation (8.6) is scaled by means of a parameter η. We will define the potential as $\phi_{x,y}$, suppressing time t. The probability of growth at the interface, $p_{x,y}$, is now given as

$$p_{xy} = \frac{\phi_{x,y}^{\eta}}{\sum\limits_{x,y \in C} \phi_{x,y}^{\eta}}, \tag{8.8}$$

where the summation is over all those sites (x, y) which are part of C, the interface to the pattern of discharge at time t. Before we show how the form is affected by the parameter η, we will summarize the classic case where $\eta = 1$. In Figure 8.1, the lattice on which the discharge takes place is illustrated with the solid dots and bonds showing the pattern of discharge so far, and the open dots and broken bonds showing the sites adjacent to the discharge for which the probabilities of selection are computed as in equation (8.8). Niemeyer, Pietronero and Wiesmann (1984) compute the fractal dimension of DBM as $D = 1.75 \pm 0.02$.

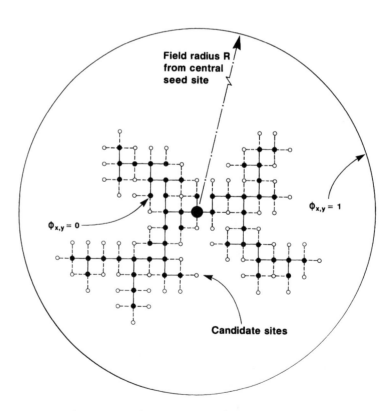

Figure 8.1. Cluster growth on a square lattice.

8.3 Analogies and Solutions

Comparisons with existing diffusion models of urban location which have developed as a part of social physics are instructive. Diffusion usually occurs from points of higher to lower potential, the highest point being the central site or CBD in the case of a city. Population potential as suggested by Stewart and Warntz (1958) is sometimes used to define a field analogous to gravitational potential, and diffusion thus takes place according to geographical distance decay, sometimes combined with a local or neighborhood effect (Hagerstrand, 1965). The DLA model is quite different. The highest potential is farthest away from the central site, and once a site has been occupied, its potential for reoccupation is zero. In fact, the potential measures the amount of space available at a distance from the central seed site and this captures the notion that it is the environment around a city which is the source of growth, not the city itself.

However, the city grows by finding areas of highest potential adjacent to existing development, and this constrains the development to remain as a connected aggregate. The DLA model is a less useful analog than DBM because the process of random walking is less realistic than the discharge process with respect to urban form. As Nittmann, Daccord and Stanley (1986) also state: "DLA has the purely phenomenological drawback that the cluster growth occurs by aggregation, whereas in RVF [radial viscous fingering], growth originates from the center of the structure". It is useful to think of the potential function $\phi(x, y, t)$ as reflecting available space in the immediate vicinity of the site (x, y) but also influenced by the growing cluster. In this sense, it is clear that the branch tips of the cluster are 'closest' to the points of highest potential, and it is easy to see why growth would occur there, thus reinforcing the dendritic nature of the structure. Once sites are occupied they have no further space potential, and this ensures the irreversibility of the process. Moreover, the basic constraint that the cluster must remain connected enables the process to be one of balancing the achievement of maximum space potential against the need to generate the scale economies associated with a connected spatial cluster.

The concepts of flow and potential appear extensively in social physics, but the restrictive nature of the Laplace equation governing the smoothness of the potential field has not been widely invoked. In fact, Sheppard (1979) suggests that the general form of Poisson's equation where $\nabla^2\phi(x, y, t) = g(x, y, t)$, is more appropriate, $g(x, y, t)$ representing some local source of variation at (x, y). Tobler (1981) and Dorigo and Tobler (1983) have used Poisson's equation in their models of movement, where $g(x, y, t)$ represents differences in spatial attraction. In modeling migration, Dorigo and Tobler minimize $\nabla^2\phi(x, y, t)$ to derive migration potentials and flows, and it is possible that a related interaction–flow interpretation might be given to DLA and DBM. In fact, Niemeyer, Pietronero and Wiesmann (1984) note that a length scale can be introduced into the simulation if $\nabla^2\phi(x, y, t)$ is assumed to be a positive constant over all (x, y). However, it is probably more useful to think of the Laplace equation as imposing a smoothness criterion across the field which balances local and global effects. This interpretation has also been exploited by Tobler (1979a) in modeling general geographic fields.

We can now speculate on the continuum of urban forms which might be generated using DBM through equations (8.7) and (8.8). The fractal case, $\eta = 1$, can be regarded as the baseline where the spatial potential function remains undistorted. As $\eta \to 0$, the sites which might be occupied around the boundary of the cluster become more evenly distributed, with the implication that the cluster will grow in a much less branch-like fashion. When $\eta \gg 1$, structures based on lines of particles across the space will emerge, and the implication is that the fractal dimension D will tend towards 1. In other words, 'linear cities' will be generated for $\eta \gg 1$, dendrites for $\eta = 1$, and circular cities for $0 \leq \eta \ll 1$. A continuum of forms will emerge where the parameter η in the range 0 to ∞ maps onto the range of fractal dimension D from 2 to 1.

There is one last speculation to be made before the discrete form of the model is discussed. The parameter η which distorts the potential field $\phi_{x,y}$ might be regarded as a measure of 'planning control'. To produce linear cities, certain sites have to be given exclusive preference for development and this can only occur if planning control is absolute and the market for land is in the hands of a single agent. At the other extreme, where there is a different type of control, the market might consist of many agents each bidding for development sites. This is consistent with a city which grows amorphously. The extremes of the linear and amorphous cities reflect the parameter values from $\eta \to \infty$ and $\eta \to 0$, respectively. The baseline case where $\eta = 1$ thus consists of a few large land agents and many small ones, thus mirroring the kind of markets that might characterize Western industrialized cities. To go further with this speculation would not be wise, but in general it fruitful to think of η as embodying a measure of planning control.

The major disadvantage to formulating the model in DBM rather than DLA terms relates to its solution. For each additional particle which is added to the cluster, the Laplace equation (8.7) must be solved subject to the previously given boundary conditions. For a lattice of 500×500 points say, there are up to 250,000 non-linear partial differential equations to be solved. These can only be solved iteratively and experience suggests it takes at least ten iterations to effect a solution. Where there is a cluster of 10,000 particles to be grown, this will involve the solution of 25 billion equations. In terms of computer time the problem is likely to take ten times as long as its equivalent formulation as a DLA model, thus requiring amounts of supercomputer time simply not available for these experiments. However, the model must be solved in DBM terms if the effects of varying the control parameter η are to be evaluated. Consequently smaller lattices will be used for growing particle clusters, in contrast to those demonstrated previously for the DLA model in Chapter 7.

The discrete approximation to Laplace's equation will now be restated, with the time subscript t omitted. Then

$$\phi_{x,y} = \tfrac{1}{4}(\phi_{x+1,y} + \phi_{x-1,y} + \phi_{x,y+1} + \phi_{x,y-1}). \tag{8.9}$$

Equation (8.9) can be generated as an approximation based on forward differences, and, for any iteration of its solution, the difference between the right-hand and left-hand sides of equation (8.9) is given as

$$\Phi_{x,y} = \phi_{x,y} - \tfrac{1}{4}(\phi_{x+1,y} + \phi_{x-1,y} + \phi_{x,y+1} + \phi_{x,y-1}). \qquad (8.10)$$

The method of solution used to solve equation (8.9) involves identifying the differences $\Phi_{x,y}$ across the lattice, and relaxing values of $\phi_{x,y}$ according to the largest differences adjacent to each point (x, y) (Williams, 1987). In the simulations to be reported here, once the original potential field $\phi_{x,y}$ has been computed at time $t = 0$, it takes an average of 13 iterations of equation (8.9) to bring each potential value $\phi_{x,y}$ to within 0.5% of its averaged neighboring values. Formally, the iteration on equation (8.9) (and (8.10)) using relaxation methods ceases when

$$\max_{(x,y)} \frac{\Phi_{x,y}}{\phi_{x,y}} \leq 0.005. \qquad (8.11)$$

At each time t, once the field $\phi(x, y, t)$ has been computed to the criterion set in equation (8.11), the probabilities of the candidate sites adjacent to the cluster are computed from equation (8.8), and one is selected for growth using a randomly generated number. This changes the boundary condition on the interface which in turn necessitates that the field $\phi(x, y, t)$ be recomputed, and so the process continues until the cluster has been grown to the required size.

The structures generated by the continuum model do of course follow the same scaling laws as those used to describe the distribution of particles in the DLA model regardless of the values of the parameter η. The four scaling relations linking the size characteristics of the cluster to the radial distance R from the cluster's center are those which relate $N(R)$, $dN(R)/dR$, $\rho(R)$, and $dN(R)/d\hat{A}(R)$ $(= Q(R))$ to R, given previously as equations (7.23), (7.24), (7.25) and (7.26), in that order. $N(R)$ is the cumulative count of the particle or population, $dN(R)/dR$ the actual population at R, which as Pietronero, Evertsz and Wiesmann (1986) note, gives the number of branches or bonds in the discharge pattern or cluster at a given distance, $\rho(R)$ is the cumulative density, and $dN(R)/d\hat{A}(R)$ is one measure of the actual density at R. The parameters of these relations are all simple functions of the fractal dimension D, easily computed through logarithmic regression as in Chapter 7.

The discrete measures used for the dependent variables in each of these relations are of two forms: either a simple count of the number of particles and their density with respect to the central seed site, these being known as one-point measures; or averages of the same counts but taken over all possible sites in the cluster, these being the two-point measures. The computation of these one-point measures is given in equations (7.27) to (7.33) and the two-point measures in (7.34) to (7.40), and we will make use of these equations again in this chapter. The one-point measures for fixed distance bands R are defined as $N(R)$, $\Delta N(R)$, $\rho(R)$ and $Q(R)$ and, as in Chapter 7, the two-point measures are notated similarly with bars indicating that these are averages, that is $\bar{N}(R)$, $\Delta\bar{N}(R)$, $\bar{\rho}(R)$ and $\bar{Q}(R)$.

The use of two-point averages is standard practice as approximations to density–density correlation functions (Meakin, 1986b: Witten and Sander, 1983), and both two-point and one-point measures can be used to find the parameters of the scaling relationships given in equations (7.23) to (7.26). In logarithmic form, these relations, given in equations (7.49), are repeated here for convenience as

$$\left.\begin{array}{rcl} \log N(R) &=& \alpha_1 + \beta_1 \log R, \\ \log n(R) &=& \alpha_2 + \beta_2 \log R, \\ \log \rho(R) &=& \alpha_3 + \beta_3 \log R, \\ \log Q(R) &=& \alpha_4 + \beta_4 \log R. \end{array}\right\} \tag{7.49}$$

Note that one-point measures are stated here, and it is assumed that the distance bands associated with R are equal. Last, the fractal dimensions can be computed from the slope parameters in equations (7.49) as $D = \beta_1$, $D = 1 + \beta_2$, $D = 2 + \beta_3$, and $D = 2 + \beta_4$, respectively. Use of the two-point measures, however, is a problem because of the computer time involved, and the use of regression analysis is extremely sensitive to the range of distance bands selected. It is well known that these occupancy and density functions are highly variable over a short range in the vicinity of the origin, and there are marked edge effects over the larger scale because of the fact that the clusters are still developing in a wide area of their periphery. Regression analysis is able to cope well with these edge effects, but it is difficult to identify the short-range effects. This suggests the need for both faster and more robust methods of estimation which we briefly presented in the last chapter. As these methods are used widely in this chapter, we will restate them.

As all measurements and simulations take place on a square lattice with unit spacing, it is expected that $N(R) \sim \pi R^D$, and $\hat{A}(R) \sim \pi R^2$. Therefore the density in equation (7.25) can be specified as

$$\rho(R) = \frac{N(R)}{\hat{A}(R)} \sim R^{D-2}. \tag{8.12}$$

For any value of R, it is thus possible to count $N(R)$ and measure $\hat{A}(R)$ and to manipulate equation (8.12) to provide an approximation to D which we will call $D(R)$. Then

$$D(R) \sim 2 + \frac{\log \rho(R)}{\log R}. \tag{8.13}$$

In a real example or typical simulation, we are likely to have a very large number of values of density associated with distances R, and from the first distance $R = r$ to the boundary of the cluster where $R = R_m$, we can compute values of $D(R)$. For example, if we begin at the seed site and measure density $\rho(R)$ with increasing distance from this center, we might expect $D(R)$ to be volatile over the short range in the vicinity of the seed site but to settle down gradually as the cluster grows outwards. Towards the edge of the cluster, a change in $D(R)$ may occur, thus revealing that this is still an area of growth and that the cluster is incomplete.

A plot of $D(R)$ against R will reveal the stability of the dimension, and we will refer to this somewhat loosely as the 'signature' of the fractal cluster. We might expect different fractal forms to exhibit different signatures, but as yet, we still have to explore this possibility. However, we would expect $D(R_m)$ to be a biased estimate of D for this pertains to the entire cluster. A more appropriate value of D for the cluster would be $D(\bar{R})$, where $\bar{R}$ is the mean distance about the seed site in the cluster, defined as

$$\bar{R} = \frac{1}{N} \sum_{r=R_0}^{R_m} \bar{n}(r)r, \; k = 1. \tag{8.14}$$

The seed site or center of the cluster is at $k = 1$, and R_0 represents the first distance for which occupancy around the seed site occurs.

This fast estimation procedure given in equation (8.13) is possible because the constants of proportionality defining the scaling relations cancel. It is possible to construct other measures which normalize estimation in this fashion, and we will note two. First we can normalize equation (7.23) as

$$\frac{N(R)}{N(R_m)} = \left(\frac{R}{R_m}\right)^D, \tag{8.15}$$

from which $D_N(R/R_m)$ can be estimated as

$$D_N(R/R_m) = \frac{N(R)}{N(R_m)} \Big/ \log\left(\frac{R}{R_m}\right), \tag{8.16}$$

In a similar manner, the same can be done for density in equation (7.25). Then

$$\frac{\rho(R)}{\rho(R_m)} = \left(\frac{R}{R_m}\right)^{D-2}, \tag{8.17}$$

from which $D_\rho(R/R_m)$ can be predicted as

$$D_\rho(R/R_m) = 2 + \left[\frac{\rho(R)}{\rho(R_m)} \Big/ \log\left(\frac{R}{R_m}\right)\right]. \tag{8.18}$$

We will use equations (8.16) to (8.18) below, but to anticipate our conclusions, equation (8.13) is the most useful estimation technique found so far.

8.4 Form and Dimension of the Baseline Model

Our previous simulations with the DLA model used a square lattice of 500×500 points and grew clusters of 10,000 particles achieving an average density of occupation of the lattice of 4%. These simulations each took 10 hours of CPU time on a MicroVax which was dedicated to these runs. To solve the continuum model at the same level of resolution and cluster size would take at least 12 days. Although supercomputer facilities were available, the amount of supercomputer time required was too great, and the only way to proceed was to work with coarser lattices and smaller clusters. As an example, we will first show a simulation of the DBM for a 300×300 lattice with a cluster size of 4157 particles. This simulation took one day, 21 hours and two minutes CPU time on the MicroVax, and thus in the more extensive analysis following this section we were forced to reduce the resolution of the lattice even further to 150×150 so that CPU time could be contained within five hours or so for each simulation run.

As already reported, the model was solved by iterating equations (8.9) to (8.11) for each time period and randomly allocating particles to lattice sites according to the probabilities given in equation (8.8) with $\eta = 1$. The number of particles generated in the examples reported here was not fixed in advance, for each cluster was grown up to about two thirds of the maximum radius of the lattice, which for a 300×300 lattice with the seed site fixed at $x = y = 150$, is $R_m = 100$. In this case, the model generates a cluster of 4157 particles. As η changes, however, the number of particles will change because η controls the compactness and density of the cluster. The other critical issue which affects the simulations involves the location of the outer boundary defining the highest points of potential. This boundary is fixed at the maximum radius of the lattice, in the case of the 300×300 lattice, at $R_{max} = 150$. Thus the cluster is grown two thirds of the way towards this boundary. In the experiments reported, it would appear that the cluster is not distorted with R_{max} set at $\frac{3}{2} R_m$ or greater. We have examined the smoothness of the field as the cluster grows and it seems that the isotropy of the field outside the cluster is maintained. However, we are conscious that we are working at the limits of acceptable cluster growth and this problem can only be resolved by running the model on an appropriate supercomputer.

The forms produced by this simulation are shown in Figures 8.2 and 8.3. Figure 8.2 shows the way sites are selected in the cluster with respect to their bonding to the various occupied lattice points. This clearly reveals the dendritic structure as in Figure 8.1 and it is obvious that the graph of this structure is simply connected. Figure 8.3 shows the order or dynamics in which sites are occupied. Twelve gray scales are used to show this order with the darkest sites being the earliest to locate, the lightest the latest; because of difficulties in capturing these images photographically and reproducing the gray scales, this and other similar figures are impression-

Figure 8.2.   Dendritic fractal growth as a simply connected graph.

Figure 8.3.   A system history of fractal growth using the continuum model.

istic, but nevertheless this does provide a clear illustration of the history of the system. Comparison of Figures 8.2 and 8.3 also shows that the dendritic pattern in Figure 8.2 is blurred by the coloring in Figure 8.3, thus leading to some cells appearing as though they are surrounded.

The structural characteristics of urban form will be measured using various indices of size and density. The total number of lattice points, N_L is 90,000, that is 300×300. The number of points occupied is given as N and the density N/N_L reflects the degree of sparseness of the structure. R_{max} the maximum radius of the lattice, R_m the maximum radius of the cluster ($\approx 0.66 R_{max}$), and $\bar{R}$ the mean distance within the cluster have already been defined. Three other measures describe the compactness of the structure. First the average density is defined as

$$\rho = \frac{N}{\pi R_m^2}.$$

The number of particles on the boundary of the cluster can be counted directly as N_b and the ratio of boundary to total occupied points defined as

$$\vartheta = \frac{N_b}{N}.$$

The proportion of interior points in the cluster is then $1 - \vartheta$. The last measure of consequence is the average number of nearest neighbors defined as

$$\xi = \frac{N_n}{N},$$

where N_n is the total number of nearest neighbors for all particles in the system; each particle has eight possible neighbors according to the eight compass points around the point in question on the lattice.

Table 8.1 presents these various measures for the 300×300 lattice example simulated here, and the 150×150 lattice model presented in the next section. These models will be referred to henceforth as the baseline models. These will act as a basis for comparison when the potential field is distorted and when areas of the lattice are absent from the spatial system. This table is largely self-explanatory. However, it is worth noting that the lattice density N/N_L and the average density ρ decline as the system gets larger. This is an obvious consequence of the model and is consistent with the density in equation (7.25) which embodies a negative fractional power law. In later comparisons where the lattice is of the same size, variations in these densities will become relevant. The boundary ratio ϑ is slightly less than 1, despite the fact that Figure 8.2 reveals that all the particles are on the boundary of the structure. This is simply a consequence of the way the boundary is represented which is as in Figure 8.3, not Figure 8.2. Lastly, the average number of nearest neighbors can range from 0 to 8 and this represents a measure of the compactness of the structure.

The parameters which give rise to different dimensions D are a function of the four power laws given in equations (7.23) to (7.26). These equations can be linearized as in equations (7.49) and parameters β_1, β_2, β_3 and β_4 estimated using regression analysis. The fractal dimensions are derived as $D = \beta_1$, $D = 1 + \beta_2$, $D = 2 + \beta_3$ and $D = 2 + \beta_4$, and these can be computed for two sets of measures; the one-point (or two-point measures) $N(R)$, $\Delta N(R)$, $\rho(R)$ and $Q(R)$ are then used in their respective regressions. We will begin with the one-point measures, and these are plotted in their logarithmic form in Figure 8.4. The edge effect posed by the incompleteness of the cluster is easily detectable, but identifying the short-range effect is much more problematic. These graphs are based on dividing the range of distance up to R_m into 30 distance bands where each band is of equal width $R_m/30$.

Table 8.1. Characteristics of the baseline model

System characteristic	Fine resolution baseline	Coarse resolution baseline
Dimension	300×300	150×150
Lattice points, N_L	90,000	22,500
Occupied points, N	4157	1856
N/N_L	0.046	0.082
Lattice radius, R_{max}	150	75
Cluster radius, R_m	101.356	49.366
R_m/R_{max}	0.676	0.658
Mean distance, $\bar{R}$	45.734	27.183
$\bar{R}/R_m$	0.451	0.544
Average density, ρ	0.129	0.236
Boundary ratio, ϑ	0.957	0.959
Nearest neighbors, ξ	4.943	4.862

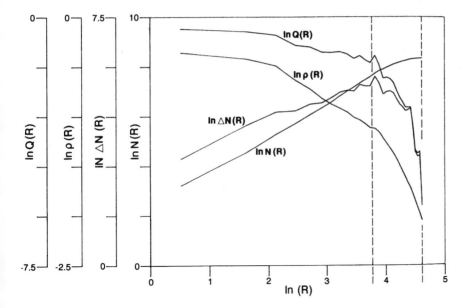

Figure 8.4. Logarithmic one-point functions.

These plots in Figure 8.4 are very similar to their respective plots for the DLA simulation shown in the previous chapter. Table 8.2 presents the dimensions D computed from each regression estimate, the standard errors of the regression slope coefficients, and the r^2 goodness-of-fit statistics. The first results are poor; these are then reestimated taking out the long-range effects by restricting the data to the first 13 distance bands. Although the standard errors and r^2 statistics improve dramatically in every case, the variation in dimension from $D = 1.376$ to $D = 1.737$ indicates that it is the method of estimation which is volatile with respect to the functions fitted and the data used.

The equivalent two-point functions are plotted in Figure 8.5. These are widely regarded as being better measures to be used in estimation, and the functions are clearly much smoother, being formed from averages of points associated with all distinct distances within the lattice. These functions

Table 8.2.   One-point estimates for the fine resolution model

Distance bands	$D = \beta_1$	$D = 1 + \beta_2$	$D = 2 + \beta_3$	$D = 2 + \beta_4$
1–30	1.317	0.994	1.554	0.994
	0.023	0.166	0.038	0.166
	0.991	0.000	0.834	0.568
1–13	1.376	1.660	1.737	1.660
	0.019	0.031	0.023	0.031
	0.998	0.997	0.916	0.917

Note: the first line of results for each distance band gives the fractal dimension, the second line the standard error, and the third the adjusted coefficient of determination r^2. These definitions are used for all subsequent tables of this type in this chapter.

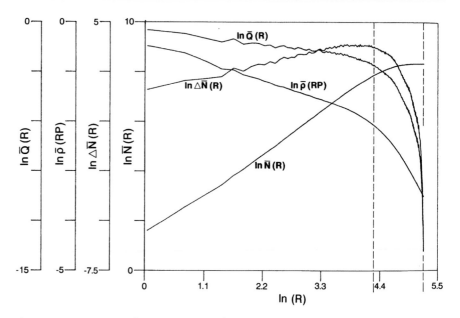

Figure 8.5. Logarithmic two-point functions.

appear similar to those computed in the last chapter for the DLA model. There are 187 distinct distance bands and, again, the long-range edge effect is clear. The first regressions shown in Table 8.3 are for all these distance bands, and the results are poor. Restricting the estimation to the first 55 distances improves the performance dramatically, but the fractal dimensions vary between 1.537 and 1.646, again suggesting that the methods of estimation are unreliable. It is quite clear that the regression methods are too sensitive to the functions used, and the data averages and aggregations made. There is need for a simpler, more robust method of estimation, and we will use that which we introduced earlier in equations (8.12) to (8.16). First, equation (8.13) has been plotted for R up to R_m, the cluster radius, thus producing a 'signature' of the form shown in Figures 8.2 and 8.3. This in effect is a cumulative computation of the fractal dimension D from the center to the edge of the cluster, and it is shown in Figure 8.6. It is quite clear that this signature is extremely volatile in the vicinity of the origin or center site and that once it settles down, the fractal dimension D is virtually

Table 8.3. Two-point estimates for the fine resolution model

Distance bands	$D = \beta_1$	$D = 1 + \beta_2$	$D = 2 + \beta_3$	$D = 2 + \beta_4$
1–187	1.257	0.005	1.311	0.058
	0.019	0.143	0.021	0.134
	0.959	0.258	0.853	0.533
1–55	1.537	1.588	1.646	1.588
	0.007	0.012	0.003	0.012
	0.999	0.977	0.996	0.954

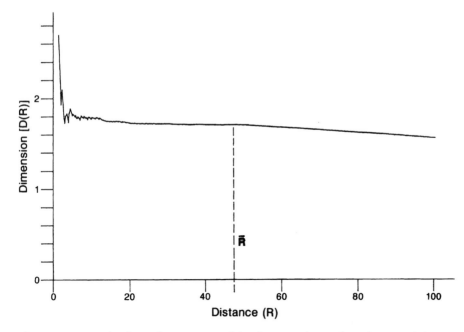

Figure 8.6. The fractal signature of the fine resolution baseline model.

constant over most of the cluster, beginning to fall as the incomplete area at the edge of the cluster is approached. From Figure 8.6, it is immediately clear that a good estimate of D is obtained at the mean distance $\bar{R}$.

At $\bar{R}$, $D(\bar{R}) = 1.708$ in comparison with $D(R_m) = 1.556$ at the edge of the cluster. It is also possible to form the average of all the dimensions $D(R)$ up to R_m, and this gives $D = 1.681$, biased towards the value of 1.708, an approximation to this value prevailing over most of the radius of the cluster. In Figure 8.6, the range of $D(R)$ is from 2.697 to 1.556, where R varies from 1.414 to 101.356, the cluster edge. By the time R has reached 13.342, the dimension has fallen to 1.756, indicating that the appropriate dimension of the cluster is about 1.7. This is close to the universal value of 1.71, and as we shall see, it is a remarkably robust procedure for determining such values. Last, we will examine the dimensions produced using equations (8.16) and (8.18). We can compute signatures based on these equations, but these appear to give values of D which are too low. For example, $D_N(\bar{R}/R_m)$ = 0.829 and a similar value is given for $D_\rho(\bar{R}/R_m)$. In fact, the edge of the cluster is not a good basis for estimation, and thus in future examples, we will restrict the estimation to the use of equation (8.13) in plotting the signature of the form and to $\bar{R}$ in determining the most appropriate fractal dimension.

8.5 The Effect of Randomness on Form and Dimension

Before we begin to demonstrate how the control parameter η can generate very different forms of structure, we need to investigate two features of the simulation which affect its fractal dimension. In this section, we will explore the effect of randomness on the model, and in the next, we will investigate how reducing the lattice space available for growth alters the fractal dimension and constrains urban form. The field equations which enable the potential $\phi_{x,y}$ to be evaluated define the probabilities that the candidate sites on the boundary of the cluster will receive growth. Whether or not one of these candidate sites receives a unit of development in the given time period depends upon the random number generated. In this sense, then, the resultant cluster, although structured in the large according to the potential field, develops in the small through random decision-making. Each run will thus yield a different form, although it is hoped that variations in these forms will have little effect on their dimension. It is this that we will explore in this section. To do so effectively, we require a large number of runs of the model, say at least 30, and this would require about two months of computer time were we to use the fine resolution model. Therefore we will compute a new coarse resolution model based on a 150×150 lattice which will henceforth act as our baseline.

The physical characteristics of this model have already been listed in Table 8.1. The urban form produced will not be shown in this section, but readers who wish to view this now can find it in Plate 8.1 (see color section). The structure is quite similar to that in Figures 8.2 and 8.3. Its fractal dimensions have been estimated from both the one-point and two-point measures whose plots are similar to those shown earlier in Figures 8.4 and 8.5. The dimensions are listed for the one-point measures in Table 8.4 where the original 30-band distance data and the reduction to 20 bands to exclude long-range edge effects are shown. The two-point measures are shown in Table 8.5, and it is immediately obvious that the results are similar to those for the fine resolution baseline. In fact, the ranking of dimension values from the full and part one-point and two-point measures is identical to the ranking in Tables 8.2 and 8.3, and the final values produced in the part two-point measures in Table 8.5 are similar in absolute terms to those in Table 8.3. Similar comments with regard to the volatility of these methods to those made previously apply.

We have also used the fast method of estimation in which we first plot the signature of the model based on the graph of $D(R)$ against R using equation (8.13). This is shown in Figure 8.7, and it is fairly similar to the signature of the fine resolution model shown in Figure 8.6: the short-range variation and long-range decline in $D(R)$ are apparent, with $D(R)$ varying

Table 8.4. One-point estimates for the coarse resolution model

Distance bands	$D = \beta_1$	$D = 1 + \beta_2$	$D = 2 + \beta_3$	$D = 2 + \beta_4$
1–30	1.467	1.431	1.704	1.431
	0.019	0.107	0.017	0.017
	0.995	0.368	0.917	0.503
1–20	1.458	1.718	1.751	1.718
	0.027	0.030	0.012	0.030
	0.994	0.970	0.960	0.833

Table 8.5. Two-point estimates for the course resolution model

Distance bands	$D = \beta_1$	$D = 1 + \beta_2$	$D = 2 + \beta_3$	$D = 2 + \beta_4$
1–98	1.311	0.219	1.390	0.219
	0.022	0.179	0.025	0.179
	0.974	0.165	0.862	0.508
1–34	1.504	1.602	1.644	1.602
	0.008	0.014	0.005	0.014
	0.999	0.982	0.994	0.960

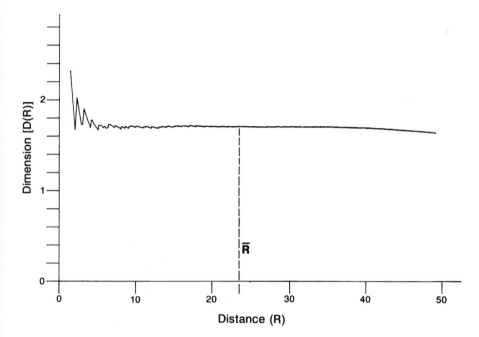

Figure 8.7. The fractal signature of the coarse resolution baseline model.

from 2.312 for the first distance R, to 1.631 for $R_m = 49.163$. $D(R)$ falls to 1.751 by $R = 14.765$, and the mean $\bar{R}$ generates a value of $D(R) = 1.701$, about the same as that for the fine resolution cluster. $D(R_m) = 1.631$ and the average over all $D(R)$ generates 1.698. Last, the values of $D_N(\bar{R}/R_m) = 1.251$ and $D_\rho(\bar{R}/R_m) = 1.254$. These confirm the comments made on these methods of estimation for the fine resolution model, and generate values of $D(R)$ almost identical to those of other researchers (Feder, 1988; Jullien and Botet, 1987).

Including the model run just reported, we have made a total of 30 runs of the coarse resolution baseline model, seeding the random number generator with a random start value on each simulation. All the signatures produced mirror that in Figure 8.7 with similar volatility in the vicinity of the seed site and a gradual fall in dimension at the edge of the cluster. We have computed equation (8.13) for R_m, $\bar{R}$ and the average over $D(R)$ for each run, and we have also formed the averages of these dimensions with respect to all 30 simulations. In Figure 8.8, the frequency graphs of the dimensions produced are plotted, and it is clear that variation around the means of these dimensions is extremely narrow. The averages are as follows: for $D(R_m)$, 1.548 ± 0.042; for $D(\bar{R})$, 1.701 ± 0.025; and for $D(\bar{R})$ averaged over the averages, the dimension is 1.679 ± 0.023. It is quite clear from Figures 8.6 and 8.7 that in this work, the most appropriate dimension to choose is based on the mean $\bar{R}$.

These values are also confirmed by other research. In the original statement of the model by Witten and Sander (1983), $D = 1.70 \pm 0.02$, and this was computed by averaging the results of six aggregates. Meakin (1986d) reports a value of $D = 1.695 \pm 0.002$ over 500 aggregates for the DLA model, and he also reports that Stanley (1977) has estimated $D = 1.715 \pm 0.002$ for 1000 runs of a 50,000 particle system. These simulations are all based on the DLA algorithm, although it is now clear that D is likely to vary according to the number of the particles and size of the system used (Meakin, 1986c). Nevertheless, comparison of Figures 8.6 and 8.7, as well as the frequencies

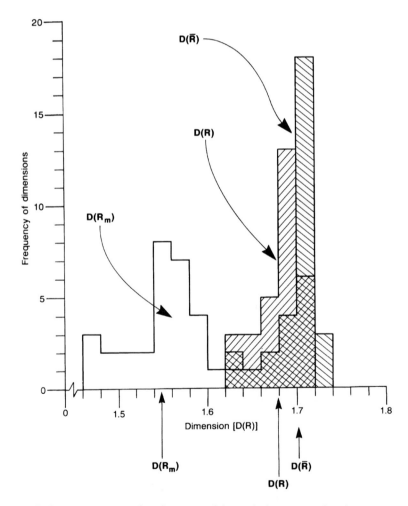

Figure 8.8. Frequency distributions of fractal dimension for the coarse resolution baseline model.

shown in Figure 8.8 does confirm the reliability of estimating fractal dimension from information on the mean occupancy, $N(\bar{R})$ and density, $\rho(\bar{R})$.

8.6 Physical Constraints on the Simulation

Fractal dimension will clearly change as the control parameter varies from very small to very large positive values, but this dimension is also affected by the shape of the 'container' or lattice in which growth is initiated. If we begin with a circular field (on a square lattice) and systematically reduce its size by taking out larger and larger sectors, the growth of the cluster will be increasingly constrained or 'compressed' within the available space. In the limit, one might envisage that the excluded sector approaches the circle itself, and all that is left for the cluster to grow on is a line of lattice points. Thus the dimension of the cluster is likely to be progressively reduced from 1.7 to 1 in the case of the baseline model. This effect, however, is not as easily imagined as one might first think because it depends on the scale of the lattice. Fractals are self-similar across a range of scales, and although the lattice might be compressed at one scale, if the scale is magnified over many orders, a lattice would be reached which to all intents and purposes would not be so constrained. Measurement of the fractal dimension of the baseline model at this scale would then reveal no change from $D = 1.7$. This simply shows that, although we argue that fractal dimension is a measure of self-similarity across many scales, it is still dependent upon the finest scale available which in this context is the 150×150 lattice.

A clear example of the effect of the 'container' on fractal dimension is provided by Nittmann, Daccord and Stanley (1985). These researchers set up an experiment to force a liquid of low viscosity into one of high viscosity using a Hele–Shaw cell whose geometry was a rectangle 10 units in length by three in width. The liquid of low viscosity entered the cell at the midpoint on its shorter side and the well-known fingers of liquid then began to spread through the cell. The estimated fractal dimension of the viscous fingering was $D = 1.40 \pm 0.04$, and Nittmann, Daccord and Stanley (1985) clearly show how the DBM style of simulation can generate a similar dendritic structure with a fractal dimension of $D = 1.41 \pm 0.05$. Other examples of growing clusters from edges rather than central points in space exist (Voss, 1984), and there is fairly wide agreement that, if the shape of the basic lattice is distorted, the fractal dimension will alter. There is some research by Kondo, Matsushita and Ohnishi (1986) who examine the relationship between the cluster grown in a wedge-shaped sector of varying angle θ, and there is some discussion of the types of barrier used in such systems to absorb or reflect particles. However, these are for the DLA model. What follows here is a systematic examination of the effects of reducing the size of the space within which the DBM operates.

We will divide the circular plane into eight equal sectors, and proceed to apply the coarse resolution baseline model to the following degrees of arc: 2π (the complete baseline model), 1.75π, 1.5π, π, 0.75π, 0.5π and 0.25π. We thus move from a complete circular baseline simulation (the one reported in the previous section) to a simulation based on a 45° wedge of the circle. It is important to note how the potential field is evaluated with respect to the lattice points which form the edges of these sectors. Equation (8.9) shows that the potential $\phi_{x,y}$ depends upon an average of its four immediate neighboring potential values. If any of these potential values fall into the omitted sector, the potential average is then formed by excluding these values. In other words, the omitted sector is not treated as a boundary constraint but as a natural boundary to the system, outside of which no potential exists.

The forms produced by the simulations on these eight systems are shown in Plate 8.2, and it is immediately clear that the geometry of each system has a marked compressing effect on the growing clusters. In each of these clusters, we can measure physical characteristics of size and density as we have done previously in Table 8.1. Table 8.6 shows quite clearly that, as the degree of arc is progressively reduced and larger sectors are excluded, the lattice and average densities remain roughly the same. These densities range from 0.057 to 0.089 for N/N_L and from 0.165 to 0.248 for ρ. In all cases, the boundary ratio remains near 1 and the average number of nearest neighbors is approximately 4.8. In short, although the forms are constrained, there is no evidence to suggest that the basic diffusion process at work is distorted by changing the space in which the process operates.

In Figure 8.9, we show the 'signatures' for each of the eight structures, and it is quite clear that as the angle of arc θ decreases, the fractal dimension D falls, In fact, in the vicinity of the central seed site, over-estimation of the dimension for the more complete systems changes to under-estimation as the wedge within which the system is contained decreases in angle. The dimensions based on $D(\bar{R}_m)$, $D(R)$ and the averages over $D(R)$ are given in Table 8.7 where it is clear that D falls towards unity as the system is constrained. These changes in D have not been plotted here, but will be later in Figure 8.11. However, Table 8.7 suggests that we might easily find a

Table 8.6. Characteristics of the physically constrained baseline simulations

System characteristic	System shape based on degrees of Arc							
	2π	1.75π	1.5π	1.25π	π	0.75π	0.5π	0.25π
Lattice dimension	All lattices based on the original 150×150 grid							
Lattice points, N_L	22,500	19,687	16,875	14,062	11,250	8437	5625	2812
Occupied points, N	1856	1433	1108	792	672	639	451	251
N/N_L	0.082	0.073	0.066	0.057	0.059	0.076	0.080	0.089
Lattice radius, R_{max}	All $R_{max} = 75$							
Cluster radius, R_m	49.366	50.000	50.804	49.396	50.448	50.290	51.400	51.088
R_m/R_{max}	0.658	0.660	0.677	0.659	0.673	0.670	0.685	0.681
Mean distance, $\bar{R}$	27.183	24.635	22.559	19.609	22.617	25.331	31.662	33.526
$\bar{R}/R_m$	0.544	0.493	0.444	0.397	0.448	0.504	0.616	0.656
Average density, ρ	0.236	0.208	0.183	0.165	0.168	0.213	0.216	0.248
Boundary ratio, ϑ	0.959	0.959	0.960	0.965	0.979	0.972	0.969	0.952
Nearest neighbors, ξ	4.862	4.868	4.839	4.828	4.812	4.789	4.896	4.741

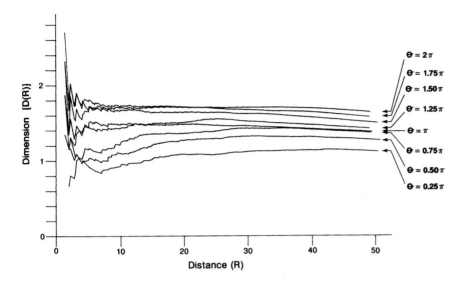

Figure 8.9. Fractal signatures of the sectorally constrained simulations.

Table 8.7. Fractal dimensions associated with the physically constrained baseline simulations

Angular variation θ	$D(R_m)$	$D(\bar{R})$	Average over all $D(R)$
2.00π (360°)	1.556	1.708	1.681
1.75π (315°)	1.516	1.707	1.647
0.50π (270°)	1.479	1.677	1.628
1.25π (225°)	1.508	1.637	1.591
1.00π (180°)	1.387	1.499	1.483
0.75π (135°)	1.417	1.413	1.355
0.50π (90°)	1.234	1.249	1.164
0.25π (45°)	1.093	0.945	0.974

well-fitting function relating D to θ. This is as we expected, but it also reveals that fractal dimension depends not only upon process but upon the geometry of the space within which the process takes place. Thus in explaining real urban form we must attempt to separate out the effects of both system geometry and the diffusion process control parameter η on spatial structure.

8.7 Generating the Continuum of Urban Forms

We are at last in a position to explore how different urban forms can be generated by varying the control parameter η. The effect of η on form has already been explained, but we will summarize it briefly for convenience. In equation (8.8) which determines the probabilities of sites being selected for growth on the boundary of the cluster, as η increases, sites with the greatest probability of selection become dominant. As $\eta \to 0$, sites become more equiprobable for selection, whereas the baseline case where $\eta = 1$, implies a measure of normal control. As $\eta \to \infty$, the form generated becomes linear because the branch tips become highly probable for selection, whereas as $\eta \to 0$, a more amorphous, compact form emerges. As $\eta \to \infty$, $D \to 1$, and as $\eta \to 0$, $D \to 2$. If η is treated as a planning control, where control becomes total, it is possible to develop highly geometric city forms similar to the linear and grid cities of the urban idealists such as Le Corbusier and Frank Lloyd Wright which we introduced in the Chapter 1. When control is relaxed and $\eta = 1$, the city grows as a fractal structure, whereas when $\eta \to 0$, it could be argued that this too is a measure of control in which all sites are treated equally by the control agency.

We will generate nine urban forms, again including our coarse resolution simulation as the baseline. We will set η at 0, 0.25, 0.50, 0.75, at the baseline of $\eta = 1$, and at 2, 3, 4 and 5. The constraint on growth is as previously specified in that, once the cluster reaches $0.66 R_{max}$ (≈ 50) units of distance from the central seed site, growth will terminate. This means that there are many more particles contained in structures with low values of η. The nine forms generated are shown in Plates 8.3 and 8.4. There is little need for comment as the forms bear out all the prior speculation which we made earlier. The range is from linear to concentric with the dendritic fractal structures forming the middle of the continuum. In Table 8.8, we show the physical characteristics of these nine forms, and we also note the computer time used to simulate each. The number of particles varies quite widely from $N = 4735$ when $\eta = 0$ to $N = 121$ when $\eta = 5$. This is reflected in the CPU times reported which range from between five and seven hours when $\eta < 1$ to only 22 minutes for $\eta = 5$. As we have shown previously, the densities depend upon the number of particles allocated and these range widely from $\rho = 0.627$ to $\rho = 0.016$, thus illustrating how η affects the compactness of the resulting cluster. The percentage of particles on the bound-

Table 8.8. Characteristics of the continuum of urban forms

System characteristic	Urban form based on the control parameter η								
	$\eta = 0$	$\eta = 0.25$	$\eta = 0.50$	$\eta = 0.75$	$\eta = 1$	$\eta = 2$	$\eta = 3$	$\eta = 4$	$\eta = 5$
CPU time (h:min)	6:45	7:17	6:14	5:41	5:02	1:04	0:40	0:23	0:22
Lattice points, N_L	All $N_L = 22,500$								
Occupied points, N	4735	3792	2639	2154	1856	404	252	132	121
N/N_L	0.210	0.169	0.117	0.096	0.082	0.018	0.011	0.006	0.005
Lattice radius, R_{max}	All $R_{max} = 75$								
Cluster radius, R_m	49.041	50.010	51.478	49.366	49.336	49.031	49.010	49.092	49.366
R_m/R_{max}	0.654	0.667	0.686	0.658	0.667	0.654	0.653	0.654	0.658
Mean distance, $\bar{R}$	27.436	26.239	24.844	25.773	27.183	19.332	22.439	18.433	20.323
$\bar{R}/R_m$	0.559	0.525	0.483	0.522	0.544	0.394	0.458	0.376	0.412
Average density, ρ	0.627	0.483	0.317	0.281	0.236	0.053	0.033	0.017	0.016
Boundary ratio, ϑ	0.552	0.719	0.878	0.926	0.959	1.000	1.000	1.000	1.000
Nearest neighbors, ξ	7.103	6.488	5.729	5.255	4.862	3.832	3.444	3.152	2.909

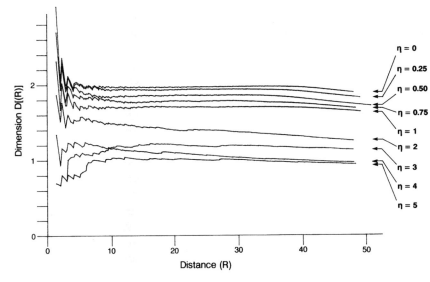

Figure 8.10. Fractal signatures of the distorted field simulations.

ary of the cluster is also affected by the type of form generated with an increasing number of interior points as the structure becomes more compact and $\eta \rightarrow 0$. The average number of nearest neighbors is a good measure of compactness and this ranges from 7.103 when $\eta = 0$ to 2.909 when $\eta = 5$. All these measures reflect the change in density and the increasing size of the cluster as $\eta \rightarrow 0$.

The next and most crucial stage of our investigation is to estimate the fractal dimensions of these nine clusters. Using equation (8.13), we have plotted the signatures for each of these forms in Figure 8.10. As expected, the average fractal dimensions fall as $\eta \rightarrow \infty$ and in Table 8.9, these values are shown for each cluster based on the use of equation (8.13) for R_m, $\bar{R}$ and the average of $D(\bar{R})$ over the profiles shown in Figure 8.10. As in the case of the fractal dimensions computed for different angular spatial systems and shown earlier in Table 8.7, it is easy to find a function which

Table 8.9. Fractal dimensions associated with the continuum of urban forms

Control parameter η	$D(R_m)$	$D(\bar{R})$	Average over all $D(R)$
0	1.879	1.971	1.964
0.25	1.814	1.938	1.924
0.50	1.708	1.858	1.847
0.75	1.675	1.782	1.769
1.00	1.631	1.701	1.698
2.00	1.248	1.409	1.417
3.00	1.127	1.187	1.185
4.00	0.960	1.110	1.060
5.00	0.776	1.009	0.976

predicts D from η. In Figure 8.11, we have plotted these dimensions from $D(\bar{R})$ in Table 8.9 against η, and from Table 8.7 against θ. One obvious problem in any real structure for which its fractal dimension can be computed, is to isolate the effects of control η from spatial constraint, measured here by θ. This will preoccupy us in the next section when we apply these ideas to the medium-sized town of Cardiff. We have also applied one-point and two-point estimation procedures to these nine forms and, although the estimated dimensions follow the same graphs as those shown in Figure 8.11, the results are poor, the procedures somewhat volatile; it thus of little worth to report them here.

8.8 Measuring and Simulating Urban Form in Medium-Sized Towns: Applications to Cardiff

We have now developed enough insight into the continuum model to make comparisons with real urban growth and to consider how the processes of growth embedded in the model might enable simulation of real forms. In the last chapter, we simply contrasted the DLA model and the form generated with the form of the medium-sized English town of Taunton. Several of the measurements of both the theoretical and actual forms were similar,

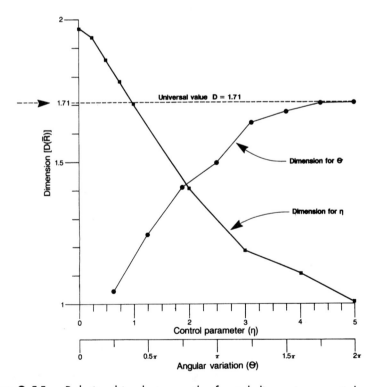

Figure 8.11. Relationships between the fractal dimension, spatial constraint parameter θ, and the planning control parameter η.

but their fractal dimensions were not. We now have a much more robust method of estimation, we have a parameter which enables us to control the compactness, hence fractal dimension of the resultant forms, and we have some insight into the way geometry and physical constraints on the growth space affect dimension. Thus it should be possible to begin some simulations of a real urban system. As a first stage in this quest, we will measure the physical characteristics of Cardiff, and estimate its fractal dimension.

Cardiff was digitized from the 1:50,000 scale map, the area being divided into 50 m grid squares which yielded a 150×150 lattice, making comparison with our theoretical structures possible. The extent of urban growth is shown in Figure 8.12 where it is clear that the center of the urban area which is the original Roman site and the site of the medieval castle, is not at the center of the lattice. In terms of the 150×150 grid, this location is at $(x = 81, y = 66)$. Moreover, the digitized urban area which comprises all land uses except open space, covers the entire extent of the lattice because there are many villages and disconnected clusters of urban development around the town. The maximum lattice radius R_{max} is not meaningful for a cluster which is off-center on the lattice, and because of the extent of urban development, the maximum cluster radius from the center is $R_m \approx$ 110 units of distance. This is twice the size of the clusters used in the simulations, and must be taken into account when comparisons are made below. Of the 22,500 lattice points, only 18,245 constitute the area for measurement and simulation: of the remaining points, 3849 are in the sea and 406 are inland waterways (rivers, canals and lakes).

The physical characteristics of Cardiff with respect to size and density

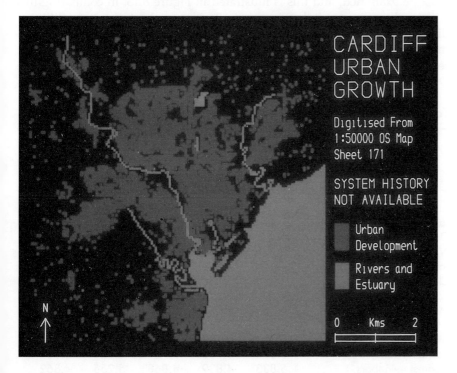

Figure 8.12. The urban development of Cardiff.

are shown in Table 8.10. As R_{max} is not relevant, related statistics have not been computed. It is worth saying that we have explored ways in which the lattice can be extended to make the form symmetric so that some of the previous measures can be computed. This involves 'guessing' the composition of areas outside the map area in Figure 8.12, and although some useful techniques have been developed, these will not be reported here. From the measures for Cardiff in Table 8.10 and from the visual appreciation of urban form shown in Figure 8.12 and Plate 8.5, we need to speculate on the type of structure Cardiff displays with respect to the theoretical forms discussed previously. In Table 8.10, we have included three of the forms presented earlier in that these forms seem 'close' to Cardiff in some way. We have also included the coarse resolution $\eta = 1$ model, which acts as the baseline. Examination of the shape of Cardiff in Figure 8.12 indicates that the urban form is similar to that shown in Plate 8.2 based on the angular sector $\theta = 1.25\pi$ simulation. However, with respect to the percentage of lattice cells excluded, the simulation based on $\theta = 1.75\pi$ is closer, and thus this has also been included in Table 8.10. We will comment on the inclusion of the $\eta = 0.75$ model in this table below, but note also that the average number of nearest neighbors in Cardiff and the boundary ratio suggest a form based on $\eta = 0.50$. Last, it is clear that Cardiff has much more development than most of the theoretical simulations here, and this indicates that in future work, some thought should be given to growing larger theoretical clusters or excluding development clearly not part of the main cluster under analysis in real applications.

To proceed with this comparison, the 'signature' of the Cardiff cluster must be examined, and this is illustrated in Figure 8.13. In comparing this with earlier figures, it has some similarities – short-range volatility of dimension in the vicinity of the origin and a long-range edge effect but in the inner area around the seed point, the dimension drops sharply, quickly recovering to a stable value over most of its profile. At the edge of the

Table 8.10. Characteristics of Cardiff and relevant urban forms

System characteristic	Cardiff	Closest comparators			
		1.25π	1.75π	$\eta=0.75$	$\eta=1$
Lattice dimension	All lattices based on the original 150×150 grid				
Lattice points, N_L	18,245	16,875	19,687	22,500	22,500
Occupied points, N	5067	1108	1433	2154	1856
N/N_L	0.278	0.066	0.073	0.096	0.082
Lattice radius, R_{max}	—	75	75	75	75
Cluster radius, R_m	110.318	50.804	50.000	49.366	49.366
R_m/R_{max}	—	0.677	0.666	0.658	0.667
Mean distance, $\bar{R}$	41.539	22.559	24.635	25.773	27.183
$\bar{R}/R_m$	0.377	0.444	0.493	0.522	0.544
Average density, ρ	0.164	0.183	0.208	0.281	0.236
Boundary ratio, ϑ	0.612	0.960	0.959	0.926	0.959
Nearest neighbors, ξ	5.833	4.839	4.868	5.255	4.862

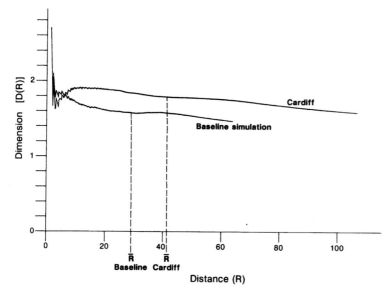

Figure 8.13. Fractal signatures of Cardiff and the baseline simulations in Cardiff's urban field.

cluster, $D(R_m) = 1.570$ whereas at the mean, $D(\bar{R}) = 1.786$. The average over all dimensions shown in Figure 8.13 is 1.772 and thus it is clear that the fractal dimension of Cardiff is higher than the fractal $\eta = 1$ case, thus suggesting that $\eta < 1$. From the earlier analysis, a fractal dimension in the order of 1.78 suggests that the control parameter η is more likely to be 0.75 than 1, hence the inclusion of this in Table 8.10.

However, examining the level of physical constraint in Table 8.7 seems to suggest that the fractal dimension associated with the physical characteristics of Cardiff would be around 1.60. To generate such a form through simulation would probably require η to be set much lower, perhaps at 0.5 or even below this, implying a much more even potential field than the $\eta = 1$ fractal case is able to generate. This will be explored below in the simulations, but first it is worth making one last point on estimation. We have also computed the one-point and two-point measures for Cardiff and used these to estimate fractal dimensions using regression. The results are disappointing as in other cases tested in this chapter. However, what is more worrying is that the dimensions produced are lower than the universal value of $D = 1.7$. For the one-point measures, D varies from 1.29 to 1.49. This also brings into doubt the results in the previous chapter where the fractal dimensions of Taunton were also lower than 1.7. However, the purpose of this research is not to aim for consensus with respect to dimension, but to derive better methods of estimation and simulation. The estimation procedure introduced in equation (8.13) clearly enables such progress to be made.

The ultimate focus of this research is on the design of a physical simulation model built on simple and thus intuitively attractive processes which govern urban growth. To this end, it is worth summarizing the assumptions of the continuum model. First, there is diffusion from a source of low to high potential, but constrained so that the resulting cluster remains intact or connected. In short, higher potential exists in areas away from the source where there is more space for expansion, but the cluster must remain intact as it realizes this higher potential through growth. Second, physical constraints which reduce space must act as barriers to development, but must not reduce potential *per se*. Third, the resultant form based on the best realization of space potential can be distorted by a control parameter which modifies the relative distribution of potential for growth on the boundary of the cluster. Last, the number of seed sites which initiate growth should be kept to a minimum, ideally to one site.

The first simulation attempted simply uses the fractal ($\eta = 1$) baseline model with its seed site at ($x = 81$, $y = 66$) on the 150×150 lattice, with the physical constraints of rivers and sea acting as limits on the area of the lattice in which it is legitimate for growth to take place. The resulting form is shown in Figure 8.14 from which several points immediately emerge. Cardiff does not grow towards its port which is some two miles from the medieval center and on the coast. This port only opened up in the mid-19th century as the South Wales coalfield developed (Daunton, 1977), and this would suggest that another 'seed' site is required. The town also grows in the area between the River Taff (the longest, middle river in Figure 8.12) and the eastern River Rhymney. Because of these physical constraints, growth is unable to spread across these barriers and thus the need for bridging is identified. Last, the cluster grown in Figure 8.14 consists of only 808, not 5067 particles, and this reinforces the requirement that more areas be opened up to growth.

Four more simulations have been attempted in which a second seed site

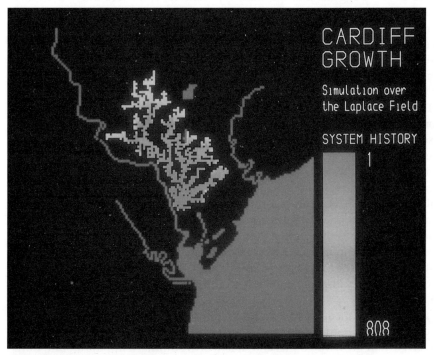

Figure 8.14. The baseline simulation in Cardiff's urban field.

is planted in the Cardiff docklands after 80 particles have been generated. Two bridges (breaks in the river constraint) have been established across the River Taff west of the medieval center and docklands, and one bridge has been made across the River Rhymney in the east. It would be easily possible to build in decision rules to generate bridges at suitable points if the pressures of growth became substantial, but in the interests of parsimony, these changes have been kept to a minimum. Simulations of the continuum model on the Cardiff lattice have been run with $\eta = 1, 0.75, 0.50$ and 0.25, and the resultant urban forms are shown in Plate 8.6. It is clear now that growth spans the rivers, and on the west bank of the Taff, development occurs later than in sites at a similar distance north of the center. But it is only when $\eta < 0.5$ that sufficient growth is generated, and the docklands begin to exert a major effect upon development.

If we examine the fractal dimensions of these four simulations, we find that the physical constraints exert a powerful effect. For the case of the single-seed-site simulation shown in Figure 8.14, we have plotted its signature earlier alongside that of Cardiff in Figure 8.13. For this simulation, $D(\bar{R}) = 1.460$. In Figure 8.15, the signature profiles are shown for the four simulations based on $\eta = 1$, $\eta = 0.75$, $\eta = 0.50$ and $\eta = 0.25$ which incorporate the two seed sites and bridging developments. These generate fractal dimensions of $D(\bar{R}) = 1.574, 1.595. 1.704$ and 1.820 respectively in comparison to their non-constrained equivalents $D(\bar{R}) = 1.701, 1.782, 1.858$ and 1.938 given earlier in Table 8.9. On this basis, we might speculate that a model with η about 0.35 might provide the best simulation for Cardiff. This implies a degree of control which might be exercised by many single landowners in competition or, perhaps, large landowners in collusion.

These simulations are designed to be suggestive, not definitive. They indicate how we might proceed. When these models are demonstrated, they tend to evoke considerable reaction, especially when it is realized that

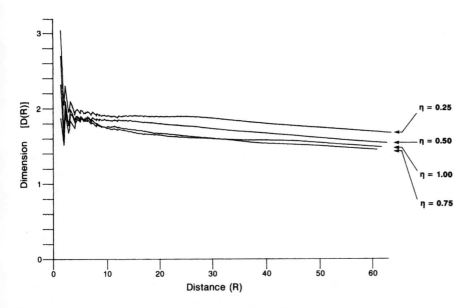

Figure 8.15. Fractal signatures of the Cardiff simulations.

physical constraints guide the simulation. Colleagues are quick to point out many obvious extensions which might make the growth processes more realistic. But the value of the model as it stands is in its *parsimony*. Rather than introduce more decision rules into the structure, there is an urgent need to examine the role of seed sites, and explore the dynamics of the model further. For this, we need better data on the historical evolution of the city, and if we had this, the importance of seed sites could be better assessed. We would then be in a position to examine thoroughly the role of physical constraints on urban growth, and to progress the model towards more realistic simulations. As it stands, our simulations indicate the importance of DLA and DBM to the generation of entire classes of city, but as yet, such simulations are far from the point where they might be used to make explicit forecasts.

8.9 Towards More Realistic Models

The continuum model based on DBM which uses Laplace's equation, its consequent solution, and the way the potential field can be controlled or distorted, clearly produces a model which is much easier to explore than the random walk version of DLA. Indeed, this specification of the model is an essential step in the process of moving towards simulation of real urban systems as has been demonstrated here for Cardiff. There are, however, several urgent developments to initiate. It is necessary to treat much larger lattices and readers with supercomputer resources such as Connection Machines whose architecture is adapted to Laplace field problems, must be encouraged to explore 1000×1000 lattices or even larger ones for this type of problem (Dewar and Harris, 1986). It is also necessary to think about three-dimensional lattices and DLA simulation, which might capture some of the characteristics of urban systems, but, wherever this research seems to offer promising insights, the issue of computer resources and time is paramount. More realistic DBM models are also possible, and it would be useful to adapt many of these to the simulation of city systems (Wiesmann, 1989).

We need to extend our research into the interaction between physical constraints on space and the control of the potential field and probabilities of occupancy around cluster boundaries. We have not rigorously examined the types of forms generated for different combinations of θ and η, although the inferences made here on the basis of our partial explorations are unlikely to be badly wrong. We also require a better investigation of physical indices, and it would be useful if we could classify different urban forms with respect to a variety of such indices as well as the spatial (θ) and planning control (η) parameters. Many of these developments are already taking place in the burgeoning field of cluster growth modeling within mathematical physics, and there is much to learn from current and future developments in those domains. But by adapting cluster models more closely to the characteristics of urban development such as discontiguous form, reversible aggregation and the possible interaction of different cluster processes, that is interlocking and interacting DLA processes operating with different types of development but in the same system, considerable progress can be made with the approach we have begun to outline here.

Finally, we need better measurements of urban development and density. In the last chapter, we were concerned that our measurement of real form was at too coarse a level to pick up the appropriate pattern of urban structure. The same difficulties apply here, and there is no substitute for finer resolution to our detection of development patterns. All this demonstrates is that once again, in the search for universals, whether it be in qualitative matters or in the social physics which we are espousing here, it is necessary to proceed with rigor on all fronts. In this chapter, we have clearly demonstrated that the same fractal dimensions can be generated through different combinations of physical constraint and planning control. This in turn brings into question the role of a fixed scale from which all measurements are taken and simulations initiated. To make further progress, it is necessary to explore the interaction of physical constraints at different scales more rigorously, and to this end, many more real urban applications are required.

In the next chapter, we will change tack once again, but in the quest to extend the ideas of this and the last chapter to more mainstream urban theory and analysis. We have almost unwittingly begun to home in upon the idea of urban density, and as a first step in showing how our theory of the fractal city might inform the mainstream, we will explore how existing approaches to urban density analysis can be enriched and reformulated in Chapter 9. This will involve us in theories of urban allometry, and these we will take further in Chapter 10 when we will move full circle to show how fractal geometry can begin to inform questions of city size and distribution, so long the traditional preserve of human geography through central place theory.

Form Follows Function:
Reformulating Population Density
Functions

A simple isolated bit of evidence, however striking, is always open to doubt. It is the accumulation of several different lines of evidence that is compelling. (Crick, 1990, p. 37.)

9.1 Cities as Population Density Functions

We could have written this book by beginning with existing theories of city size, shape and distribution and then gradually showing how fractal geometry could be used to reinterpret, generalize and extend the body of theory which geographers, economists and planners have been working with for the last hundred years. But instead we chose a different tack, introducing fractal geometry first and tracing out its implications for how cities might be organized, before we embarked upon the ways in which our theory of the fractal city might link to the mainstream of urban studies. Without our having reviewed the multitude of urban theories in other than cursory terms, it is already clear that fractal geometry has appealing properties with respect to cities in ideas concerning space-filling, self-similarity and density. In fact as Crick (1990) implies above, although these lines of evidence for a fractal theory of cities are highly suggestive, they become compelling when it is realized that much of what has been developed in the mainstream is entirely consistent with fractal geometry.

We are now at the point where we can begin to make these connections, in this chapter to the distribution of population and other activities within the city, in the next to the distribution of population sizes and shapes across cities. In fact as we have implied throughout this book, our foray into the fractal geometry of cities is but a beginning and we anticipate that entire areas of urban theory might be reworked using fractals in the coming years. Here we will confine our efforts to the most basic applications starting with simple gravitational density models which constitute the heart of what has been called social physics. Ever since Newton published his celebrated Laws of Motion in the late 17th century have there been attempts to apply classical physics to social systems in general, city systems in particular.

Social forces between populations in space were described explicitly by Carey in the mid-19th century using gravitational analogies, while the notion that the density of economic activity declines with increasing distance from its market is implicit in the work of von Thunen, circa 1830 (Hall, 1966). In the study of population densities, it is now just over 100 years since Bleicher (1892) wrote: "The rapid decrease in population density with distance from the center is highly characteristic of an old city such as ours" (Edmonston, 1975; Mogridge, 1984).

However another 50 years were to elapse before these observations were associated with specific mathematical functions. There is some evidence that such functions were being used in the 1940s (Ajo, 1944), but it is Colin Clark (1951, 1967) who is accredited with the first use of the negative exponential function as the basic model for population densities. Since then, many variants of this model have been developed. The negative exponential density function is consistent with the theories of strict utility-maximizing associated with urban economic theory (Beckmann, 1969; Muth, 1969), while the development of operational urban models based on entropy-maximizing (Wilson, 1970) and discrete choice theory (Anas, 1982) which we introduced, albeit briefly, in Chapter 4, make widespread use of such functions. Although early analogies with gravitational models based on the inverse square function of distance formed the foundations of social physics in the 1940s and 1950s (Stewart, 1941, 1950), these power functions were quickly replaced with the negative exponential in the 1960s and 1970s due to the analytical convenience of such functions in problems of economic and statistical optimization, as well as to the elegance of the mathematical forms produced.

These developments, however, appear to have lost sight of the fact that the density and flow of economic activity across space must be fundamentally constrained and thus determined by the geometrical properties of their physical systems. It is clear that there is much misunderstanding of these issues, as Stewart (1950) was never slow to point out. Others such as Coleman (1964) who have considered the foundations of social physics have reinforced the point that power functions in their inverse form are the most obvious ones which embody the physical properties of the correct systems of interest (Batty and March, 1976). But such views have never attracted much attention and have remained apart from the mainstream of urban analysis during the last three decades. What a fractal theory of cities offers is a coherent approach to these earlier traditions.

Here we will argue forcibly that the use of the negative exponential function as a model of population densities is fundamentally flawed. We will argue that its use is based on its convenience in problems of optimization, on the elegance of its mathematical properties, not on its appropriateness to empirical data, and certainly not upon our ability to make sensible interpretations of its parameters. Our thesis here is based on the identification of appropriate scaling laws for urban systems based on ideas associated with allometry, although our principal concern will be with linking these laws to the principles of fractal geometry which shows how form follows function. As we demonstrated in Chapter 7, scaling laws based on power functions have been given a new lease of life of late in that their parameters can now be unambiguously associated with the size, shape and form of the systems they describe. In short, their parameters can be associated with the extent to which their systems exploit the space in which they exist, the fractal dimension being directly associated with these parameters and with the extent to which the form fills the space available. The form or morphology of the system is no longer a prerequisite to models of its functioning, but a consequence of the way the system works in space. In this sense then, we will be dealing with systems in which 'form follows function'.

This chapter will attempt to weave several diverse themes together. Once again, we will note the work on urban allometry in which the size of the urban system is related to the space it occupies (Stewart and Warntz, 1958; Dutton, 1973), we will show how densities based on power functions arise as a natural consequence of such allometry, and we will cast our argument in terms of the new physics of fractional dimension (Davies, 1989) which uses the empirical ideas of Chapter 7 explicitly and the DLA and DBM models implicitly. We will first examine the properties of the negative exponential and inverse power functions, showing that the inverse power function has certain properties for describing urban population densities which have hitherto been overlooked. These properties can be easily exploited through scaling laws appropriate to urban systems, and accordingly, we show how urban form follows quite naturally from such functional descriptions. In this sense, we are also able to show that the density parameters associated with these functions are directly related to the fractional or fractal dimensions of the space within which these city systems exist.

These arguments have profound implications for the way we should measure population density in cities, and thus we then set out to estimate these functions in a variety of forms. The data set we use is for the city of Seoul in South Korea for the year 1982 (Kim, 1985); four variants on the base data set are used in estimating the density parameters of inverse power functions which we also represent in four related forms. These forms are estimated using three methods: the first two – regression of their log–linear forms, and the so-called signature of the underlying fractal growth process – were introduced in Chapters 7 and 8, but a third, conventional method based on entropy-maximizing, is also introduced here. The many variants of data and estimation which we use produce a range of density parameters and fractal dimensions which show remarkable consistency. From the theoretical arguments developed in the last two chapters, we argue that the fractal dimension of a typical city such as Seoul will have a value between 1 and 2, probably between 1.5 and 1.8, and a density parameter between 0.2 and 0.5. We show that this is indeed the case, and this suggests that many previous estimates of population density functions should be reworked with power functions to reveal parameter values which if consistent, could be used to derive more meaningful taxonomies of city size and shape.

9.2 Exponential Functions of Urban Density

Clark's (1951) original model assumes that population density $\rho(r)$ at distance r from the center of the city ($r = 0$) declines monotonically according to the following negative exponential

$$\rho(r) = K \exp(-\lambda r), \tag{9.1}$$

where K is a constant of proportionality which is equal to the central density $\rho(0)$ and λ is a rate at which the effect of distance attenuates. Note that in this chapter we will use λ for the density parameter of the negative exponential and α for the inverse power function. β will be used as previously as a general regression parameter of various scaling relations from which the fractal dimension D can be derived. As previously, we will use the variable r to indicate a variable distance from the CBD, whereas R will be used to define the accumulation of distance which is an integral of r up to the radius R. r should not be confused with its use as a measure of scale in earlier chapters, but its use should be obvious from the context.

Clark's (1951) paper was wide-ranging, idiosyncratic and brilliant; he not only fitted the log transform of equation (9.1) to over 20 cities using linear regression but also speculated on how the parameter λ changed through time, thus charting from the beginning, the direction for all subsequent empirical work on urban density functions. It is still not clear why Clark chose the negative exponential function for he was unaware of Ajo's (1944) doctoral dissertation in which a negative exponential function was used to model traffic flow in the Finnish city of Tampere. It is likely, however, that this function was chosen because it was popular in mathematical economics in models of capital depreciation and the like of which Clark was probably aware.

In the parallel development of social physics, inverse power functions of distance were being widely exploited in gravitational models of traffic flow and in rank-size relations. But there were no attempts to collapse such gravitational models to models of population density until the early 1960s when Smeed (1961, 1963) suggested a suitable such model might be based on

$$\rho(r) = Kr^{-\alpha}, \tag{9.2}$$

where K is the constant of proportionality as in equation (9.1) above (but not defined where $r = 0$) and α is the parameter on distance. However, by this time, there was already a major groundswell in urban economics and transport modeling seeking to replace power functions with the negative exponential. The use of log–linear utility functions in urban economics from the work of Alonso (1964) on, and the development of gravity models using entropy-maximizing (Wilson, 1970) both led to the use of the negative exponential. The generalization of spatial interaction models into location as well as traffic distribution models and their collapsing to a single origin and many destinations led quite naturally to Clark's (1951) model (Bussiere and Snickars, 1970). Furthermore, important empirical work by Mills (1970), by Bussiere (1972b) and Bussiere and Stovall (1981), and by Mogridge (1984) drowned out any further attempts to model population densities by anything other than negative exponential functions.

So far, the body of work concerned with population density models is almost exclusively based on the negative exponential function or its generalization. As Zielinski (1979) points out, attempts at demonstrating the precedence of one function over another in this field are quite inconclusive and in the absence of further empirical evidence, theoretical considerations suggest the negative exponential function as being superior. There have been some dissenting voices. Smeed's (1961) work has been noted, and Blumenfeld (1972) (summarized in Vaughan, 1987) and Saviranta (1973) have both argued for inverse power functions of density. However, there has been more work at seeking a generalized function such as the gamma whose typical form is

$$\rho(r) = Kr^{-\alpha} \exp(-\lambda r), \tag{9.3}$$

where the parameters K, α and λ fulfill the same roles as in equations (9.1) and (9.2). Tanner (1961), March (1971) and Angel and Hyman (1976) have suggested that functions such as (9.3) are general enough to encompass the various debates about one functional form or the other. Finally, it is worth noting that Parr (1985a, b) amongst others has suggested that the negative exponential function is more appropriate for describing density in the urban area itself, while the inverse power function is more appropriate to the urban fringe and hinterland. In later work, Parr and his colleagues have argued that the most appropriate generalized function of density is the log–normal (Parr, O'Neill and Nairn, 1988: Parr and O'Neill, 1989); this relates to processes which generate such functions, which in turn relate to the use of such functions in fractal geometry.

The most obvious interpretation of the parameter λ in the negative exponential can be made by taking the first derivative of equation (9.1). Then

$$\frac{d\rho(r)}{dr} = -\lambda K \exp(-\lambda r)$$
$$= -\lambda \rho(r), \tag{9.4}$$

and thus

$$\frac{d\rho(r)}{\rho(r)} = -\lambda dr, \tag{9.5}$$

which implies that λ is the percentage change in density for a small change in distance dr. In this sense then, the parameter plays a crucial role in the calculation of elasticities in the fully-fledged urban economic theory of the housing market which gives rise to this function (Muth, 1969).

To find an explicitly spatial interpretation of the parameter λ in equations (9.4) and (9.5), we need to examine how the density function behaves with respect to distance. There are two ways of proceeding. First, we will consider $\rho(r)$ as a one-directional function on a single line of distance from the center $r = 0$, and second we will consider how the same function behaves in the field around its center which involves two directions; this latter possibility involves formulating the density in polar coordinates as $\rho(r, \theta)$ where

r is the line of distance and θ is the angular variation, both about the center. Note that we will use the terms one-directional and two-directional only in those contexts where it is necessary to draw distinctions between direction and dimension. In all other contexts, the term dimension will suffice for both (Batty and Sikdar, 1982).

We will first examine the one-directional function. Note that in the sequel, we will normalize the density over its space to sum to unity. Then

$$\int_0^{R_b} \rho(r) \, dr = \int_0^{R_b} K \exp(-\lambda r) \, dr = 1, \tag{9.6}$$

where R_b marks the distance to the boundary of the spatial system. Evaluating equation (9.6) gives the constant K as

$$K = \frac{\lambda}{1 - \exp(-\lambda R_b)}, \tag{9.7}$$

and therefore the density becomes

$$\rho(r) = \frac{\lambda \exp(-\lambda r)}{1 - \exp(-\lambda R_b)}. \tag{9.8}$$

Clearly when $R_b \to \infty$, the value of $K = \lambda$. The cumulative distribution of $\rho(r)$, $N(R)$, is given as

$$N(R) = \int_0^R \rho(r) \, dr$$

$$= \frac{1 - \exp(-\lambda R)}{1 - \exp(-\lambda R_b)} \approx 1 - \exp(-\lambda R). \tag{9.9}$$

However, it is the mean density in the city which is of most interest, and this is defined as

$$C(R_b) = \int_0^{R_b} \rho(r) \, r \, dr$$

$$= \frac{1}{\lambda} - \frac{R_b \exp(-\lambda R_b)}{1 - \exp(-\lambda R_b)}. \tag{9.10}$$

In equation (9.10), if $R_b \to \infty$, then $C(\infty) = 1/\lambda$ and the interpretation of λ is as an inverse measure of the mean density, thus controlling the spread of the function in the linear direction.

The same type of analysis as presented in equations (9.6) to (9.10) can be developed for the two-directional model which we stated earlier in polar coordinates as $\rho(r, \theta)$. The density function is now given as

$$\rho(r, \theta) = K \exp(-\lambda r), \tag{9.11}$$

and its normalization as

$$\int_0^{2\pi} \int_0^{R_b} \rho(r, \theta) \, r \, d\theta \, dr = 2\pi K \int_0^{R_b} \exp(-\lambda r) \, r \, dr = 1. \tag{9.12}$$

The normalizing constant K can be evaluated as

$$K = \frac{\lambda^2}{2\pi \, \{1 - (1 + \lambda R_b) \exp(-\lambda R_b)\}}. \tag{9.13}$$

From equation (9.13) when $R_b \rightarrow \infty$, then $K = \lambda^2/2\pi$. The cumulative distribution function $N(R)$ is

$$N(R) = \frac{1 - (1 + \lambda R) \exp(-\lambda R)}{1 - (1 + \lambda R_b) \exp(-\lambda R_b)}$$

$$\approx 1 - (1 + \lambda R) \exp(-\lambda R). \tag{9.14}$$

and the mean density

$$C(R_b) = \int_0^{2\pi} \int_0^{R_b} \rho(r, \theta)\, r^2 \, d\theta \, dr$$

$$= \frac{2}{\lambda} - \frac{\lambda R_b^2 \exp(-\lambda R_b)}{1 - (1 + \lambda R_b) \exp(-\lambda R_b)}. \tag{9.15}$$

As $R_b \rightarrow \infty$, $C(\infty) = 2/\lambda$, thus implying that λ is also an inverse measure of mean density controlling the spread of the function over the two directions of space (Batty, 1974).

When the boundary distance $R_b \rightarrow \infty$, $\lambda C = 1$ for the one-directional function and $\lambda C = 2$ for the two-directional. In this context, it is possible to associate direction with dimension, the dimension of the spatial system entering the calculation of the parameter λ directly. To anticipate an argument of a later section, the spread of development is unlikely to be over the entire two-dimensional space, but it is likely to be spread over more area than the one-dimensional line. Therefore it is likely that $1 < \lambda C < 2$, and thus the value of λC is a measure of the extent to which the density fills two-dimensional space, if and only if R_b defines a good approximation to the spread across space of the density function. We will now develop the same analysis as contained in equations (9.6) to (9.10) and (9.11) to (9.15) for the inverse power function.

9.3 Power Functions of Urban Density

An immediate interpretation of the parameter α in the scaling function in equation (9.2) is provided by its first derivative

$$\frac{d\rho(r)}{dr} = -\frac{\alpha}{r}\, \rho(r) = -\alpha K^{-\alpha-1}, \tag{9.16}$$

which can be written as

$$\frac{d\rho(r)}{\rho(r)} \bigg/ \frac{dr}{r} = -\alpha, \tag{9.17}$$

where α is clearly an elasticity, the ratio of the percentage change in density $d\rho(r)/\rho(r)$ to the percentage change in distance dr/r. In equations (9.16) and (9.17), α has a more precise interpretation than the negative exponential parameter λ in equations (9.4) and (9.5), but its role is similar.

The difficulty with the inverse power function emerges when it is normalized. As previously we will begin with the one-directional form of the model and then repeat the analysis for two. The normalization of equation (9.2) is given by

$$\int_0^{R_b} \rho(r)\, dr = Kr^{-\alpha}\, dr = 1.$$ (9.18)

The integral in equation (9.18) cannot be evaluated when $r = 0$, for the function $\rho(0)$ is infinite at this value. This has been one of the main reasons for researchers preferring the negative exponential. However, the problem can easily be dealt with by translating the origin of system to a value of $r > 0$, $r = 1$ being the obvious lower limit. Some have argued that population density is not defined at the center of the city in any case or that population density at a point is meaningless although neither of these assumptions are necessary to the shift of the origin which is arbitrary. Evaluating the integral in equation (9.18) from $r = 1$ to $r = R_b$ gives

$$K = \frac{1 - \alpha}{R_b^{1-\alpha} - 1}$$ (9.19)

and

$$\rho(r) = \frac{(1 - \alpha)r^{-\alpha}}{R_b^{1-\alpha} - 1}.$$ (9.20)

As Zielinski (1979) points out, the normalization in equations (9.19) and (9.20) is still "analytically awkward", and further indefinite integrals are impossible to evaluate. With a little simplification, however, it is possible to proceed. First if the boundary of the system $r = R_b$ is much greater than $r = 1$, then it is possible to ignore the lower limit; second if it is assumed that α lies between 0 and 1, then equation (9.20) will always act as an inverse power function. Moreover, if $\alpha \geq 1$, then the function breaks down, and is no longer meaningful as a model of population density. Thus the use of equation (9.20) implies that there are tight bounds on the value of α. With these assumptions, the cumulative density function can be written as

$$N(R) = \int_1^R \rho(r)\, dr$$

$$= \frac{R^{(1-\alpha)}}{R_b^{(1-\alpha)}} \approx R^{(1-\alpha)}.$$ (9.21)

Finally the mean density $C(R_b)$ is evaluated as

$$C(R_b) = \int_1^{R_b} \rho(r)\, r\, dr$$

$$= \frac{1 - \alpha}{2 - \alpha} R_b.$$ (9.22)

and this shows that the parameter α depends directly upon the value of the system boundary R_b. From equation (9.22), the parameter α can be computed as

$$\alpha = \frac{2C(R_b) - R_b}{C(R_b) - R_b},$$ (9.23)

but this is still an approximation whose relevance cannot be judged in advance of any particular application. However, equation (9.23) does provide some bounds on the value of α, namely that as $R_b > C(R_b)$, then $\alpha \leq 1$. The analysis for the two-directional model follows directly. The normalization is given as

$$\int_0^{2\pi} \int_1^{R_b} \rho(r, \theta)\, r\, dr\, d\theta = 2\pi K \int_1^{R_b} r^{-\alpha}\, r\, dr = 1, \tag{9.24}$$

from which K can be evaluated as

$$K = \frac{2 - \alpha}{2\pi\, (R_b^{2-\alpha} - 1)}. \tag{9.25}$$

Assuming that $R_b \gg 1$, then the density $\rho(r, \theta)$ becomes

$$\rho(r, \theta) = \frac{(2 - \alpha)\, r^{-\alpha}}{2\pi R_b^{2-\alpha}} \tag{9.26}$$

and the cumulative density is

$$N(R) = \int_0^{2\pi} \int_1^R \rho(r, \theta)\, r\, dr\, d\theta$$

$$= \frac{R^{2-\alpha}}{R_b^{2-\alpha}} \approx R^{2-\alpha}. \tag{9.27}$$

The mean density $C(R_b)$ is now evaluated as

$$C(R_b) = \int_0^{2\pi} \int_1^{R_b} \rho(r, \theta)\, r^2\, dr\, d\theta$$

$$= \frac{2 - \alpha}{3 - \alpha}\, R_b, \tag{9.28}$$

and this has the same structure as equation (9.22) for the one-directional model. It is possible to compute α from equation (9.28) as

$$\alpha = \frac{3C(R_b) - 2R_b}{C(R_b) - R_b}, \tag{9.29}$$

and from this, it is clear that α is unlikely to be greater than 2. The real significance of equations (9.23) and (9.29) however is that they show that the parameter α of the inverse power model is critically dependent on the boundary of the system R_b, and in certain empirical contexts, it will be possible to estimate α from these equations.

Although the differences between the two functions elaborated through equations (9.4) to (9.15) and (9.16) to (9.29) are substantial in mathematical terms, in practice both have been shown to fit empirical data equally well (or equally badly). In this section we will seek to demonstrate this. In Figure 9.1, one-dimensional negative exponential and inverse power functions from equations (9.8) and (9.20) respectively are plotted up to a regional boundary $R_b = 50$ units of distance. The parameters λ and α have been chosen to fit a mean density $C(R_b) = 20$ units; values of $\lambda = 0.025$ and

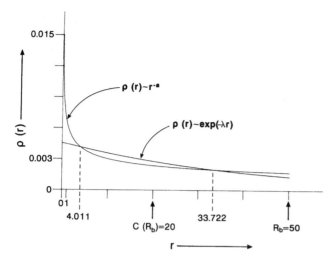

Figure 9.1. A comparison of the negative exponential and inverse power functions.

$\alpha = 0.349$ have been estimated which give simulated mean densities for both functions within 0.01% of the predetermined mean. Before we explore these functions further, it is worth noting for the inverse power function that if equation (9.23) is used to predict α, which is based on the assumption that the lower limit of r is 1, then the value of this parameter is 0.333 which is within 5% of the computed value.

No simple solution for the parameter λ exists for the negative exponential model. A first approximation to λ based on $1/C$ gives 0.05 while the use of the two-dimensional equation $2/C$ gives 0.1. The actual computed value is half the one-dimensional approximation, thus implying that the negative exponential over the given range from $r = 0$ to $r = 50$ provides only a partial approximation to its overall spread. This can be easily seen in Figure 9.1 where the inverse power function is much steeper in the area of its origin compared to the negative exponential which has a more gradual slope over the same distance to which it is applied. A more direct comparison of these functions can be made over their intermediate ranges where, from Figure 9.1, it is clear that the functions are similar. These functions will cross at $r = 4.011$ and $r = 33.722$, which are solutions to the equation of the two model functions $\{\lambda \exp(-\lambda r)/[1 - \exp(-\lambda R_b)]\} = \{(1 - \alpha)r^{1-\alpha}/R_b^{1-\alpha}\}$. It is between these two values that the functions are similar.

From Figure 9.1, it is quite clear that both functions are likely to be poor predictors of the central densities in the neighborhood of the origin $r = 0$. The inverse power function will overpredict while the negative exponential is unlikely to give a good prediction for there is little flexibility in controlling the value it takes when $r = 0$. Figure 9.1 also shows the problem with the negative exponential at the regional boundary. The fall-off in density from this model is likely to be too great. The pattern of population density in the hinterlands of western cities has been shown to be more even and higher than the negative exponential is able to predict, hence the suggestion that the negative exponential be only used to model intraurban variation in density, the inverse power being used to model peripheral variation (Parr, 1985a).

One of the main reasons for the popularity of the negative exponential function in population density models relates to its elegant properties. In fact, as we have shown above, these properties can only be fully exploited when it is assumed that the regional boundary distance is infinite; in short, this is only the case when the infinite boundary provides a good approximation to the observed density field. In the given hypothetical example as well as in the applications to Seoul which follow, this is clearly not the case and it is the inverse power model which yields more tractable equations which can be exploited in rapid estimation. Furthermore, although the negative exponential emerges 'naturally' from entropy-maximizing, this is due to the constraint on total travel distance adopted. There is in fact considerable evidence to suggest that distance perception is logarithmic, this being the basis of the Weber–Fechner law in psychology. If the logarithmic constraint on travel distance is used, then it is easy to show that the inverse power function is the appropriate derivation using entropy-maximizing. On balance, it is our view that both functions are useful in different contexts. Moreover, we should not ignore Zielinski's (1980) comment: "Since both (functions) can give practically identical fits to data, what criteria should be adopted to prefer one to the other? In this case the pragmatist must take the back seat to the theoretician. And theoreticians must endeavor to prove their assumptions". This we will attempt to do in the following sections.

9.4 Urban Allometry, Density and Dimension

In the growth and evolution of natural systems, there has been considerable research into the ways various features of such systems scale with increasing size, the study of relative sizes being allometry (Gould, 1966). We briefly alluded to this line of research in Chapters 2, 6 and 7, but here we provide a more complete summary in preparation for this and the next chapter. Allometric relationships relate the size of an object to a familiar yardstick such as length. For example, taking a measure of size in terms of the dimension of a system E, in Euclidean geometry we can define points where $E = 0$, lines where $E = 1$, planes where $E = 2$ and so on. If we take the yardstick as a measure of length in one dimension, that is R say, then objects which scale as a point vary as R^0, as length itself R^1, as the plane R^2 and so on, in general the scaling relation being R^E. If the size of the object in question is expected to scale as R^E, we refer to this as isometric scaling. If the object scales as R^D with $D < E$, then this is called negative allometry and if $D > E$, this is positive allometry.

In its most basic form, population density can be considered as the scaling between population $N(R)$ and area $A(R)$, however defined, where R is some measure of the linear dimension of the space. Then the key scaling relation between $N(R)$ and $A(R)$ can be written as

$$N(R) \sim A(R)^\phi. \tag{9.30}$$

From *a priori* considerations, we can argue that the value of the parameter ϕ indicates how population fills the two-dimensional space available to it. If $\phi > 1$, then the population fills more than the two dimensions of the space, while if $\phi < 1$, population is filling less than its available space. There have been several studies of this allometric relation over different sizes of cities based on the general assumption that as cities grow into the third dimension, then equation (9.30) should exhibit positive allometry. This is borne out in the work of Stewart (1947) and Stewart and Warntz (1958) where they show that $\phi = 4/3$ for British and American cities with 1951 data. With Swedish data for 1966, Nordbeck (1971) concludes that $\phi = 1.506$ which is a little larger than $3/2$ which would be the value if cities filled the three dimensions available to their development. More recently, Jones (1975) following work by Best, Jones and Rogers (1974), has derived ϕ as 1.193 for cities in England and Wales from the 1971 Population Census, and Craig and Haskey (1978) who reworked these data concluded that ϕ has remained approximately stable since 1951 with a value between 1.41 and 1.45. However, Woldenberg (1973) using data for American cities has shown that ϕ varies from around 0.8 to 1.2 depending upon the data set used.

All these studies refer to data sets based on wide ranges of city size. In the intra-urban case, where population densities decline with increasing distance from the center, equation (9.30) will show negative allometry. First we will replace the measure of area in equation (9.30) with the yardstick of length R which enables us to link this analysis to population density functions introduced above. Then equation (9.30) can now be written

$$N(R) = \gamma A^\phi$$

$$= \gamma(\pi R^2)^\phi = \varphi R^D, \tag{9.31}$$

where we have assumed that the distance associated with the area is given as $R = \sqrt{A}$, and γ and φ are constants of proportionality. From equation (9.31) it is clear that $D = 2\phi$ and if $\phi < 1$, then $D < 2$. Takayasu (1989) refers to D as the 'effective dimension', but to anticipate our argument, this of course is the fractal dimension. As in the two previous chapters, the value of D is thus a measure of the extent to which the city fills its two-dimensional area.

Without anticipating the value of D for any particular city, we can now present the equation for population density in terms of the scaling relation based on the yardstick of length R and explicitly containing the parameter D. From equations (9.30) and (9.31), we will write the density as in equations (2.33) and (7.9)

$$\rho(R) = \frac{N(R)}{A(R)} \sim A(R)^{\phi-1}, \tag{9.32}$$

and from this it is clear that if population is isometric with area and $\phi = 1$, then $\rho(R)$ is constant. For population density to decline with increasing distance from the center, then the exponent in equation (9.32) must be less than 0, that is $\phi - 1 < 1$, while it is most unlikely that ϕ would be greater than 1 which would imply increasing density with distance from the center. Writing (9.32) explicitly in terms of the yardstick R gives

$$\rho(R) = \frac{\varphi R^D}{\pi R^2} = \xi R^{D-2}, \qquad (9.33)$$

and for the density to decline with distance, it is clear that the fractal dimension D should be less than 2, implying that the city will not fill the two-dimensional space available.

The real value of this analysis is in revealing how density should be defined. Casual observation should suggest whether the city is filling two or three dimensions. If the city fills less than the plane, then the appropriate space on which to compute density is the plane; thus the definition of area as $A(R) = \pi R^2$ in equation (9.32) is correct and the value of D will be less than 2. However, if the city is filling three dimensions of space then the appropriate normalization by area would be $A(R) = \pi R^3$, the volume, and then the value of D would probably be greater than 2 but less than 3. In this case, the more general form of density equation in (7.18) would be appropriate. In fact, in all studies of density to date (of which the authors are aware), the implicit assumption is that cities fill the plane, not the volume, thus suggesting that the argument made by Nordbeck (1971) amongst others that cities fill the third dimension is spurious.

The other important conclusion from this analysis is that the measure of area to be used represents the space within which the city grows, its field, not the more restricted area which is associated with its built-up form; in fact most studies of density based on the population and area of Census tracts treat the area of the field, although in some studies which use built-up area, the parameters derived cannot be compared with those here. What is certain, however, is that in most studies of population density to date, researchers have paid very little attention to the definition of area, thus throwing into question the validity of the parameter values estimated, at least in terms of the sorts of theory invoked here. Comparisons between different studies are therefore difficult to make.

9.5 The Basic Scaling Relations Revisited

We are now in a position to relate the density equations stated earlier in terms of the inverse power functions, to those derived from urban allometry. We will use the two-directional function given in equation (9.26). Equating this to the density in equation (9.33), we will integrate over θ. Then

$$\rho(R) = \int_0^{2\pi} \rho(R, \theta)\, d\theta = K'R^{-\alpha} = \xi R^{D-2}, \qquad (9.34)$$

and if the equation holds, then $D - 2 = -\alpha$ or $\alpha = 2 - D$. As D is a measure of the extent to which space is filled, then it is expected to be less than 2, and thus α is its complement, a measure of the extent to which the available space is not filled. The cumulative density functions can also be equated, and the same conclusions drawn. Comparing equation (9.27) with (9.31) and using appropriate notation, then

$$N(R) = K''R^{2-\alpha} = \varphi R^D. \tag{9.35}$$

Equations (9.34) and (9.35) suggest a coherent and useful coincidence between the fractal dimension D and the parameter of the associated inverse power function of population density; that is, that the two dimensions of the associated space can be divided into a space-filling component D and a non-space-filling component α which sum to the Euclidean dimension E of the space within which the city exists, in short, that $E = D + \alpha = 2$.

We have already defined three scaling relations, namely the population–area relation in equation (9.30), the population–radius relation in equations (9.31) and (9.35), and the density relation in equations (9.33) and (9.34). We will add to these a fourth relation, based on the first derivative of the cumulative population–radius relation in equation (9.35). This relation, referred to as the incremental population–radius equation, is derived as

$$n(R) = \frac{dN(R)}{dR} = hR^{D-1} = hR^{\eta}. \tag{9.36}$$

h is a constant of proportionality and η is the scaling parameter. We now have four scaling relations; three of these which relate the cumulative population $N(R)$, the incremental population $n(R)$, and the density $\rho(R)$ to the radius R and based on equations (9.31), (9.36) and (9.33), are those used in Chapters 7 and 8 to describe the distribution of particles in the DLA and DBM simulations. These will be used here in the empirical analysis of density in Seoul, but note that the alternate density variable $Q(R)$ which was used in Chapters 7 and 8 and defined previously in equation (7.26) is not used. The fourth relation is the classic allometric equation which relates $N(R)$ to $A(R)$ as in equation (9.30).

Before we broach the question of estimation, we must make clear the fact that we expect the value of the fractal dimension estimated from the Seoul data to be similar to that of the DLA simulations, that is $D \approx 1.7$, as implied in many of the estimates given earlier in Table 7.1. Thus the value of the density parameter would be around -0.3, that is $\alpha = D - 2$. Earlier we speculated that in the case of the negative exponential density function, the dimension of the system would fall between $1 < \lambda C < 2$ from arguments relating to the mean density in one- and two-dimensional systems. We can now speculate that $\lambda C \approx 1.7$, a result which has already been borne out in work by one of the authors almost 20 years ago (Batty, 1976). Similar relations are not obvious for the inverse power function, although D and α are immediate results of their estimation and further insights must await further research. To provide some sense of closure to this theoretical section and to progress the research to applications, methods of estimating equations (9.31), (9.36), (9.33) and (9.30) in that order will now be discussed.

9.6 Methods of Parameter Estimation

There are two main issues to clarify before we embark on fitting the basic scaling relations to the empirical data: these deal with aggregating the data, and choosing appropriate estimation methods. We will deal with these issues in turn. Researchers fitting population density models have either dealt with the data in their raw form by Census tracts or have aggregated the data into concentric rings. The latter method produces better fits and hence more reliable estimates because local variations in the data are reduced, but the use of one or the other data set ultimately depends upon the purpose for which the analysis is undertaken. Here we will employ both, but we consider that the method of concentric rings is likely to give much 'truer' estimates of the values of the parameters D and α which is of most interest to the analysis performed here. In fact, this was the method which we used to organize the data in Chapters 7 and 8 for comparing the theoretical simulations with Taunton and Cardiff. A related issue involves the way the data are aggregated over distance and whether relationships are fitted in their cumulative or incremental form. Cumulative relations are bound to give better fits and this will be our emphasis although we will also examine some incremental estimates. In this sense then, we will follow the practice of Bussiere (1972) and Bussiere and Stovall (1981), rather than the traditional treatment used by Clark (1951).

The first method of estimation we will use and one that will act as our baseline, involves taking logarithmic transformations of equations (9.31), (9.36), (9.33) and (9.30) and estimating their parameters using linear regression. The four relations can now be summarized in discrete form as

$$\log N_i = \alpha_1 + \beta_1 \log R_i, \tag{9.37}$$

$$\log n_i = \alpha_2 + \beta_2 \log R_i, \tag{9.38}$$

$$\log \rho_i = \alpha_3 + \beta_3 \log R_i, \tag{9.39}$$

$$\log N_i = \alpha_4 + \beta_4 \log A_i. \tag{9.40}$$

Note first that the intercepts or constant terms α_1, α_2, α_3 and α_4 are not directly related to the parameter α of the inverse power function but are so defined to make them consistent with their usage in Chapters 7 and 8 through equations (7.49). Throughout the analysis, distances are ordered so that $R_i < R_{i+1} < R_{i+2}$, the cumulative populations are given as $N_i = \Sigma_j n_j$, ($j = 1, \ldots, i$), the areas for each cumulative ring as $A_i = \pi R_i^2$, the actual area of each ring as $a_i = A_i - A_{i-1}$, ($i > 0$ and $A_0 = 0$), and the density $\rho_i = n_i/a_i$. We also need to be clear about the various parameter estimates in these equations and the look-up table reproduced as Table 9.1 shows the conver-

Table 9.1.   Relationships between the parameters

Equation number[1]	Intercept parameter	Slope parameter	Dimension D	Density coefficient α
9.37 (9.31)	$\alpha_1 = \log \varphi$	$\beta_1 = D$	β_1	$2 - \beta_1$
9.38 (9.36)	$\alpha_2 = \log h$	$\beta_2 = \eta$	$1 + \beta_2$	$1 - \beta_2$
9.39 (9.33)	$\alpha_3 = \log \xi$	$\beta_3 = D - 2$	$2 + \beta_3$	β_3
9.40 (9.30)	$\alpha_4 = \log \gamma$	$\beta_4 = \phi$	$2\beta_4$	$2(1 - \beta_4)$

[1] The first equation number in each row is the number of the log transform of the second equation number (which is in brackets).

sion between these parameters, the dimension D and the coefficient α. In the sequel, all estimates are given to three decimal places.

There are several other methods of estimation which we consider less reliable than log–linear regression. Mills (1970), Mills and Tan (1980), and Weiss (1961) all use methods which involve only two values of density or population given at two different points within the city. For example, if the density $\rho(R)$ or the cumulative population $N(R)$ are known at, say, distances R and R_b, then using equations (9.26) or (9.27) in the two-dimensional case, the constant and scaling parameters can be found from the solution of two equations in two unknowns using the Newton–Raphson method (Batty, 1976). There is little work on how reliable these types of estimates are in comparison with those from regression, but we consider that such methods are really only appropriate when no more than two observations are available.

There are, however, two other methods which we will use, the first of which was introduced in Chapters 7 and 8 and which can only be used if population data are available on a very fine lattice. Where each occupied lattice point is the location of a single equal-sized household, then a good approximation to the density in equation (9.33) is $\rho(R) \sim R^{D-2}$ where the constant of proportionality is approximately equal to unity. Then for any distance R from the center, D can be calculated from a log transform of this equation, given earlier in equation (8.13) which is restated as

$$D(R) = 2 + \frac{\log \rho(R)}{\log R}. \tag{8.13}$$

In earlier chapters we called the graph of $D(R)$ against R the 'signature' of the density function. In the vicinity of its origin, $D(R)$ can fluctuate wildly, but it soon settles down to a characteristic value ($D(R) \approx 1.7$ for the case of a DLA cluster). At the edge of the cluster, the value of the dimension is also unreliable because this is the area where the city is likely to be developing most rapidly. Thus the best value of the dimension will be given at the distance value of the mean density, that is at $D\{C(R_b)\}$. We have not yet said anything about the data in the applications which follow, but two of the four data sets we will use are based on a crude approximation to the shape of the city using lattice point data which reveals the morphology of the city in question. This will become clear in the sequel.

The last method is well-known in that it is based on deriving the density and population model by entropy-maximizing. Formulating the model in terms of the location of population n_i in individual zones i, the model can be stated as

$$n_i = N \frac{R_i^\eta}{\sum\limits_i R_i^\eta}, \left(\sum\limits_i n_i = N\right), \tag{9.41}$$

where N is the total population in its absolute value (or normalized form where $N = 1$). The parameter η in equation (9.41) is found by solving the model subject to either of the following two constraint equations

$$\bar{C} = \sum_i \frac{n_i}{N} R_i \qquad\qquad (9.42)$$

or

$$\bar{C}_{\log} = \sum_i \frac{n_i}{N} \log R_i. \qquad\qquad (9.43)$$

Strictly speaking, equation (9.41) is associated with constraint equation (9.43) not (9.42); that is, equation (9.41) is derived by maximizing entropy subject to equation (9.43), thus leading to the derivation of the inverse power function (Wilson, 1970). In fact, we will fit equation (9.41) by separately solving for both equation (9.42) and (9.43), thus giving two estimates of η (and thence of D and α through Table 9.1). We will not concern ourselves any further with entropy-maximizing except to point out that there is a strong relationship between entropy, information and fractal dimension which finds its clearest expression in the derivation of power functions such as those treated here (Batty and Sikdar, 1982; Takayasu, 1989).

9.7 Applications to Large Cities: the Seoul Data Base

Seoul was selected for our empirical work because the negative exponential model has already been fitted to its population density, thus giving us the opportunity of making some casual comparisons to the inverse power density models which we will estimate here (Kim, 1985). We also had access to reasonable population data for the city at three dates 1970, 1977 and 1982 from which we selected the 1982 data for our applications. Moreover, Seoul is a rapidly growing city, its population increasing from around 5.5 million in 1970 to almost nine million in 1982, and we consider that cities such as this one where rapid growth has taken place under few market imperfections to be ideal testing ground for the ideas introduced here. The basic set of zones for the 1982 population data are shown in Figure 9.2(a) which are aggregations of Census tract data. In the analysis, the center of the city was found using centrographic analysis on the 1982 data (Kim, 1985). Distances to all other zones were then defined as crow-fly distances from this center to each individual zone centroid. From this original data set, the zones are ranked according to distance from the center and these are aggregated in the given order for estimating three of the four scaling relations.

The second data set used is quite different. The urban form of Seoul taken from a 1982 cadastral map was defined by placing a 72×72 lattice across the built-up area and coding each lattice point according to whether the surrounding cell was developed or undeveloped. The size of the lattice spacing was half a kilometer, and a lattice point was classified as developed if more than half the surrounding cell was built up. The basic logic behind this type of coding is that if the lattice spacing is fine enough, the lattice will detect the location of population in such a manner as to provide a

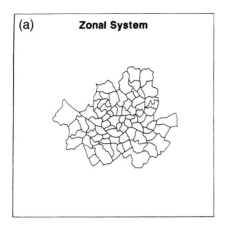

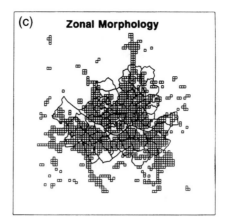

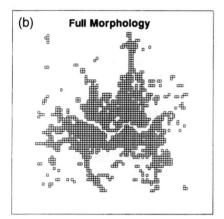

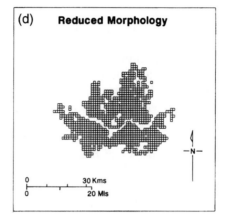

Figure 9.2. Zonal and lattice systems for the four data sets.

detailed morphology of the city. In short, although each lattice point is assumed to have an identical population density, when aggregated for purposes of analysis into concentric rings say, then the variable density of population will be detected. This is clearly not the case here where the lattice is far too coarse; for it to pick up the kind of variation needed, the spacing should be as fine as 10 m × 10 m. Our gross approximation here is thus illustrative rather than definitive, and although it does pick up the morphology and variable density at a crude scale, the results of using this data set must be interpreted with caution. The coding is shown in Figure 9.2(b).

Two related data sets have also been produced. First, by combining the measured population in the first 80 zone data set with the morphology defined by the second, a third data set in which the actual population is allocated to the points of the lattice can be defined. This is done by overlaying the zonal structure in Figure 9.2(a) on the morphology in 9.2(b), associating each lattice point with one of the original 80 zones, and counting the number of lattice points in each zone. The population in each original zone is then allocated equally to as many lattice points as there are in the zone in question. Figure 9.2(c) shows the overlay of the two zoning systems which produces the third, noting that the periphery of the city is excluded from the original urban morphology shown in Figure 9.2(b) due to the fact that population data is not available for these outer areas. The fourth and last data set is similar to the second except for the peripheral areas which have been excluded. This is simply formed by overlaying the first data set on the second, excluding the peripheral areas, thus forming a reduced morphology based on lattice spacing. This is shown in Figure 9.2(d).

For the second, third and fourth data sets which are all based in some way on the lattice morphology, concentric rings can be easily defined at increasing units of equal distance around the center. In these cases, we have divided the greatest radial distance to the edge of the city into 25 equal units on which we have arranged 25 concentric rings. The populations and related variables for each ring have then been derived by counting the number of lattice units (and their populations in the case of the third data set) which fall into each ring. In subsequent analysis, we will refer to these four data sets as follows; the first data set based on the zones shown in Figure 9.2(a) is called the Zonal System, the second in Figure 9.2(b) the Full Morphology, the third in Figure 9.2(c) the Zonal Morphology, and the fourth in Figure 9.2(d) the Reduced Morphology.

It is also important to be clear about which estimation method is to be applied to which data set at this stage. All four scaling relations in equations (9.31), (9.36), (9.33) and (9.30) will be fitted to all four data sets using the logarithmic transformations given in equations (9.37) to (9.40). This will represent our set of baseline estimates for we consider this type of estimation as providing us with the most comprehensive set of estimates. This will generate four estimates of the dimension D and the density parameter α for each of the data sets. The estimates based on solving the entropy-maximizing constraint equations in (9.42) and (9.43) will also be applied to each of the four data sets. This will provide us with two sets of parameters D and α derived from η, one for each solution of the appropriate constraint equation. Finally, the method of calculating D (and hence α) from the signature given in equation (8.13) is only valid for the Full and Reduced Morphology data sets, the second and fourth, because this requires that the data be based on equally dense lattice points. This concludes our survey of the data and we will now embark on presenting the baseline estimates.

9.8 The Density Model Estimates

Throughout the process of fitting the baseline equations in (9.37) to (9.40) to the four data sets, the analysis was aided by frequent graphical interpretations of the base data, model predictions and residuals. To provide some sense of the similarities between the data sets, we have plotted the cumulative population $\{N_i\}$ against the radius $\{R_i\}$ as given in equation (9.37). The graphs of these data are plotted in Figure 9.3 and show very characteristic profiles which go some way to indicating that the four data sets are detecting the rudiments of the urban form and density of Seoul, as well as being similar to related profiles in other cities (for example, see the exten-

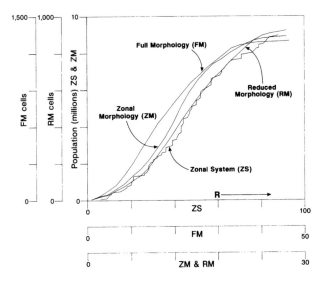

Figure 9.3. Cumulative population profiles for the four data sets.

sive examples in Bussiere and Stovall, 1981). Using Figure 9.3, if a detailed analysis is made of the variation in density and population in the vicinity of the origin and at the edge of the city, it is clear that density is volatile and shows no characteristic trend in these areas. Population density is notoriously difficult to model near the center of the city, while at the edge, the city is growing at its fastest rate, and the density is nowhere close to the density which will ultimately prevail.

The models therefore should not be applied in these areas; at the center whatever function is used is likely to be inappropriate, while at the edge, densities are likely to be too low, and thus the function will underpredict these. We will use these characteristics to exclude certain observations from our data set in the results presented below as we did with the simulation results and the empirical data pertaining to Taunton and Cardiff in Chapters 7 and 8. This is a particularly important issue in modeling population density, for we must assume that wherever the density function applies, the city must be in equilibrium. In previous work, this issue has been entirely ignored for most research has not been cast into an appropriate dynamic framework which indicates that densities in the areas of the origin and periphery of a growing city are likely to be subject to rapid change. The theory of the growing city which we have alluded to here based on DLA simulations provides a strong rationale for systematically excluding these areas from our estimation and accordingly, we will proceed by doing so.

Table 9.2 presents the results of fitting equations (9.37) to (9.40) to the Zonal System data whose spatial system is subdivided as in Figure 9.2(a). In the sequel, all parameter estimates from these equations will be converted into their appropriate fractal dimension D using Table 9.1, and the reader can easily note the density parameter α by calculating it as $D - 2$. Table 9.2 shows immediately that the fit of the cumulative populations with respect to area and radius are much better than those of the incremental population and the density. This difference has been widely observed in

Table 9.2. Dimensions associated with the Zonal System data

Number of zones	Population–radius (9.37)	Incremental population (9.38)	Population density (9.39)	Population–area (9.40)
80	1.765 97.7	1.096 00.9	1.633 18.9	1.504 87.0
77 less 1–3	1.667 98.0	1.088 00.5	1.490 25.9	1.352 84.2
71 less 72–80	1.850 98.5	1.203 04.8	1.976 02.3	1.976 99.3
68 less 1–3, 72–80	1.758 98.9	1.228 04.9	1.932 23.7	1.914 99.4

Note: The statistics shown below each of the estimates of dimension are coefficients of determination $100r^2$ calculated for each set of dependent and independent variables. These are also shown in Tables 9.3, 9.4 and 9.5.

the literature and results from aggregating variables, thus reducing their variance (Muth, 1969). However, our quest is to increase the fit of all four equations by systematically removing those observations which are most suspect. To this end, we have first removed the three central zones, then the nine peripheral zones, and then these central and peripheral zones together. The fit of all the equations is improved by these exclusions, although the estimates of dimension for the incremental population equation (9.38) differ most from the other three whose values are closest to one another. The best fits occur for all four equations when both the central and peripheral zones are excluded with the cumulative population–radius relation giving a dimension value closest to that of the DLA model (1.758 compared to 1.71), with all four of its dimensions for the four variants on this data set, falling between 1.667 and 1.850. What is extremely encouraging for this data set is that all the dimensions lie between 1 and 2, the range which suggests that cities do not fill their entire two-dimensional space. As we will see, our confidence that the 'true' dimension of Seoul lies between 1.5 and 1.8 will be progressively increased as we examine each data set.

The second set of data – the Full Morphology – detects the form of the city, but is based on the assumption that each lattice cell has the same density of population. These 1300 cells have been aggregated into 25 equally spaced concentric rings, and the same type of progressive reduction in the rings used is made in the attempt to exclude the most problematic observations. The rationale for these exclusions only becomes clear when the data are plotted, which has been done in every case but is not illustrated here for lack of space. The results are shown in Table 9.3, and these indicate once again that it is the incremental population relation in equation (9.38) which has the lowest fit, and the cumulative population relation (9.37) which has the best. Of the 24 estimates of dimension given in Table 9.3, only two of these fall outside the range of $1 < D < 2$. The average of all dimensions in this table is 1.551, and once again, the estimates from this data set which detect only the form are similar to those in the first set which

Table 9.3. Dimensions associated with the Full Morphology data

Number of concentric rings	Population–radius (9.37)	Incremental population (9.38)	Population density (9.39)	Population–area (9.40)
25	1.333	0.668	1.593	1.513
	97.3	06.2	63.2	95.5
24	1.290	0.148	1.449	1.389
less 1	95.5	25.1	73.9	94.3
15	1.498	1.597	1.835	1.793
less 16–25	99.5	71.3	55.6	99.2
14	1.552	1.384	1.753	1.721
less 1, 16–25	99.2	41.7	65.8	98.8
9	1.529	1.918	1.957	1.943
less 10–25	99.3	98.1	60.1	99.9
8	1.682	1.876	1.940	1.930
less 1, 10–25	99.7	94.8	54.6	99.9

detect only the density. In Table 9.3, the best estimates across all four scaling equations are given by the data which excludes the 16 peripheral zones.

Perhaps the most consistent data set for the models developed here is the third – the Zonal Morphology – which combines both density and form and which is shown in Figure 9.2(c). The results of fitting the four equations to this set are shown in Table 9.4 where it is clear that all dimensions estimated, with the exception of one, fall between the limits of 1 and 2. As observations are excluded, the performance of the models increases significantly with the best fitting range of estimates achieved when the 15 periph-

Table 9.4. Dimensions associated with the Zonal Morphology data

Number of concentric rings	Population–radius (9.37)	Incremental population (9.38)	Population density (9.39)	Population–area (9.40)
25	1.434	1.048	1.694	1.641
	98.4	00.2	68.3	98.1
24	1.477	0.725	1.632	1.597
less 1	97.7	04.6	68.1	97.3
13	1.486	1.873	1.846	1.817
less 14–25	98.5	93.7	78.1	99.7
12	1.640	1.941	1.856	1.842
less 1, 14–25	98.9	89.5	59.3	99.4
10	1.416	1.831	1.822	1.780
less 11–25	98.6	92.2	82.2	99.6
9	1.566	1.887	1.810	1.788
less 1, 11–25	98.7	84.6	67.8	99.3

eral rings are excluded. Here the dimensions vary from 1.416 to 1.822, and if the central ring is excluded as well, the range narrows to 1.566 to 1.810 with an average of 1.763, again close to our theoretical value of 1.71. The last data set – the Reduced Morphology, shown in Figure 9.2(d), is simply the Full Morphology reduced by the exclusion of the periphery. However, the data are still organized into 25 concentric rings, and as such, this represents a scaled-up version of the Full Morphology. The model estimates for the progressive exclusion of rings from this data set are shown in Table 9.5 where all 24 dimensions computed lie between 1.140 and 1.899. The same sorts of interpretation as in the previous three data sets emerge again here: the incremental population and density relations show the poorest fits with the population–area and population–radius the best. The overall best fit occurs when 11 peripheral rings are excluded, and the average dimension when the central ring is excluded as well is 1.798.

The range of dimension values computed from these four data sets is remarkably narrow, with only three values from the 88 estimated falling outside the range of $1 < D < 2$, these values being less than 1 in each case. This is fairly conclusive evidence that the inverse power density function when fitted to population density data computed with respect to the urban field (and not just the residential built-up area) will yield a fractional dimension between 1 and 2, with the likely value between 1.5 and 1.8. This also implies that the density parameter should lie between 0.2 and 0.5. We would argue that if estimates of the inverse power function yield values of $\alpha > 1$ or $\alpha < 0$, the data or the estimation procedure is likely to be suspect, or the data in question implies an urban morphology which is unusual. However, before we conclude, we will also present the other two methods of estimation, the first based on the signature equation in (8.13), the second on the entropy estimation method relating to equations (9.41) to (9.43).

We are only able to estimate dimensions for the signature of the density

Table 9.5. Dimensions associated with the Reduced Morphology data

Number of concentric rings	Population–radius (9.37)	Incremental population (9.38)	Population density (9.39)	Population–area (9.40)
25	1.472	1.330	1.733	1.689
	98.8	16.3	76.5	99.1
24	1.545	1.140	1.699	1.673
less 1	98.7	02.3	72.4	98.6
18	1.504	1.724	1.812	1.781
less 19–25	98.6	86.3	83.0	99.7
17	1.663	1.707	1.817	1.800
less 1, 19–25	99.1	76.0	71.1	99.5
14	1.475	1.835	1.823	1.791
less 15–25	98.3	92.7	78.6	99.6
13	1.630	1.899	1.838	1.824
less 1, 15–25	98.7	88.2	59.8	99.3

for the Full and Reduced Morphologies, the second and fourth data sets as presented in Figure 9.2(b) and (d). From equation (8.13), we have plotted the signature $D(R)$ against R and this is shown in Figure 9.4. This signature relates to the Full Morphology, but as the Reduced Morphology is a subset of this, the figure is relevant to both. The regional boundaries differ in that $R_b = 47.424$ for the Full, $R_b = 28.071$ for the Reduced, and these are also indicated in Figure 9.4. At these values of R, the dimension for the Full system can be calculated as 1.756 in comparison with 1.704 for the Reduced. However, it is clear from Figure 9.4 that a better value of R to take would be the mean value $C(R_b)$, and these yield dimensions of $D\{C(R_b)\}$ of 1.845 for $C(18.590)$, the Full data set, in contrast to 1.856 for $C(14.185)$ for the Reduced set. These estimates are close to and consistent with the regression estimates in Tables 9.2 to 9.5, and some exploration of the signature in Figure 9.4 reveals that in the region of the origin, the estimates of dimension are volatile, although by $R = 9$, these estimates have settled to around $D(9) = 1.85$. Clearly the mean values of $C(R_b)$ are the most appropriate to use. Together with the estimates of the simulations using the DLA and DBM methods in the two previous chapters, these signature functions have proved to be the most robust methods of estimation.

The entropy estimation also produces well-fitting models with dimension values which accord to the results so far. These estimations involve solving equations (9.42) or (9.43) for the parameter η by some non-linear method – here we use the Newton–Raphson method – then using Table 9.1 to calculate the dimensions D ($= 1 + \eta$). Two estimates are made for each of the four data sets, these estimates being based on solving for the constraint in equation (9.42), then (9.43). All four data sets with their exclusions as given previously in Tables 9.2 to 9.5 are used in the estimation, thus giving 44 estimates of D in total. These results are shown in Table 9.6. In this table, under each dimension value, we first give the coefficient of determination $(100r^2)$ for the predictions of the incremental population model which is

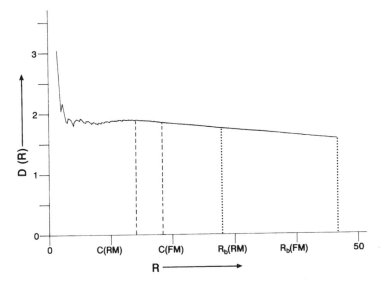

Figure 9.4. The signature of the full and reduced morphologies.

Table 9.6. Entropy estimates of the dimension

	Zonal system			Full Morphology			Zonal Morphology			Reduced Morphology		
No. of zones	Equations (9.42)	(9.43)	No. of rings	Equations (9.42)	(9.43)	No. of rings	Equations (9.42)	(9.43)	No. of rings	Equations (9.42)	(9.43)
80	1.132 01.8 99.8	1.703 01.9 99.8	25	0.898 00.9 94.6	0.621 00.1 96.5	25	1.085 00.8 95.1	0.822 00.3 96.1	25	1.245 08.1 97.6	1.029 01.7 98.0
77	1.134 01.3 99.8	1.064 01.4 99.8	24	0.698 08.4 95.9	0.422 04.1 97.1	24	0.940 00.2 95.6	0.689 00.1 96.4	24	1.151 02.7 97.7	0.947 04.8 98.1
71	1.188 03.5 99.8	1.134 03.6 99.8	15	1.405 39.4 98.7	1.252 44.2 99.1	13	1.942 94.3 99.9	1.973 94.4 99.9	18	1.640 66.5 99.3	1.544 68.2 99.4
68	1.199 02.8 99.8	1.130 02.9 99.8	14	1.283 21.7 98.9	1.157 24.5 99.2	12	1.972 93.1 99.9	1.990 93.1 99.9	17	1.614 59.2 99.3	1.152 60.8 99.4
			9	1.870 93.3 99.8	1.829 93.6 99.8	10	1.882 94.3 99.9	1.912 94.4 99.9	14	1.881 90.6 99.8	1.870 90.6 99.8
			8	1.838 90.3 99.8	1.803 90.5 99.8	9	1.910 92.6 99.9	1.931 93.0 99.9	13	1.903 88.4 99.8	1.890 88.4 99.8

Note: the first line of each cell is the fractal dimension, the second line is $100r^2$ for the increment of population, and the third line is $100r^2$ for the cumulative population.

the form in which the model is specified in equation (9.41), and below this, we give the same coefficient for the population in cumulative form.

The results are similar to those in Tables 9.2 to 9.5 in that the Zonal System data performs least well. The Full, Zonal and Reduced Morphology data sets give parameter values and fits which are both good and similar to one another, and there is a consistent increase in the performance of all models as zones or rings are progressively excluded from the estimation. Of the 44 estimates, eight fall below $D = 1$ and none is greater than 2. As in previous estimates using regression, the best fits are those obtained when the most zones or rings are excluded. These results again strengthen our confidence in various hypotheses that suggest that cities never fill their two-dimensional space in which they grow, regardless of any vertical growth into the third dimension which has occurred within the last century, and that their fractional dimension lies between 1.5 and 1.8. Moreover, if the models and data sets to which they are applied are correctly specified, it is easy to give order of magnitude estimates for the density and dimension parameter values before the analysis begins.

9.9 Fractals and City Size

The theoretical analysis with which we introduced this chapter concentrated on the relative advantages and limitations of the two classical functional forms which have dominated social physics, the negative exponential which has become the conventional wisdom for representing density and interaction, and the inverse power which was associated with much early research. Notwithstanding our view that the inverse power function has less direct but important properties which have hitherto hardly been exploited or even recognized, the parameters of both functions reflect the properties of the space within which such functions are defined. However, it is clear that the parameters of the inverse power function are direct measures of the extent to which the phenomena whose density is being measured, fills the space available, and using arguments from urban allometry, the link between such functions and fractal geometry can be made. Thus the function used determines the form of the system being modeled, and it is in this sense that we say 'form follows function'.

The empirical work in this chapter in which the inverse power function has been fitted to population density profiles in the city of Seoul has produced quite startling results. Although all the theory we have developed in the last three chapters suggests that cities have a fractional dimension between 1 and 2, we did not expect our results to be quite so conclusive, over such a large range of scaling relations and estimation methods. Using the four data sets and variants of these based on excluding certain observations, we have provided 136 estimates of the dimension D and density parameter α. Of these, only 11 fall outside the postulated range $1 < D < 2$, and these are all less than 1. If we look at the results based on excluding the most problematic observations, of the 24 values of the dimension produced, 21 fall within the range 1.566 to 1.940, thus suggesting that the 'true' value of the dimension must be nearer 2 than 1.

However, perhaps the most important value of this analysis is not in demonstrating the consistency of results produced by both theoretical and empirical analysis, but in the need to be extremely careful in the way data are collected and density defined. Strictly, we need data bases in which every household and household size is recorded in terms of its location before we can develop any definitive analysis of density which exploits the fractal model most appropriately. This represents an immense task, but with better data and data systems becoming available, it is now within the bounds of feasibility. On both the theoretical and empirical sides of this argument, we also need to explore the link between entropy, information and dimension (Takayasu, 1989); for in doing so, we are likely to generate a clearer picture of the role of the conventional model of population density based on the negative exponential, as well as exploring further the properties of the inverse power function. This will also enable us to link our approach to the mainstream where entropy and utility maximizing are widely used in the derivation and estimation of spatial economic, urban and transportation models.

Finally, we need to explore the relationship between city size, fractal dimension, changing densities and changing form. This implies once again that we broach directly the question of an appropriate model dynamics which encompasses processes of fractal growth (and decline), as well as questions of reversibility. Only in this way will we be able to connect these ideas to the large body of knowledge originally developed by Clark (1951) which concerns the changing shape of population density profiles over time. If we can make progress here, it may be possible to begin to fashion a theory of city size, shape and form which enables us to classify cities in terms of the efficiency and perhaps economy of their form. This will be the goal of our next and final chapter where we will speculate upon the groundwork which is required for a fractal theory of city size.

Extending the Geometry to Systems of Fractal Cities

... in the final analysis, fractal methods can serve to analyze any 'system', whether natural or artificial, that decomposes into 'parts' articulated in a self-similar fashion, and such that the properties of the parts are less important than the rules of the articulation. (Mandelbrot, 1983, p. 114.)

10.1 Articulating Systems of Cities

Throughout most of this book, our concern has been with using fractal geometry to describe and model the shape and distribution of population within individual cities. In Chapter 6, we focussed upon treating individual land uses as fractal objects, and examining how fractal geometry could be used to infer the dimensional properties of the entire distribution of land use shapes. In Chapter 1, we alluded to the manner in which the spatial hierarchy of cities gave rise to a rank-size distribution, but as yet, we have not explored how this geometry might be extended to entire systems of cities. This will be the quest of the present chapter. There is of course a well-worked-out theory of city size known as central place theory which we referred to in Chapter 1 (Christaller, 1933, 1966) and to which we must relate our extensions of this geometry. Just as we articulated a city in terms of a hierarchy of development and free space using the Sierpinski carpet model in Chapters 2 and 7, it is possible to generate a hierarchy of cities, beginning with a primate city as generator and then partitioning its hinterland or sphere of influence successively, generating a distribution of city sizes and frequencies from the largest to the smallest. In central place theory, the space of the largest city and its hinterland is first exhaustively partitioned into a series of equal and lesser-sized hinterlands, which in turn are subdivided into lower levels of hierarchy, thus generating a size distribution often referred to as the rank-size rule. From considerations relating to the optimal packing of hinterland shapes, the hexagonal hinterland area emerges, and in terms of these shapes, a nested set of hexagonal market areas is the result. Various size distributions can be generated depending upon the partitioning used, while overlapping hinterlands are also possible as we illustrated in Chapter 1.

To illustrate this idealized system, assume that the largest hinterland, which will be our starting point, has a linear measure L_0. Now let us define a scaling ratio ε_k which when applied to the original measure L, generates a measure of the size of a lower order hinterland L_k where k is the order or rank of the city and its hinterland in question:

$$L_k = L_0 \, \varepsilon_k. \tag{10.1}$$

Assume that the hinterland of the largest city associated with $k = 0$ is square, that is, its field area $U = L_0^2$, that each successive hinterland associated with the partitioning is also square, and that its subdivision ratio from level to level is given as r. Note that this ratio must be positive but less than 1, for it must yield a smaller measure L_k when applied to L_{k-1}, that is

$$L_k = L_{k-1}r. \tag{10.2}$$

Moreover, through recursion from L_0, equation (10.2) can be written as

$$L_k = L_0 r^k, \tag{10.3}$$

where it is now clear that $\varepsilon_k = r^k$ in equation (10.1).

Because the original hinterland is assumed to be square, the number of cities and their hinterlands generated by this process is given as

$$n_k = [(r^k) \, (r^k)]^{-1} = r^{-2k}, \tag{10.4}$$

and the area U_k of each city hinterland in this grid-based hierarchy is thus

$$U_k = L_k^2 = L_0 r^{2k} = L_0 n_k^{-1}. \tag{10.5}$$

A couple of examples illustrate the typical size distribution which can be generated. If we assume that the original area L_0 (= 1 unit of measure) is subdivided into four subspaces at the first level of hierarchy implying that $r = 1/2$, then the number of cities generated from (10.4) are 1, 4, 16, 64, 256, and so on, with their associated linear dimensions as 1, 1/2, 1/4, 1/8, 1/16 ... and their areas as 1, 1/4, 1/16, 1/64, 1/256 .... If the subdivision were 1/3 as in the Sierpinski carpet (see Chapter 2 or Chapter 7), then the frequency distribution would be 1, 9, 81, 729, 6561, and so on. Of course, it would be possible to generalize this process using a non-square space such as the hexagon and also a packing parameter which did not assume square subdivision, that is generalizing equation (10.4) as $n_k = r^{-\gamma k}$, where γ is a now parameter of the system in question. But these are details which we do not have time to pursue here, nor are they essential to our quest.

The most important assumption which we will make, however, relates to the populations which are associated with this system of generating cities. We will in fact assume that the population of each city in the hierarchy is generated within its space using a DLA-like process which assumes that population N_k scales with the linear size of its space L_k according to the fractal dimension D. Using this notation our classic scaling relation which we have previously specified in equations (2.32), (7.6) and (9.31) is

$$N_k = \varphi L_k^D, \tag{10.6}$$

where $1 < D < 2$. Then from equation (10.3) or (10.5)

$$N_k = \varphi L_0^D r^{Dk} = \varphi N_0 r^{Dk}. \tag{10.7}$$

where N_0 is the population of the primate city in the hierarchy. If we now note that r can be written as $1/z$ where z is the number of additional cities generated from one level of the hierarchy to the next, then

$$N_k = \varphi \, \frac{N_0}{z^{Dk}}. \tag{10.8}$$

Equation (10.8) can be considered as a generalized rank-size equation in which population size is solely a function of rank, assuming that the parameter D is constant. The only way, however, that we are able to generate a strict rank-size rule of the form $N_k = \varphi \, N_0/k^\tau$ from equation (10.8) is by assuming that the fractal dimension D varies with rank, that is that $D = (\log k)/k$. This implies that as city size increases, the fractal dimension also increases in value. In turn, this implies that the density parameter α would decrease in value with city size and this would appear to be mildly consistent with some empirical evidence (Clark, 1951; Mills, 1970; Mogridge, 1984), although the question remains ill-defined. In fact, although this analysis is highly suggestive of the way we might connect up central place theory to fractal geometry and to urban density functions, its implications are well beyond what we are able to pursue in this book and must await further sustained research. The analysis, however, is rich with implications for the way we might begin to fuse intra- and inter-urban theory, theories of what happens inside the city with those which seek to show how systems of cities develop. As such, it represents a major direction for future work in human geography and urban economics.

What we have begun to sketch here is a basis for a preliminary exploration of the relationship between population size and linear dimension over a system of cities. What we have not yet examined is the possibility that the fractal dimension might actually vary systematically over this size distribution for this is something we wish to first test. The city size distributions generated here like those we generated earlier within individual cities using the Sierpinski carpet model, are based on a top-down approach, and there are no implications for how cities might actually change their position within the hierarchy through growth or decline. We will, in fact, assume that the fractal scaling laws governing the population and its distribution within the individual city, can be extended in a straightforward way to a system of cities as we have already adopted in equations (10.6) to (10.8) above. If the traditional rank-size rule were an accurate portrayal of city size distribution, then this would imply that D would increase in value as cities grew, but we consider that these speculations are so uncertain and the models postulated no more than examples of the fractal approach, that we have confidence in proceeding by assuming the constancy of D.

Before we begin to show how our theoretical model might be tested on different systems of urban settlements, we need to note its relation to the concept of allometry which we alluded to in earlier chapters. Allometry, according to Gould (1966), is used "to designate the differences in proportions correlated with changes in absolute magnitude of the total organism or of the specific parts under investigation". More commonly, the term is used to describe scaling relations between two 'size' measures of an organism or system under study (Mark and Peuker, 1978). One relation linking perimeter length of an urban boundary to its area was stated in

Chapter 2 as equation (2.29) and used extensively in Chapter 6. In Chapter 9, the relation between population and the size of its urban field was also examined in equations (9.30) and (9.31). But a much stricter and more conventional view of the allometric relation between population and its actual area of occupation will be developed here. From equations (10.6) and (10.7), it is clear that the area occupied by the population – its development – must vary with the population itself assuming that the density of occupancy of the elemental unit is the same, regardless of city size. Thus $N_k \propto A_k$ where A_k is the occupied, developed or built-up area. This is the relation that we will also test in the sequel with a view to determining whether the city system displays positive or negative allometry, or even isometry. On this basis we might speculate as to whether cities truly grow into their third dimension or not.

A related theme in this chapter concerns the measurement of size and shape, area and density. In particular, we will make a central distinction between the concepts of the built-up urban area and the urban field, focussing upon the need to relate the particular measurement in question to the purpose of the analysis. It is already very clear to us from the literature on the measurement of urban density reviewed in Chapter 9 that conventional practice is confused, and our confidence in previous empirical estimates of allometric and other scaling relationships in urban studies is low. Another theme, but one which is of different import, involves the representation of spatial shape and area in computer models and information systems which are concerned with spatial manipulation, analysis and display. Thus our models which are based on describing size and shape, also have some more practical implications for the representation of digital data.

In this chapter then, we will work towards a consistent theory of urban growth and form in a system of urban settlements, combining allometric relationships and fractal geometries. We will illustrate our theory with data on the size, shape and spacing of urban settlements in two case studies: in the County of Norfolk in the English region of East Anglia, and then in the whole of the South East region of England where we will explore the extent to which the growth of the settlement pattern has been constrained by planning policies, specifically those instruments of early 20th century planning known as 'green belts'. We will introduce a standard data base for both case studies, briefly reviewing the principal means by which urban shapes and areas are represented through boundaries or 'envelopes'. We will then apply the various scaling relationships which we consider of major importance in linking size to shape through dimension, to the urban settlement system in Norfolk, validating the hypotheses which we will set out in the next section. We will then present a more refined but more speculative analysis using the same scaling relations, attempting to classify settlements according to their various dimensions with a view to determining whether some settlements have been affected by explicit planning policies in terms of their size and shape. In this way, we will conclude our introduction to the fractal city by showing how we might use the geometry presented here to inquire into the impact of ongoing planning policies and other forms of public decision-making.

10.2 Scaling Relations for City Size Distributions

The two basic measures of size which we will use are population and area. Our task will be to seek relationships between these variables, first by researching how these variables might best be defined, and second, by exploring how the scaling model of the previous section might be used to illuminate the postulated relations. In the rest of this chapter, we will explore these relations first using data from the pattern of urban settlement in the English County of Norfolk in the region of East Anglia, and then with a much wider set of the same data for the whole of South East England. Associated with the population N_k of any urban cluster k, there might be several definitions of area. Note that as each cluster is of a different size, and if these are ordered by population, then the index k, in fact, is consistent with rank-size.

We will use two distinctive measures of area here: first there is the occupied area called A_k which can loosely be defined as the built-up or developed area, and is likely to covary to an extent with population. Second, there is the urban field whose area U_k can be defined as the hinterland immediately associated with the greatest radial extent of the cluster (Hagerstrand, 1952). This may be the immediate circle of area within which growth has already taken place, or as in the theoretical model in the previous section, the square area defined by equation (10.5). There is also a fourth variable of interest which relates area A_k to field size U_k, and this is the urban envelope E_k defined as the length of the boundary or perimeter which marks the greatest extent of the built-up area, and which we used extensively in Chapters 6 and 7 in our early forays into the geometry of the fractal city. To provide some meaning to these concepts, we have illustrated their spatial definition using the example of the largest town from our data set, Norwich; these definitions are shown in Figure 10.1.

Figure 10.1(a) shows the built-up urban area whose extent A_k is indicated by the cross hatch, and it is this area that contains the population N_k. The urban field is shown in Figure 10.1(b), and this is the bounding circle based on the center of the cluster, marked by the maximum radius R_k which contains the whole cluster. The area of the cluster is given as $U_k = \pi R_k^2$ and $U_k > A_k$. The urban envelope is shown in Figure 10.1(c), its length E_k being a measure of both the size and the shape of the cluster. In Figure 10.1(d), the maximum spanning distance across the cluster – 'Feret's diameter' – was defined earlier in equation (5.12) (Kaye, 1989b); the length of this span is defined as F_k, and this will be used later in estimating and approximating the radius R_k. Note that in the sequel, we will use the radius R_k in preference to the linear measure L_k introduced earlier. We will examine two types of relationship between these variables, first relating population N_k to area A_k and to field radius R_k, second relating the length of the envelope E_k to these same variables. These types of relationship are central to allometry or 'relative size' relationships (Gould, 1966), and by relating size and length to area, this enables us to explore questions of density. In this way, we are able once again to relate our work to the mainstream literature on urban allometry (Dutton, 1973) which we have already introduced in Chapters 7 to 9 in the study of urban population density and form. Here, however, our

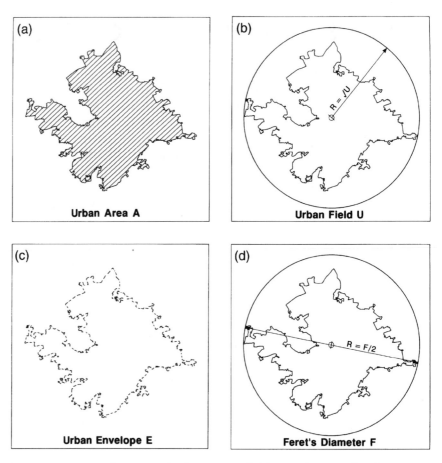

Figure 10.1. Definitions of urban area, field, envelope and radius.

use of allometric relations will be more conventional, with our emphasis on fitting such relations to sets of different sized objects – towns and cities in this case, in contrast to our previous use of these relations for examining changes in the size of the individual city.

The classic allometric relation we will begin with involves the relationship between population size N_k and occupied area A_k which we can write as

$$N_k = \gamma A_k^\beta = \gamma A_k^{\Delta/2}. \tag{10.9}$$

γ is a constant of proportionality and β is a scaling constant. In equation (10.9), we have also written β as $\Delta/2$ where Δ can be interpreted as a 'dimension' of the occupied area, scaling the radius R_k of such an area ($R_k = A_k^{1/2}$) to population. The use of this convention will become clear in the sequel when all the scaling parameters have been introduced. As we pointed out in Chapter 9, there is obviously a strong relationship between population and area, although the precise form of the scaling is problematic. Nordbeck (1965, 1971) suggests that the scaling constant β should be $3/2$ using the argument that population growth takes place in three dimensions; thus if $R_k = A_k^{1/2}$ is taken as the linear size of area, then $N_k =$

$\gamma R_k^3 = \gamma A_k^{3/2}$. This hypothesis is borne out in an analysis of the urban population of Sweden in 1960 and 1965 (Nordbeck, 1971). Results from urban density theory also suggest that as cities get bigger, their average density increases but the empirical evidence on this is mixed and is much complicated by the definitions of urban area used (see Muth, 1969). However, Woldenberg (1973) shows quite unequivocally that $\beta \approx 1$ from an analysis of two large population–area data sets for American cities.

In the case of the scaling model introduced earlier, it is clear that the area occupied by the population N_k varies as the population itself. This point was also made in equation (7.7) where the same analysis was applied to the individual city. For the growing fractal, the area of each occupied cell is assumed to be identical, say ε^2, thus the total urban area is $A_k = N_k \varepsilon^2$. In short, the population density $N_k/A_k = \varepsilon^{-2}$ is constant regardless of scale or the stage reached in the growth process. In summary then, we might expect the empirical relation between N_k and A_k to be of the simplest kind – perfect scaling – with both the theoretical model and much empirical evidence suggesting that $\beta \approx 1$ and $\Delta \approx 2$.

With respect to the urban field, the scaling between N_k and U_k is more complicated. As cities grow, their field becomes correspondingly larger, growing at a more than proportionate rate, and in the case of very large cities, the urban field is often considered to be global. This implies that as cities grow, their field density N_k/U_k always decreases. As in previous chapters, it is more appropriate to represent the field area U_k in terms of its radius $R_k = U_k^{1/2}$. Thus the field relationship can be stated as

$$N_k = \varphi R_k^D = \varphi U_k^{D/2}. \tag{10.10}$$

φ is a constant of proportionality and D is the scaling constant, the fractal dimension which will be less than 2 but always greater than 1 as can be seen from Figure 10.1(b). In terms of the idealized central place theory model of the previous section, equation (10.10) is equivalent to equation (10.6) and this is the basic scaling relation linking population to the size of its city which we used earlier in equations (2.32), (7.6) and (9.31).

Relationships between the length E_k of the bounding envelope of urban development and the area A_k and field radius R_k will also be explored here. It is important to note that the bounding envelope is not the perimeter of the cluster in that any undeveloped interior of the cluster is not detected by the envelope (see Figure 10.1(a) and (b)). In fact, the perimeter of a DLA cluster varies directly with its population as we indicated in Chapter 7 (see equation (7.7)). As the envelope defines the outer edge of the cluster, it is likely to be smoother and less circuitous than the perimeter, and this suggests that any measure of the fractal dimension of such a line is likely to be less than the fractal dimension of the cluster. In the case of the urban area A_k, we can relate the envelope to the assumed radius $R_k = A_k^{1/2}$ of occupied area, giving

$$E_k = \zeta A_k^\omega = \zeta A_k^{\delta/2}, \tag{10.11}$$

while for the field radius, a similar relation is postulated:

$$E_k = \nu R_k^{\check{D}}, \tag{10.12}$$

where ω, hence δ in equation (10.11) and $\check{D}$ in equation (10.12) can be regarded as 'dimensions' with ζ and v as constants of proportionality.

Before we summarize the relationships which we seek to validate empirically, it is worth noting the theoretical bounds within which our analysis will take place. It is clear that cities with a variety of forms of development from the linear to the compact circular are consistent with the theoretical model we outlined in the first section. In the case of the completely compact cluster, its occupied area and its field are coincident with $N_k = \gamma A_k = \varphi U_k \propto \pi R_k^2$ and with $\Delta = D = 2$. The growing zone at the edge of the cluster is the same as the perimeter, and this is defined as the derivative of N_k with respect to radius R_k, that is $dN_k/dR_k \propto \pi R_k$. The envelope is also the perimeter in this case with $E_k = \zeta A_k^{1/2} = v R_k \propto \pi R_k$ and $\delta = \check{D} = 1$. In the case where the cluster is linear $N_k = \gamma A_k^{1/2} = \varphi U_k^{1/2} \propto \pi R_k$ and $\Delta = D = 1$, while the derivative of N_k does not provide the formula for the perimeter, just the growing zone which is always a point of zero dimension, implying in this case that $\delta = \check{D} = 0$. In the case of a real urban cluster which does not completely fill its available space, area, perimeter and envelope can be approximated by space-filling lines which suggest that all the dimensions of significance – Δ, D, $\check{D}$, and δ – will be between 1 and 2. The only examples we are aware of where the dimensions of urban envelopes have been estimated are those we illustrated in Chapters 5 and 6 which yielded values between about 1.1 and 1.5, in contrast to those for the population–radius relations which from Table 7.1 lie between about 1.5 and 1.9.

Pulling all these threads together, we will hypothesize that the four dimensions associated with the four scaling relationships given in equations (10.9) to (10.12) should be ordered as $1 < \check{D} < \delta < D < \Delta$, where $\check{D}$, $\delta \approx 1.26$, $D \approx 1.71$ and $\Delta \approx 2$. The constants associated with these four relationships can be estimated from regressions of their log-linearized forms. We will refer to these relationships as being of allometric or DLA (diffusion-limited aggregation) type, involving independent variables of occupied area or urban field. The log-linearized forms of equations (10.9) to (10.12) are given as

$$\log N_k = \log \gamma + \beta \log A_k, \ (\Delta = 2\beta), \tag{10.13}$$

$$\log N_k = \log \varphi + D \log R_k, \tag{10.14}$$

$$\log E_k = \log \zeta + \omega \log A_k, \ (\delta = 2\omega), \tag{10.15}$$

$$\log E_k = \log v + \check{D} \log R_k. \tag{10.16}$$

Equations (10.13) to (10.16) will be those whose parameters will be estimated in the sequel and used to establish the consistency between the form of the urban settlement systems in Norfolk, and in South East England, and the theoretical allometric and DLA relationships outlined in this and the previous section.

10.3 The Representation of Urban Areas

We have already focussed upon some of the difficulties of measuring the relationship between the size and form of urban settlements. Early work on the size relations within settlement systems was necessarily restricted by the quality of the measures of the precise extent and population size of constituent areas. Naroll and von Bertalanffy (1956) attributed much of the variation in international urban–rural population ratios to differing national definitions of 'urbanity' and the differing areal extent of data collection units which together comprise urban areas. Newling (1966) encountered problems of the changing areal basis of data collection in his study of the evolution of intra-urban population density gradients over time. And as we have noted, Woldenberg (1973) obtained some quite radically different estimates of population–size relations in his cross-sectional study of the US settlement system, which depended upon his use of one or other of two atlases to source his urban area measurements. In the face of such vagaries and inconsistencies, it is scarcely surprising that the nature of the theoretical relationship between size and spatial form remains obscure. We have already begun to clarify some of these issues in earlier sections, and our empirical analysis which follows is designed to cast further light on these questions.

The causes of these discrepancies and sources of possible measurement errors are increasingly understood, and the routine innovation of digital databases holds the prospect of greater precision in the delineation of urban areas and monitoring of the areal impacts of change (Shepherd and Congdon, 1990). But nevertheless, there remains cause for concern that even in the data-rich environment of the 1990s, the effects of different measurements of areal units will go undetected in spatial analysis. Moreover, there exist acute definitional difficulties with respect to what is and what is not unambiguously 'urban', and the distance threshold beyond which outlying urban parcels should be classified as physically (and possibly, by extension, functionally) separate from main urban areas. Our own investigations in the examples used throughout this book using comparable boundary data recorded at different spatial scales, but based upon slightly different digitizing criteria, suggest that areal discrepancies of the order of 20% to 30% are likely to be quite common for most settlement sizes. Taken together, this makes it difficult to assess precisely how marginal increments in population lead to changed boundaries of urban forms through the process of accretion, and there is a clear need to develop stronger links between measurement and theory.

In this context however, all our data are represented in the theoretically more accurate vector mode. The data source used in both the Norfolk and South East England examples, is the Office of Population Census Statistics (OPCS) urban areas data base (OPCS, 1984) in which urban areas are defined as follows: land on which permanent structures are situated; transportation corridors (roads, railways and canals) which have built-up sites on one or both sides, or which link built-up sites which are less than 50 m apart; transportation features such as railway yards, motorway service areas, car parks as well as operational airfields and airports; mineral workings and quarries, and any area completely surrounded by built-up sites. The areas were identified using the 1:10,560 Ordnance Survey series in conjunction with Population Census Enumeration District (ED) base maps. These maps were used to ascertain which areas of urban land contained four or more EDs, and on this basis, these qualified as urban areas.

Population figures from EDs which had 50% or more of their population within an urban area were included in the population total for that area. Further general information and details of the treatment of small areas of population and discontiguous urban land can be found in OPCS (1984). These boundaries were then reduced to the 1:50,000 scale and computer digitized to an accuracy of 0.5 mm permitting inaccuracies of up to 250 m on the ground. Our first case study uses data for the County of Norfolk, our second for the 13 counties composing the standard region of South East England, both of which have been extracted from this source.

10.4 Initial Analysis of the Norfolk Settlement Pattern

The data comprise 86 distinct urban settlements from populations as small as 45 to the major county town of Norwich which has about 186,000 people. The pattern and form of these urban settlements are shown in Figure 10.2. We have already alluded to the difficulty of defining and adhering to definitions of urban land which are both unambiguous and appropriate to any specific task, and it is likely that the original decision by OPCS to include some of the smallest settlements was in practice an arbitrary one. We anticipate that the population and area of these smallest settlements would not closely correspond to any empirical regularities extant elsewhere in the data set, as a result of disproportionate errors in the measurement of their populations and bounding envelopes. Settlements whose form is dominated by transportation infrastructure are also likely to be 'unusual' in both geo-

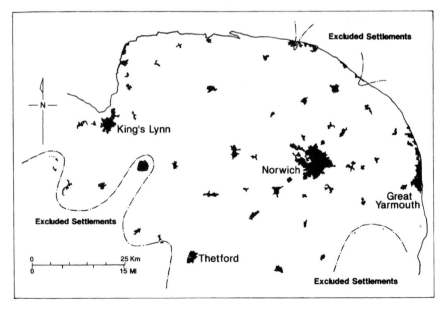

Figure 10.2.   The pattern of urban settlement in Norfolk.

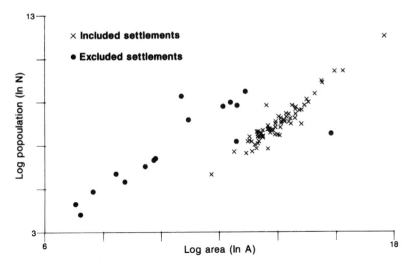

Figure 10.3. The population–area relation for the Norfolk settlement system.

metrical and population terms, with such settlements primarily, but not exclusively, small in size and scale.

Our theory posits that population and area covary in a systematic way, and thus our preliminary analysis began by assessing whether this was indeed the case. Figure 10.3 illustrates the relationship between population and urban area for the entire Norfolk settlement system. This figure depicts an unambiguous relationship across most of the range of settlement areas, although this relationship breaks down amongst the 15 smaller settlements. These settlements are shown in Figure 10.3 by the solid circles. Several related criteria were used for their exclusion: all 15 settlements are those which have less than 50 digitized pairs of coordinates defining their urban areas, thus making computation of their fractal dimensions unreliable using

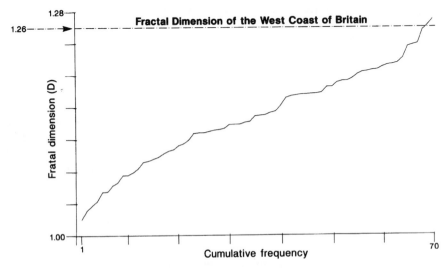

Figure 10.4. The cumulative distribution of fractal dimensions.

the Richardson (1961) 'walking dividers' method. These settlements were also amongst the smallest in terms of population and area, and are mainly located on the edge of the region. Some are cut by the regional boundary, hence form only parts of settlements, thus requiring their exclusion from the data set.

It is reasonable to anticipate this on *a priori* grounds since the form of small settlements is likely to be dominated by the transport network rather than by density–size relations. Although there is visual evidence to suggest that a different relationship holds for these smaller settlements, we nevertheless simply disregarded them in our subsequent analysis since our focus is upon the growth of settlements which might be unambiguously described as 'urban'. We can also note that the dominant population–area relation only appears to establish itself above a rough area threshold and thus suggests that this is a consequence of the dominant impact of transport infrastructure beneath this threshold. The single other settlement whose shape is unquestionably distorted by transport infrastructure is Marham Airfield. This 'settlement' has large area but low population and thus constitutes an outlier to the main relationship: as such it too was removed from the subsequent analysis which was based on the remaining 70 settlements.

We initially computed fractal dimensions for each of these 70 settlements. Calculation of such dimensions is now an established diagnostic for identifying the structure and character of digitized curves (Muller, 1986, 1987). The fractal dimensions of each individual settlement were first computed using the 'structured walk' algorithm based on Richardson's (1961) method of spanning each digitized curve at different scales and calculating their associated lengths. This algorithm which we first outlined in Chapter 5, entails measurement of the boundary envelope of each area at a range of successively finer scales, thus yielding correspondingly increased length measurements as more and more detail on the base curve is picked up. The range of scaled measurements obtained for each parcel was set at between half the mean digitizing intensity for that parcel and one-half of Feret's diameter, the maximum spanning distance between any two points on the digitized base curve (Kaye, 1989a), shown earlier in Figure 10.1(d) for Norwich. Regression analysis was then performed on the paired envelope–scale length points to establish whether the envelope is indeed fractal from the value of its (fractal) dimension. In Chapters 6 and 7, we found that the structured walk method is the most reliable and robust procedure for computing such dimensions.

Figure 10.4 illustrates the distribution of fractal dimensions for the subset of 70 settlements, in terms of their cumulative frequency, also indicating the fractal dimension of the west coast of Britain ($D \approx 1.26$) for comparison (Richardson, 1961). The mean value of our settlements is rather lower at 1.148 with a standard deviation of 0.059 and this would appear to reflect the less intricate nature of man-made boundaries. These dimensional measurements are not directly comparable with the other measurements reported below due to the fact that our subsequent analysis is based on computing fractal dimensions using the set of 70 settlements as observations of the changing size of the fractal city, not scale changes derived by aggregating curves for individual settlements.

However, the dimensions reported here are likely to have the same order of magnitude as those we will compute in the next sections for the envelope–area and envelope–field relations, and these, as we argued earlier, will be less than those which we will compute from the population–area and population–field relations. This is a consequence of the different ways in which the urban boundary is represented as an envelope rather than a perimeter, and strikes at the heart of the argument as to which 'development' should be included in analyses of urban density. The urban envelopes which make up the OPCS data base each include urban areas which nevertheless have zero population density through space occupied by industrial, commercial or educational land uses, by transport infrastructure or by public open space. By contrast, fine resolution raster representations of urban areas maintain 'holes' of unoccupied land within the outermost urban boundary. This explains why analysis of vectorized urban envelopes yields lower fractal dimensions, although the measurements will remain internally consistent between settlements. Moreover, when we examine the distribution of the individual fractal dimensions computed here, there is no real evidence of any spatial patterning, suggesting that boundary geometry alone is not a sufficiently strong criterion to enable classification of urban form.

10.5 Estimates of Allometric and Fractal Dimension in Norfolk

Central to the assessment of urban shape and form is the notion that the growth of urban areas is fuelled by the functions that each area performs in relation to the rest of the urban system. As we noted earlier, established thinking on the nature of urban densities has paid scant attention either to the juxtapositioning of settlements or to the relationship between population growth and boundary shape. However, the development of analogies between growth through diffusion-limited aggregation (DLA) and processes of urban development offers some prospect for understanding how urban forms and densities evolve within a clearly-specified pattern, whilst investigation of envelope–area relations may reveal how growth occurs at the margins of settlements. Thus both may be seen to complement those more established allometric approaches which reduce form to a simple area measure; hence our approach may contribute towards a more sensitive and comprehensive treatment of urban population size and form.

Our present empirical analysis is restricted in the degree to which the artifacts of urban growth can be clearly identified. We have already defined the set of urban area data $\{A_k\}$ through the digitized envelope data $\{E_k\}$ in the OPCS urban areas data set, and population $\{N_k\}$ is also a part of this data set. However, with respect to our DLA analogies, we do not have data on the field area U_k or the radius R_k ($= \sqrt{U}$). In the absence of information as to where the historical 'seed' of each settlement is likely to lie, we can calculate a crude approximation to its radius, using Feret's diameter (F_k) shown in Figure 10.1(d) for Norwich; this enables us to devise a rudimentary 'field' for each of the settlements, and a 'radius' R_k which is taken as $F_k/2$. A further problem is that the rate of urban growth is likely to be uneven at different places around our envelopes, and it remains to be seen whether any signals attributable to characteristic growth patterns might be detectable from aggregate measures of the structure and character of the entire set of boundaries. To provide some indication of the way the urban area data set $\{A_k\}$ relates to the calculated field areas $\{U_k\}$, Figure 10.5 illustrates that the relationship between built-up area and field across the range of settlement sizes is quite erratic, although there is a low positive correlation as might be expected. What Figure 10.5 does show, however, is that urban fields are everywhere much larger than urban areas, thus indicating that none of the settlements in the data set is compact, and that all must be irregular, possibly dendritic, and thus fractal in some sense.

In our empirical analysis of the Norfolk data set, we will examine the four sets of relations identified previously. These are: the population–urban area relation based on equation (10.9) in accordance with established allometric analysis; the population–radius relation based on equation (10.10) in analogy with urban forms generated by DLA; the envelope–area relation based on equation (10.11) which enables us to identify whether there is any detectable evidence that boundaries are characteristic of growth processes; and the envelope–radius relation based on equation (10.12) to identify whether the boundaries of the settlements can be related to fractal growth. Figure 10.6 illustrates each of these relations for the 70 settlements based on logarithmic transforms of the data as implied by equations (10.13) to (10.16), and we have fitted regression lines to the scatters shown in Figure 10.6. The results are shown in Table 10.1.

These results generally confirm our *a priori* expectations. The dimension Δ of the allometric population–urban area relationship is 2.085, close enough to our hypothesized value of 2 to suggest that density is more or less constant with settlement size. Our analysis was carried out for a smaller range of settlement size than previous analyses, and the implication of this

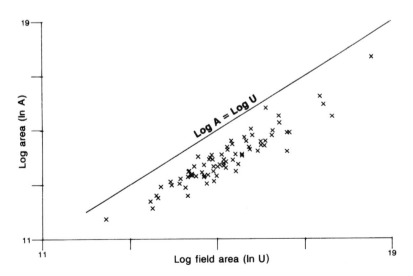

Figure 10.5. The relation between urban area and urban field.

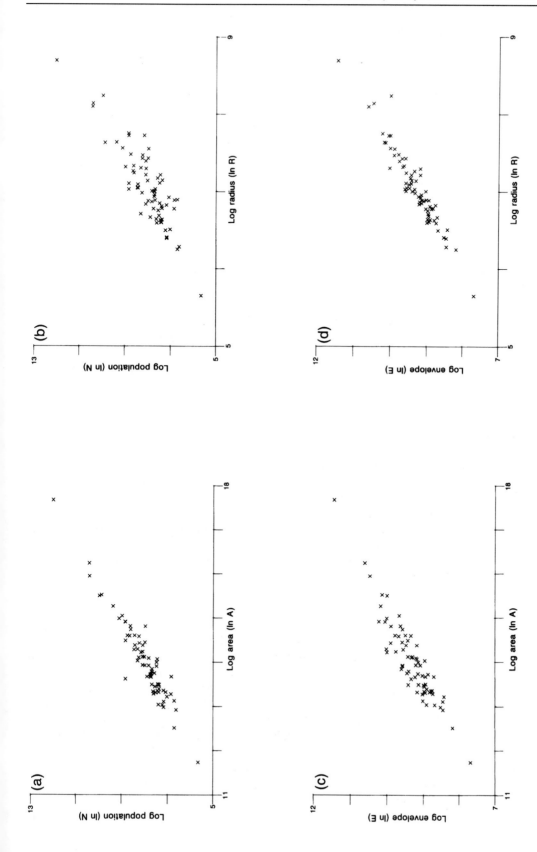

Figure 10.6. Allometric and DLA relations for the 70 urban settlements.

Table 10.1. Estimated dimensions for 70 urban settlements

Statistic	Population–area $\Delta \approx 2$	Population–radius $D \approx 1.7$	Envelope–area $\delta \approx 1.3$	Envelope–radius $\check{D} \approx 1.2$
Slope coefficient	1.043	1.738	0.613	1.152
r^2	90.3	76.1	85.7	91.5
Dimension	2.085	1.738	1.227	1.152

Note: in this and subsequent tables in this chapter, the r^2 statistic is the coefficient of determination which gives the percentage of the covariation explained by the relationship.

finding is to reinforce the simple scaling hypothesis based on an area–area relation found by Woldenberg (1973) and Dutton (1973), rather than the area–volume hypothesis argued by Nordbeck (1971). The r^2 statistic suggests a high global goodness-of-fit, although the high degree of potential leverage exerted by the three largest settlements is a potential source of uncertainty. The dimension estimated from the population–radius analysis is very close to that of a classic DLA structure with $D = 1.738$, and this is an encouraging result, particularly in view of the crudity of the approximation to settlement radius. However, the level of overall statistical fit is lower, with only 76% of the variance explained, and high potential leverage effects can again be detected from Figure 10.6(b). Both of the envelope analyses produced high fitting estimates of their dimensions with $\delta = 1.227$ and $\check{D} = 1.152$. It is interesting to note that the average dimension of the individual settlement dimensions computed by applying Richardson's (1961) method to the envelopes of each settlement discussed earlier, was 1.148, and this compares quite favorably with the value of $\check{D}$ which is its closest comparator.

Although these results are most encouraging, confirming our initial hypotheses and demonstrating, at least to us, the value of prior theoretical analysis in establishing such hypotheses, we are also concerned to identify whether or not our results can be disaggregated and generalized to subsets of settlements of different sizes and in different locations. Accordingly, we carried out two further sets of analyses on the data. First, the two largest outlying settlements representing Norwich and King's Lynn in the graphs of Figure 10.6 were removed from the data set, first individually and then together. In a statistical sense, this was carried out in order to verify that the high potential leverage effect of these observations was not exerted too strongly against the dominant trend in the data points. In a theoretical sense, this was also important in so far as all of the size and area relations confirm that these two settlements are the most important in the study area, and thus that they might exhibit different relations between density and form. The results of this analysis are shown in Table 10.2(a)–(c). The r^2 statistics shown there are consistently lower than the corresponding values in Table 10.1, indicating that the major settlements accord with the general trend in the rest of the data. With the exception of the envelope–urban area relation, all of the analyses which exclude Norwich and/or King's Lynn

Table 10.2. Estimated dimensions of the urban settlements excluding the largest towns

Statistic	Population–area $\Delta \approx 2$	Population–radius $D \approx 1.7$	Envelope–area $\delta \approx 1.3$	Envelope–radius $\check{D} \approx 1.2$
(a) Excluding Norwich				
Slope coefficient	1.024	1.603	0.624	1.125
r^2	87.4	71.7	82.6	89.9
Dimension	2.048	1.603	1.247	1.125
(b) Excluding King's Lynn				
Slope coefficient	1.038	1.698	0.616	1.146
r^2	89.4	74.5	84.7	90.9
Dimension	2.075	1.698	1.233	1.146
(c) Excluding Norwich and King's Lynn				
Slope coefficient	1.014	1.541	0.629	1.115
r^2	85.7	69.3	81.0	89.1
Dimension	2.029	1.541	1.259	1.115

produce lower fractal dimensions, suggesting that the global figure is boosted by the particularly tentacular structure of these two settlements.

The second set of disaggregate analyses considered the relations within several subsets of settlements defined *a priori*. Three classes were identified: two regions were delineated around the hinterlands of Norwich and King's Lynn, whilst a third was drawn to embrace all of the settlements along the coast. Settlements which did not clearly fall into any of these categories were omitted. This regionalization is shown in Figure 10.7. The rationale for the first two functional regionalizations was twofold: first, to identify whether the settlements *within* two more broadly-defined urban fields, approximating the sphere of influence of each of the two largest settlements, shared common characteristics; and, second, to make a first attempt at identifying common characteristics between them. The results shown in Table 10.3(a)–(c) suggest that although the Norwich region appears to generate higher dimensions than the King's Lynn area and the full set of 70 settlements (Table 10.1), no startling differences emerge.

The rationale for separating out the coastal region was to identify how the constraining impact of the sea restricts the shape and form of the settlements. All of the four dimensions – Δ, D, δ and $\check{D}$ – will fall in value if the space within which any settlement can grow is restricted. This is an obvious consequence of constraining the geometry and this effect has been clearly demonstrated by the simulated urban growth patterns using DLA presented in Chapter 8. In fact, this effect can be seen in Table 10.3 for the

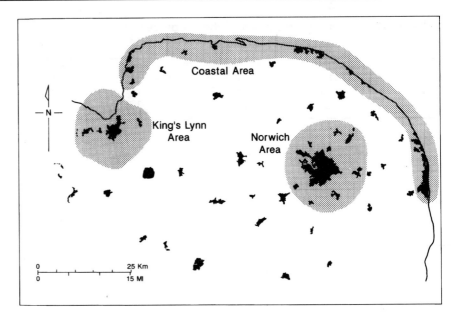

Figure 10.7. Regionalization of the Norfolk settlement pattern.

Table 10.3. Estimated dimensions for three regionalizations of the urban settlement pattern

Statistic	Population–area $\Delta \approx 2$	Population–radius $D \approx 1.7$	Envelope–area $\delta \approx 1.3$	Envelope–radius $\check{D} \approx 1.2$
(a) Norwich region				
Slope coefficient	1.040	1.980	0.601	1.300
r^2	96.3	83.9	86.5	97.2
Dimension	2.080	1.980	1.202	1.300
(b) King's Lynn region				
Slope coefficient	1.010	1.750	0.623	1.260
r^2	94.0	74.4	90.4	97.6
Dimension	2.020	1.750	1.246	1.260
(c) Coastal region				
Slope coefficient	1.010	1.630	0.634	1.030
r^2	75.4	72.3	90.8	87.9
Dimension	2.020	1.630	1.268	1.030

DLA dimension associated with the form of the Norfolk coastal settlements. The slightly higher dimension of the envelope–area relation reflects increased concentration of growth upon the inland portion of each of the settlements, although the dimension of the envelope–radius relation is lower, reflecting the restrictions upon the growth field. From Tables 10.2 and 10.3, it is also significant that it is the DLA dimension D which shows the greatest sensitivity to our regionalization varying from 1.603 to 1.980, in contrast to the other three dimensions where the range of variation is much narrower.

10.6 Constraining Urban Form Through Green Belts

A major problem which we have in one sense avoided, apart from in our theoretical simulations in Chapter 8, concerns the effect of geometric constraints on the city system; these involve the extent to which space is filled, the density of development, and the parameter values of the scaling relations. Clearly, *ceteris paribus*, the less space available, the lower the fractal dimension, and this is especially clear when we consider cities that develop in coastal regions or in areas where a major part of their hinterland or field is constrained from development. However, notwithstanding the problems of assessing these effects, we can turn these problems to our advantage in exploring the impact which known constraints might have had on the development of cities. A particularly important constraint on the form of the city system in Britain has been the impact of planning policies which have sought to constrain and inhibit development around major cities during the last 60 years. The most explicit policy instrument used to effect these policies has been the 'Green Belt', and using our scaling analysis, we will now attempt to measure this impact.

The idea of a 'Green Belt' of open land encircling a major city and embracing both small and medium-sized settlements located in the hinterland of a 'core' city is one of the main philosophical and practical underpinnings of the British Town and Country Planning system (Ravetz, 1980). As such, both the idea and the practice of Green Belts as a planning policy instrument have been debated and implemented most extensively in relation to the Metropolitan Green Belt (MGB), an annular tract of land now extending for between 25–40 km in width around the Greater London conurbation. Not unnaturally, given both its scale and importance and the nature of the development pressures upon it, the MGB has, over the years, been the subject of considerable research. Attention has been focussed on such matters as the distribution of land uses within it, its impact on land prices within urban areas, the function it performs in terms of human activities and who gains and who loses from its continued existence (Hall *et al.*, 1973; Munton, 1983; Elson, 1986; Evans, 1989).

Although the origins of the MGB (and indeed of Green Belts generally) can be traced to the Garden City Movement pioneered by Ebenezer Howard (1898, 1965) and the more conceptually based work of Raymond Unwin for the Greater London Regional Planning Committee (1927–36), the main postwar impetus for the implementation of a complete *cordon sanitaire* around London came from Sir Patrick Abercrombie's 1944 Greater London Plan (Abercrombie, 1945). This had the multiple aims of stopping the outward growth of London itself, preserving open land for agriculture and recreation and preventing the coalescence of towns contained within it. In 1946 the multiplicity of aims contained within Abercrombie's Green Belt proposals were accepted by central government, although the over-riding objective was, and continues to be, to contain the growth of urban areas (Elson, 1986). The broader policy was to be effected through the development plan provisions of the Town and Country Planning Act 1947, and its proposals were implemented with a certain enthusiasm by the seven county planning authorities surrounding London (Mandelker, 1962). The present extent of the MGB was basically established in the Structure Plans of the mid-1970s (SERPLAN, 1976) and although there were four main categories of Green Belt in operational terms (i.e. originally submitted and approved, approved extensions, extensions with interim approval and areas where Green Belt controls were operated with central government acceptance), to all intents and purposes broadly similar restraint measures became operative over the whole MGB area (Elson, 1986).

The context and the means for containing growth was set out in two circulars issued by the Ministry of Housing and Local Government in 1955 and 1957. The first established the objectives of Green Belt controls. These were: to check the further growth of a large built-up area; to prevent neighboring towns from merging into one another; and to preserve the special character of a town (MHLG, 1955). From this point on, therefore, the statutory support for operating development controls within Green Belts rested ultimately on concerns about urban form (and, working indirectly through form on urban functions) and not on the preservation of urban land for agriculture or recreation (Elson, 1986). The second circular (MHLG, 1957) introduced, among other things, the concept of 'white land' parcels between the town and the Green Belt which would not be developed in the contemporary plan period but which could be developed later without prejudice to the strategic and local objectives of a Green Belt. Thus whilst the objective of Green Belt planning was to be the control of urban form, there was also scope for some locally declared policy which might, in the longer term, result in a changed settlement pattern (Elson, 1986).

We might anticipate that this dual strategy of central direction about aims and local autonomy about means has had an impact upon the nature and form of settlements, yet this is a subject which has never yet been researched in anything but superficially descriptive terms. The only extensive studies of the impact of Green Belts upon urban form are those carried out by Elson and his colleagues, and these show that, for a very small number of settlements, the provision of 'white land' on the periphery of settlements was indeed a significant local determinant of change in the pattern of urban land uses (Elson, 1986). Clearly, however, there is a need for a more broadly based and systematic empirical analysis of the impact of physical planning controls such as Green Belts on the form of urban settlements.

In this chapter, we will make a first attempt to address this issue, using the Office of Population Censuses and Surveys (OPCS) urban areas database (OPCS, 1984) which we used for the Norfolk example. Using again the four scaling relations based on the allometric and fractal growth of a system of cities and given earlier in equations (10.9) to (10.12), we will consider the degree to which the form and density of urban settlements has been influenced by Green Belt designation, and we will attempt to discern apparent variations in the spatial manifestations of what is first and foremost a national development policy. To this end, we will develop a straightforward analysis of the physical extent of urban areas in South East England and attempt to interpret shapes and forms with respect to the presence or absence of direct Green Belt Policy on their development. We will also draw some general conclusions as to the prospects for devising more coherent settlement classification systems which incorporate quantitative measures of shape, dimension and density. Our analysis thus seeks to link our new measures of urban shape and form to the practical consequences of policies which seek to mold and constrain urban development. It is in this sense that our analysis is preliminary, and thus represents only a starting point for a broader research agenda.

In defining the impact of physical planning policies, particularly those involving restricting urban development using instruments such as Green Belts, it is essential to evaluate their effects by examining the extent to which the physical form of development departs from the 'norm'. In this quest, we need to define urban form not only in terms of the size of development but also in terms of its shape. This is important because policy instruments such as New Towns and Green Belts have often been implemented in terms of idealized forms such as those characterizing the British New Towns and Garden Cities. But a rigorous study of the size and shape of urban settlements, however, is in its infancy. Despite the emphasis in land use planning upon controlling and influencing the size and shape of towns, most work has hitherto been cast in a somewhat idealistic mold, reflecting a fascination with form and shape for its own sake rather than as a consequence of the processes and decisions which condition the spread of urban settlement.

We are now in a position to make clear our strategy for the analysis of the impacts of Green Belts on urban form using scaling relations. In essence, what we will do is compute these measures for different classes of settlement, each of which is classified according to the policy instruments which have been applied in the control of their development. As we do not have parameter values of the four relationships for a given baseline, we will also be concerned with estimating the parameters of this baseline. In short, we need to develop the following estimates of values associated with the entire data set of settlements, the values associated with those settlements which are unlikely to have been affected by Green Belt Policy, and then those that have been so affected. It is thus the differences in parameter values between these various sets that we will be focussing upon. Before we present these, it is worth noting that the analysis could be inconclusive if our estimates of the values associated with the control baseline – the set of settlements not affected by policy instruments – are not significant or imply a poor performance of the model relationships. The same might be true of other sets of estimates, and thus there is always the possibility that our assessment of impact will be dwarfed by poor performance or contradictory results from the various estimations.

Before we develop the analysis, we must explain briefly the data set which we will present in the same way as we did the Norfolk data. A subset of the OPCS data base pertaining to all of the urban areas in the South East England planning region is shown in Figure 10.8, and it is useful to compare this to Bracken's (1993) visualization illustrated in Plate 7.1. Although the largest urban areas (notably London) are broken down into boroughs and districts in the original data set, these administrative divisions have been removed for purposes of our analysis. What remains for these largest settlements is a number of large polygons which describe the bounding envelopes of contiguous urban development. We recognized at the outset of our analysis that our posited relationships between settlement populations and the shapes of urban areas are unlikely to hold over the entire range of settlement sizes. Specifically, the geometry of those smallest settlements which comprise a mere handful of inhabited buildings are likely to be dominated by the intersection of transport links, and thus will reflect the nature of the local and regional transport network rather than the intrinsic characteristics of growing settlements *per se*. As previously, the smallest settlements in the data base were thus deemed irrelevant in terms of both population size and areal extent, and thus removed.

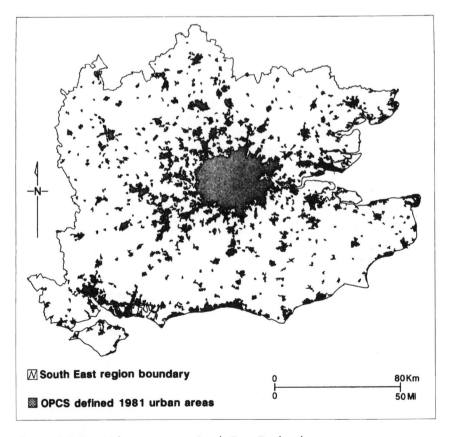

☒ **South East region boundary**

▨ **OPCS defined 1981 urban areas**

0   80 Km

0   50 MI

Figure 10.8. Urban areas in South East England.

Figure 10.9 illustrates this for the relationship between population and area in the whole digitized settlement system of the South East. There is a reasonably clear break in the dominant relationship amongst the very smallest settlements, and although we have estimated empirical relationships using the entire data set (Table 10.4), these results are neither statistically efficient nor theoretically coherent. In the bulk of our analysis, we have adopted the practice of excluding all settlements whose form was encoded using 15 or fewer digitized points, since such settlements were deemed too small for our specific purposes. This amounts to a fairly minor amendment of the Department of the Environment definition of 'urban' land use and reduced our data set from the original 701 observations to 686 settlements.

Since the historical center point of each urban area is not digitized as part of the data set, we have approximated the settlement radius as being equal to half of the spanning distance joining the two widest spaced digitized points on the settlement boundary (that is, half the Feret diameter). A further complication in the data set is that the population figures for the urban areas are not assigned to all of the individual parcels which together comprise a single named settlement. This means that exact population figures cannot be attributed to approximately 60 settlements. In practice, this was resolved by allocating population to physically split named settlements in direct proportion to the area of the constituent parcels. This does not affect the weighting of such parcels in our regressions, although if such named settlements are outliers to the main scatter of points, this does result in the appearance of a parallel scatter of points about the main trend in the data, as is clearly seen in Figure 10.9.

10.7 The Impact of Green Belts Using Scaling Relations

Figure 10.10(a)–(d) illustrates each of the logarithmically transformed scaling relations given in equations (10.13) to (10.16) for the 686 settlements

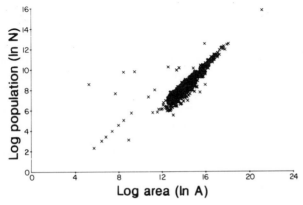

Figure 10.9. The population–area relation for the entire South East England settlement system.

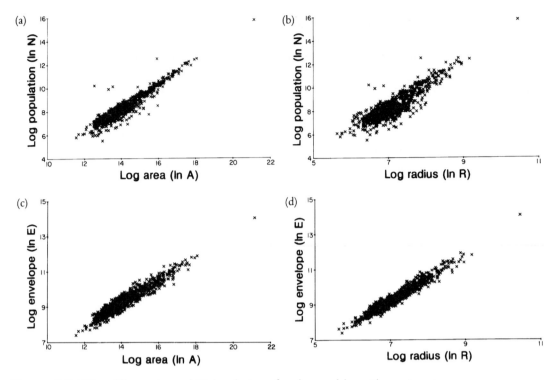

Figure 10.10. Allometric and DLA relations for the usable settlement system.

which were captured with 16 or more coordinate pairs. The results of fitting regressions to the scatters shown in Figure 10.10 are given in Table 10.4, and the 95% confidence intervals about the dimensional estimates are reproduced in diagrammatic form in Figure 10.11(a)–(d). In interpreting these results, we will also draw comparisons with our previous empirical study of the settlement structure of Norfolk. It was recognized at the outset that no region of England even approximates the isotropic surface on which, for example, central place theory is developed, although Norfolk was chosen for our first analysis because of the comparative homogeneity of its terrain and the absence of abnormal planning restrictions upon urban growth.

The results of our analyses of the South East England data generally conform to our *a priori* expectations. There are evident differences in the parameter and dimensional estimates between the analyses embracing all (701) settlements and those (686) settlements comprising 16 or more coordinate pairs. In the cases of the population–area, population–radius and envelope–area relations, these differences are statistically significant. The classic population–area relationship has dimension 2.046, which is quite close to (although, at conventional confidence levels, just above) the widely mooted value of 2. We made a similar finding in our Norfolk study, where a similar degree of overall statistical fit (r^2, corrected for degrees of freedom) was discerned. This general consistency between study areas is encouraging, particularly in view of the inclusion of London as an observation. London clearly constitutes a high potential leverage point in the analysis, although it is theoretically suspect to exclude the observation purely on grounds of

Table 10.4.   Estimated dimensions for settlements in the South East region[1]

Statistic	Population–area $\Delta \approx 2$	Population–radius $D \approx 1.7$	Envelope–area $\delta \approx 1.3$	Envelope–radius $\check{D} \approx 1.2$
(a) All settlements (701)				
Slope coefficient	0.808	1.569	0.619	1.258
r^2	75.6	70.8	93.1	95.6
Dimension	1.616	1.569	1.238	1.258
(b) All usable settlements (686)				
Slope coefficient	1.023	1.872	0.645	1.271
r^2	89.0	79.0	91.1	93.9
Dimension	2.046	1.872	1.290	1.271
(c) Outside the Green Belt (389)				
Slope coefficient	1.047	1.868	0.635	1.236
r^2	89.1	77.6	89.8	93.0
Dimension	2.093	1.868	1.271	1.236
(d) Partly in the Green Belt (15)				
Slope coefficient	1.083	1.890	0.719	1.317
r^2	94.1	84.3	92.9	92.4
Dimension	2.167	1.890	1.439	1.317
(e) Within the Green Belt (237)				
Slope coefficient	0.994	1.875	0.663	1.323
r^2	93.7	86.0	93.3	95.8
Dimension	1.988	1.875	1.326	1.323

[1]In Tables 10.4 to 10.6, data pertaining to settlements that lie within or astride the Oxford and the Southampton Green Belt boundaries have been omitted from the analyses. The number in parentheses after the analysis label is the number of settlements in that category.

size, since the impact of the Green Belt is likely to be most significant along and around the boundary of this area. In practice, however, this potential leverage transpires not to be against the trend in the rest of the data, and an exploratory analysis carried out with this dominant central settlement excluded, yielded results which were neither more consistent in substantive terms nor were significantly improved in terms of statistical fit.

The result of the population–radius regression yields a significantly higher dimension than was anticipated on *a priori* grounds, suggesting that settlements in the South East fill more of their urban fields than does the classic space-filling diffusion-limited aggregation model. This was not the case in any of our previous studies in which the DLA structure provided

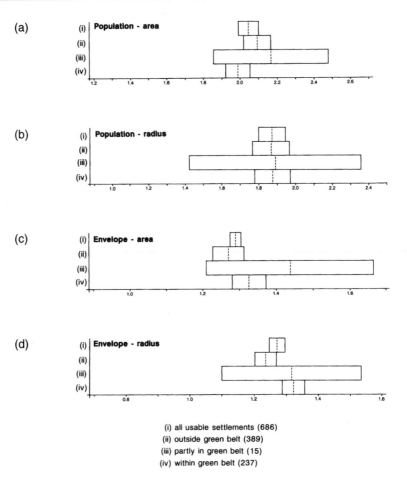

(i) all usable settlements (686)
(ii) outside green belt (389)
(iii) partly in green belt (15)
(iv) within green belt (237)

Figure 10.11. Confidence intervals about the dimension estimates (a) population–area; (b) population–radius; (c) envelope–area; (d) envelope–radius.

a plausible theoretical baseline model, and may be taken to imply that pressures conspire to encourage the development of more intricate settlement forms within the urban fields of settlements in this region. The purely geometrical analyses yield values consistent with our expectations, and high levels of statistical fit characterize these relationships.

As the next step, the South East settlements were divided into three groups according to their position relative to the Greater London Green Belt: those (237) settlements which lay entirely within it; those (389) that lay entirely outside of it; and those (15) that lay astride the boundary. The South East region includes two other Green Belts, centered upon Oxford and Southampton. For purposes of our present analyses, it was considered that these Green Belts were different in spatial and temporal terms from the London Green Belt, and thus settlements that lay either within or astride the Oxford and Southampton Green Belt boundaries were omitted from our analysis at this stage. This classification is shown in Figure 10.12. The results of separate regression analyses upon these subareas are shown in

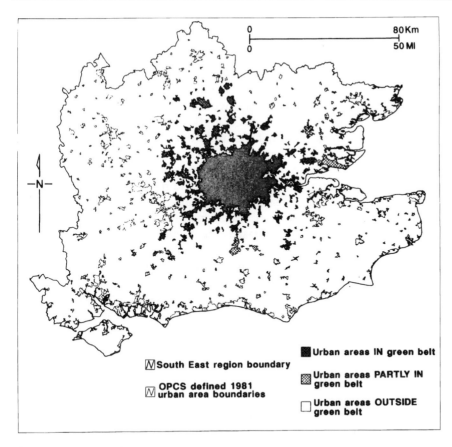

Figure 10.12.   The Green Belt status of settlements in South East England.

Table 10.4 and Figure 10.11. There is no significant difference between the estimated dimensions for the population–area relation, although the wider confidence intervals and the lower r^2 value for the extra-Green Belt settlements are indicative of greater variation in the effects of forces governing this relation. The lower estimated dimension for the population–area relation for the intra-Green Belt settlements is indicative of a disproportionately small increase in area amongst larger Green Belt settlements, although the global level of statistical fit is insufficient to confirm an unequivocal difference.

Neither are clear distinctions apparent when considering the population–radius relationship. Here, the estimated dimension and the extent of the confidence limits are remarkably similar for all of the settlement classes, although the modified r^2 statistic suggests greater heterogeneity amongst the extra-Green Belt settlements. Regarding the envelope–area relation, there is very limited evidence to suggest that the larger settlements which straddle the Green Belt boundary exhibit disproportionate increases in boundary length, and this might be indicative of contortions in urban form consequent upon differential planning restrictions. However, largely because of the small number of observations, no statistically significant differences are apparent. Significant differences do, however, exist, between the envelope–radius relations for extra- versus intra-Green Belt settlements.

The intra-Green Belt dimensional estimate is higher, suggesting that these settlements are more circular and compact than those outside.

These, then, are our preliminary attempts to utilize detailed vectorized boundary data in order to gauge the general spatial impact of an important component of spatial policy. Of course, this discussion presumes that settlement shapes in South East England would be free to evolve in an unconstrained manner in the absence of Green Belt planning policy. The spirit of our approach is to assume that the multitude of other factors which conspire to mold urban form (terrain, fluvial features, land ownership patterns, etc.) do not obscure the central impact of this strict planning control. One of the most obvious and important confounding influences is that of the coast, which clearly has constrained the shape, form and density of many settlements in our study region. Consequently, a separate set of analyses were carried out in which the coastal settlements illustrated in Figure 10.13 were excluded. The results are presented in Table 10.5, and show that there exist some minor differences in dimensional estimates and confidence intervals and that the previously significant difference between the 'partly in' and 'outside' dimensional estimates for the envelope–area relation disappears. The results nevertheless show the same broad relationships as identified in Table 10.4, and the maintenance of the population–radius differ-

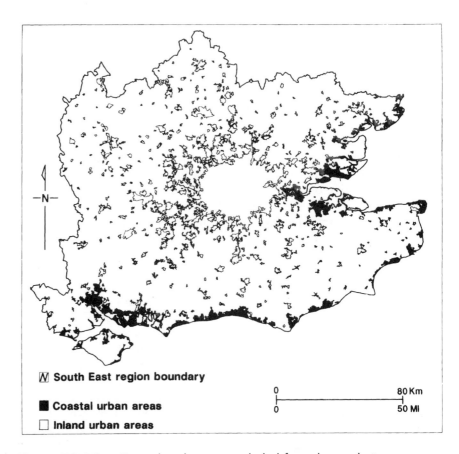

Figure 10.13. Coastal settlements excluded from the analysis.

Table 10.5. Estimated dimensions for settlements in the South East region excluding coastal settlements

Statistic	Population–area $\Delta \approx 2$	Population–radius $D \approx 1.7$	Envelope–area $\delta \approx 1.3$	Envelope–radius $\check{D} \approx 1.2$
(a) All usable settlements (592)				
Slope coefficient	0.998	1.836	0.645	1.289
r^2	88.0	77.6	90.3	93.9
Dimension	1.996	1.836	1.290	1.289
(b) Outside the Green Belt				
Slope coefficient	0.996	1.744	0.628	1.250
r^2	84.4	69.8	86.1	92.3
Dimension	1.992	1.744	1.256	1.250
(c) Partly in the Green Belt (8)				
Slope coefficient	1.005	2.270	0.650	1.486
r^2	96.5	93.9	92.6	92.6
Dimension	2.010	2.270	1.300	1.486
(d) Within the Green Belt (222)				
Slope coefficient	0.997	1.903	0.661	1.323
r^2	94.2	87.2	94.0	95.8
Dimension	1.995	1.903	1.321	1.323

ences suggests that the distorting impact of the sea is less than that generated by Green Belt planning policy.

In a final series of analyses, we have begun to investigate whether our empirical settlement relations vary between County Planning Authorities. It is conceivable that, over half a century, different County Planning Authorities have evolved consistently different interpretations of Green Belt Policy. Our four relations were thus estimated for each of the 13 county divisions within the South East Region (see Figure 10.14), although the small number of usable observations for a few of these counties leads to quite wide confidence intervals. In the case of Greater London, the four relations were estimated for each of 36 administrative divisions of the area, and so these results are not strictly comparable with those of the other counties. The results of this county-based analysis are reproduced in Table 10.6 and Figure 10.15. There are no evident significant differences amongst the population–area and population–radius results, suggesting that population pressures across different counties have not had the effect of distorting regional population density norms.

However, there is evidence that the settlement geometry differs between

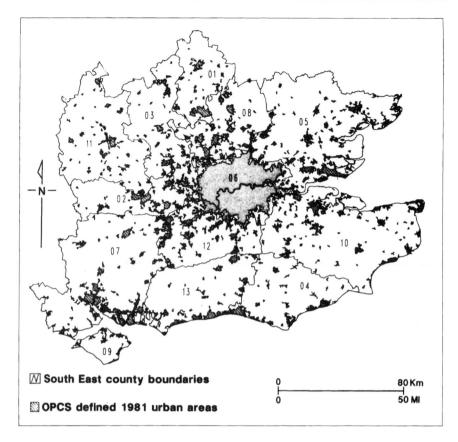

Figure 10.14. County divisions in South East England.

individual counties. First, the envelope–area relation suggests that bounding envelopes are significantly shorter for a given settlement area in Oxfordshire and Hertfordshire than in any of Kent, Surrey, Greater London and (for the case of Oxfordshire only) Berkshire. The envelope–area relations for these two counties are also significantly smaller than the estimates derived from the complete set of (686) settlements (Table 10.4). This can be seen as indicative that growth has been contained within more compact areas in these two counties. The envelope–radius relation for Oxfordshire also exhibits a significantly lower dimensional estimate than for the set of all settlements and than for the individual counties of Berkshire, Essex, Hertfordshire, Kent, Surrey and Greater London, suggesting that growth in Oxfordshire has been contained within more compact areas than has been the case in these other counties. A significant difference in the envelope–area relation also exists between Buckinghamshire and Surrey.

10.8 An Unfinished Agenda

So far we have identified statistical differences between the various sub-groupings of settlements based on the implementation of Green Belt

Table 10.6 Estimated dimensions for the County-based settlement analysis

Statistic	Population–area $\Delta \approx 2$	Population–radius $D \approx 1.7$	Envelope–area $\delta \approx 1.3$	Envelope–radius $\check{D} \approx 1.2$
(a) Bedfordshire (33)				
Slope coefficient	0.854	1.564	0.622	1.208
r^2	64.3	57.7	93.7	95.2
Dimension	1.709	1.564	1.244	1.208
(b) Berkshire (41)				
Slope coefficient	1.027	1.908	0.663	1.272
r^2	95.0	90.3	94.7	96.0
Dimension	2.055	1.908	1.327	1.272
(c) Buckinghamshire (51)				
Slope coefficient	0.995	1.733	0.644	1.205
r^2	96.1	87.4	90.6	95.2
Dimension	1.989	1.733	1.289	1.205
(d) East Sussex (29)				
Slope coefficient	1.150	1.971	0.595	1.187
r^2	94.8	72.8	84.8	89.5
Dimension	2.300	1.971	1.190	1.187
(e) Essex (87)				
Slope coefficient	1.046	1.891	0.648	1.277
r^2	91.2	78.5	91.7	93.9
Dimension	2.092	1.891	1.296	1.277
(f) Greater London (42)				
Slope coefficient	1.011	1.993	0.683	1.376
r^2	98.4	94.7	96.4	96.9
Dimension	2.022	1.993	1.367	1.376
(g) Hampshire (96)				
Slope coefficient	1.072	1.986	0.629	1.269
r^2	84.1	73.5	89.7	93.1
Dimension	2.144	1.986	1.258	1.269
(h) Hertfordshire (40)				
Slope coefficient	1.040	2.192	0.577	1.311
r^2	97.5	87.0	90.6	94.4
Dimension	2.079	2.192	1.153	1.311

Table 10.6. Continued

Statistic	Population–area $\Delta \approx 2$	Population–radius $D \approx 1.7$	Envelope–area $\delta \approx 1.3$	Envelope–radius $\check{D} \approx 1.2$
(i) Isle of Wight (13)				
Slope coefficient	1.097	1.643	0.637	1.053
r^2	90.7	66.5	86.8	79.4
Dimension	2.194	1.643	1.273	1.053
(j) Kent (93)				
Slope coefficient	0.995	1.759	0.694	1.343
r^2	85.4	72.5	90.5	92.4
Dimension	1.990	1.759	1.388	1.343
(k) Oxfordshire (56)				
Slope coefficient	0.931	1.748	0.530	1.089
r^2	78.1	69.1	84.8	90.3
Dimension	1.861	1.748	1.060	1.089
(l) Surrey (40)				
Slope coefficient	0.965	1.756	0.705	1.389
r^2	93.7	81.7	93.1	95.5
Dimension	1.929	1.756	1.410	1.389
(m) West Sussex (46)				
Slope coefficient	1.124	1.914	0.644	1.202
r^2	90.5	77.7	90.2	93.5
Dimension	2.248	1.914	1.287	1.202

policies, geometrical constraints such as those posed by the coastline, and administrative differences in the operation of planning policies, but we have not commented on the substantive differences which our analysis has revealed. In *a priori* terms, we might expect that where Green Belt Policy is rigidly enforced, this would constrain the form of settlement and development, and in turn would make the boundaries of such settlement more irregular in contrast to development not so constrained. However, such constraints also imply that the amount of space in the field about such settlements would be reduced by Green Belt Policy. This implies that the value of D associated with the population–field relation would be less than that for the unconstrained growth, while the value of $\check{D}$ for the constrained case would be greater than for the unconstrained case. In fact, these hypothesized values are borne out in Table 10.4, although the variance in the parameters of the Green Belt affected settlements is much greater than the unconstrained set of settlements. In the case of the population–area relation,

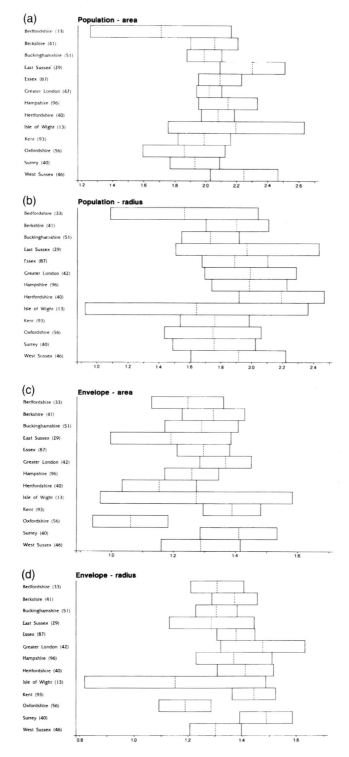

Figure 10.15. Confidence intervals for the county-based dimension estimates (a) population–area; (b) population–radius; (c) envelope–area; (d) envelope–radius.

the parameter of the constrained case is just less than 2, while for the unconstrained it is a little greater than 2. The same degree of difference is borne out in the envelope–area parameter values. In the case of the county-based analysis, there is very wide variation between the purely geometrical dimensions, whereas population-based relations are more stable across counties. This suggests the paramount importance of form in the implementation of planning policy. What is clear is that it is geometrical relations which exhibit the greatest diversity, and that such relations should be incorporated into classifications of settlements *vis-à-vis* planning policy. More detailed interpretations are possible, but these must await further research and analysis and more meaningful classifications of settlements with respect to both morphology and planning policy.

In this chapter, we have been content simply to develop descriptive measures of settlement form based on standard methods of scaling and dimensionality which underpin the study of morphology, through allometry and fractal geometry. We have not implied, in any sense, that settlement forms which are characterized by particular dimensions indicating their density and space-filling properties, provide any indicator of their optimality or efficiency. In fact, one of the most controversial issues in the study of urban form has been over questions of whether very different forms such as linear versus concentric, high versus low density, radial versus grid, are more optimal than one another. For example, from the point of view of transport accessibility, indices can be derived which show that these various forms all embody some ideal attributes of such accessibility. Questions of optimal urban form from the point of view of energy use also provide contradictory conclusions depending upon what measures are constructed. Moreover in this context, it could be argued that Green Belt Policy has both increased the journey to work at a cost but increased access to the countryside as a benefit, and so on and so forth. In future studies, we might address these issues, but we feel that at this point that we have at least provided a rich source of suggestions which might condition future research, which involves a reworking and extension of the ideas presented here.

Conclusions

Insofar as the statements of geometry speak about reality, they are not certain, and insofar as they are certain, they do not speak about reality. (Einstein, 1921, p. 3.)

Fractal geometry has emerged in direct response to the need for better mathematical descriptions of reality, and there is little doubt that it provides a powerful tool for interpreting and rendering natural systems. Yet in its wake has come, once again, the realization that all knowledge is contingent upon its context in time and space, that good theory is relative to what we already have and have had before, thus reminding us of Einstein's (1921) thoughts on the limitations of any geometry, indeed of all mathematics. Although extending our abilities to model both natural and artificial systems, fractals impress even further upon us the inherent complexity and uncertainty of the world we live in. In this sense, one kind of uncertainty – that involving the inapplicability of Euclidean geometry to many real systems – has been replaced with another – a more appropriate geometry for simulating reality, but one which is based on the notion that reality itself has infinite complexity in the geometric sense.

In this conclusion, we will attempt to pull the diverse threads which we have woven in this book together, and suggest directions in which the application of fractal geometry to cities as well as the theory of the fractal city might develop. Throughout, we have made many suggestions and identified many problems, all of these being worthy of further research, and we will not attempt to list these again. What we will do, is summarize the theory as it has emerged here, thus providing readers with both a sense of closure as well as some directions in which we feel this work should be taken further. In one sense, we can see this book in two parts: first in the early chapters, we presented the rudiments of fractal geometry and mildly suggested ways in which it might pertain to the physical form or morphology of cities. In the second part, from Chapter 5 onwards, we argued that the city itself is fractal and the new geometry the obvious medium for its measurement and simulation. In this second part, we also drew a major distinction between fractals as applied to single cities and to systems of cities, to intra-urban and to inter-urban spatial structure. But our exposition has been mainly from the standpoint of fractals as they are applicable to cities, and not the other way around. Perhaps it is time to change and rework the edifice of urban spatial theory, noting the ways in which fractals arise naturally and spontaneously, once we now have this new geometry in place. This has not been our quest here, but doubtless in time, the map will be completed in this way by others.

We are now able to provide a reasonably coherent summary of the ways in which fractal geometry is applicable to cities in general, urban growth and form in particular, but before we do so, a word about dimension. The concepts of Euclidean dimension are so deeply ingrained that we use them and will continue to do so as a shorthand to describe the magnitude and complexity of many systems of interest. For example, notwithstanding the fact that we now know that the dimension of any real system is fractional, we still refer to it as existing in n dimensions where n is an integer (usually the integral part of the fractal dimension). This is important here in that we can articulate cities as having properties that can still be measured as points, lines, areas and volumes, from zero to three dimensions, or even beyond if our geometry is one that results from urban processes which can be visualized in mathematical space. However, in this context, most of our ideas are based on conceiving of the city as sets of lines and areas, and thus our geometry is based upon one and two dimensions, not zero or three, although there are arguments which suggest that cities might be treated as points or volumes, thus composing fruitful extensions to the new geometry.

The way we have represented the geometry of the city has been central to our analysis. In essence, cities are conceived as filling two-dimensional space, as sets of connected points and lines which form areas, less than the entire space in which they might exist but more than simply the straight line; their fractal dimensions must therefore fall between one and two. It was only in Chapter 7 that we began to treat cities in this way for we first introduced a simplification to the geometry, approximating areas as boundaries which we dealt with in Chapters 5 and 6. In short, we proposed that a growth model for the city based on diffusion-limited aggregation (DLA) with a dimension $D \approx 1.71$, represents an idealized model of the way in which urban space is filled, while a simplified form for the boundary of the space filled was based on the Koch curve with a dimension $D \approx 1.26$. We did not provide a rigorous link between DLA and the Koch curve, but we did present sufficient examples to show that the dimensions of idealized and real boundaries are less in value than those for the entire cities from which they are formed.

In developing fractal geometry, we introduced two methods for deriving dimensions, the first based on changing the scale over which an object is measured, the second based on changing its size. We mainly used the first method for urban boundaries although it can be used for areas (Batty and Xie, 1994), whereas the second method is appropriate to systems where we can grow the city into the space which it fills. In another sense, our distinction between boundaries and areas filled is one between treating the city in static as opposed to dynamic terms, the Koch model being a static model of the way scale is varied, the DLA model being a dynamic one where the object is grown by varying its size. The relations between the object, the city, and scale and size are generally the same in that population N, measured by the number of elements composing the urban boundary or space filled, is related to scale r or size R through power laws involving the fractal dimension D. All subsequent analysis flows from these premises.

The critical relations for boundaries relate number of elements and their length to scale but there are few substantive implications for urban theory.

For growing cities, however, the link to urban theory is much stronger and more suggestive. Population as a function of linear size is easily generalizable to area which is at the basis of allometry, the study of relative size, while once area is invoked, density can be defined. This relates the entire analysis to mainstream urban economics where classic density profiles for cities are outcomes of diverse market clearing processes based on the conventional micro-economic behavior of the land market. In short, the key relations for the city which involve fractal dimension, relate population and its density to linear size and area, these relations being structured in incremental or cumulative form. Moreover, we showed in Chapter 9 that these relations appear to have greater rationale than those used traditionally, and what is more, that the whole approach shows how careful one must be in defining and measuring densities. One conclusion is that much of the work on urban density theory and its applications over the last 40 years should be reworked in the light of these developments.

There are many extensions to this geometry which we have pondered since we began this work. The obvious one which we have explored in part elsewhere, involves growing cities based on more than one seed or center, that is moving from a monocentric to a multicentric context. We explored the influence of two cities planted from separate seeds growing towards one another, thus forming a larger urban aggregate in terms of the consequent mixing of dimensions (Fotheringham, Batty and Longley, 1989), but we barely touched the surface of these ideas, and there is all still to be done. We have also begun to explore DLA in three dimensions, and to speculate on what a three-dimensional urban fractal might be like, but so far, we have not had the resources to pursue this line of attack to any conclusion. We have explored many modifications to the growth processes in DLA-like models which give rise to different urban forms, hence fractal dimensions, we have mixed processes and dimensions, and we have considered ways in which our growth models might incorporate reversibility. However, we have but scratched the tip of an iceberg, and to extract even the smallest kernel of knowledge which will advance our understanding of urban form, there is an enormous research program to initiate.

Extending fractal geometry to systems of cities is comparatively straightforward. Hints have been provided in Chapters 1 and 10, but a thorough analysis is yet to be attempted. We have shown how the central place hierarchy is fractal as evidenced by the rank-size distribution, and we have speculated that population densities must fall, and fractal dimensions increase as cities move up their hierarchy. But we have not shown how this possibility is consistent with the growth of the single city and its size; for the analysis of a single growing city implies nothing about the way cities might grow and compete within a hierarchy. In this book, our analysis has been largely confined to the single city, to intra-urban spatial structure, and extensions to systems of cities must therefore be high on any research agenda.

We began this book by examining visual perceptions of urban form, the traditional starting point for understanding the city. Indeed, our initial forays into the geometry of cities were in terms of how we might render their form through data and models so that we might generate more realistic and more communicable pictures using computer graphics. This somewhat serendipitous approach (which incidentally has been largely responsible for the general awakening of interest in fractals) did, however, introduce the idea that computers are laboratories for visualizing urban form, with great potential to enhance our understanding as well as to communicate complex ideas in manageable form. Throughout, we have been intent upon developing computer models which can ultimately be used, in such laboratory settings, to visualize different urban forms, with very different degrees of realism and prospects for realization. Now we have come to the end, we must admit that our models are still highly simplistic, yet do contain the rudiments of reasonable explanation, particularly those which we examined in Chapter 8.

The question some will ask is whether or not these ideas have any relevance for real policy making and planning. The answer we must give is, of course, contingent upon context, but we would argue that these ideas are as relevant in thinking about current urban problems such as energy, transportation, spatial polarization and segregation, planning control and so on as those currently advocated. But they are certainly less accessible, although our quest has been to make them a little more so and computer graphics is central to this. What fractal geometry does establish is that cities like most other real systems manifest a myriad of infinite complexity and this must change our responses to urban planning which have hitherto been simplistic and unrealistic, to say the least. Barnsley (1988a) who we quoted at the beginning of this book, says that "Fractal geometry will make you see everything differently", but it also changes our perceptions concerning the certainty of the reality and how we might manipulate it. There is now renewed hope that we might be able to forge a more conclusive link between the physical form of cities and the various social, economic and institutional processes that are central to their functioning.

Bibliography

Abercrombie, P. (1945) *Greater London Plan 1944*, HMSO, London.

Ajo, R. (1944) *Tampereen Liikennealue*, Tutkimuksia XIII, Kansantaloudellisia, Helsinki, Finland.

Alexander, C. (1964) *Notes on the Synthesis of Form*, Harvard University Press, Cambridge, MA.

Alexander, C. (1965) A city is not a tree, *Architectural Forum*, **122** (1), 58–61 and (2), 58–62.

Alexander, C. (1979) *The Timeless Way of Building*, Oxford University Press, New York.

Alexander, C., Ishiwaka, S., Silverstein, M., Jacobson, M., Fiksdahl-King, I. and Angel, S. (1977) *A Pattern Language: Towns, Buildings, Construction*, Oxford University Press, New York.

Allen, P. M. (1982) Evolution, modelling and design in a complex world, *Environment and Planning B*, **9**, 95–111.

Alonso, W. (1964) *Location and Land Use: Toward a General Theory Land Rent*, Harvard University Press, Cambridge, MA.

Anas, A. (1981) The estimation of multinomial logit models of joint location and travel mode choice from aggregated data, *Journal of Regional Science*, **21**, 223–242.

Anas, A. (1982) *Residential Location Markets and Urban Transportation: Economic Theory, Econometrics and Policy Analysis with Discrete Choice Models*, Academic Press, New York.

Anas, A. (1983) Discrete choice theory, information theory and the multinomial logit and gravity models, *Transportation Research B*, **17**, 13–23.

Angel, S. and Hyman, G. M. (1976) *Urban Fields: A Geometry of Movement for Regional Science*, Pion Press, London.

Aono, M. and Kunii, T. L. (1984) Botanical tree image generation, *IEEE Computer Graphics and Applications*, **4**, 10–33.

Arlinghaus, S. L. (1985) Fractals take a central place, *Geografiska Annaler*, **67B**, 83–88.

Arlinghaus, S. L. and Nysteun, J. D. (1990) Geometry of boundary exchanges, *The Geographical Review*, **80**, 21–31.

Arnheim, R. (1968) Gestalt psychology and artistic form, in L. L. Whyte (Editor) *Aspects of Form*, Lund Humphries, London, pp. 196–208.

Bacon, E. N. (1967) *Design of Cities*, The Viking Press, New York.

Ball, R. C. (1986) DLA in the real world, in H. E. Stanley and N. Ostrowsky (Editors) *On Growth and Form: Fractal and Non-Fractal Patterns in Physics*, Martinus-Nijhoff Publishers, Dordrecht, pp. 69–78.

Barnsley, M. F. (1988a) *Fractals Everywhere*, Academic Press, San Diego, CA.

Barnsley, M. F. (1988b) Fractal modelling of real world images, in H.-O. Peitgen and D. Saupe (Editors) *The Science of Fractal Images*, Springer-Verlag, New York, pp. 219–242.

Barnsley, M. F. and Demko, S. G. (1985) Iterated function schemes and the global construction of fractals, *Proceedings of the Royal Society A*, **399**, 243–275.

Barnsley, M. and Hurd, L. (1993) *Fractal Image Compression*, A. K. Peters, New York.

Barnsley, M. F. and Sloan, A. D. (1988) A better way to compress images, *Byte*, **13**, 215–223.

Batty, M. (1974) Spatial entropy, *Geographical Analysis*, **6**, 1–31.

Batty, M. (1976) *Urban Modelling: Algorithms, Calibrations, Predictions*, Cambridge University Press, Cambridge, UK.

Batty, M. (1991) Cities as fractals: simulating growth and form, in T. Crilly, R. A. Earnshaw and H. Jones (Editors) *Fractals and Chaos*, Springer-Verlag, New York, pp. 41–69.

Batty, M. (1992) Physical phenomena, *Geographical Magazine*, **64** (7), 35–37.

Batty, M. and Longley, P. A. (1987) Urban shapes as fractals, *Area*, **19**, 215–221.

Batty, M. and March, L. (1976) The method of residues in urban modelling, *Environment and Planning A*, **8**, 189–214.

Batty, M. and Sikdar, P. K. (1982) Spatial aggregation in gravity models: 2. One-dimensional population density models, *Environment and Planning A*, **14**, 525–553.

Batty, M. and Xie, Y. (1994) Preliminary evidence for a theory of the fractal city, unpublished paper, National Center for Geographic Information and Analysis, State University of New York, Buffalo, NY.

Beckmann, M. J. (1969) On the distribution of urban rent and residential density, *Journal of Economic Theory*, **1**, 60–67.

Ben Akiva, M. and Lerman, S. R. (1985) *Discrete Choice Analysis: Applications to Travel Demand*, The MIT Press, Cambridge, MA.

Benevolo, L. (1980) *The History of the City*, The MIT Press, Cambridge, MA.

Benguigui, L. and Daoud, M. (1991) Is the suburban railway system a fractal? *Geographical Analysis*, **23**, 362–368.

Berry, B. J. L. (1964) Cities as systems within systems of cities, in J. Freidmann and W. Alonso (Editors) *Regional Planning and Development: A Reader*, The MIT Press, Cambridge, MA, pp. 116–137.

Berry, B. J. L. and Horton, F. E. (Editors) (1970) *Geographic Perspectives on Urban Systems*, Prentice-Hall, Englewood Cliffs, NJ.

Berthon, S. and Robinson, A. (1991) *The Shape of the World: The Mapping and Discovery of the Earth*, Rand McNally, Chicago, IL.

Best, R. H., Jones, A. R. and Rogers, A. W. (1974) The density-size rule, *Urban Studies*, **11**, 201–208.

Bleicher, H. (1892) *Statistiche Beschreibung der Stadt Frankfurt am Main und Ihrer Bevolkerung*, J. D. Sauerlander's Verlag, Frankfurt am Main.

Blumenfeld, D. E. (1972) Effects of road system designs on congestion and journey times in cities, unpublished PhD Thesis, University College, London.

Bracken, I. (1993) An extensive surface model database for population-related information: concept and application, *Environment and Planning B*, **20**, 13–27.

Bracken, I., Holdstock, S. and Martin, D. (1987) Map manager: intelligent software for the display of spatial information, *Technical Reports in Geo-Information Systems, Computing and Cartography, 3*, Wales and South West Regional Research Laboratory, University of Wales, Cardiff.

Bronowski, J. (1973) *The Ascent of Man*, BBC Publications, London.

Buchanan, C. *et al.* (1963) *Traffic in Towns: A Study of the Long Term Problems of Traffic in Urban Areas*, HMSO, London.

Bunde, A. and Havlin, S (Editors) (1991) *Fractals and Disordered Systems*, Springer-Verlag, New York.

Burrough, P. A. (1981) Fractal dimensions of landscapes and other environmental data, *Nature*, **294**, 240–242.

Burrough, P. A. (1984) The application of fractal ideas to geophysical phenomena, *The Institute of Mathematics and Its Applications*, **20**, 36–42.

Bussiere, R. (1972a) Static and dynamic characteristics of the negative exponential model of urban population distributions, *London Papers in Regional Science*, **3**, 83–113.

Bussiere, R. (Editor) (1972b) *Models Mathematiques de Repartition des Populations Urbaines*, Centre de Recherche et de Rencontres d'Urbanisme, Paris, France.

Bussiere, R. and Snickars, F. (1970) Derivation of the negative exponential model by an entropy maximizing method, *Environment and Planning*, **2**, 295–301.

Bussiere, R. and Stovall, T. (1981) *Systemes Evolutifs Urbains et Regionaux a L'Etat D'Equilibre*, Centre de Recherche et de Rencontres D'Urbanisme, Paris, France.

Buttenfield, B. P. (1985) Treatment of the cartographic line, *Cartographica*, **22**, 1–26.

Carpenter, L. (1980) Computer rendering of fractal curves and surfaces, *Computer Graphics*, **10**, 90–97.

Chapin, F. S. and Weiss, S. F. (Editors) (1962) *Urban Growth Dynamics: In a Regional Cluster of Cities*, John Wiley and Sons, New York.

Chapin, F. S. and Weiss, S. F. (1968) A probabilistic model for residential growth, *Transportation Research*, **2**, 375–390.

Christaller, W. (1933, 1966) *Central Places in Southern Germany*, Prentice Hall, Englewood Cliffs, NJ.

Clark, C. (1951) Urban population densities, *Journal of the Royal Statistical Society (Series A)*, **114**, 490–496.

Clark, C. (1967) *Population Growth and Land Use*, Macmillan at the St. Martin's Press, London.

Clark, N. N. (1986) Three techniques for implementing digital fractal analysis of particle shape, *Powder Technology*, **46**, 45–52.

Coleman, J. S. (1964) *Introduction to Mathematical Sociology*, The Free Press, New York.

Couclelis, H. (1985) Cellular worlds: a framework for modeling micro-macro dynamics, *Environment and Planning A*, **17**, 585–596.

Coyne, R. D., Rosenman, M. A., Radford, A. D., Balachandran, M. and Gero, J. S. (1990) *Knowledge-Based Design Systems*, Addison-Wesley Publishing Company, Reading, MA.

Craig, J. and Haskey, J. (1978) The relationships between the population, area and density of urban areas, *Urban Studies*, **15**, 101–107.

Crick, F. (1990) *What Mad Pursuit: A Personal View of Scientific Discovery*, Penguin Books, Harmondsworth.

Curry, L. (1972) A spatial analysis of gravity flows, *Regional Studies*, **6**, 131–147.

Dam, A. van (1984) Computer software for graphics, *Scientific American*, **251**, 102–113.

Dantzig, G. B. and Saaty, T. L. (1973) *Compact City: A Plan for a Livable Urban Environment*, W. H. Freeman and Company, San Francisco, CA.

Daunton, M. J. (1977) *Coal Metropolis: Cardiff 1870–1914*, Leicester University Press, Leicester.

Davies, P. (Editor) (1989) *The New Physics*, Cambridge University Press, Cambridge, UK.

Dawkins, R. (1986) *The Blind Watchmaker*, Longmans Scientific and Technical, London.

Dearnley, R. (1985) Effects of resolution on the measurement of grain 'size', *Mineralogical Magazine*, **49**, 539–546.

Dell'Orco, P. and Ghiron, M. (1983) Shape representations by rectangles preserving fractality, *Auto-Carto*, **6**, 299–308.

Demko, S., Hodges, L. and Naylor, B. (1985) Construction of fractal objects with iterated function systems, *Computer Graphics*, **19**, 271–278.

Devaney, R. L. (1990) *Chaos, Fractals and Dynamics: Computer Experiments in Mathematics*, Addison-Wesley Publishing Company, New York.

Dewar, R. and Harris, C. K. (1986) Percolation on the DAP, in L. Pietronero and E.

Tosatti (Editors) *Fractals in Physics*, North-Holland Publishing Company, Amsterdam, pp. 145–148.

Dodge, C. and Bahn, C. R. (1986) Musical fractals, *Byte*, **11**, 185–196.

DoE (1978) *Housing Survey Reports 10: English House Condition Survey 1976: Part 1: Report of the Physical Condition Survey*, Department of the Environment, HMSO, London.

DoE (1979) *Housing Survey Reports 11: English House Condition Survey 1976: Part 2: Report of the Social Survey*, Department of the Environment, HMSO, London.

Dorigo, G. and Tobler, W. (1983) Push-pull migration laws, *Annals of the Association of American Geographers*, **73**, 1–17.

Doxiadis, C. A. (1968) *Ekistics: An Introduction to the Science of Human Settlements*, Hutchinson, London.

Dutton, G. (1973) Criteria of growth in urban systems, *Ekistics*, **36**, 298–306.

Dutton, G. H. (1981) Fractal enhancement of cartographic line detail, *American Cartographer*, **8**, 23–40.

Edmonston, B. (1975) *Population Distribution in American Cities*, D. C. Heath and Company, Lexington, MA.

Einstein, A. (1921) *Geometrie und Erfahrung*, J. Springer, Berlin.

Elson, M. (1986) *Green Belts*, Heinemann, London.

Evans, A.W. (1989) South East England in the eighties: explanations for a house price explosion, in M. Breheny and P. Congdon (Editors) *Growth and Change in a Core Region*, Pion Press, London.

Falconer, K. (1990) *Fractal Geometry: Mathematical Foundations and Applications*, John Wiley and Sons, Chichester.

Feder, J. (1988) *Fractals*, Plenum Press, New York.

Feller, W. (1950) *An Introduction to Probability Theory and Its Applications: Volume 1*, John Wiley and Sons, New York.

Feynman, R. (1965) *The Character of Physical Law*, The MIT Press, Cambridge, MA.

Flook, A. G. (1978) The use of dilation logic on the quantimet to achieve fractal dimension characterisation of textured and structured profiles, *Powder Technology*, **21**, 295–298.

Forrest, S. R. and Witten, T. A. (1979) Long-range correlations in smoke-particle aggregates, *Journal of Physics A*, **12**, 1109–1117.

Fotheringham, A. S., Batty, M. and Longley, P. A. (1989) Diffusion-limited aggregation and the fractal nature of urban growth, *Papers of the Regional Science Association*, **67**, 55–69.

Fournier, A., Fussell, D. and Carpenter, L. (1982) Computer rendering of stochastic models, *Communications of the ACM*, **25**, 371–384.

Frankhauser, P. (1988) Fractal aspects of urban structures, *International Symposium des Sonderforschungsbereich 230: Naturliche Konstruktionen-Leichtbau in Architektur und Natur: Teil 1*, Universities of Stuttgart and Tubingen, West Germany.

Frankhauser, P. (1990) Aspects fractals des structures urbaines, *L'Espace Geographique*, **19**, 45–69.

Frankhauser, P. (1991) Fraktales Stadtwachstum, *Archiv und Zeitschrift für Architektur und Stadtebau*, **109**, 84–89.

Frankhauser, P. (1992) Fractal properties of settlement structures, paper presented at the First International Seminar on Structural Morphology, Montpellier, France, 7–11 September 1992.

Frankhauser, P. (1994) *La Fractalite des Structures Urbaines*, Collection Villes, Anthropos, Paris, France.

Frankhauser, P. and Sadler, G. (1991) Fractal analysis of agglomerations, *International Symposium des Sonderforschungsbereich 230: Naturliche Konstruktionen-Leichtbau in Architektur und Natur: Teil 2*, Universities of Stuttgart and Tubingen, West Germany.

Gallion, A. B. and Eisner, S. (1950, 1975) *The Urban Pattern: City Planning and Design*, Van Nostrand Reinhold Company, New York.

Garreau, J. (1991) *Edge City: Life on the New Frontier*, Doubleday, New York.

Geddes, P. (1915, 1949) *Cities in Evolution*, Williams and Norgate, London.

GLC (1985) *London: Facts and Figures*, Greater London Council Intelligence Unit, County Hall, London.

Goodchild, M. F. (1980) Fractals and the accuracy of geographical measures, *Mathematical Geology*, **12**, 85–98.

Goodchild, M. F. (1982) The fractional Brownian process as a terrain simulation model, *Modeling and Simulation*, **13**, 1133–1137.

Goodchild, M. F. and Mark, D. M. (1987) The fractal nature of geographic phenomena, *Annals of the Association of American Geographers*, **77**, 265–278.

Gottman, J. (1961) *Megalopolis: The Urbanized Northeastern Seaboard of the United States*, The Twentieth Century Fund, New York.

Gould, S.J. (1966) Allometry and size in ontogeny and phylogeny, *Biological Review*, **41**, 587–640.

Hagerstrand, T. (1952) The propagation of innovation waves, *Lund Studies in Geography: Series B: Human Geography*, **4**, 3–19.

Hagerstrand, T. (1965) A Monte Carlo approach to diffusion, *European Journal of Sociology*, **6**, 43–67.

Haggett, P., Cliff, A. D. and Frey, A. (1977) *Locational Analysis in Human Geography*, John Wiley and Sons, New York.

Hall, P. (Editor) (1966) *Isolated State: An English Edition of Der Isolierte Staat, by Johann Heinrich von Thunen*, Pergamon Press, Oxford.

Hall, P., Gracey, H., Drewett, R. and Thomas, R. (1973) *The Containment of Urban England*, Allen and Unwin, London.

Hayashi, Y. and Isobe, T. (1985) Modelling the long term effects of transport policies on industrial location behaviour, paper presented at the International Conference on Transport Behaviour, 16–19 April, Noordwijk, The Netherlands.

Hensher, D. A. and Johnson, L. W. (1981) *Applied Discrete-Choice Modelling*, Croom Helm, London.

Hill, F. S. and Walker, S. E. (1982) On the use of fractals for efficient map generation, *Graphics Interface '82*, 17–21 May, Toronto, Ontario, pp. 283–289.

Hillier, B. and Hanson, J. (1984) *The Social Logic of Space*, Cambridge University Press, Cambridge, UK.

Howard, E. (1898, 1965) *To-Morrow: A Peaceful Path to Real Reform*, Swan Sonnenschein, London, republished (1965) *Garden Cities of ToMorrow*, The MIT Press, Cambridge, MA.

Hutchinson, J. E. (1981) Fractals and self-similarity, *Indiana University Journal of Mathematics*, **30**, 713–747.

Isard, W. (1956) *Location and Space-Economy*, The MIT Press, Cambridge, MA.

Jacobs, J. (1961) *The Death and Life of Great American Cities*, Vintage Books, New York.

Jenks, G. F. (1981) Lines, computers and human frailties, *Annals of the Association of American Geographers*, **71**, 1–10.

Johnson, J. H. (1984) Hierarchical structure in design, in R. Langdon and P. Purcell (Editors) *Design Theory and Practice*, Design Council, London, pp. 51–59.

Jones, A. R. (1975) Density-size rule, a further note, *Urban Studies*, **12**, 225–228.

Jullien, R. and Botet, R. (1987) *Aggregation and Fractal Aggregates*, World Scientific Company, Singapore.

Kadanoff, L. P. (1986) Fractals: where's the physics? *Physics Today*, **39**, 6–7.

Kaproff, J. (1986) The geometry of coastlines: a study in fractals, in K. Hargittai (Editor) *Symmetry: Unifying Human Understanding*, Pergamon Press, Oxford, UK, pp. 655–671.

Kaye, B. H. (1978) Specification of the ruggedness and/or texture of a fineparticle profile by its fractal dimension, *Powder Technology*, **21**, 1–16.

Kaye, B. H. (1984) Multifractal description of a rugged fineparticle profile, *Particle Characterization*, **11**, 14–21.

Kaye, B. H. (1989a) *A Random Walk Through Fractal Dimensions*, VCH Publishers, New York.

Kaye, B. H. (1989b) Image analysis techniques for characterizing fractal structures, in D. Avnir (Editor), *The Fractal Approach to Heterogeneous Chemistry: Surfaces, Colloids, Polymers*, John Wiley and Sons, New York, pp. 55–66.

Kaye, B. H. and Clark, G. G. (1985) Fractal description of extra terrestrial fineparticles, Department of Physics, Laurentian University, Sudbury, Ontario.

Kaye, B. H., Leblanc, J. E. and Abbot, P. (1985) Fractal dimension of the structure of fresh and eroded aluminum shot fineparticles, *Particle Characterization*, **2**, 56–61.

Keeble, L. (1959) *Principles and Practice of Town and Country Planning*, The Estates Gazette, London.

Kent, C. and Wong, J. (1982) An index of littoral zone complexity and its measurement, *Canadian Journal of Fisheries and Aquatic Sciences*, **39**, 847–853.

Kim, K. S. (1985) *Urban Form Measures and Their Application to the Seoul Metropolitan Area*, Sung Kyun Kwan University, Seoul, Korea (in Korean).

Kondo, H., Matsushita, M. and Ohnishi, S. (1986) Diffusion-limited aggregation with a restriction of growth direction, in Y. Kato, R. Takaki and J. Toriwaki (Editors) *Science of Form*, KTK Scientific Publishers, Tokyo, pp. 33–38.

Kostof, S. (1991) *The City Shaped: Urban Patterns and Meanings Throughout History*, Little, Brown and Company, Boston, MA.

Lam, N. and Quattrochi, D. A. (1992) On issues of scale, resolution and fractal analysis in the mapping sciences, *The Professional Geographer*, **44**, 88–98.

Lauwerier, H. (1991) *Fractals: Endlessly Repeated Geometrical Figures*, Princeton University Press, Princeton, NJ.

Lerman, S. R. (1985) Random utility models of spatial choice, in B. G. Hutchinson, M. Batty and P. Nijkamp (Editors) *Optimization and Discrete Choice in Urban Systems*, Springer-Verlag, Berlin, pp. 200–217.

Levy, S. (1992) *Artificial Life: The Quest for a New Creation*, Pantheon, New York.

Lewin, R. (1992) *Complexity: Life at the Edge of Chaos*, Macmillan Publishing Company, New York.

Longley, P. A. (1984) Comparing discrete choice models: some housing market examples, in D. E. Pitfield (Editor) *Discrete Choice Models in Regional Science*, Pion Press, London, pp. 163–180.

Lovejoy, S. (1982) Area–perimeter relation for rain and cloud areas, *Science*, **216**, 185–187.

Lovejoy, S., Schertzer, D. and Ladoy, P. (1986) Fractal characterization of inhomogeneous geophysical measuring networks, *Nature*, **319**, 43–44.

MacDonald, N. (1983) *Trees and Networks in Biological Models*, John Wiley and Sons, Chichester, UK.

Mandelbrot, B. B. (1967) How long is the coast of Britain? Statistical self-similarity and fractal dimension, *Science*, **155**, 636–638.

Mandelbrot, B. B. (1975) Stochastic models for the earth's relief, the shape and fractal dimension of coastlines and the number-area rule for islands, *Proceedings of the National Academy of Sciences USA*, **72**, 3825–3828.

Mandelbrot, B. B. (1982) Comment of computer rendering of fractal stochastic models, *Communications of the ACM*, **25**, 581–583.

Mandelbrot, B. B. (1983) *The Fractal Geometry of Nature*, W. H. Freeman and Company, San Francisco, CA.

Mandelbrot, B. B. (1984) On fractal geometry and a few of the mathematical questions it has raised, *Proceedings of the International Congress of Mathematicians*, 16–24 August, Warsaw, Poland, pp. 1661–1675.

Mandelbrot, B. B. (1988) Appendix A: fractal landscapes without creases and with rivers, in H.-O. Peitgen and D. Saupe (Editors) *The Science of Fractal Images*, Springer-Verlag, New York, pp. 243–260.

Mandelbrot, B. B. (1990) Fractals – a geometry of nature, *New Scientist*, **127**, 38–43.

Mandelker, D. (1962) *Green Belts and Urban Growth*, University of Wisconsin Press, Madison, WI.

March, L. (1971) Urban systems: a generalized distribution function, *London Papers in Regional Science*, **2**, 156–170.

March, L. and Steadman, P. (1971) *The Geometry of Environment: An Introduction to Spatial Organization in Design*, RIBA Publications, London.

March, L. and Stiny, G. (1985) Spatial systems in architecture and design: some history and logic, *Environment and Planning B*, **12**, 31–53.

Mark, D. M. (1984) Fractal dimension of a coral reef at ecological scales: a discussion, *Marine Ecology Progress Series*, **14**, 293–294.

Mark D. M. and Aronson, P. B. (1984) Scale-dependent fractal dimensions of topographic surfaces: an empirical investigation with applications in geomorphology and computer mapping, *Mathematical Geology*, **16**, 671–683.

Mark, D.M. and Peucker, T.K. (1978) Regression analysis and geographic models, *Canadian Geographer*, **22**, 51–64.

McFadden, D. (1979) Quantitative methods for analyzing travel behavior of individuals: some recent developments, in D. A. Hensher and P. R. Stopher (Editors) *Behavioural Travel Demand Modelling*, Croom Helm, London, pp. 279–318.

McGuire, M. (1991) *An Eye For Fractals: A Graphic and Photographic Essay*, Addison-Wesley Publishing Company, New York.

McMahon, T. A. (1975) The mechanical design of trees, *Scientific American*, **233**, 92–102.

Meakin, P. (1983a) Diffusion-controlled cluster formation in two, three and four dimensions, *Physical Review A*, **27**, 604–607.

Meakin, P. (1983b) Diffusion-controlled cluster formation in 2–6 dimensional space, *Physical Review A*, **27**, 1495–1507.

Meakin, P. (1985) The structure of two-dimensional Witten–Sander aggregates, *Journal of Physics A*, **18**, L661–L666.

Meakin, P. (1986a) Some recent advances in the simulation of diffusion-limited aggregation and related processes, in L. Pietronero and E. Tosatti (Editors) *Fractals in Physics*, North-Holland Publishing Company, Amsterdam, pp. 205–212.

Meakin, P. (1986b) Computer simulation of growth and aggregation processes, in H. E. Stanley and N. Ostrowsky (Editors) *On Growth and Form: Fractal and Non-Fractal Patterns in Physics*, Martinus-Nijhoff Publishers, Dordrecht, pp. 111–135.

Meakin, P. (1986c) Universality, non-universality and the effects of anisotropy on diffusion-limited aggregation, *Physical Review A*, **33**, 3371–3382.

Meakin, P. (1986d) A new model for biological pattern formation, *Journal of Theoretical Biology*, **118**, 101–113.

Meakin, P. and Tolman, S. (1989) Diffusion-limited aggregation: recent developments, in L. Pietronero (Editor) *Fractals' Physical Origins and Properties*, Plenum Press, New York, pp. 137–168.

MHLG (Ministry of Housing and Local Government) (1955) *Green Belts*, Circular 42/55, HMSO, London.

MHLG (Ministry of Housing and Local Government) (1957) *The Green Belts*, Circular 50/57, HMSO, London.

Mills, E. S. (1970) Urban density functions, *Urban Studies*, **7**, 5–20.

Mills, E. S. and Tan, J. P. (1980) A comparison of urban population density functions in developed and developing countries, *Urban Studies*, **17**, 313–321.

Mogridge, M. J. H. (1984) Strategic population forecasting for a conurbation using the negative exponential density model, paper presented to the British Section of the Regional Science Association's Annual Meeting, September 1984, The Transport Studies Group, University College, London.

Morris, A. E. J. (1979) *History of Urban Form: Before the Industrial Revolutions*, Longmans Scientific and Technical, London.

Morse, D. R., Lawton, J. H., Dodson, M. M. and Williamson, M. H. (1985) Fractal dimension of vegetation and the distribution of arthropod body lengths, *Nature*, **314**, 731–733.

Muller, J. C. (1986) Fractal dimension and inconsistencies in cartographic line representations, *The Cartographic Journal*, **23**, 123–130.

Muller, J. C. (1987) Fractal and automated line generalisation, *The Cartographic Journal*, **24**, 27–34.

Munton, R. (1983) *London's Green Belt: Containment in Practice*, Allen and Unwin, London.

Musgrave, F. K., Kolb, C. E. and Mace, R. S. (1989) The synthesis and rendering of eroded fractal terrains, *Computer Graphics*, **23**, 41–50.

Muth, R. (1969) *Cities and Housing: The Spatial Pattern of Urban Residential Land Use*, Chicago University Press, Chicago, IL.

Muthukumar, M. (1983) Mean field theory for diffusion-limited cluster formation, *Physical Review Letters*, **50**, 839–842.

Nakano, T. (1983) A 'fractal' study of some rias coastlines in Japan, *Annual Reports of the Institute of Geosciences, University of Tsukuba*, **9**, 75–80.

Nakano, T. (1984) A systematics of 'transient fractals' of rias coastlines: an example of rias coast from Kamaishi to Shizugawa, North-Eastern Japan, *Annual Reports of the Institute of Geosciences, University of Tsukuba*, **10**, 66–68.

Naroll, R. S. and Bertalanffy, L. von (1956) The principle of allometry in biology and the social sciences, *General Systems Yearbook*, **1**, 76–89.

Nelson, T. R. and Manchester, D. K. (1988) Modeling of lung morphogenesis using fractal geometry, *IEEE Transactions on Medical Imaging*, **7**, 321–327.

Newling, B. E. (1966) Urban growth and spatial structure: mathematical models and empirical evidence, *Geographical Review*, **56**, 213–225.

Niemeyer, L., Pietronero, L. and Wiesmann, H. J. (1984) Fractal dimension of dielectric breakdown, *Physical Review Letters*, **52**, 1033–1036.

Nittmann, J. Daccord, G. and Stanley, H. E. (1985) Fractal growth of viscous fingers: quantitative characterization of a fluid instability phenomenon, *Nature*, **314**, 141–144.

Nittmann, J., Daccord, G. and Stanley, H. E. (1986) When viscous fingers are fractal, in L. Pietronero and E. Tosatti (Editors) *Fractals in Physics*, North-Holland Publishing Company, Amsterdam, pp. 193–202.

Nittmann, J. and Stanley, H. E. (1986) Tip splitting without interfacial tension and dendritic growth patterns arising from molecular anisotropy, *Nature*, **321**, 663–668.

Nordbeck, S. (1965) The law of allometric growth, *Discussion Paper No. 7*, Michigan Inter-University Community of Mathematical Geographers, University of Michigan, Ann Arbor, MI.

Nordbeck, S. (1971) Urban allometric growth, *Geografiska Annaler*, **53B**, 54–67.

Nysteun, J. (1966) Effects of boundary shape and the concept of local convexity, *Discussion Paper No. 10*, Michigan Inter-University Community of Mathematical Geographers, Department of Geography, University of Michigan, Ann Arbor, MI.

OPCS (1984) *Key Statistics for Urban Areas*, Office of Population Census and Surveys, HMSO, London.

Orbach, R. (1986) Dynamics of fractal networks, *Science*, **231**, 814–819.

Orford, J. D. and Whalley, W. B. (1983) The use of the fractal dimension to quantify the morphology of irregular-shaped particles, *Sedimentology*, **30**, 655–668.

Parr, J. B. (1985a) A population-density approach to regional spatial structure, *Urban Studies*, **22**, 289–303.

Parr, J. B. (1985b) The form of the regional density function, *Regional Studies*, **19**, 535–546.

Parr, J. B., O'Neill, G. J. and Nairn, A. G. M. (1988) Metropolitan density functions: a further exploration, *Regional Science and Urban Economics*, **18**, 463–478.

Parr, J. B. and O'Neill, G. J. (1989) Aspects of the lognormal function in the analysis of regional population distribution, *Environment and Planning A*, **21**, 961–973.

Paterson, L. (1984) Diffusion-limited aggregation and two-fluid displacements in porous media, *Physical Review Letters*, **52**, 1621–1624.

Peitgen, H.-O., Jurgens, H. and Saupe, D. (1990) The language of fractals, *Scientific American*, **263**, 40–47.

Peitgen, H.-O., Jurgens, H. and Saupe, D. (1992) *Fractals for the Classroom: Part 1: Introduction to Fractals and Chaos*, Springer-Verlag, New York.

Peitgen, H.-O. and Richter, P. H. (Editors) (1986) *The Beauty of Fractals: Images of Complex Dynamical Systems*, Springer-Verlag, New York.

Penck, A. (1894) *Morphologie der Erdoberflache*, Stuttgart, Germany, quoted in Perkal (1958a)

Pentland, A. D. (1984) Fractal-based description of natural scenes, *IEEE Transactions of Pattern Analysis and Machine Intelligence*, **6**, 661–674.

Perkal, J. (1958a) O Dlugosci Krzywych Empirycznych, *Zastosowania Matematyki*, **3**, 257–286; translated 1966 by W. Jackowski as 'On the length of empirical curves', in *Discussion Paper No. 10*, Michigan Inter-University Community of Mathematical Geographers, Ann Arbor, MI.

Perkal, J. (1958b) Proba Obiektywnej Generalizacji, *Geodezja i Kartografia*, **7**, 130–142; translated 1966 by W. Jackowski as 'An attempt at objective generalization', in *Discussion Paper No. 10*, Michigan Inter-University Community of Mathematical Geographers, Ann Arbor, MI.

Peucker, T. K. (1975) A theory of the cartographic line, *AutoCarto*, **2**, 508–518.

Pietronero, L. (Editor)(1989) *Fractals' Physical Origin and Properties*, Plenum Press, New York.

Pietronero, L., Evertsz, C. and Wiesmann, H. J. (1986) Scaling properties of growing zone and capacity of Laplacian fractals, in L. Pietronero and E. Tosatti (Editors) *Fractals in Physics*, North-Holland Publishing Company, Amsterdam, pp. 159–163.

Porter, E. and Gleick, J. (1990) *Nature's Chaos*, Viking Penguin, New York.

Prusinkiewicz, P. and Lindenmayer, A. (1990) *The Algorithmic Beauty of Plants*, Springer-Verlag, New York.

Ravetz, A. (1980) *Remaking Cities*, Croom Helm, London.

Reps, J. W. (1965) *The Making of Urban America: A History of City Planning in the United States*, Princeton University Press, Princeton, NJ.

Richardson, L. F. (1961) The problem of contiguity: an appendix of 'Statistics of deadly quarrels', *General Systems Yearbook*, **6**, 139–187.

Richter, P. H. and Peitgen, H. O. (1985) Morphology of complex boundaries, *Berichte der Bunsengesellschaft fur Physikalische Chemie*, **89**, 571–588.

Rickaby, P. (1987) An approach to the assessment of energy efficiency of urban built form, in D. Hawkes, J. Owers, P. Rickaby and P. Steadman (Editor) *Energy and Urban Built Form*, Butterworth, Sevenoaks, pp. 43–61.

Rosenau, H. (1983) *The Ideal City: Its Architectural Evolution in Europe*, Routledge and Kegan Paul, London.

Roy, J. R. (1983) Estimation of singly-constrained nested spatial interaction models, *Environment and Planning B*, **10**, 269–274.

Ruelle, R. (1991) *Chance and Chaos*, Princeton University Press, Princeton, NJ.

Saaty, T. L. (1980) *The Analytic Hierarchy Process: Planning, Priority Setting, Resource Allocation*, McGraw-Hill, New York.

Sander, L. M. (1987) Fractal growth, *Scientific American*, **256**, 82–88.

Satpathy, S. (1986) Dielectric breakdown in three dimensions, in L. Pietronero and E. Tosatti (Editors) *Fractals in Physics*, North-Holland Publishing Company, Amsterdam, pp. 173–176.

Saupe, D. (1988) Algorithms for random fractals, in H.-O. Peitgen and D. Saupe (Editors) *The Science of Fractal Images*, Springer-Verlag, New York, pp. 71–136.

Saupe, D. (1991) Random fractals in image synthesis, in A. J. Crilly, R. A. Earnshaw and H. Jones (Editors) *Fractals and Chaos*, Springer-Verlag, New York, pp. 89–118.

Saviranta, J. (1973) Chorological matrices and gravity models in human geography, *Fennia*, **121**, 5–51.

SERPLAN (Standing Conference on London and South East Regional Planning) (1976) *The Improvement of London's Green Belt*, SC620, HMSO, London.

Shelberg, M. C., Moellering, H. and Lam, N. (1982) Measuring the fractal dimensions of empirical cartographic curves, *Auto Carto*, **5**, 481–490.

Shepherd, J. and Congdon, P. (1990) *Small Town England: An Investigation into Population Change among Small and Medium-Sized Urban Areas*, Progress in Planning Series, Pergamon, Oxford.

Sheppard, E. S. (1979) Geographic potentials, *Annals of the Association of American Geographers*, **69**, 438–447.

Simon, H. A. (1969) *The Sciences of the Artificial*, The MIT Press, Cambridge, MA.

Sitte, C. (1889, 1965) *City Planning, According to Artistic Principles*, Random House, New York.

Smeed, R. J. (1961) The traffic problem in towns, *Manchester Statistical Society Papers*, Norbury Lockwood, Manchester.

Smeed, R. J. (1963) Road development in urban areas, *Journal of the Institution of Highway Engineers*, **10**, 5–30.

Smith, A. R. (1982) The genesis demo: instant evolution with computer graphics, *American Cinematographer*, **63**, 1038–1039 and 1048–1050.

Smith, B. (1991) Morphological similarities: Taunton, England and Guatemala City, Guatemala, unpublished paper, Department of Geography, State University of New York, Buffalo, NY.

Stanley, H. E. (1977) Cluster shapes at the percolation threshold: an effective cluster dimensionality and its connection with critical-point exponents, *Journal of Physics A*, **10**, L211–L219.

Stanley, H. E. and Ostrowsky, N. (Editors)(1986) *On Growth and Form: Fractal and Non-Fractal Patterns in Physics*, Martinus-Nijhoff Publishers, Dordrecht.

Steadman, P. (1979) *The Evolution of Designs: Biological Analogy in Architecture and the Applied Arts*, Cambridge University Press, Cambridge, UK.

Steadman, P. (1983) *Architectural Morphology: An Introduction to the Geometry of Building Plans*, Pion Press, London.

Steinhaus, H. (1954) Length, shape and area, *Colloquium Mathematicum*, **3**, 1–13.

Steinhaus, H. (1960) *Mathematical Snapshots*, Oxford University Press, Oxford.

Stevens, P. S. (1974) *Patterns in Nature*, Penguin Books, Harmondsworth.

Stewart, J. Q. (1941) An inverse distance variation for certain social influences, *Science*, **93**, 89–90.

Stewart, J. Q. (1947) Suggested principles of "Social Physics", *Science*, **106**, 179–180.

Stewart, J. Q. (1950) The development of social physics, *American Journal of Physics*, **18**, 239–253.

Stewart, J. Q. and Warntz, W. (1958) Physics of population distribution, *Journal of Regional Science*, **1**, 99–123.

Suzuki, M. (1984) Finite size scaling for transient similarity and fractals, *Progress in Theoretical Physics*, **71**, 1397–1400.

Takayasu, H. (1990) *Fractals in the Physical Sciences*, Manchester University Press, Manchester.

Tanner, J. C. (1961) Factors affecting the amount of travel, *Road Research Laboratory Technical Paper No. 51*, HMSO (Department of Scientific and Industrial Research), London.

Thibault, S. and Marchand, A. (1987) Reseaux et Topologie, Institut National Des Sciences Appliquees de Lyon, Villeurbanne, France.

Thompson, D'A. W. (1917, 1961) *On Growth and Form*, Cambridge University Press, Cambridge, UK.

Thomson, J. M. (1977) *Great Cities and Their Traffic*, Victor Gollancz, London.

Tobler, W. (1979a) Smooth pycnophylactic interpolation for geographical regions, *Journal of the American Statistical Association*, **74**, 519–530.

Tobler, W. R. (1979b) Cellular geography, in S. Gale and G. Olsson (Editors) *Philosophy in Geography*, D. Reidel, Dordrecht, pp. 279–386.

Tobler, W. (1981) A model of geographical movement, *Geographical Analysis*, **13**, 1–20.

Toffler, A. (1981) *The Third Wave*, Bantam Books, New York.

Turcotte, D. L. (1992) *Fractals and Chaos in Geology and Geophysics*, Cambridge University Press, Cambridge, UK.

Turkevitch, L. A. and Scher, H. (1985) Occupancy-probability scaling in diffusion-limited aggregation, *Physical Review Letters*, **55**, 1026–1029.

Vance, J. E. (1990) *The Continuing City: Urban Morphology in Western Civilization*, The Johns Hopkins University Press, Baltimore, MD.

Vaughan, R. (1987) *Urban Spatial Traffic Patterns*. Pion Press, London.

Vicsek, T. (1989) *Fractal Growth Phenomena*, World Scientific Company, Singapore.

Voss, R. F. (1984) Multi-particle fractal aggregation, *Journal of Statistical Physics*, **36**, 861–872.

Voss, R. F. (1985) Random fractal forgeries, in R. A. Earnshaw (Editor) *Fundamental Algorithms for Computer Graphics*, Springer-Verlag, New York, pp. 805–835.

Voss, R. F. (1988) Fractals in nature: from characterization to simulation, in H.-O. Peitgen and D. Saupe (Editors) *The Science of Fractal Images*, Springer-Verlag, New York, pp. 21–70.

Waldrop, M. M. (1992) *Complexity: The Emerging Science at the Edge of Order and Chaos*, Simon and Schuster, New York.

Weaver, W. (1967) *Science and Imagination: Selected Papers*, Basic Books, New York.

Weiss, H. K. (1961) The distribution of urban population and an application to a servicing problem, *Operations Research*, **9**, 860–874.

West, B. J. and Goldberger, A. L. (1987) Physiology in fractal dimensions, *American Scientist*, **75**, 354–365.

Whyte, L. L. (1968) Introduction, in L. L. Whyte (Editor) *Aspects of Form*, Lund Humphries, London, pp. 1–7.

Wiesmann, H. J. (1989) Realistic models of dielectric breakdown, in L. Pietronero (Editor) *Fractals' Physical Origins and Properties*, Plenum Press, New York, pp. 243–257.

Williams, G. (1987) An introduction to relaxation methods, *Byte*, **12**, 111–123.

Wilson, A. G. (1969) The use of analogies in geography, *Geographical Analysis*, **1**, 225–233.

Wilson, A. G. (1970) *Entropy in Urban and Regional Modelling*, Pion Press, London.

Witten, T. A. (1986) Scale-invariant diffusive growth, in H. E. Stanley and N. Ostrowsky (Editors) *On Growth and Form: Fractal and Non-Fractal Patterns in Physics*, Martinus-Nijhoff Publishers, Dordrecht, Holland, pp. 54–68.

Witten, T. A. and Sander, L. M. (1981) Diffusion-limited aggregation: a kinetic critical phenomenon, *Physical Review Letters*, **47**, 1400–1403.

Witten, T. A. and Sander, L. M. (1983) Diffusion-limited aggregation, *Physical Review B*, **27**, 5686–5697.

Woldenberg, M. J. (1968) Hierarchical systems: cities, rivers, Alpine glaciers, bovine livers and trees, unpublished PhD thesis, Department of Geography, Columbia University, New York.

Woldenberg, M. J. (1973) An allometric analysis of urban land use in the United States, *Ekistics*, **36**, 282–290.

Woldenberg, M. J. and Berry, B. J. L. (1967) Rivers and central places: analogous systems? *Journal of Regional Science*, **7**, 129–139.

Wong, D. W. S. and Fotheringham, A. S. (1990) Urban systems as examples of bounded chaos: exploring the relationship between fractal dimension, rank size and rural-to-urban migration, *Geografiska Annaler*, **72B**, 89–99.

Woolley, B. (1988) In search of a postmodern maths, *The Guardian (London)*, Friday 10 June, p. 29.

Woronow, A. (1981) Morphometric consistency with the Hausdorff–Besicovitch dimension, *Mathematical Geology*, **13**, 201–216.

Wrigley, N. (1985) *Categorical Data Analysis for Geographers and Environmental Scientists*, Longmans Technical and Scientific, London.

Wrigley, N. and Longley, P. A (1984) Discrete choice modelling in urban analysis, in D. T. Herbert and R. J. Johnston (Editors) *Geography and the Urban Environment: Volume 6: Progress in Research and Applications*, John Wiley and Sons, Chichester, pp. 45–94.

Wycherley, R. E. (1962) *How the Greeks Built Cities*, W. W. Norton and Company, New York.

Zielinski, K. (1979) Experimental analysis of eleven models of population density, *Environment and Planning A*, **11**, 629–641.

Zielinski, K. (1980) The modelling of urban population density: a survey, *Environment and Planning A*, **12**, 135–154.

Zipf, G. K. (1949) *Human Behavior and the Principle of Least Effort*, Addison-Wesley Publishing Company, Cambridge, MA.

Author Index

Subject Index